HITLER'S EXILES

Also by Mark M. Anderson

Kafka's Clothes: Ornament and Aestheticism in the Habsburg Fin de Siecle, Oxford: The Clarendon Press, 1992.

Reading Kafka: Prague, Politics, and the Fin de Siecle (editor), New York: Schocken Books, 1989.

In the Storm of Roses: Selected Poetry of Ingeborg Bachmann (editor and translator), Princeton: Princeton University Press, 1986.

Hitler's EXILES

PERSONAL STORIES OF THE
Flight from Nazi Germany to America

Edited by
MARK M. ANDERSON

THE NEW PRESS
NEW YORK

per laura, l'archivista del cuore

Excerpt from "Concerning the Label Emigrant" by Bertolt Brecht is © 1976, 1979 by Methuen London, Ltd. From *Bertolt Brecht's Poems, 1913–1956*, edited by John Willett and Ralph Manheim. Reproduced by permission of Routledge, Inc.

Published in the United States by The New Press, New York, 1998
New Press paperback edition, revised with a new preface, 2000
Distributed by W. W. Norton, New York

LIBRARY OF CONGRESS CATALOGING-IN-PUBLICATION DATA

Hitler's exiles : personal stories of the flight from Nazi Germany to
America / edited by Mark M. Anderson.
    p.   cm.
Includes bibliographical references (p. 345) and index.
ISBN 1-56584-394-0 (h.c.)
ISBN 1-56584-591-9 (pbk.)
    1. German Americans — Biography. 2. Exiles — United States —
Biography. 3. Germany — Social conditions — 1933–1945. 4. United
States — Emigration and immigration — History — 20th century.
5. Germany — Emigration and immigration — History — 20th century.
6. Exiles' writings, German — United States. I. Anderson, Mark M.
E184.G3H56 1998
304.873043 — dc21   98-91189

The New Press was established in 1990 as a not-for-profit alternative to the large, commercial publishing houses currently dominating the book publishing industry. The New Press operates in the public interest rather than for private gain, and is committed to publishing, in innovative ways, works of educational, cultural, and community value that might not be considered sufficiently profitable.

The New Press
450 West 41st Street, 6th Floor
New York, NY 10036

www.thenewpress.com

Printed in the United States of America

9 8 7 6 5 4 3 2 1

I always found the name false which they gave us: Emigrants.

That means those who leave their country. But we

Did not leave, of our own free will

Choosing another land. Nor did we enter

Into a land, to stay there, if possible for ever.

Merely, we fled. We are driven out, banned.

Not a home, but an exile, shall the land be that took us in.

—Bertolt Brecht, from "Concerning the Label Emigrant"

(1939, translated by Stephen Spender)

Contents

PART III: New Worlds

CHAPTER FIVE
New Lives

CHAPTER SIX
Looking Homeward

Preface to the Paperback Edition

B risk sales and reviews in daily newspapers are something of a novelty for someone accustomed to the world of university presses, where a book may wait years before receiving scholarly attention and barely reaches an audience outside academia. But the most gratifying and moving aspect of the reception to *Hitler's Exiles* has been the response of the protagonists themselves. While researching and editing my book, I had made countless efforts to trace the lives of my subjects after they arrived in the United States. Where had they settled and found work? Had they raised a family? Where were the children, and what were their views of their parents' experiences? Too often it was impossible to answer these questions; too often a letter of inquiry sent to the author's last known address came back to my office unopened and unread. But the publication of *Hitler's Exiles* found many of the families. Children, relatives and friends got in touch with me, excitedly relating their discovery that a long-forgotten or unknown family manuscript was suddenly in print and available for the world to see. I keenly remember the moment I heard on my answering machine the simple words of Pierre Schoenheimer—whose mother recounts in "Fleeing through Occupied France" how her young, French-born child is shot in the neck by Nazi warplanes—"I'm the son." I sensed in his and other responses a feeling of pride and vindication. After decades of indifference or even hostility, a broad swath of American readers is now acutely interested in hearing the stories of these "ordinary exiles."

I would be remiss, however, if I didn't report a persistent criticism of the book's title. At a number of public lectures I gave in the past year, people who themselves had fled Nazi Germany pointed out that they didn't consider themselves "exiles." "Refugees" was their status back then; afterwards, they became Americans and considered themselves immigrants. My only reply was, and is, that the Germans who came to this country because of Hitler did so for many reasons and viewed their relation to America in different ways. Writers like Bertolt Brecht and Thomas Mann looked to the United States as a temporary, more or less hospitable haven from the storm, and never seriously considered not returning to Germany or Europe. In fact, a good number of intellectuals and professional writers eventually returned; for them, the noble, if not grandiloquent, title of "exile" was a badge they wore proudly, one that helped shore up their meager, isolated existences far from their homelands.

Statistically, however, the overwhelming majority of German-speaking people who fled Hitler for America wound up settling here for good. Indeed, many left Germany already determined never to return again, and for them the term "exile" is inappropriate both in meaning and in tone. The question of names is therefore substantial, and I see no solution other than to acknowledge the impossibility of encompassing the exile/refugee/emigrant experience—or however one chooses to describe it—with a single term.

This paperback edition brings about the welcome prospect that the book will reach new readers, especially students in the increasingly numerous high school and university courses on Holocaust-related subjects. It has also allowed me to emend a number of errors that crept into the hardcover edition. My sincere thanks go to Peter Crane and Robert H. Silverman for their generous assistance in correcting and clarifying the original text.

New York
October 1999

Acknowledgments

In a book with so many stories to tell, the individuals and institutions who helped me along the way were numerous and invaluable. A virtual novice venturing into unfamiliar territory, I benefitted immeasurably from previous work on exile, German history, and American immigration, often done by writers who were exiles themselves and whose direct knowledge of the period is unrivaled. A partial list of these scholars is included in the bibliography, but the pioneering work of Kurt Grossmann, Egon Schwarz, John Spalek, Guy Stern, and, certainly not least, Will Schaber and Herbert A. Strauss deserves explicit mention here. Younger scholars, including Stephanie Barron, Wolfgang Benz, Anthony Heilbut, Jean-Michel Palmier, Sibylle Quack, Monika Richarz and others have influenced this volume in profound if often subterranean ways. My thanks also go to archivists at the Leo Baeck Institute (especially Diane Spielman and Frank Mecklenburg), at YIVO and Butler Library of Columbia University in New York; at the Houghton Library of Harvard University; and at the Institute for Research on Anti-Semitism at the Technische Universität, Berlin.

Finally, a word of thanks must be said to all those who believed in the power of the written word to convey the struggle against the political, social, and emotional costs of exile. The stories contained in this volume represent only a tiny portion of the writing that Hitler's exiles produced in response to their experiences. One should also remember the authors and assistants of the vast corpus of unpublished texts of exile: the interviewers who patiently transcribed the halting sentences of newly arrived victims of Nazi persecution; the Harvard professors who had the foresight in 1940 to sponsor an essay contest on the theme of "My Life in Germany Before and After January 30, 1933," which resulted in over 200 fascinating and (with a few exceptions) still unpublished manuscripts; the children and grandchildren of exiles who saved the memoirs and old letters they found in desk drawers and attic trunks; the archivists, librarians, and scholars who gave these documents a catalogued, climate-controlled afterlife for future generations.

I gratefully acknowledge the generous financial support of the Alexander von Humboldt Foundation for research in Germany. Like other similarly enlightened German institutions, it allows the recipients of its largesse complete intellectual freedom and did not protest when my work took an unexpected turn. My home institution, Columbia University, provided two much-appreciated sabbatical leaves and an intellectual base for all my work.

I am also indebted to the Director of The New Press, André Schiffrin, without whose initial prompting, encouragement, and understanding silences this book would not have seen the light of day. His efforts on behalf of a broad history of emigration to the United States, of which this anthology comprises a small part, are a rare example of vision and civic responsibility in the contemporary publishing world. I also thank my unstintingly patient and supportive editor Matt Weiland, who provided expert advice throughout this project and once rescued it at a critical juncture.

At an early stage, Dorothea von Moltke provided crucial bibliographical assistance; the traces of her labor and intelligence are still evident in the final product. For their unflagging intellectual and emotional support I think my friends and colleagues, especially Marion Kaplan, Alessandro Fambrini, Jennifer Lyons, Frank Wolf, Philip Boehm, Sara Bershtel, Ritchie Robertson, Andrée Hayum, and Andreas Huyssen. Laura De Angelis first showed me the way to an archive many years ago in Florence; her willingness to set aside her own work and listen to these stories made it possible for others to hear them now.

Introduction

O f the roughly half-million German-speaking emigrants who fled Germany and Austria during Hitler's reign of terror from 1933 to 1945, about 132,000 eventually made their way to the United States. It is one of the largest and most dramatic mass migrations to this country in the twentieth century. The great majority of those who came were educated, prosperous, middle- and upper-class citizens before the Nazis came to power, who surely never dreamed of moving to a country whose language they didn't speak, whose customs they didn't understand, whose hard-nosed capitalist values they didn't share. Germany was home to them—even (or especially) to those of Jewish origin whose ancestors had only recently become German citizens. They had fought for the Fatherland in the First World War. The classics of German literature, Goethe, Schiller and Lessing, stood in their libraries; they went to concerts by Mozart, Beethoven, and Brahms; and they named their children after Wagnerian heroes.

Flight was not their first choice, nor was the United States their preferred destination. Most of them would have opted to stay in Europe, especially in a nearby country such as Switzerland or Czechoslovakia where German was spoken, or in France, the classic refuge for Germans seeking political asylum since the nineteenth century. But as National Socialism tightened its grip over an increasingly large portion of Europe; as other countries either closed their borders or made clear the limited economic resources for new arrivals; and as Britain carefully limited the number of Jews allowed into Palestine, these newfound exiles turned to the traditional land of immigration whose democratic government, thriving economy, egalitarian educational system, and, not least, vast physical size could best accommodate them.

Not that the United States accepted them willingly. Historians have amply documented the "paper walls" of anti-immigrant legislation that a xenophobic Congress and its bureaucratic executors erected to keep out the exiles, some seventy-five percent of whom were Jews. The professional associations that closed ranks, the "restricted" hotels that refused Jewish guests, the Nazi sympathizers of the German-American "Bund" who goose-stepped their way down Broadway—too many people did their part to make sure that those who did enter would not feel welcome. But no matter. From 1933 to 1945, this large group of educated, energetic, and productive emigrants arrived in the United States and stayed here, transforming themselves as much as they transformed postwar America.

The story of a few of the most famous exiles has of course been told: images of a disheveled Albert Einstein in Princeton or of Thomas Mann in a dapper white suit in the Pacific Palisades belong to our collective memory of the immediate postwar era. Some readers will recall the novelists Franz Werfel and Lion Feuchtwanger arriving in New York to great popular acclaim, or Bertolt Brecht testifying before the House Committee on Un-American Activities. Yet these are only the most famous exiles. More than a hundred thousand other exiles—doctors, lawyers, businessmen, journalists, university professors, and others came with their families and rebuilt (or tried to rebuild) their lives, most of them fleeing Germany forever and all of them transferring their skills and energies to the United States. But until now, their stories have largely been hidden from view, left untranslated in obscure archives or in early publications that never found an audience.

Hitler's Exiles brings together the collective voices—many in English for the first time—of this extraordinary migration. Famous and unfamous, men and women, political radicals and conservatives, Jews and non-Jews: together they recount a fascinating and heartbreaking story of persecution and isolation in their home countries, of a desperate search for legal papers, money and safe passage to the United States, of their arrival and first steps in a foreign land. Neither a statistical survey nor a comprehensive historical account of the German refugees, *Hitler's Exiles* is rather a personal, multi-voiced account of the exile experience, first in deciding to leave Germany, then in negotiating the perilous route to America, and finally in starting a new life in a foreign world. What triggered the decision to dissolve a household, remove one's children from school, and abandon homes and property for an uncertain, possibly impoverished life across the ocean? What obstacles confronted the exiles along the way? What were their impressions of America before and after arrival? How did they make a living and adjust to a new language, a new (and usually lower) job, a new social condition? And how did they respond to the tragic events unfolding back home in Germany, to the loss of relatives and friends, to the destruction of their world?

Broadly speaking, there were two emigrations from Germany, a political and a "racial" immigration. The first wave of exiles included the political opponents of Hitler, those who had fought against National Socialism and who could expect reprisals once the Nazis seized power and who could accept exile as the logical consequence of their political beliefs. For these highly visible critics of the Nazis—journalists, Communist and Socialist politicians, writers and artists—Hitler's rise to power on January 30, 1933, the burning of the Reichstag at the end of February and the public burning of "un-German" books on May 10, marked the beginning of their exile from Germany. Many left the country immediately or, finding themselves abroad, decided not to return.

Despite the high drama and patent danger of those months, many of these people initially regarded their "flight" as something of a lark or a vacation, certainly not as "exile." When he heard the news of the Reichstag fire on the radio, Alfred Döblin (a medical physician as well as the author of *Berlin Alexanderplatz*) had to be persuaded to leave for Switzerland that evening. "It will just be a brief trip abroad," his wife said. "You'll let the storm pass over you, just three or four months, and the Nazis will be gone." He left, but during the entire trip he felt foolish for running away from nothing. The physician and Berlin politician Käte Frankenthal, when she heard the news of the Reichstag fire, was in Switzerland on vacation but decided to return to Berlin immediately, rescuing compromising political documents from her office before the Nazis searched it. Only a month later did she realize how dangerous her situation was and left for Prague.

But for the vast majority of Germans who emigrated to America, the political events in early 1933 were not a reason to leave their homeland. Most fled Germany only after the National Socialist government had defined them as "aliens" or "undesirables" on "racial" grounds, excluding them from German schools, businesses, and government employment (which included school teachers, university professors and many scientific researchers) and subjecting them to increasingly severe harassment and persecution.

Though the Nazi authorities persecuted Jews from the start, from 1933 to 1938 their efforts were inconsistent. Pressure from the international community increased in 1936, for example, when the United States and other Western democracies were scheduled to participate in the Summer Olympic Games in Berlin. Eager to enhance their international reputation (and perhaps fearing a boycott), Nazi authorities avoided overt political actions against Jews. In this confusing interlude, as Peter Gay reports, many future exiles made leisurely plans for a gradual emigration from Germany or argued among themselves whether emigration was necessary at all. Among Jews, it was often housewives who recognized the danger sooner and more clearly; they saw how they and their children were being mistreated by their neighbors and shopkeepers, whereas men and professional women tended to be insulated by their work situations from a direct expression of prejudice, or simply reluctant to abandon the fruit of decades of work. As the powerful head of a large steamship line, Arnold Bernstein was initially protected by his wealth and social connections from Nazi persecution. In 1937 the Nazis finally decided to arrest him, sending a high-level Gestapo agent who respectfully sat next to Bernstein and his guests while they finished lunch in an exclusive Berlin hotel. Alice Salomon, one of the leading figures in the German women's movement for thirty years as well as an international authority on social work, had no thought of leaving Germany until the Gestapo called her into their offices in 1937 and told her she must emigrate or face deportment to a concentration camp.

For the overwhelming majority of German exiles, the pogrom of November 9–10, 1938, known as *Kristallnacht* (sometimes called the "Night of Broken Glass") signaled a definitive rupture in their relation to Germany and triggered their decision to emigrate. In response to the murder of a German consular official in Paris by a Polish Jew (whose parents had just been deported from Germany to the Polish border), the Nazis set synagogues on fire and shattered the shop windows of Jewish merchants throughout Germany and Austria; widespread looting and pillaging followed. Hertha Nathorff's first impression of *Kristallnacht* was of her telephone ringing off the hook because so many of her husband's patients had suffered heart attacks. He spent the first day racing from one patient to the next until finally he returned home and was arrested by the Nazis who, following the pogrom, systematically rounded up all Jewish male adults and sent them to "work" camps where they were tortured and sometimes murdered. Nathorff recounts her anxious waiting in this period as she begins a desperate search for the necessary travel documents and tax releases for emigration even before she knows if her husband will return alive. Annemarie Wolfram, a child at the time, recounts that she went to school as usual the morning after *Kristallnacht* only to be sent home at once, her teachers having been arrested; her father was also arrested and sent to a concentration camp. The family applied for an American visa while he was still interned and left Germany upon his release.

Tragically, the U.S. Congress and the State Department were less and less inclined to allow foreigners into the country; consular officials were under strict orders to let in fewer Germans and Austrians than the allowed quotas, themselves dramatically reduced with regard to immigration in the first three decades of the century. Thus, when Hitler's opponents suddenly realized the impossibility of staying in Germany, they were confronted with the impossibility of securing permission to leave it. Few countries would let them in, especially since new currency restrictions and taxes imposed by the Nazis ensured that those leaving the Reich would arrive completely destitute, thus posing a financial burden to the countries accepting them. Because children were allowed to emigrate more easily—a rescue operation to England in 1939 saved approximately 10,000 Jewish children —many families were separated as the children were sent abroad and the parents remained behind to work and wait for a visa to the United States. This was Elisabeth Freund's situation, whose stark depiction of her forced labor in an armament factory in Berlin in 1941 closes the first section of this volume. She got out on the last train to France, later traveling to Cuba and finally to the United States where she rejoined her children. "Four days later the German government forbids departure for all Jews, and the army command discontinues the release of freight cars for the journey through France. But the deportation of Jews to Poland goes on."

The paths of exile from Nazi Germany to the United States were varied and often tortuous. Because of the large number of Germans living in Paris (at least until the Nazi occupation of France in 1940), one of the most common itineraries of flight went from the north to nonoccupied Southern France. In Marseille, however, the port was easily controlled by Vichy and, later, Nazi officials, thus forcing many to cross the Spanish border illegally and make their way to Lisbon where they could board steamers leaving for America. Whichever way they went, those who left earliest had the easiest time; they even often managed to bring some of their belongings and savings with them. But those who left later, and especially those who left after November 1938, were often forced to sell their property at a fraction of its real value, required to pay a so-called "retribution tax," and forbidden to export anything of value. American immigration laws allowed foreigners with "start-up capital" to enter the country on a capitalist visa, but those without means—by far the majority of those who came—were required to obtain an "affidavit" from someone legally residing in the United States who would guarantee that the newcomers would not become a burden to the state. For this reason many German exiles who wished to go directly to the United States were forced to wait in transit countries, such as France, Sweden, Cuba, and the Dominican Republic, for the necessary papers to be assembled.

The German refugees constitute a singular chapter in the history of American immigration. Most immigrants to this country have arrived dirt poor. They too had given up their homes and, in most cases, their languages, but most often they merely traded the bottom of one social ladder for another. The middle-class, educated Germans arrived in America looking backwards, lamenting what they had lost and whom they had left behind. Many insisted on maintaining their language and the external appurtenances of their lives back home, from the massive German furniture they stuffed into tiny New York apartments to the afternoon cake-and-coffee gatherings they held in decidedly uncongenial American cafeterias. They became "those queer refugees" with the funny German clothes and the heavy accents, complaining how much better things had been *"bei uns"* (with us) back home, thus earning for themselves the title of "byunskys." A classic joke of German emigration has two dachshunds walking down Broadway in New York City. One says to the other: *You know, here I'm just a dachshund, but back home in Germany I was a St. Bernard . . .* The joke rings true not just because of the exile's need to inflate or romanticize his past, but because so many dachshunds *were* in fact St. Bernards. As the novelist Lion Feuchtwanger notes, "There were doctors and lawyers who now sold ties door to door, did secretarial work, or tried—

illegally, hounded by the police—to make use of their professional training. There were women with a university education who earned their keep as sales clerks, cleaning ladies, and masseuses." In her first years in this country Käte Frankenthal—in Germany a prominent physician, author and politician— was reduced to selling ice cream on the streets of New York, hiding her head when she recognized someone she had met at a lecture or medical conference. The consequence of exile for those fleeing Hitler was therefore a profound social uprooting and *déclassement*, a loss of social caste, not just in a few isolated cases but in a large majority.

Another difference vis-à-vis other immigrant groups is that many Germans also wrote their stories down. This might be expected of the professional writers who used their often harrowing, dramatic experiences as raw material for journalism, novels, plays, poetry, or even scholarly studies. But it was true of housewives and businessmen as well. They wrote down their life stories, even if only for their immediate families and without thought of publication or even conservation in an archive or university library. In part this is the result of their German education, which was intensely literary and tended to instill a desire for extensive documentation. In part it is a natural consequence of the dramatic events that had befallen them, a bewildering, unexpected persecution that so defied belief that it needed to be written down and preserved for future generations. One must also consider the long periods of anxious waiting for an exit or entry visa, of joblessness or social isolation: writing served as a vital outlet for people with oppressive time on their hands. In any case, no matter where they wound up in America, in big cities such as New York and San Francisco or small towns in New England and the Midwest, a paper trail remains to tell their stories.

Earlier immigrants to America had tended to be young, unattached males, but the Germans fleeing Hitler included a high proportion of women and children, as well as older people of both sexes. This diversity of perspectives had a direct influence on the narratives generated by German exiles. Judges, businessmen, professors—their careers suddenly interrupted—reflected and wrote about their experiences while at the height of their mental powers and looking back at decades of work. Children of all ages wrote from their perspective, diaries and poetry and letters, with great openness and spontaneity. Housewives and professional women (including nurses, doctors, teachers) often wrote with an eye for everyday details and emotions that male writers frequently failed to observe. And although we also have the narratives and personal reflections of some of the most gifted writers, artists, musicians, intellectuals, and scientists in Germany, they too at the height of their abilities or growing into them while in exile—Thomas Mann, Lion Feuchtwanger, Hannah Arendt, Bertolt Brecht, Theodor Adorno, and many others—the number is not as high as one might expect. Professionals tended to channel their energy into their work, not into personal reflections on the exile experience *per se*. Albert Einstein (to cite only the most famous instance) was often asked to write about political and moral questions concerning Nazi Germany and emigration, but one searches in vain among his writings for a sustained personal narrative of his expulsion from the German university and his adaptation to life in the United States. And even among the professional writers who did address the exile question, gender marks their perspective, as a comparison between the very different pieces by Hannah Arendt and Thomas Mann in this volume makes clear. By and large, however, the most compelling, personal accounts of the exile experience stem from the pens of "ordinary" exiles who were suddenly thrust into extraordinary, life-changing circumstances.

Once they arrived in America, the German exiles generally preferred to gather in large cities where other exiles were located, especially New York, despite the attempts of refugee-settlement organizations to distribute them throughout the country. (According to one study, more than eighteen percent of all German refugees in 1940 were in New York City, the largest single center of refugee settlement.) And although many of the refugees were of Jewish origin, perhaps as many as seventy-five to eighty percent, the Jewish German intellectuals had relatively little contact with New York Jewish intellectuals, preferring to maintain the older friendships and intellectual relationships in German, even when they no longer lived in the same place and had to correspond by letter. Age obviously played a crucial role in the extent of integration with other Americans, with younger refugees assimilating and adapting more quickly. But even someone like Hannah Arendt, who was twenty-seven when she left Germany, whose career flourished in this country and who had numerous American friends, colleagues, and students, maintained her closest ties with other German exiles.

This attachment to Germany, and after Germany to Europe, marks another trait of the German exiles that differentiates their story from the classic pattern of immigrants seeking a new and better life in America. "I would have preferred emigrating anywhere," remarks the writer and theater critic Ludwig Marcuse, "just not to the New World, which struck me less as new than as uncanny. [. . .] Young people today have no idea that, fifty years ago, educated Europeans lived in a world whose center was Paris. New York and the colonial territory surrounding it were further away than Africa . . ." Jews were particularly attached to their homes in Germany, perhaps because their identities as Germans was of relatively recent date and uncertain status. A story is told of the Gestapo visiting the German writer Erich Maria Remarque in exile in Switzerland to convince him to return to Germany. Remarque adamantly refused, prompting the Gestapo officer to exclaim: "But don't you feel homesick?" The German writer is said to have replied: "Homesick? Do you take me for a Jew?" Since the nineteenth century, German Jews had believed in Germany and German culture with a conviction that was noticeably lacking in relations between Eastern European Jews and their host countries. This made Nazi Germany's betrayal of them all the more incomprehensible, and conditioned their attitudes to life in America years later, as both William Niederland and Peter Gay relate.

Not every figure of exile, nor every art form or profession or academic discipline, is represented here. The sheer bulk and diversity of Hitler's exiles preclude comprehensive treatment. Nor is the collection without its biases: the decision to focus on strong, first-person narratives conveying the texture of the exile experience tends to favor professional writers or at least able diarists, as well as those most sensitive to the subtle details of everyday life. The number of working-class exiles is also limited, not just because those who successfully emigrated to the United States tended to be from the middle- and upper-middle classes but also because the workers who did emigrate generally lacked the education and training to write effectively about their experiences. A few oral histories have been included to address this gap.

But unlike other anthologies that focus on a particular exile group, whether the "illustrious exiles" who first claimed public attention or subgroups such as Jewish refugees or "women of exile," *Hitler's Exiles* features a broad range of voices whose differences as well as similarities provide a much larger, variegated, though necessarily incomplete account of this dramatic migration. A common language and the common experience of fleeing from Hitler to America provide the twin pillars on which all these exile narratives rest; "Germany" and "German" in this collection are used in a cultural, linguistic sense extending to Austria and the German-speaking regions of Central Europe. But what mainly unifies these exiles is the immediacy and vibrance of their "personal stories." This is not to suggest that we are dealing with spontaneous, uncensored, historically objective accounts of exile. Virtually all of these narratives were fashioned after the fact. Elisabeth Freund writes of her forced labor in Berlin while waiting in Cuba for a visa to the United States. Peter Gay writes of his journey from the vantage point of the American bicentennial in 1976; Richard Plant was interviewed in 1996, shortly before he died. Even Hertha Nathorff's diaries, the originals having been lost in transit, were recomposed from memory after her arrival in America. However, the point of *Hitler's Exiles* is not to provide an objective historical account of the flight from Hitler to America, but a kaleidoscope of subjective, internal voices narrating history as they experienced it. Though only some of these voices are the result of oral interviews, in the end I hope *Hitler's Exiles* provides a history of German exile from what Studs Terkel called, in his account of the Great Depression *Hard Times*, "an improvised battalion of survivors."

Few chapters of the history of American immigration are as richly documented as that of Hitler's exiles. May the following accounts remind us of the untold number of written lives still waiting to be rediscovered—and thereby brought back to life.

Chronology of Events*

1933

30 January
Hitler becomes chancellor of the German Reich by invitation of President Hindenburg; heads coalition in which National Socialist Party has minority of votes.

23 February
Homosexual rights groups banned.

27 February
In Berlin the Reichstag (German Parliament building) burns down. Dutch Communist Marinus van der Lubbe is arrested and charged with crime. Many German Communists arrested and beaten afterwards.

4 March
Franklin D. Roosevelt inaugurated president of the United States.

U.S. immigration quota allows 25,957 Germans to enter the country each year. Special provisions made for "off quota" immigrants such as university professors, scientists, clergymen, etc.

5 March
National Socialists win forty-four percent of national votes; Hitler given dictatorial power.

---

* This chronology provides only selective information directly related to German emigration to the United States as it appears in the present collection. Many important, indeed crucial events in the broader history of Hitler's regime and the Holocaust have not been included. Ed.

8 March
German interior minister announces creation of concentration camps.

1 April
Nationwide Nazi-organized boycott of Jewish businesses, physicians, dentists, lawyers.

7 April
Law passed for the "Restoration of the Professional Civil Service," allowing government to dismiss Jewish and "politically unreliable" civil servants or force them into retirement.

10 April
Jewish lawyers excluded from German Bar Association

22 April
Jewish doctors excluded from national medical insurance system; over 3000 Jewish doctors lose their practices.

10 May
Burning of books by "un-German" authors at the Opera Square in Berlin; Goebbels holds speech praising the action, attends later burnings throughout Germany.

June
Formation of Jewish *Kulturbund* (cultural association) that organizes cultural events by and for Jews; eventually counts over 70,000 members, has its own orchestra, opera, chorus, and several theater companies.

July
All political parties (except National Socialists), trade unions, and strikes outlawed. 27,000 political prisoners held in concentration camps.

September
10,000 German refugees have entered Switzerland.

October
Heinrich Mann named honorary president of the Defense League of German Writers.

30 November
The Gestapo (abbreviation for *geheime Staatspolizei,* secret state police) is created.

In 1933 a total of 65,000 Germans leave Germany, four-fifths of whom are Jewish; forty percent go to France. 6,000 of the 30,000 immigrants who enter Palestine are from Germany.

1934

February
In Austria Parliament is dissolved and Social Democrats banned. Civil war breaks out and is stopped with help of Austrian Fascist Party, leading to emigration of thousands of Austrians, many to Paris.

10 May
One year after Berlin book burning, the German Library of Freedom is founded in Paris by Lion Feuchtwanger, Heinrich Mann, and others with the object of preserving literature banned by the Nazis.

18 May
The Reich Emigration Tax of 25 percent is applied to all transfers abroad above 50,000 marks.

June
Beginning of sterilization of eugenically "unfit" or "asocial" Germans, resulting in 300- to 400,000 sterilizations in all.

23 June
Prospective emigrants allowed to purchase only 2,000 marks in foreign currency (rather than previous 10,000 marks).

30 June
"Night of the Long Knives," in which SS (Hitler's elite guard) murder members of the SA, including its leader, Ernst Röhm.

25 July
Austrian Chancellor Engelbert Dollfuss is murdered in a Nazi putsch in Vienna.

2 August
Death of President Hindenburg. Hitler becomes president, appointing himself *Führer* and chancellor of the Reich two weeks later.

October–November
Nationwide arrests of homosexuals.

December

The first issue of *Aufbau-Reconstruction*, a weekly newspaper in German, appears as a newsletter of the German Jewish Club in New York City. The newspaper will become a vital forum for German-speaking refugees in America.

1935

Reichsbank pays only 30 percent of market rate for foreign currency to prospective emigrants; this figure steadily reduced until it reaches four percent in 1939.

13 January

Saarland plebiscite brings about its reunification with Germany. 7,000 refugees—Social Democrats, Communists, Jews—now leave the Saarland, most of them to France.

16 March

Germany repudiates the disarmament clause of Versailles Treaty. German military service reestablished.

May–August

Escalation of anti-Jewish propaganda in Germany.

21–25 June

In Paris the International Conference of Writers for the Defense of Culture brings together prominent left-wing German writers to fight against fascism (Bertolt Brecht, Max Brod, Lion Feuchtwanger, Heinrich and Klaus Mann are among the participants).

September 15

At party conference in Nuremberg, Hitler announces creation of "racial" laws giving Jews a lower class of citizenship and prohibiting marriage or sexual relations between Jews and Aryans. A "racial Jew" is defined as anyone with three or more Jewish grandparents, independent of religious belief.

14 November

Jews dismissed from public service.

Approximately 80,000 refugees have left the German Reich, most of them to neighboring European countries.

1936

10 February
Gestapo actions placed above the law.

March–April
German army moves into demilitarized Rhineland.

July
German government begins interning gypsies in concentration camp in Dachau, near Munich.

17–18 July
Civil war breaks out in Spain between Fascist and Popular Front forces; United States announces policy of nonintervention.

July–August
The Olympic Summer Games are held in Berlin with Hitler in attendance. Overt action against Jews beforehand held back for fear of adverse international attention.

Summer
Popular Front government in France introduces liberal immigration policy.

1 November
Rome-Berlin axis is announced.

November
The German Cultural Ministry is declared "free of Jews."

1937

British government reduces Jewish immigration to Palestine, thereby closing down one of the chief escape routes for German refugees.

23 June
Germany signs military treaty with Franco, while the United States, France, and Britain remain neutral.

June–July
Campaign against "degenerate art" in German museums results in confisca-

tion of 12,000 prints and 5,000 paintings. Two exhibitions open in Munich, one with "degenerate artworks," the other with artworks endorsed by the Nazis.

July
In United States, the Works Progress Administration (WPA), founded in 1935 to put millions of unemployed back to work, passes a rule restricting employment to American citizens.

November
Exhibition "The Eternal Jew" opens in Munich on purported Jewish destruction of German culture.

10,895 Germans enter United States during 1936–37, seventy percent more than in previous year, but still far below official quota of nearly 26,000.

1938

11 March
German invasion of Austria. Annexation (*Anschluss*) made into law on March 13. Widespread persecution of Austrian Jews (roughly 200,000), "Aryanization" of Jewish firms (forced transfer to "Aryan" owners at depressed prices), expulsion of Jews from German territory, etc., results in new wave of emigration. Britain and France tighten immigration quotas and temporary-residence permits.

15 June
1,500 Jews in Germany interned in concentration camps.

July
"Evian Conference" of thirty countries led by United States in order to confront refugee problem. United States and Britain unwilling to increase their refugee-immigration quotas. Britain refuses to open Palestine to Jewish immigration. Dominican Republic agrees to accept 100,000 Jews, although less than one thousand actually emigrate there.

17 August
As of January 1, 1939 Jews required to add "Sara" or "Israel" to their names.

29–30 September
Britain and France sign so-called Munich agreement allowing Germany to take over Sudetenland.

28 October
17,000 Jews with Polish citizenship expelled from Germany and transported to Polish border, where they are refused entry by Poland.

7 November
Ernst vom Rath, German diplomat in Paris, shot by Herschel Grynzspan (whose parents were among the 17,000 Polish Jews forced to leave Germany).

9–10 November
Kristallnacht (Night of Broken Glass), large-scale pogrom instigated by the Nazi Party against German Jews. Almost 200 synagogues set on fire, Jewish cemeteries desecrated, thousands of Jews physically abused, approximately ninety murdered. 30,000 Jewish men between eighteen and sixty-five arrested and imprisoned in work camps. New wave of Jewish emigration, including special children's transports to England.

28 November
Jewish houses and apartments seized.

3 December
Compulsory "Aryanization" of Jewish businesses begins.

According to French government report, 30,000 German and Austrian Jews are living illegally in France.

1939

Great Britain relaxes immigration laws, admitting 10,000 Jewish children and large number of Social Democrats from Sudetenland, some of whom eventually emigrate to the United States.

15 March
German army invades Czechoslovakia.

30 April
Jews are evicted from their homes throughout the Reich and forced to live in *Judenhäuser* (Jewish houses) in cramped conditions.

1 July
U.S. Congress decides not to admit 20,000 Jewish children from Germany.

1 September
German invasion of Poland, where more than five million Jews reside.

3 September
Britain and France declare war on Germany.

4 November
Roosevelt signs Neutrality Act allowing arms sales to Britain and France, thus asserting U.S. support of war against Nazi Germany.

By end of 1939 about 6,000 Jehovah's witnesses are in prison or in concentration camps.

1940

5 June
German army invades France; Marshall Pétain becomes head of government on June 16.

25 June
Emergency Rescue Committee is founded in New York as private refugee organization. In August Varian Fry travels to Marseilles, where he eventually helps over 2,000 refugees to escape occupied France.

28 June
U.S. Congress passes Alien Registration Act requiring foreigners to register periodically.

29 June
U.S. Secretary of State Hull issues memorandum advising all consular and diplomatic officials to tighten regulations on foreigners applying for entry visa; drastic reduction in number of visas issued.

14 November
Aliens residing in United States prohibited from leaving without an exit permit.

18 December
U.S. State Department allows intellectual and artistic refugees special "visitors" visas outside normal quota regulations.

1941

22 June
Germany invades Soviet Union, simultaneously beginning mass killings of Jews in Polish and Soviet territories.

1 July
Applications for immigrant and nonimmigrant visas must be approved by U.S. State Department.

September 19
All Jews in Greater German Reich required to wear the Yellow Star.

October
Beginning of systematic deportations of all Jews in Germany to extermination camps in the east. According to German statistics, just under 164,000 "racial Jews" are living in Germany, roughly half of them in Berlin.

23 October
Jewish emigration from German territory is forbidden by German law.

1942

14 January
Roosevelt orders all "enemy aliens" in the United States to register with government.

20 January
Wansee Conference outside Berlin organizes "final solution" to Jewish problem through systematic policy of forced labor and mass murder in all areas controlled by Germany; by December 1942 almost four million Jews have been killed.

13 February
Letter to Roosevelt from Albert Einstein, Thomas Mann, and other prominent refugees protesting treatment of anti-Fascist refugees as enemy aliens.

July
French police arrest 13,000 stateless Jews in Paris; 9,000 are sent to Auschwitz.

11–12 November
German occupation of Vichy France.

1943

30 April
Jews lose German citizenship.

19 June
Goebbels declares Berlin "free of Jews."

23,725 immigrants from Germany enter United States during 1942–43; almost 26,000 places for German immigrants allowed by quota regulations remain unfilled.

1944

Treasury Secretary Henry Morgenthau, Jr., persuades Roosevelt to set up War Refugee Board to try to rescue victims of Nazi oppression; however, most of these victims are in death camps and cannot be evacuated.

6 June
D-Day. American forces land in Normandy.

August
Intergovernmental Committee on Refugees claims there are between one and two million stateless individuals in the world.

1945

12 April
Roosevelt dies.

7–9 May
Unconditional surrender of Germany to Allied Forces.

5 June
Allied Control Commission assumes control over Germany.

August 14
Japan surrenders after atomic bombs dropped on Hiroshima and Nagasaki (6–9 August), thereby ending World War II.

Between 1933–45, approximately 132,000 refugees from Germany and Austria enter the United States (figure does not include persons entering with visitor visas); roughly 100,000 of these refugees are of Jewish descent.

PART ONE

Leaving Home

INTRODUCTION

When Hitler came to power in late January 1933, only a small percentage of the people who would eventually flee Germany were in immediate danger: left-wing politicians, intellectuals, artists, and journalists who had publicly opposed National Socialism during the Weimar Republic. For most of these targeted individuals, the burning of the Reichstag or Parliament building in Berlin in late February sounded the alarm to go underground or flee the country, for the Nazis used the arson as an excuse to conduct mass arrests and brutal "interrogations" of their political enemies. Persecution of specific individuals and groups escalated during the following months: concentration camps were created in early March; a nationwide boycott of Jewish shops, dentists, lawyers, and doctors took place on April 1; Jews were excluded from the civil service, the German law bar and the German medical insurance program in April; books of "undesirable" authors were burned on public squares throughout the Reich in May with Minister of Culture Goebbels in attendance; all political parties (except the National Socialists), trade unions, and strikes were prohibited in July. By the end of 1933, 27,000 political prisoners were in concentration camps while 65,000 Germans had managed to flee the country (forty percent of them to France). This group of political exiles, among whom were some of the most famous figures of Germany's academic and intellectual elite (Albert Einstein, Thomas Mann, Siegfried Kracauer), is represented here through the selections by Alfred Döblin, Ernst Toller, and Käte Frankenthal, all of whom were in immediate danger in 1933 for their outspoken opposition to the Nazis.

The vast majority of eventual refugees, however, remained in Germany and learned to adjust to each new discriminatory practice. For instance, Jews responded to their exclusion from German cultural life by forming the Jewish *Kulturbund* (cultural association) in the summer of 1933, thereby allowing suddenly unemployed Jewish musicians and actors to perform before Jewish audiences throughout the pre-war years of Hitler's reign. Some people became active in underground anti-Fascist movements or engaged in individual acts of resistance (see the account by the anonymous housewife in this section) or were already planning their emigration (A farmer from south Germany, Marta Appel, Peter Gay). In September 1935 the so-called Nuremberg racial laws were enacted, defining Jews on "racial" rather than religious grounds and prohibiting marriage and sexual relations between Jews and non-Jews. At the beginning of 1936, Nazi repression eased somewhat because the regime wanted to enhance its image abroad before the Summer Olympic Games in Berlin, which took place with Hitler in attendance. But the first gypsies were sent to Dachau in July, followed by the mass arrest of Jehovah's Witnesses in late August.

The year 1938 brought a massive change in the political situation of German-speaking Jews in Germany and Austria. On March 11 the Germans invaded Austria, and two days later the annexation of Austria (*Anschluss*) was made into law, resulting in the compulsory "Aryanization" of many Jewish firms and the expulsion of Jews into neighboring states. Then, on November 9–10, following the assassination of a German diplomat in Paris by a Polish Jew, the Nazis organized a massive pogrom of Jewish businesses and synagogues throughout the Reich (including Austria), which resulted in the destruction of almost two hundred synagogues, approximately ninety murders, and the arrest of thousands of Jewish men between the ages of eighteen and sixty-five who were kept in concentrations camps for weeks afterward (see the account by the unnamed accountant from Vienna and, from a wife's perspective, the diary of Hertha Nathorff). This event, known as *Kristallnacht* (Night of Broken Glass), marked a turning point in the lives of all German Jews and provoked a massive rush to emigrate (see the accounts by Nathorff and Wolfram). However, visa restrictions in foreign countries had become much stricter than they were in 1933, while the German authorities imposed horrendous taxes, currency regulations, and bureaucratic restrictions, including an "emigration tax for fleeing Germany" amounting to twenty-five percent of one's entire fortune (this was increased to eighty percent in 1941). Germans were allowed to leave Germany with only ten marks in their possession. The struggle to obtain the necessary permits and official stamps took on Kafkaesque dimensions, as did the legal system, which organized show trials of influential Jewish industrialists on trumped-up charges of financial improprieties (see the account of the shipping magnate Arnold Bernstein, arrested in 1937 just as he was about to emigrate).

Although many Jews were trapped in Germany and Austria after 1938, some children were allowed to emigrate to England, which led to the division of many families (Hertha Nathorff's son was sent abroad, as were Elisabeth Freund's three children). The parents left behind were subjected to increasingly severe living conditions, forced to give up their homes and live in cramped quarters in so-called "Jewish houses" while working in factories and other heavy-labor employment for below-market wages. As of September 19, 1941, all Jews were forced to wear the Yellow Star; on October 23 emigration was officially forbidden for the duration of the war. According to Nazi statistics for the year 1941, some 164,000 "racial" Jews were living in Germany. A small number managed to emigrate abroad, while the majority of remaining Jews, unable to obtain proper immigration papers, were deported to extermination camps in Poland (see the account by Elisabeth Freund).

CHAPTER ONE

"The Reichstag is burning . . ."

Alfred Döblin }

THE REICHSTAG IS BURNING

Although support for the Nazis had been growing throughout the 1930s, and although Hitler had been named chancellor of the Reich on January 30, it was the burning of the Reichstag, the German Parliament building in Berlin, on February 27, 1933, that signaled the beginning of police terror and sent many of Hitler's enemies into exile. Alfred Döblin, author of Berlin Alexanderplatz, *of Jewish origin and a highly visible critic of the Nazis, was among those who fled immediately. Yet despite the danger he was in, a sense of unreality and even of festive renewal pervades the perception of his flight.*

At nine in the morning I heard on the radio that the Reichstag had been set on fire, that the firemen had been able to extinguish the blaze, that the police had succeeded in arresting the arsonists on the spot, that it was the result of a Communist plot—an unspeakable crime committed against the German people, etc. I turned off the radio, speechless. I was already used to the radio and its new owners, but this was the limit. Apparently the Reichstag had actually been set on fire—but by the Communists? They expect us to believe such patent lies? One must first ask *cui bono?*—who profits from the fire? The answer was obvious.

Although deeply disturbed and angry, I wasn't worried for myself—until someone called me and asked what I planned to do. I was astonished. Why? Well, the arrests. I should be careful. Ridiculous, I thought to myself. But the telephone didn't stop ringing. Then people came to see me, always with the same plea that I should make myself scarce, at least for a while. I was in danger, the Nazis had lists, etc. I couldn't see the logic in all this. At first I wasn't able to make the mental leap from a constitutional democracy to a dictatorship and pirate state. By that evening I was capable. My wife also thought I should leave. It would just be a brief trip abroad. You'll let the storm pass over you, just three or four months, and the Nazis will be gone. My friends came to visit, tears were shed. I was calm and laughed. I left with one small suitcase, alone.

Downstairs I was in for a surprise. A Nazi wearing a civilian coat over his uniform was standing in front of the physician's sign with my name on it. He stared at me—and then followed me into the subway. He waited for me to get on the train and then entered my compartment. At the Gleisdreieck Station I got out; he did too. He was following me. A train pulled in and a crowd of people were getting off, so I ran downstairs and took a train from another platform in another direction, and only later to my real destination, the Möckern Bridge at Potsdamer Square. I wanted to get to the Anhalter Railway Station where a train was leaving for Stuttgart at ten. I managed to get a ticket in a sleeping car. (Throughout the twelve years of my emigration, I would carry that ticket around with me in my briefcase.) As the train pulled out of the station, I stood at the window in the corridor. It was dark. I had traveled this route many times. The lights of the city—I've always liked that sight. It was always the same when I returned to Berlin from somewhere else: I saw the lights, I would breathe a sigh of relief and know I was home. Well, I'm on my way now, I should lie down and sleep. It was a strange situation that had nothing to do with me, really.

A few hours in Stuttgart. Life is calm, the Nazis are announcing some big rallies. It's crazy. Why am I running away? So naïve. Later I'll be ashamed of myself. I get to Überlingen [near the Swiss border], where I spend the night, a boat trip across Lake [Constance] to Kreuzlingen. Now comes the border crossing, by car; everything goes perfectly. In Kreuzlingen I paid a visit to the physician of a private clinic who had invited me and my wife the year before to stay with him (what a fresh, happy time). Now I was coming as a refugee, a role which struck me as absurd and meaningless. So who was running away? From what?

Everything looked so peaceful, normal, completely normal! Until one day I was called outside the clinic; someone was asking to see me. It was March 3, 1933: 3/3/33 (I have a slight superstition about numbers). Outside, with the exception of one son, stood my entire family. Now that was a completely different situation. My wife, extremely agitated, told me about the awful things that were happening in Berlin, the terrible harassment, the things she had heard on the train. The whole family was in danger, they couldn't stay. Well, they were all here. I was terrified by the date, 3/3/33. It made me think. But I got over the shock. I had other things to worry about, such as where we would live, or our walks and conversations, our plans for the future. Had I really left, or was I just waiting? I didn't know. I didn't really care. My wife saw the true situation we were in. She knew she had taken leave of her home for good, that the children had been ripped from everything, she saw the mountain of cares, the cloud of uncertainty awaiting us. She cried a lot. On the other hand (what could I do against myself?), I felt elated. Yes, elated. How so? In those months I kept thinking about the quote from Schiller's ballad "The Diver": "Yet it became my salvation, it pulled me on high."

What did my salvation consist in? Everything in Germany, not just politics, had become intellectually intolerable. It was as if the political battles, the stagnation, had taken hold of German culture and paralyzed it. I fought against it in my own way. But finally, at the end of 1932, an image had appeared to me that I couldn't shake off: an ancient, rotting god, close to complete putrefaction, takes leave of his seat in heaven and flies down to the people on earth to renew himself and atone for his old sins. Once a god and ruler, now he is a mortal like the rest of us. This image was the intuition of my exile.

Yes, exile: the separation and isolation, the escape from the dead end, this sense of falling and sinking—it appeared to me as a kind of salvation. In my heart I could hear the music: "It pulled me on high." I couldn't keep myself from feeling this way. I was elated (a state which carried over into the book I was working on that whole year).

This is how I went into exile. This is how I felt when I "took my leave" of Germany.

BERLIN, 1933

Käte Frankenthal (1889–1976) was one of the first female physicians in Wilhelmine Germany, a member of the Socialist Party in the Prussian Landtag and an elected representative of the Berlin City Council. On vacation in Switzerland when the Reichstag was set on fire, her first impulse was not to flee Germany but to return to Berlin to use her authority to help her patients, friends, and political colleagues endangered by the Nazis. The following is taken from her memoirs, written in early 1940 for an essay contest sponsored by Harvard University on the theme: "My Life in Germany Before and After January 30, 1933."

In February [1933] I took a few days vacation and traveled to Switzerland. I had barely arrived when I heard the news of the Reichstag fire. Among the first people to be arrested was the communist city councilor of Neukölln.* I took the next train back. I had barely entered my apartment when the telephone rang. Communist colleagues of mine wished to speak to me at once. They had been calling every hour for the last twenty-four hours in the vague hope that I might return home.

They were afraid that there were important party documents in the city councilor's office. The names and addresses he might have in his desk would make people suspect they were Communists and lead to their arrest. The Nazis could come at any minute to search the office and had already been in his apartment. The mayor of Neukölln, a Socialist, still believed that the persecution of the Communists wouldn't be extended to other groups. He remained an obedient civil servant, even under Göring, and wouldn't allow anyone without proper authority to enter the councilor's office.

In the absence of the city councilor I immediately became his representative and thus had official authority to take his place. I called the mayor and said

---

* Neukölln is the working-class district where Käte Frankenthal resided and served in the municipal government. In Berlin each district had its own mayor and autonomous city hall. Ed.

that because of the political events I had cut short my vacation and was returning to work.

"Yes, thank you. That's very nice."

"Should I come to see you?"

"No thank you, that won't be necessary. There's nothing special happening."

He wasn't the only one who didn't notice that something special was happening before it hit him in the face.

I went to the office and sat down at the city councilor's desk. I was carrying a briefcase of the sort that almost all professional people in Germany carry with them everywhere. Immediately an official [*Beamte*] came in and put Göring's last proclamation on the desk: "Whoever shreds or removes official documents will be punished by imprisonment."

I said that I wished to look through the mail that had accumulated and didn't want to be disturbed for several hours. I knew what the official's political views were. But obedience is something so ingrained for Prussian civil servants that they couldn't shift gears fast enough and disobey their superiors.

After a few hours a female physician who worked in the office requested to see me on official business. She was carrying a briefcase similar to mine. When she left the office, we had exchanged briefcases. Now the Nazis were free to come. They found nothing.[. . .]

My removal from office was announced in the paper under the headline "Cleansing in Neukölln." None of my friends checked up on me, and they were right not to. Staying in touch was dangerous and there was no time for sentimentality. The only person to call was my housekeeper of many years who had married in the meantime but who still saw to it that the new servants did everything the way it had always been done. I think she was the only person in Germany who was committed to me unconditionally.

"I just read the paper," she said on the phone. "They must be totally crazy."

"Ida, hang up and come here," I answered. It was even our task to make it clear to our few remaining friends that they could no longer voice their loyalty.

Everything was dangerous now. Even before Hitler's seizure of power, I couldn't stand it when one of the screaming Nazi voices came over the radio. "Shut up," I called from the other room, and the maid understood what I meant. She went and turned the radio off. (I suppose we were much more liberal with such expletives in Germany than in other countries). Whenever Nazi speeches came on after the seizure of power, the maid would call out: "Should I make him shut up, Doctor?" That could cost her her life if the window was open and someone heard her. It could cost me my life, too, if she had a Nazi boyfriend and told him she had learned this from me. Life was cheap in Germany.

I visited some of the Socialist groups in the rest of Germany. Everywhere I found the same picture: complete disintegration and despair, arrests and desertions. Several groups had been totally destroyed because they had hidden a handful of useless weapons that were then found. To the very end they didn't want to believe that they weren't being called upon to fight.

The "brief National Socialist education" began. People were arrested for twenty-four hours, beaten half to death, then sent home. They didn't even dare call a doctor. People would slip me their house keys with the request to come late, when it was dark. I took some pictures of the horribly battered bodies and will always regret that I didn't make it out of Germany with them.

I had no more business in Germany and knew that with every passing hour I was uselessly exposing myself to danger. Already, the terror had struck in great proximity to me: close colleagues of mine had been arrested. I decided to look around for a place where I could emigrate. Austria, Czechoslovakia, or Switzerland were possibilities. I prepared to travel around for approximately two weeks in order to assess the situation. After that, I wanted to return, dispose of my belongings, pack up the things I wished to keep, and emigrate.

I left on March 31, 1933. It was one day before the boycott of the Jews officially ordered by the government. I had withdrawn a sizable amount of money, but then I worried about taking it along, since so many Jews were departing on that day and we could expect to be searched. I had already made arrangements to have all my savings transferred abroad.

We were only allowed to take fifty marks with us when leaving the country. Of course that wasn't enough for two weeks of traveling. In order to export more than that, formal steps were required, but I didn't want to draw the administration's attention to my travel plans. I was prepared to find the emigrants in a desperate state and also had to have some money available for them. I folded up a thousand mark bill and buried it in a glass container that I had carefully filled to the brim with powder. I put the container in a bag that contained only a few toiletries and a book—something almost any traveler carried. A container with powder belonged in every lady's bag, and since this one was made of glass and you could see from the outside that it was filled with powder, the money was safe.

I kept the rolls of film with the torture evidence in the inside pocket of my jacket. I planned to give them to the papers in Prague.

Besides this, I took only a small suitcase with some clothes and the few things that I might need in two weeks' time. I wasn't going to be attending any parties, after all. I debated whether to take my fur coat along, which I especially loved. Its value was far beyond my means. The friends I mentioned earlier, the owners of a clothing store, had gotten it for me at a good price and I hoped that its life span would be as long as mine. Unfortunately, I thought it was already too warm for the coat. I was never to see Germany and my things again.

In Dresden I was arrested. Nazis stormed the train, went from compartment to compartment, picking out the ones to be arrested—between twenty and thirty people. I don't know how they were selected. Probably it was everyone whose destination lay outside Germany or whose passport was relatively old. Mine had been issued two years earlier.

The police were on hand to herd us into trucks. There were several elderly people among the arrested and some who were frightened out of their wits, and were crying and screaming. The police officers remained calm and helped the elderly climb into the trucks. The tone that followed then was very different. A high-ranking Nazi came and yelled: "What are you doing, police officers?! You're helping those Jewish pigs? A kick in the a . . . to send them flying onto the truck is what they should get!"

The first thing I noticed was that the relationship between the police and the SA, which Göring had only recently declared as an auxiliary police force, was extremely tense. The police didn't want to be given orders by the SA and insisted that the people under arrest were in their custody. The SA men screamed the worst insults and threats. A woman had seizures. The police took care of her and had a calming effect on all of us. Some young SA men chose the oldest one of the group, a gray-haired man, to help them carry a crate. One policeman suggested, "Maybe one of the younger men should do that?" The police liked its auxiliary police even less than it did the people under arrest.

I was completely calm. I had been carrying cyanide in my purse for weeks, as accessible as my handkerchief. I had seen too much of the Nazi methods to submit to them, and was fully aware how horribly effective these methods of terror were. I was no more courageous than the people who were crying like children. I simply was protected from what they feared. There were millions in Germany whose life was cut short with the Nazi seizure of power. They would not have feared death in their efforts to undermine Nazi power. The death penalty would not have deterred these resistance fighters. But under inhuman torture many became traitors to their friends and even confessed to what wasn't true. The Nazis denied their methods only to foreign countries. In Germany they utilized the unfortunate ones whom they sent home bloodied and beaten up as examples; to add insult to injury, the victims were scorned and shunned by their friends. I do not view these people as traitors or slanderers, and in Germany I offered them medical assistance. Inhuman suffering is stronger than human character. I believe that many of them would have gone to their own executions as heroes.

We were taken to the Trade-Union Building of Dresden, which I knew well since it adjoined a fine hotel where I had stayed on several occasions. Now it was occupied by the SA and the police, and was being used for the first interrogations accompanying the mass arrests. Later, when we were called into various rooms for interrogations and searches, we were always told to take note of the beautiful rooms and of the fact that this was how the union bureaucrats lived off of the workers.

We were taken into a large room where we sat on the floor. This is where we spent the night. The whole thing seemed improvised and wasn't very systematically organized. In response to the question of what we were charged with, the police said that there were no charges and that it was just a formality.

Two foreigners were arrested who made loud, insistent demands that their consul be informed. One of the consuls arrived in the middle of the night and the foreigners were released immediately. I noticed that the incident had been an embarrassment and led to reciprocal accusations between the police and the SA.

I thought of the gruesome pictures I was carrying in my pocket as evidence of the Nazi terror and thought I was doomed. But then I saw my chance. People were asking if they could go to the bathroom and the policeman nodded his head indifferently. I went to the bathroom immediately. When I returned, the incriminating evidence was no longer in my pocket. It wasn't a minute too soon. Female and male officers arrived and everyone was accompanied to the bathroom.

In the next twenty-four hours, my things were searched five times by five different officials. Five times they touched the fateful glass jar with the facial powder and I looked about indifferently, as was appropriate for someone whose pocketbook contains nothing of value except the stipulated fifty marks in cash. No infringement of the currency regulations. I almost enjoyed the body search which followed. They discovered the inside pocket of my jacket and emptied it out—it contained nothing but a pencil.

More interrogations followed. By now all our luggage was piled up in a big heap in the entrance hall. I couldn't very well show much interest in an unimportant pocketbook and carry it around wherever I went. It might yet get lost or stolen. But it would probably no longer kill me. Late at night we were gathered together and told that everyone was free to leave with the exception of a few unlucky souls who had been found to be carrying money or incriminating evidence. All our passports were being kept and would be returned to our local authorities. Those with a clear conscience, they said, might retrieve their passports from their hometown.

I didn't have a clear conscience and couldn't go to the Berlin offices. I was glad they hadn't yet come to me. Moreover, I already knew from the reports of other emigrants that it was a terrible problem to live in a foreign country without a passport. I could neither advance nor retreat.

But obviously this insight did little to cheer me up in my present predicament. Then it occurred to me that I was actually very lucky to be exactly where I was, namely, on the streets of the beautiful city of Dresden and not on my way to a concentration camp. For today I had made it incredibly far and seemed in fact to be having a streak of good fortune. Tomorrow I could even visit the Sistine Madonna, which I hadn't seen in a long time. (I never got around to it.) In the past I had usually regretted being so pressed for time and having to rush back to Berlin. Now I actually had a reason to celebrate that I could neither advance nor retreat. We had been given some soup and bread under arrest, but I hadn't had anything decent to eat since lunch the day before and had spent the night mostly on my feet. So I went to the best hotel in Dresden, ordered a very good dinner, and drank an entire bottle of excellent wine. Then I slept wonderfully, in a decent room, for the first time in a long while. That was just the psychological treatment I needed.

The following morning I ordered a good breakfast and read the paper at my leisure. That was what saved me. A new decree had been issued by the Nazis stating that no one was allowed to leave the country without permission. The decree went into effect immediately. But anyone already traveling was to be let through!

This cut off the route to Berlin for good. Apparently the Nazis were trying to prevent potential enemies from leaving the country with passports issued by an earlier government. That was exactly my case. But the notice in the paper opened up a different path. It stated that anyone already traveling was to be let through. The officials in Dresden apparently hadn't even determined the identity of the people they had arrested. Otherwise I, along with a well-known Communist who had been arrested with me, would never have been released. We had found a moment in which to agree that in case one of us should happen to get out, the other would pass on a message to Berlin, telling our friends what had happened to us.

I had nothing to lose and took a taxi back to the Nazis instead of to the Sistine Madonna. Later it often occurred to me that one is only capable of doing something truly rational if one is alone in life. A friend would not have let me return to the lion's den, which I had escaped because they happened not to know who I was. I probably wouldn't have let a friend return either.

I was greeted by the Nazis as I had expected: "What does the Jewish pig want?" By the time I left, they would say: "It's been a pleasure, Doctor. Till the next time." Hopefully there will be no next time, I thought to myself.

In my best government-official tone of voice, I told the Nazi who had greeted me so kindly that I urgently wished to see his superior. He went into a room to announce me and I immediately followed him just in case. It was a Sunday, and the head Nazi was soaking his feet. "Oh, how embarrassing to have a lady come in here," he said. I managed a smile and said, "That's quite all right, I'm a doctor—and a *Beamte* (civil servant) at that." (That was no longer true, I had been a *Beamte*.) "You're a *Beamte* too and know what it's like. You can't choose your vacation but must travel whenever you have a spare moment. It would ruin my entire vacation if I had to return to Berlin now. Here is a decree from Adolf Hitler stating that people who were already traveling yesterday should be allowed to continue their trip. Couldn't you give me back my passport?" I guess he must have been convinced that I had a clear conscience if I voluntarily came back here and referred to a decree from Adolf Hitler. He struck up a friendly, Sunday morning kind of chat. In the end he said he would check whether the passports were still there, though he didn't think so. He came back holding mine in his hand.

I was terribly sorry I couldn't reach the Communist woman to tell her of my experience. She had continued on immediately and wanted to try to get across the border at night. Later I met her in Prague. Her escape had been successful, but later she encountered great difficulties because she had no passport.

I took the next train [on April 2, 1933] across the border. All the seats in the compartment were taken. Nobody said a word, and nobody seemed to take an interest in his fellow travelers. After we crossed the border, a woman interrupted the silence with a deep sigh: Thank God! From that moment on a lively conversation ensued. Everyone on the train was fleeing.

An Open Letter
to Herr Goebbels

Fire, whether the burning of the Reichstag in February 1933 or the burn-
ing of German synagogues in November 1938 (Kristallnacht), was can-
nily used by the Nazis as a physical means of destruction as well as a potent
political symbol. On May 10, 1933, right-wing students in Berlin set fire to
a huge pile of books by authors that had been labeled as "undesirable" by the
Nazis; Propaganda Minister Joseph Goebbels held a speech hailing the de-
struction. Ernst Toller, a well-known dramatist and left-wing political ac-
tivist who had taken a leading role in the Socialist Revolution in Bavaria
following World War I, was particularly hated by the Nazis. Like Döblin,
he fled Germany in 1933 and arrived in New York in 1936, where he com-
mitted suicide in 1939.

When, on the tenth of May [1933], the works of German writers, philosophers, and scientists were thrown onto the funeral pyre, you, Herr
Goebbels, protected and welcomed this barbaric act. In a speech you named
the burned works of those men, who represent a more noble Germany than
you, "intellectual garbage."

You have burned the works of German publishing houses, theaters, book-
stores, libraries, and schools; you persecute their authors, lock them up, or
drive them from their native country.

You are driving out the best teachers from German universities.

The conductors and composers from the concert halls.

The painters, architects, and sculptors from their studios and academies.

You're not satisfied with torturing those whom you have locked up in your
prisons and concentration camps. You personally persecute the emigrants
with the many weapons in your power; you wish to destroy them intellectually
and physically (to use your language) "in a brutal and merciless way."

And what is the cause of such unbounded hatred?

These men believe in a world of freedom, humanity, social justice; these
men are true Socialists, Communists, or believing Christians; these men are
not willing to deny the voice of truth or to bow before brute force.

The persecutions and harassment are a great honor for those of us who are being hounded; many of us will now have to prove that they deserve this honor.

You claim to save German culture, and you destroy the purest work of German culture.

You claim to awaken Germany's youth, and you blind their spirit, their eyes, their senses.

You claim to save German children, and you poison their hearts with the defaming slogans of a stupid nationalism and racism.

You claim to free the working classes, and you lock them up in the chains of social and intellectual slavery.

You claim to purify Germany from its "criminals," and you persecute the weakest ones, the Jews.

You claim that you and the German spirit are identical, but your deeds are the contradiction of the ideas of Goethe and Lessing, Herder and Schiller, Wieland and Ranke, and all those men who have fought for the purest values of Germany and borne them into the world. Recently I read your literary works. I won't reproach you for your poor style in German; power doesn't automatically lead to talent. But the fact that you force German theaters to put on these miserable plays is pitiful.

You speak so often of heroism—where have you shown it? We too are familiar with heroism—the heroism of work, of character, of the principled individual who stands by his ideas.

You speak so often of the cowardice of your opponents. We promise you that your persecutions will make us harder, your hatred more mature, your battle more combative.

We are not without fault in our fate. We've made many errors, and the greatest was our patience.

Thanks to the lesson you have given us, we will overcome our errors. And that is your merit.

CHAPTER TWO

Lives Transformed

Anonymous }

A FARMER FROM SOUTH GERMANY

The following statement was first published in 1941 in a volume entitled We Escaped, *which contained twelve personal accounts of the flight to America. The farmer from south Germany is not identified other than by this generic title; apparently this original oral narrative was translated (or brought into idiomatic English) by the American editors.*

In 1933 we had just built a new house. It was a good brick house, near the town but in the country. I had fifteen acres of vineyards, which produced about 60,000 litres of wine every year, and we sold it to a dealer who came round to buy wine wholesale from the farmers. I also dealt in cattle—making trips to neighboring provinces to buy them, and of course we had chickens, a big garden, a house for chilling the grapes, and stables with all the newest equipment. The house had central heating and electric light.

My family was Jewish, and came originally from Spain, but we have found records mentioning them as far back as 1570 in our district. The household consisted of my wife and me, my mother-in-law, our two children—a boy and a girl—a maid, and two hired men. We were respected in that district, and I really had no enemies except people who would have liked to have my farm. It was the best farm around there. But in 1933, when Hitler came in, they started arresting people such as the mayor of the town, who was a democrat. Then they came and took me and the hired man. It was the busy time of year when we were setting out the potatoes. They took us before the *Ortsgruppenleiter.* I said to him:

"What do you mean by arresting me—I was a volunteer in the last war and served four years!"

Immediately I was let go.

We stayed on the farm, and people on the whole were very decent. I was allowed to trade freely. They sent police to search the house, but they didn't find anything. We went ahead with the farming as usual, until June— *Fronleichnamstag* (Corpus Christi Day) it was. Then because they couldn't find any legal grounds to arrest me, they just sent two policemen to get me, at

4:30 in the morning. They always made arrests at times like that, because they were sure of catching a person at home.

I was taken to a nearby town, where it was demanded that I undergo a medical examination. I refused, saying I was not sick. "What's the matter?" I asked the doctor they had there. He couldn't answer and just shook his head.

Along with a group of others, I was carried off to a bigger town, and put in a regular prison. That was the first time in my life I ever was in a prison. We stayed in it a day and a night. The guard who took me there said, "This is the worst trip I've ever taken" and gave me some money.

In the evening we were put into a common police wagon, and driven to the town of B———, where we were locked up for the night again. The next morning we were shipped to the concentration camp of Sachsenhausen.

As we were unloaded, the Gestapo explained to us, "Now your nice time's over," and we were handed to the SS men. Right away the kicking and cuffing began. We had to run for thirty or forty minutes to the barracks, and anyone trying to escape was shot at immediately. Then in the camp itself, we were introduced to the commander—the head of the whole place. He made a speech to us, something like this:

"You cowardly *Schweinehunde*—what you see here is your freedom. All you need to be relieved is a little lead in the belly. Here you'll get old and gray—you must grow beards that will go three times around the table. And remember that my soldiers are first-class shots."

We were glad when he stopped and they took us away. We had to take off all our clothing, and give up even our wedding rings. The guards would say, "Give your ring up—you'll never see your Sarah again in your life!" All our hair was cut off, and we put on criminal suits with the Jewish star on the breast. Whoever didn't cooperate was beaten to death, and if you flinched from a blow, they would give you another one. Then before we were to go to our quarters, we had to do an endurance run, singing all the time. You sang any little song—*Lore, Lore, Lore* and I don't know what else.

At night the SS men came and beat us up.

They woke us at 4:30 the next morning, and we went to work under a heavy guard. When we arrived at the working place, it was explained to us:

"At the left is 'neutral' ground—whoever steps in there will be shot immediately."

Then we started to load sand into a wagon, on which an SS man stood with his gun. All the work had to be done running. This went on till noon. Many, many were left there. Those who showed fear were forced to bow down before the SS men until they were exhausted, crying "I am a dirty Jew," and other such things. The overseer called out to me, "Hey, you tall one—you can work," and gave me the job of tipping the wagon and emptying it, in addition to running to and fro.

If anyone said he wanted a drink, they told him to go over in the direction of the neutral ground, and that meant, of course, getting shot. We were warned that if we heard a shot, we should lie down and not get up until ordered to do so. Very soon a shot came.

At twelve, they said, "The Jews haven't worked—they won't get anything to eat." As a matter of fact we got half portions. But the religious sect of *Bibelforscher** who were our fellow prisoners gave us some water secretly—there was a death penalty for that. The sun shone on our shaven heads and it was very hot.

So it went until evening.

At seven, as we left the working grounds, we had to keep up the tempo and *run* home, accompanied by blows and shots. That was probably the worst time of all—that running home at the end of the day. When we got in, an SS man came to me and to two others, and told us to follow him. We thought this is the end—we will be shot. But we were ordered to climb into an auto, taken to the neutral ground near the place we had been working, and there had to load onto the truck a dead body. It was the man who had been shot first that morning, when he went to get a drink. He had been a big merchant in Hamburg—a great fat man.

Back at the camp we put the corpse in the hall, and then expected we should have our supper and a little peace. But instead we had to stand upright without moving in the isolation barracks for the rest of the evening. At nine we could lie down, but we got no food.

That was our first day in the concentration camp of Sachsenhausen.

During the night the SS men came again and beat us up.

So it went for about five weeks. We got no mail for the first four weeks. My wife didn't know where I was—there was no sign of life from me.

Illness you couldn't report—you were just tortured to death. In those first weeks three or four people died a day. The guards were always finding excuses to shoot. If an SS man felt like shooting there was nothing to stop him really. They always tortured the fat people most—twenty-five blows, or hung them up facing the sun. Then there was one old man—between seventy-five and eight, I think—who was strong enough to keep on working. When he didn't die they took him and kept him at work until he did finally collapse and die from the effects.

After the first four weeks I got the first card from my wife, and two weeks later I was allowed to send her a printed card on which it said:

"It goes very well with me here. We must emigrate."

One was glad every evening that one still had one's life, and one was relieved at dawn that one hadn't been beaten to death in the night. The fear of death was with us all the time. It happened to me that my shovel broke while

---

* "Jehovah's Witnesses." Ed.

I was working. I reported it to the overseer. He told me to go to the carpenters and get a handle put in—the carpenters were mostly the *Bibelforscher*—very nice people. But close to the place where I went to get the shovel repaired was an SS wagon. The men in it called me over and led me away. They took me to a table, laid me over it, and started beating me on the back with a heavy stick. They beat as hard as they could.

I stood it. Then their commander came and tried his hand at it. Again I didn't speak. He ordered me to get up. I got to my feet and stood at attention in the military way. He looked at me and said:

"You were a soldier?"

"Yes."

"You are a brave young man," he said. "You can go."

I escaped all the worst punishments, since I knew where I stood and what the rules were. Yet another time I had gone with seven comrades to be photographed and fingerprinted, and reported immediately on return, saying:

"Prisoner number —, back with seven Jewish prisoners."

The officer kicked me. So I tried again, and said:

"Prisoner number —, back with seven Jewish prisoners."

It still wasn't right. I had to say:

"A work-refusing Jew with seven work-refusing Jewish prisoners reports back." Then it was all right.

Once a prisoner and I talked together, and the overseer came in and heard us. He said, "Who talked?" and we reported immediately, since otherwise the whole group would have been punished. When we were handed over to the superior officer, we both stood stiffly at attention. He recognized that we had been soldiers. He asked my companion, "What rank?" He had been a lieutenant. So he was let go without punishment, and since I too had been in the war, and had won medals, I was also let go.

But it was only faith in God and the hope of release that kept one from committing suicide.

Then they began to release those who had proof that they could emigrate, and the Jews and the *Bibelforscher* were moved from the isolation barracks where they had been, to the so-called "free" camp. This consisted of big barracks with decent beds in them, and here we were allowed to receive from outside fifteen marks a week, with which we could buy food at the canteen. The working hours were much the same—five in the morning to about seven at night. This, they told us, was "freedom."

Those last four weeks were not anywhere nearly so bad as the first five, especially for me since I was foreman of the first wagon at work, and had the luck to be on good terms with the overseer. Also we were continually being told that we could get out if we emigrated across the sea. "But," we were warned, "if you say anything against the concentration camp, the Gestapo will get you wherever you are. You'll go back, you'll be shot."

One day I was called up to headquarters to get some money and my clothes which had been checked there. But then they said to me:

"You can come into the *Gummistube* now."

That was a cellar room where about 1000 prisoners who were crazy were put to crushing stones. Some had actually gone insane, and some only pretended. I said quickly that I'd rather go back to my wagon!

Next morning they read a list of those to be released and my name was on it. I didn't step forward because I thought it was another joke—I couldn't believe it, and besides my name was a very common one and there were so many who might be meant. But they kept calling me forward, and when I did finally come out, they asked me which was my number. (All the prisoners had numbers, of course.) But I was so confused at that moment that I told them not my number but the date of my birth. Of course that was wrong, and I was sent back again.

Later they called me from work and asked me my wife's name.

"Elizabeth," I said.

"Your wife's name," they said again.

"Elizabeth."

"No—Sarah is your wife's name!"

So I had to say "Sarah."*

At last I was called and told that I was to be released. But when they told me, they said, "You're released, but you're crazy, aren't you—you swine," and again, "You—released—you'll get twenty-five blows, you will!" But by then I knew that the arrangements had all been made, and I said to them, "You'll have to let me go."

I was given a bath, shaved, got my clothes, and was examined by the camp doctor. I had bad pus-filled boils from sweating all the time. The doctor asked me if I had anything wrong with me, and I started to say:

"Yes—I've got—"

"You've got flesh on your bones, haven't you," he said. "Do you want me to heal it for you or will you do it yourself?"

"I'll do it," I said quickly.

Two hours later the commander gave all of us who were going out a lecture, and asked us questions like, "When you get out, how soon will you go to work?" If you answered "in forty-eight hours," you were pushed back again. You had to say "immediately!" Then he asked, "How did you like it here?" and things like that, and we were threatened again if we dared say anything against the camp when we were outside. But when we left, we were each given three loaves of excellent bread to take along—to impress people outside.

---

* As of January 1, 1939 the Nazi government required all Jews to take either Sarah or Israel as a middle name. Ed.

I arrived home at twelve o'clock one night. When my wife saw me, she ran away at first—she thought I was a criminal. She couldn't recognize me—I was just skin and bones.

My wife had been trying to arrange that I should emigrate at once to Cuba alone. I said no—"I'll stay here on the farm even if they beat me dead." I knew of no dishonest thing I had done in my life, and I knew I had done my duty by my country.

I was supposed to report to the police station every day, but the mayor exempted me. Some days later, though, I was ordered to come before the *Orts-bauernführer*, and he said to me—although he owed me money himself:

"Rudolf, your farm has been made into an *Erbhof* (a farm to be owned only by Aryans)—so you must sell it."

I said, "I'll think about it."

After a while an officer came up to my place and told me again that I would have to sell. I said to him:

"Who built this house—you or I?"

In my own house we almost came to blows, and he left saying that he'd put me back where I'd been.

So I decided to leave.

The date set for my emigration was September 6. I went to several different consulates for a visa, but I had no luck. I knew there was a chance in America, and tried to get on the refugee lists for the United States, but there was not enough time. Then I got a visa to Panama because I was a farmer. But my sister who lived in America sent me a newspaper clipping that said the central refugee committee was looking for a farmer to settle in a community in the U.S.A., if he already had his affidavit and a number—the number of registration at the consulate. I could get an affidavit from my sister, and I was registered at the consulate, but my number was so high that it seemed I'd have to wait for two years.

In the meantime the date set for my emigration in September had come. The local police warned me to leave and let me get out with my family although they had a warrant for my arrest in their pockets already. When we were gone our house was broken into right away, and all our good things smashed and the windows broken.

We took our auto, and for sixteen days and nights we travelled—just anywhere. We didn't know where to go. It seemed safest to stay every night in a different place. So we always kept moving—sixteen days and sixteen nights.

One day the news reached me that I was supposed to report to Berlin. I was scared to go there, so I managed to get a postponement by telephone. I was in touch with our mayor all this time by telephone and he advised me to stay away for a while still—he'd tell me when it was safe to come home. But for me it seemed impossible to keep up that life. I finally went to a police station in a large city, reported myself with my wife, and told them my case. They gave me a letter releasing me from arrest. We went back to the farm.

I had to make the trip to Berlin to get my admission to America—to see if they would accept me as one of the farmers to be settled there. I was selected from a big group of applicants, and they even gave me a special letter to hasten the granting of the American visa in Stuttgart. But the consul in Stuttgart wanted a lot of papers and complicated proofs. It took a long time, until I got a French transit visa—a four weeks' stay in France—that would make it possible for me to get out of Germany. They granted the transit visa on the old Panama visa I'd received some months before.

Alone, I set out for Strasbourg. My wife stayed behind to get our things together, pack them, and send them on. The children were also with her. In Strasbourg the American consul told me to go to Paris for my American visa. There the refugee committee supported me while I had to wait, and put me in a hotel. My wife sent our two children on to me under care of a friend, but I had no place to keep them, so I had to put the girl in an orphan asylum and the boy stayed with a French family.

That was an awful time for me. I didn't have much to eat and there was much waiting at the consulates. At last I got my wife admitted.

In the meantime our boy had had an accident. One day he burned himself very badly. He had to be rushed to the hospital and was in danger of death. That was the same day that I was to go and get my visa, which had been granted at last. I got to the offices ten minutes late, and so couldn't get it any more. They told me that I'd have to start all over again.

This was when my wife arrived. It was toward the end of August 1939. She'd had a terrible time at home. She had tried to get as many of our possessions together to take with her as possible, since you couldn't take money out. During that time great areas in our district were being evacuated for military purposes, and they wanted to put these evacuated people on the Jewish farms. Luckily for us there was a dispute among our local officials, and because of that we were able to have the sale of our farm delayed, so my wife had a little time to get ready. But she had to buy many new things, because most of our old ones had been broken when they raided our house.

When at last she was ready to go, they said she couldn't emigrate as long as the farm was still in our name. So she had to go through the business of the sale, although she couldn't take the money from it with her!

After all that, the biggest trunk with our things never got through into France, because the war broke out. When my wife arrived, she wanted first of all to rest, but had to report to the *préfecture*, and they sent her to Cherbourg. She was supposed to stay in France only eight days. But because the boy was sick she was allowed to stay with him, and then she got an extension of fourteen days more. She kept getting extensions. All around in Paris were people who had nowhere to go at this time, and you saw them leaving the *préfecture* weeping.

I was with my wife in Paris only for those first eight days. In September all Germans were interned and I was sent to a French concentration camp near Paris.

The first three or four weeks there were inhuman. Except for the beating to death, everything was just as bad as in Germany. The guards hated us because we were Germans. The quarters were very bad—we didn't even have latrines in that camp. But later I was put in a different place where we were treated very well. The commander was a nice man and very generous to the prisoners.

It had been demanded that we should enlist in the French army as colonial troops, but now we heard that those with visas might emigrate instead. The American consul in Paris got me a second visa, and on this I was granted a release. My wife meanwhile had been helped by a friend of ours who gave her food and money and told her where to get a good lawyer. She managed to get a visa to Bordeaux. There she had to stay a night, and she decided she would try to see me in the camp nearby, although she had not *sauf-conduit* and it was illegal for her to travel there without a pass. She had heard from me that we had an exceptional commander in the camp. When she came to him, he was very nice to her. He could not at that moment release me, but she was allowed to speak to me, and then the commander went with her to the local *préfecture*, helped her out there, and even found a hotel for her to stay in. When I got my release, she was allowed to accompany me part of the way to Vichy, on the train. Then we had to separate again, and she went to get the children and to buy a ship's ticket. I was taken to Paris, and from there to Le Havre—under guard right onto the boat.

For a moment we met just by chance when I was being taken through Paris. We were both in line at the station—I turned around and there she was! But we could not go to Le Havre together. It was on the boat that our whole family was united again.

Marta Appel }

FROM THE EYES OF A MOTHER

Marta Appel was born in Metz (Lorraine) in 1894 but was expelled with her family by the French after the First World War. She married Dr. Ernst Appel, a rabbi of a large congregation in Bingen, who was subsequently called to Dortmund. She escaped Germany secretly with her daughters to Holland, then emigrated to the United States. Her husband was a rabbi in Jackson, Tennessee until 1969.

The children had been advised not to come to school on April 1, 1933, the day of the boycott. Even the principal of the school thought Jewish children's lives were no longer safe. One night they placed big signs on every store or house owned by Jewish people. In front of our temple, on every square and corner, billboards were scoffing at us. Everywhere, and on all occasions, we read and heard that we were vermin and had caused the ruin of the German people. No Jewish store was closed on that day; none was willing to show fear in the face of the boycott. The only building which did not open its door as usual, since it was Saturday, was the temple. We did not want this holy place desecrated by any trouble.

I even went downtown that day to see what was going on in the city. There was no cheering crowd as the Nazis had expected, no running and smashing of Jewish businesses. I heard only words of anger and disapproval. People were massed before the Jewish stores to watch the Nazi guards who were posted there to prevent anyone from entering to buy. And there were many courageous enough to enter, although they were called rude names by the Nazi guards, and their pictures were taken to show them as enemies of the German people in the daily papers. Inside the stores, in the offices of the owners, there was another battle proceeding. Nazis were forcing those Jewish men to send wires abroad to foreign businesses, saying that there was no Jewish boycott and that nothing unusual was happening. Accompanied by two Nazi officials, one of the men was taken even to Holland to convince the foreign customers and businessmen there.

Our gentile friends and neighbors, even people whom we had scarcely known before, came to assure us of their friendship and to tell us that these horrors could not last very long. But after some months of a regime of terror, fidelity and friendship had lost their meaning, and fear and treachery had replaced them. For the sake of our gentile friends, we turned our heads so as not to greet them in the streets, for we did not want to bring upon them the danger of imprisonment for being considered a friend of Jews.

With each day of the Nazi regime, the abyss between us and our fellow citizens grew larger. Friends whom we had loved for years did not know us anymore. They suddenly saw that we were different from themselves. Of course we were different, since we were bearing the stigma of Nazi hatred, since we were hunted like deer. Through the prominent position of my husband we were in constant danger. Often we were warned to stay away from home. We were no longer safe, wherever we went.

How much our life changed in those days! Often it seemed to me I could not bear it any longer, but thinking of my children, I knew we had to be strong to make it easier for them. From then on I hated to go out, since on every corner I saw signs that the Jews were the misfortune of the people. Wherever I went, when I had to speak to people in a store I imagined how they would turn against me if they knew I was Jewish. When I was waiting for a streetcar I always thought that the driver would not stop if he knew I was Jewish. Never did anything unpleasant happen to me on the street, but I was expecting it at every moment, and it was always bothering me. I did not go into a theater or a movie for a long time before we were forbidden to,* since I could not bear to be among people who hated me so much. Therefore, when, later on, all those restrictions came, they did not take away from me anything that I had not already renounced. Nevertheless, it meant a new shame. Not to go of my own accord was very different from not being allowed to go.

In the evenings we sat at home next to the radio listening fearfully to all the new and outrageous restrictions and laws which almost daily brought further suffering to Jewish people. We no longer visited our friends, nor did they come anymore to see us. Why should we be together, since our minds were upon only one thing and, when we spoke, we heard only one story more cruel than the other? Was it not sufficient to face the cruelty during our day's work? Why should we sacrifice our sleep to hear of more and more atrocities?

Since I had lived in Dortmund, I had met every four weeks with a group of women, all of whom were born in Metz, my beloved home city. We all had been pupils or teachers in the same high school. After the Nazis came, I was afraid to go to the meetings. I did not want the presence of a Jewess to bring any trouble, since we always met publicly in a café. One day on the street I met one of my old teachers, and with tears in her eyes she begged me: "Come again

---

* The ban forbidding Jews to attend theater, concerts, movie houses, etc. was not effected until November 12, 1938. Three days later Jewish children were expelled from the public schools.

to us; we miss you; we feel ashamed that you must think we do not want you anymore. Not one of us has changed in her feeling toward you." She tried to convince me that they were still my friends, and tried to take away my doubts. I decided to go to the next meeting. It was a hard decision, and I had not slept the night before. I was afraid for my gentile friends. For nothing in the world did I wish to bring them trouble by my attendance, and I was also afraid for myself. I knew I would watch them, noticing the slightest expression of embarrassment in their eyes when I came. I knew they could not deceive me; I would be aware of every change in their voices. Would they be afraid to talk to me?

It was not necessary for me to read their eyes or listen to the change in their voices. The empty table in the little alcove which always had been reserved for us spoke the clearest language. It was even unnecessary for the waiter to come and say that a lady phoned that morning not to reserve the table thereafter. I could not blame them. Why should they risk losing a position only to prove to me that we still had friends in Germany?

I, personally, did not mind all those disappointments, but when my children had to face them, and were not spared being offended everywhere, my heart was filled with anguish. It required a great deal of inner strength, of love and harmony among the Jewish families, to make our children strong enough to bear all that persecution and hatred. [. . .] My heart was broken when I saw tears in my younger child's eyes when she had been sent home from school while all the others had been taken to a show or some other pleasure. It was not because she was denied going to the show that my little girl was weeping—she knew her mommy always could take her—but because she had to stay apart, as if she were not good enough to associate with her comrades any longer. It was this that made it hard and bitter for her. I think that even the Nazi teacher sometimes felt ashamed when she looked into the sad eyes of my little girl, since several times, when the class was going out for pleasure, she phoned not to send her to school. Maybe it was not right to hate this teacher so much, since everything she did had been upon orders, but it was she who brought so much bitterness to my child, and never can I forget it.

Almost every lesson began to be a torture for Jewish children. There was not one subject anymore which was not used to bring up the Jewish question. And in the presence of Jewish children the teachers denounced all the Jews, without exception, as scoundrels and as the most destructive force in every country where they were living. My children were not permitted to leave the room during such a talk; they were compelled to stay and to listen; they had to feel all the other children's eyes looking and staring at them, the examples of an outcast race.

Every day they had to face another degrading and offensive incident. As Mother's Day came near, the children were practicing songs at school to celebrate that day. Every year on that occasion the whole school gathered in a joint festival. It was the day before when my girls were ordered to see the music teacher. "You have to be present for the festival," the teacher told them, "but since you are Jewish, you are not allowed to join in the songs." "Why can't we sing?" my children protested with tears in their eyes. "We have a mother too, and we wish to sing for her." But it seemed the teacher did not want to understand the children's feelings. Curtly she rebuked their protest. "I know you have a mother," she said haughtily, "but she is only a Jewish mother." At that the girls had no reply; there was no use to speak any longer to the teacher, but seldom had they been so much disturbed as when they came from school that day, when someone had tried to condemn their mother.

The only hope we had was that this terror would not last very long. The day could not be far off when this nightmare would cease to hound the German people. How could anybody be happy in a land where "freedom" was an extinct word, where nobody knew that the next day he would not be taken to jail, possibly tortured to death. The Jewish people were not the only ones afraid of a loud spoken word; many others, too, were trembling for fear that somebody might listen even to their thoughts. [. . .]

We were not even allowed to hold meetings of the various organizations of our congregation without the presence of a supervisor sent by the Gestapo. Therefore we sometimes had the members assemble in our house. I always saw to it that the maid was away on such an evening. The telephone was disconnected, and our friends entered the house only singly and at different times. It was strange to see that most of the time those Nazi supervisors became very friendly with the Jews after they had come to the meetings for a while. Very much to our displeasure they liked to stay even after the lectures or the business part to have a cup of tea with us. They apparently felt so pleased in our company that they were not aware how much we wanted to get rid of them. But the Gestapo resented their "conversion." Whenever the reports of those men became too good, they were replaced by a new and better Jew hater. [. . .]

Hanukka [1934], the feast of light, was near. Now that the Jews were suffering the deepest degradation, it was a comfort to be reminded of the glorious deeds of the Maccabees when they freed the Jews from the bondage of the Syrians. We had planned that year to have at least a Hanukka play for our children. The Gestapo had given its permission, but even to the children's play they sent their supervisor. One part of the program was magical art. A boy fourteen years old played the magician. He really was splendid. Everybody liked him; he was so very witty.

At first he demonstrated some simpler tricks, but then he needed some help from the audience. He had already chosen some of the children, when he decided to have one of the adults, too. He looked around, and his eyes rested on a man who was sitting in the first line with the children. "Well," he said, "I guess you are the nearest and the best one for my experiments."

We never could decide whether it was because this young Gestapo official forgot his mission so completely in watching the show, or because he just did not know what to say. He got up very red and embarrassed, but as the boy had said, he made an excellent medium. The boy went ahead as if he were entirely unaware that this was one of the much feared Gestapo men, and he made him do the funniest things. We laughed so hard that the tears came to our eyes. The Jewish boy and the Gestapo official were the best-liked number on the program.

As in all the years before, we were very busy in all the auxiliaries making Hanukka parcels for our poor. The list of needy people had grown out of all proportion, while our contributions had become smaller and smaller. It had become a difficult task for anyone to give an adequate offering. If we wished to be of any real help to our poor, we had to give up all entertainments and lectures by out-of-town people. Prices had become so high that, since Jewish people did not get the same relief from the city as others, many were without heat and food. That winter we had to open a kitchen where we gave warm meals to the poorest of them. Besides that our B'nai B'rith women's auxiliary* furnished a lunch for all needy school children. We did all that we could, but the families that we could not help were those to whom the Gestapo brought death and hardships. We were entirely powerless against its actions. The intervention of a Jewish lawyer most of the time was not acknowledged at all, and Christian lawyers were afraid to speak up for Jews.

If God did not help, there was no help at all. And no one was sure that the next day it would not be his turn to disappear behind electrified barbed wire, to come back either in a crematory urn or bearing the marks of pitiless mistreatment on body and soul. It was an almost unbearable pain to see our friends return, their spirit so broken that they did not speak of their experiences even to their wives. Persistently I begged my husband to leave everything and to take us to a country where each day I would not be tormented by the fear of losing the dearest thing that I possessed. I used to watch nervously for my husband whenever he came late from a meeting, or when he was summoned by the secret police. The steady feeling of insecurity and uncertainty began to torture my nerves. Sometimes I was tempted to run away. [. . .]

---

* The independent Jewish order B'nai B'rith (Sons of the Covenant) was founded in 1843 in New York, and as of 1882 it also existed in Germany. In 1932 there were more than a hundred individual lodges in Germany, which were dedicated to social activities and educational and social work. As of 1897 women were members of the B'nai B'rith Sisterhood, which joined the Jüdischer Frauenbund (Jewish Women's League) in 1929. On April 19, 1937, the B'nai B'rith was dissolved by the Gestapo and its assets were confiscated.

One day, for the first time in a long while, I saw my children coming back from school with shining eyes, laughing and giggling together. Most of the classes had been gathered that morning in the big hall, since an official of the new *Rasseamt*, the office of races, had come to give a talk about the differences of races. "I asked the teacher if I could go home," my daughter was saying, "but she told me she had orders not to dismiss anyone. You may imagine it was an awful talk. He said that there are two groups of races, a high group and a low one. The high and upper race that was destined to rule the world was the Teutonic, the German race, while one of the lowest races was the Jewish race. And then, Mommy, he looked around and asked one of the girls to come to him." The children again began to giggle about their experience. "First we did not know," my girl continued, "what he intended, and we were very afraid when he picked out Eva. Then he began, and he was pointing at Eva, 'Look here, the small head of this girl, her long forehead, her very blue eyes, and blond hair,' and he was lifting one of her long blond braids. 'And look,' he said, 'at her tall and slender figure. These are the unequivocal marks of a pure and unmixed Teutonic race.' Mommy, you should have heard how at this moment all the girls burst into laughter. Even Eva could not help laughing. Then from all sides of the hall there was shouting, 'She is a Jewess!' You should have seen the officer's face! I guess he was lucky that the principal got up so quickly and, with a sign to the pupils, stopped the laughing and shouting and dismissed the man, thanking him for his interesting and very enlightening talk. At that we began again to laugh, but he stopped us immediately. Oh, I was so glad that the teacher had not dismissed me and I was there to hear it."

When my husband came home, they told him and enjoyed it again and again. And we were thankful to know that they still had not completely forgotten how to laugh and to act like happy children.

"If only I could take my children out of here!" That thought was occupying my mind more and more. I no longer hoped for any change as did my husband. Besides, even a changed Germany could not make me forget that all our friends, the whole nation, had abandoned us in our need. It was no longer the same country for me. Everything had changed, not people alone—the city, the forest, the river—the whole country looked different in my eyes.

[In the spring of 1935 a Jewish doctor flees from Dortmund, leaving all that he owned behind.]

A few days after the doctor had left with his family, we were invited to a friend's house. Of course the main subject of the evening was the doctor's flight. The discussion became heated. "He was wrong," most of the men are arguing. "It indicates a lack of courage to leave the country just now when we should stay together, firm against all hatred." "It takes more courage to leave," the ladies protested vigorously. "What good is it to stay and to wait for the slowly coming ruin? Is it not far better to go and to build up a new existence somewhere else in the world, before our strength is crippled by the everlasting strain on our nerves, on our souls? Is not our children's future more important than a fruitless holding out against Nazi cruelties and prejudices?" Unanimously we women felt that way, and took the doctor's side, while the men, with more or less vehemence, were speaking against him.

On our way home I still argued with my husband. He, like all the other men, could not imagine how it was possible to leave our beloved homeland, to leave all the duties which constitute a man's life. "Could you really leave all this behind you to enter nothingness?" From the heavy sound of his voice I realized how the mere thought was stirring him. "I could," I said frankly, and there was not a moment of hesitation on my part. "I could," I said again, "since I would go into a new life." And I really meant it.

Our private life became more and more troublesome. It was not simply that my husband always had difficulties with his sermons. Everywhere they tried to set a trap for him. There were so many regulations always being set up for a large congregation, and the rabbis had to abide by them. Every four weeks from now on we had to send revised typewritten lists of all the members of the different clubs. Whenever some of them were moving, we had to know it and inform "the party" immediately. We had to ask the Gestapo for permission for everything that went on in the temple and in the community house.

Our New Year and the Day of Atonement, the highest Jewish holy days, were approaching [1935]. Carefully my husband and I went through each of his sermons. Word for word we read aloud and considered whether they would pass the scrutiny of the Nazi supervisor who was present at every service. On the other hand, there was so much that my husband wanted to say to his people during these holy hours that he was not permitted to utter. The whole congregation would be there to get new hope out of those sacred days. He had to arrange his words in such a way that without mentioning the facts he could make his meaning clear to his audience. It was a hard task. It was not just a matter of his own safety that made my husband careful, but a case of preventing the Nazis, if possible, from getting a reason out of his sermons for closing the services and arresting the whole board of the congregation.

Two or three days before the holy days the pavement around the temple was besmeared with big white letters. "The Jews are our bad luck," and many similar signs. We cleaned the pavement on the eve of the first holy day, but the next morning it was even worse. That was not the only disturbance; a group of young Hitler Boys in their uniforms were posted at the entrance of the temple to make a deafening noise. When people entered the temple they had to walk through two lines of boys who were beating drums with all their force and sounding their trumpets in dreadful dissonance. A policeman was posted not more than ten steps away at the street corner, but when the ushers asked him to help them send the boys away, his reply was, "There is nothing I can do about it; they are sent on a special order." And the boys stayed until nobody was entering, until the tardiest arrival had come in. The sound of their raucous playing entered into the quiet of our temple, disturbing our prayers.

The next holy day passed without interference. Sometime later we learned that numerous anonymous letters had poured in to the Gestapo expressing the indignation of the Christian citizens at the disturbance of our service. At that time it still may have seemed wiser to the Nazis not to arouse too much sympathy for the Jewish people, and not to show their real intentions toward them too openly.

There were still millions of Germans who did not believe that this treatment was accorded us with the official sanction of the Hitler government. We would hear them say constantly, "If Hitler knew about such cruelty, he never would allow it. He would stop them at once. He does not know about what is going on. This is all illegal, and done by these vile Storm Troopers without his knowledge."

Many eyes were opened only when, in the fall of that year, 1935, the *Nuernberger Gesetze,* the laws of Nuremberg, were proclaimed. Only then did they believe, after reading in every paper and listening to each broadcast, that Jewish people were no longer citizens. Furthermore, the Jews remained subjects of the German Reich, with all the duties of a subject but without any of the rights of a citizen. [. . .]

Whenever we went to a meeting I saw faces which I had never seen before, while many of the old and well known were missing. Our congregation changed its members constantly now. Following the laws of Nuremberg, more and more businesses were forced to close, and the former owners left the country or went to Berlin, where they thought to lose themselves in the great mass of Jews. In spite of that our congregation did not decrease, since, from all smaller places around, Jews came to bigger cities. Life in a small town had become intolerable for Jews. They could not even buy food any longer in an Aryan store, and the Jewish ones had been closed for a long time.

Once my husband had to go to the country for a funeral service. He came back the next day sick from the cruel ordeal he had had to go through on that occasion. They had not been allowed to bring the body to the cemetery until it was dark. All Jews or Gentiles other than the immediate family were forbidden to attend the funeral. Not even a gravedigger was permitted, and members of the family had to dig the grave for the father themselves. Nazi guards were posted outside so that nobody could help.

After the funeral my husband was called before the Nazi official. "How can you dare, you dirty Jew, tell your people that they should hope for a better time to come?" the man shouted at him when my husband entered the police office.

"I was giving an interpretation of the Holy Bible. Do you have any objection to that?" my husband asked very calmly. This mean and common-looking man did not make any impression on him. His shouting did not frighten him. It made him feel only deep contempt and aversion.

"Who reads your Bible?" the man retorted. "Nobody anymore is interested in this Book. The times of the Bible are over. Our Bible is Adolf Hitler's book, *Mein Kampf*." With this confession of faith in the Nazi God, he calmed down and released my husband. [. . .]

Again it was spring [1936]. Nature, in its own new strength, was bringing new hope. But, for us, there was no hope. The restrictions were drawn tighter and tighter, strangling the life of the Jewish congregations. The budget of our congregation, which had been 800,000 marks when Hitler came to power, had diminished to 80,000 marks. Where we had had less than a quarter of our people on relief before, we now had more than three-fourths of them on our relief roll. The city relief scarcely provided for Jewish people, and now no religious or private institution was permitted to make a charity drive. The only thing to do for our paupers was to have, as the Nazis had, a weekly "pound" collection of food and another of old clothing. Week after week a truck went around and every Jewish household gave at least one pound of some foodstuff. More than once, those of us on the committee did not know what to do when nothing but sacks of dried peas and lentils came in. Even people with money could not buy what they needed. Fruit, vegetables, butter, eggs, and meat were no longer on the market in sufficient quantities. It was clear that people could give only of what they themselves had plenty. We had the same sad experience with our clothing collection. The new substitutes, which looked very nice in the show windows, did not last long. People would alter their old clothes to make them look like new, so that the wardrobe for the poor in our community house gradually became empty.

Never, in my memory, had we had so much activity in our community house. From the basement to the attic there was not a single space where a group of people was not taking a course of some sort. Men and women, boys and girls came to learn new trades and professions which they hoped would enable them to make a living abroad. Ladies who had never touched a thing in their own homes came now to learn to cook, to sew, to become a milliner, a hairdresser, or to prepare in some other way to make a living abroad. Men who had been retired for several years, or those who had had big businesses and factories of their own, came to learn to be farmers, shoemakers, or carpenters, or to fit themselves for some other vocation. And, mingled with the sounds of all these trades coming out of the various rooms, there was also a mixture of different languages echoing throughout the building. Spanish, French, English, or Hebrew could be heard whenever one passed a room.

The hardest task I had to do was to arrange for the transportation of children to foreign countries: the United States of America, Palestine, England, and Italy. It was most heartbreaking to see them separate from their parents. Yet the parents themselves came to beg and urge us to send their children away as soon as possible, since they could no longer stand to see them suffer from hatred and abuse. The unselfish love of the parents was so great that they were willing to deprive themselves of their most precious possessions so that their children might live in peace and freedom. [. . .]

Besides all other duties, we had been busy for weeks and weeks outfitting a great number of children for Palestine* The enthusiasm was as great among the Jewish children to build up a new homeland in Palestine as among the German youths to build up a new Germany. They came in throngs to enroll and were eager to be the first to go. It was not just the wish to go away from hate and slander which influenced these Jewish boys and girls. The idea of having again a great and holy task to live for made them strong and eager. In no country of the world had the idea of rebuilding Palestine been fought so desperately or caused so much opposition toward its followers as in Germany. Even now most of the older generation were strictly opposed to it. "We are Jews by religion, but our political ideals are German," was a tenet deeply rooted for centuries in the minds of the German Jews. Hatred and persecution could not destroy the love we felt for our homeland. The rising new enthusiasm of the Jewish youth for Palestine caused ill feeling in a great many homes. Often we had to smooth the friction between parents and children. The youth did not want to wait any longer, while the parents' hearts and hopes still belonged to the German fatherland.

One day I left Dortmund with a group of Jewish children to take them to Berlin, where a long train was leaving for Palestine. Our train coming from Dortmund was a little late, and I was hoping with all my heart that there would not be very much time left for me. Because I was still suffering from the tragic scenes of our departure from Dortmund, I felt I could not endure again seeing those heartbreaking farewells. In the great station at Berlin, hundreds of mothers and fathers filled the vast platform, which had been closed to everyone but the accompanying parents. By the time I reached the platform with my group, the train was already filled. All the windows were crowded with the children's shining faces. Pleasure and anticipation were written in their eyes and made them forget the pain of parting. Not so for the group of parents who were standing sad and silent, alongside the train. I tried to avoid looking at those faces. I did not want to see their grief. "What should I feel if my own children were among them?" I thought, while I guided my group to the compartment which was reserved for them.

Scarcely had they taken their seats when the whistle blew and I had barely

---

* From 1934 to the end of 1939 over 18,000 Jewish children and young people emigrated from Germany without their parents, 8100 to England and 5300 to Palestine. Emigration to Palestine was organized by the Youth Aliya, which had been initiated by Recha Freier in Berlin. In Palestine the Youth Aliya was directed by Henrietta Szold.

time for a hasty good by and the injunction that they be brave, before I descended from the train. "Greet my Mommy! Greet my Dad! They must not
worry about me," the children were calling behind me. Before I could close
the door, a boy of sixteen came near me and pushed a tiny parcel into my hand,
"Please take this to my mother," he begged me, "and tell her to wear it until we
see each other again." It was a tiny gold ring. The boy had made it himself, as
he was learning to become a goldsmith. This was his first independent work,
and he wished to dedicate it as a farewell gift to his beloved mother.

I was standing on the platform again, and as the slowly moving train passed
by me, I noticed how quiet the children had become. The beaming light had
faded from most of the young faces as they looked for a last time upon their
dear ones. I saw many little girls who had been laughing before now stretching out their hands for a last handshake with their mothers and fathers, while
the tears were running down their cheeks, and I saw many a boy's face distorted into a twisted smiling one. "We will be brave" and "Sholem Aleichem,"
the Jewish greeting, was sounded through the vast hall, while hundreds of
Jewish children left their German fatherland.

The fluttering handkerchiefs had disappeared, and the noise of the departing train had long since faded away, but still the crowd stood motionless, looking ahead where nothing was to be seen. I kept wondering numbly how many
of those parents and children would ever see each other again. Suddenly I
heard a scream, and when I turned back I saw people crowding together at
one point. "A woman fainted," I heard people saying, and the call for a doctor
went around. A few minutes of silence passed while a doctor bent down over
the poor mother, and again, low and incredible, the message came to the last of
the line, where I was standing, "She is dead." She had been strong enough to
bring her child to the threshold of a new life, but her heart could not endure
more. [. . .]

In 1937 it became more and more difficult for my husband to perform his
duties under the supervision of the Gestapo of the city. All this was wearing on
my husband's health, and besides, the uncertain, unpromising future of our
girls was upon his mind both day and night. I could not help him. What I
wished to say was, "Let us go," but I had promised not to urge him anymore,
not to make it still harder for him. So what was ever-present in our thoughts
lay unspoken between us.

"He has to take a rest," the doctor told me. "He has to go away from home
to forget all these troubles for a while." As my husband did not want to go
alone I decided to go with him, much as I hated to leave the children alone in
such a perilous time.

To make it even more painful for us to leave them in a time when they so
greatly needed someone to help them against the cruelty of Nazism, my older
girl came home the day before we left with her face pale and stunned and her
lips pressed together in a thin line. I knew this expression in my children's

faces. They tried with all their willpower not to let us know about their suffering, but the signs of pain in the girl's childlike face were too evident to escape our eyes. I thought I could spare my husband, so I did not ask my daughter anything when she came to the dinner table. But even my husband, whose mind was absorbed by the hundreds of things that he still had to arrange for his absence from the congregation, was aware of her grief.

"It is nothing, Daddy, but a headache." She tried to divert my husband's attention, but her eyes immediately filled with tears. "No, my dear," my husband said, "it is more than a headache which is bothering you. Please tell me what it is." But it was the younger one who had to tell it, since the child's resistance was now broken and, with the wild sobbing which followed, there was not one word we could understand. "Daddy, they have a new classroom," our little daughter explained, "and the benches are arranged in a different way, so that the teacher has made a new seating arrangement. And you know, Daddy," she said, "until now, sister was sitting beside her best friend, though they had not been allowed to be together on the way home, nor during the recreation hour. But now the teacher said, in the presence of all the girls, that it was no longer possible to have an Aryan girl sitting beside a Jewish girl. This would be a disgrace for an Aryan. And the teacher ordered her to take her seat in the last bench against the wall, and no Aryan girl could take a seat in this row. Now she is sitting alone in the rear of the classroom and is separated even during class from all the pupils."

My husband did not answer, but his face and his lips grew so bloodless, so pale, that even the children in their own grief were frightened.

Anonymous }

UNDERGROUND

A wealthy housewife tells of rescuing thirty-eight anti-Nazis from Germany. This material is from an oral interview conducted shortly after the speaker arrived in the United States, apparently during the war. From the archives of the YIVO Institute for Jewish Research in New York.

My story is an amazing one. With the help of two men I created the first underground in a large German city. Even my family did not know about it until recently when I became an American citizen and at last felt safe. When you have been taken before the Gestapo, you can never lose your fear.

My husband was originally a chemist and worked for I.G. Farben Industrie when I married him. My father persuaded him to come into our large pulp and paper factory and he lost touch with his chemical work. We were very rich and our only trouble was that we had too many servants and nothing to do. My children had a governess and I had little responsibility, even for them, so I devoted myself to the Jewish poor, especially the children. I was the first woman in our city to be president of our Jewish congregation.

In 1933 I sent away my eldest daughter to Paris to study. She could not continue her studies in Germany under the Nazis and the rabbi told me he thought things would get worse. The rest of us stayed on in Germany. The first thing that terrified me was that I watched the burning of the books; I was horrified as I saw the intelligentsia had joined the Nazis.

I felt that all good people should join together to help save lives. The Nazis had a grudge against certain people. The first one we thought of was a prominent Jewish lawyer who had defended an anti-Nazi in 1932. As Rabbi B. and I were leaving a meeting one day, he told me he would like me to help in getting this man out. I was going to Paris to try to make plans for some Polish orphans and also to have a visit with my older daughter who was there. In 1933 things were not too bad if you were well known and had money.

On my visit to Paris I talked to the French ministers about saving people from the Nazis but with no success. In the [train] compartment when I was returning to Germany I got into a conversation with a physician who stated he was a French Catholic. He said as a doctor he was shocked at the taking of life by the Nazis. Due to a train accident, I was slightly injured and had to be in the hospital in Strasbourg for several days. During this time I got well acquainted with the doctor who was very kind to me. It had occurred to me that he might help in smuggling people out of Germany and I finally got the courage to discuss it with the doctor and to appeal for help. When I explained my idea to the doctor, he liked it. He said he had a brother who was a forest ranger at the border of Alsace and who might be helpful. A few days after my return home, I received a letter from this doctor saying that his brother was lonesome and he hoped I would be able to send him guests. This was the signal that our work was to start.

We had a good friend Mr. S. who was Jewish but did not look like a Jew. I discussed the matter with him and he agreed to take on the very risky work of traveling back and forth and making the contacts. I told my husband nothing at all about this work. I provided all the money needed as every refugee had to be financed. I took a good deal of money and my husband used to wonder what in the world I did with it all. In all we managed to get out thirty-eight people.

While we were engaged in this work, I received a notice from the Gestapo to come to them that night. I at once got in touch with Mr. S. and with Rabbi B. as they were the ones who were working with me. Neither of them had heard from the Gestapo. I was afraid to go alone and took the children's governess with me. The cause of their summoning me was a really innocent letter which I had sent to a friend in Czechoslovakia deploring the persecution of the Jews. It was not an easy two hours that I spent with the Gestapo. There was a whole row of men, all of whom fired questions at me. Three machines were typing in the room all the time. They tried their best to confuse me but I finally convinced them of the truth that it was an innocent letter written simply as a religious Jew.

Our work constantly became more difficult and living conditions more unpleasant. In May 1938 Mr. S. called me on the phone and said that he knew I was going to the cemetery and that he would meet me there. I knew something terrible had happened and took a taxi to the cemetery immediately. Mr. S. wanted to tell me that Rabbi B. had been arrested. Later through my hospital work I learned that he had been received at the hospital in a pitiful condition after being tortured. They succeeded in sending him to Holland and he died there.

By this time we were anxious to leave Germany. I had wanted to leave much much earlier but my husband was not allowed to sell his factory, which the Germans considered vital, and he was unwilling to leave without funds. In 1938 the Nazis finally put a value on the factory but the *Gauleiter* said "the Jew can only have one-third of the sum." A Nazi was put in charge of it for six weeks and my brother and husband were not allowed to go near the place. Then the Nazis told us that they would pay nothing for the factory, because without its Jewish managers, it did not run well. During all this time we lived in the most terrible fear. Our chauffeur blackmailed us constantly. He is the only boy that I could really kill. We had done everything for him.

By this time we were making every effort to get out of Germany but we had no permission to leave and no passport. Then came the day of the terrible November pogrom [*Kristallnacht*, in 1938]. Our house filled up with women we knew who had been driven from their own homes and came to us for help and protection. Fortunately my husband was out when the Gestapo came and asked for him. I knew my telephone was tapped and I used the telephone of a gentile neighbor to reach my husband let him know not to come home. The Gestapo returned at [illegible] a.m. They looked everywhere for my husband and even knocked on the tables to see if they were solid. They made all the women who had come to the house go into the garden in the icy wintry night. The next day the Gestapo came looking for my husband again and threatened to arrest me. A Christian neighbor hid me. We had a country home in a little village where we had done a great deal for the people. That day the Burger-meister of the village took his life in his hands to bring us our passports. Through our lawyer I got word to my husband to be at the station at eleven. The lawyer met him with his passport, and my husband and I met again on the train.

Some time before this, we sent our younger daughter to England. In the meantime, my older daughter had married and left to the United States with her husband. My husband and I joined our younger daughter in England and waited for our American passports. My husband was urged to stay in England to try to get some money for his factory but the day we received our visas, we left.

We did not have any affidavits to help us to get to the United States. The way we managed to get there is a story in itself. In 1932 a loan exhibition of Dutch paintings was held in Amsterdam. We had sent about a dozen very fine paintings. They were still in Amsterdam when the Nazis came to power and the men in charge offered to keep them. Later he sold them for us and this gave us enough money so that we were able to come to this country without affidavits and had something to live on.

I can understand that when you have been through these horrible experi-ences and have lived for months with this terrible fear, it is hard to shake it off. We wanted to be sure to live in a country where we would not have to be afraid, but even in this country it takes time to lose this fear. Recently I was talking to an Austrian friend who talked rather loud in German. A man came up and said, "Oh, I see you are German." I shook like a leaf for hours. I don't trust any German gentiles and never will again. When we left Germany we had to leave the best of everything behind us. Our fine old German furniture and all our fine pictures had to be left for the Nazis. I had to give up all my silver and jewels. [. . .]

Peter Gay }

THE 1936 BERLIN OLYMPICS

Sterling Professor Emeritus of History at Yale University, Peter Gay emigrated from Berlin through Cuba to America in 1940 as a young boy. The following contribution was written in 1976 for the bicentennial of American independence as a tribute to his feeling "at home in America."

In truth, I had been infatuated with America for several years before I saw the country, before I could be sure that I would ever see it. I claim no special prescience for this anticipatory passion: it was natural for a boy entering adolescence in Nazi Germany and being told, with ugly and emphatic reiteration, that he was Jewish—which meant, in the official vocabulary, subhuman. For me Roosevelt's America was in every respect what Hitler's Germany was not: a land of justice and freedom. I have called it Roosevelt's America, for it was that to me. [. . .]

The first opportunity to act on my affection for the United States came in the summer of 1936, when I was thirteen, at the Olympic Games in Berlin. My father, a sports enthusiast both canny and resourceful, had managed to secure two tickets for them when he had been in Budapest four years earlier. So we went to the Berlin Olympics for a week—to watch the American athletes dominate the track and field events, to cheer them on, to send up a few fervent secular prayers that Hitler, whom we could see in his box across the field, should feel duly humiliated as Negroes swept one gold medal after another. Surrounded as we were by a small but noisy Hungarian contingent, we could release our feelings with impunity. I shall never forget the women's relay race—it remains one of the great moments in my life. The German sprinters, finely tuned and exhaustively trained, were clear favorites, and I grew increasingly dispirited as the final events approached. The Teutonic Amazons were going to win for the Führer, and I had to sit still to watch their triumph and his gloating face. The United States, I knew, had put together a strong team, led by Helen Stevens, but their hopes for first place were slender. As the race unfolded before us, it developed true to form: the German sprinters made, and widened, their lead. Yet for all their superb timing and military discipline, they faltered at the final transfer of the baton. Now, forty years later, my father's voice still reverberates in my ear. Jumping to his feet in his excitement, one of the first among the more than a hundred thousand spectators to see the decisive mishap, he shouted, "The Germans have dropped the baton!" And as the German women athletes trotted off the field weeping, the Americans loped home for yet another gold medal.

The story seems trivial now, but the event was beautiful then and pregnant with meaning. My love for America fed on my hatred for Germany. Here, before my astonished eyes, poetic justice had triumphed. It meant I would not have to rise with secret rage to listen to the interminable playing of the Nazis' "Horst Wessel Song," which, with "Deutschland, Deutschland über Alles," was the Third Reich's anthem. Instead it meant standing up, as so often, for the American anthem, of which I then barely understood a word: "Oh say, can you see? . . ." That, too, was beautiful.

So was Jesse Owens, running and leaping to four gold medals in his effortless but wholly authoritative way. And so was that athlete incarnate, Glenn Morris, who amassed impressive scores in the decathlon to establish a new world's record and who, between events, would lie down on the green field in the stadium under the blazing sun, in full sight of the ranked masses, put a towel over his head, and, for all I knew, nap. They all seemed splendid exemplars of America. My pantheon was an indiscriminate and democratic gathering of athletes and politicians and priests. In this bicentennial year I am persistently importuned to think of Jefferson and Franklin, and I respect, even admire, them for good and proper reasons. But they lack the resonance that only one's boyhood heroes can provide. I like to think instead of FDR and Jesse Owens, Cardinal Mundelein, and Glenn Morris.

In 1936, the year of the Berlin Olympic Games, my impractical infatuation with America assumed more realistic contours with the visit of one of my mother's older brothers, my "American uncle." His romantic history had long engaged my imagination. An unworldly, studious young man, a passionate violinist and fanatical chess player, he had met an American girl in Breslau in the early 1920s at the house of a chess partner, married her, and moved with her to her hometown in northern Florida. There he helped to manage one of the family's chain of prosperous hardware stores, played chess by correspondence, and traveled to Tallahassee with his wife, as gentle and cultivated as he, to catch an occasional touring virtuoso. In 1936 this favorite uncle— hypochondriacal, old-fashioned, and almost irrationally generous—came to Berlin to see his aging mother and to discuss with us all a schedule for emigration. It is hard to reconstruct our sober meetings of that summer; only two years later they seemed unrealistic, self-deceptive. But we could sit, my family and I, and set up a leisurely timetable by which my two cousins and I would move to the United States first, to be followed in the early 1940s by our parents and their various brothers and sisters.

My father, wholly assimilated, "Jewish" only by Nazi edict, content in his business, and reassured by loyal friends, did not then guess that the Nazis would soon brutally tear up our timetable. A moderate Social Democrat, a wounded and decorated veteran of the First World War, he felt little direct pressure on him. Had he been a politician or a journalist, he would have been dragged to a concentration camp in 1933, or forced into early exile. As it was, my father endured the usual anti-Semitic harassments and looked at the obscene world around him with a mixture of contempt and incredulity. Ironically enough, it was his gentile friends, "good" Germans all, who inadvertently disguised the reality of our situation and weakened our will to emigrate. My mother, frail, plagued by bouts with tuberculosis, was even more unwilling to leave the only world she had ever known, the country she claimed quite simply as her home. Like most other refugees from Hitler, we did not go gladly. We were forced to be free.

My uncle's visit made a caesura in my life. America, the fabulous land of opportunity, the country where you did not darn socks but threw them away, was now part of my program for the future. But it was my cousin Hanns, three years older than I, who was the first of the family to go. In 1937 he left for the United States. Among the first things he did was to translate his all-too-German, unpronounceable, and unspellable name, Fröhlich ["gay" or "merry"], into English. I do not know his motives. All I know is that when I finally managed to join him in America, I changed my own name. My reasons were more than mere convenience, more even than hatred of all reminders of the land I had barely escaped. Adopting an English-sounding name was a declaration of love for my new country, hopeful and a little pathetic at the same time. It was a statement concealing, and disclosing, a wish—the wish for a home. [. . .]

In the tortuous and eventful course of my emigration one person stands out: a physician at the American consulate in Havana. In the late 1930s, the United States showed its less forthcoming side. Confronted with desperate pleas to open its doors to Hitler's victims, U.S. officials took refuge in bureaucratic obstruction and legalist literalism. They admitted a full quota of immigrants no more, refusing to add places left unfilled from earlier years, or to borrow from other countries or from future quotas. After the *Anschluss* of Austria in March 1938, the German quota was slightly more than 28,000 a year, but the persons clamoring to be rescued were ten times that number. There were lifeboats, but not enough of them. We had made application too late to guarantee admission, and so in April 1939, when we finally got out of Germany, we went to Cuba to wait, rather than to the United States to live. And in Cuba we vegetated, idly, restlessly, glad to be alive but impatient to reach our true destination. I went to school to improve my English and my typing; my father was busy trying to rescue his remaining two sisters from the

Nazis' hands; my mother, her tuberculosis in a virulent stage, went to a Cuban sanatorium.

Then, in December 1940, we were called to the American consulate to have our papers processed. There I encountered, once again, the America of my fond imagination. Potential immigrants had to have proper papers, respectable American sponsors, and good health. My mother went to her physical examination directly from the sanatorium—doped up, as I remember, with some stimulants to keep her upright for the grueling day. Nothing is easier to detect than tuberculosis, but the physician passed my mother as though she were the sturdiest woman alive. It may have been the indifference of a doctor rusticated to a boring consular assignment; it may have been sheer incompetence. I prefer to think it was kindness, a commodity that the rulers of my native country had outlawed as decadent. Whatever it was, it struck me as a supremely appropriate prologue to our entry into the land of my fantasies.

Chapter Three

The Night
of Broken Glass

Hertha Nathorff }

A Doctor's View

On November 7, 1938, a seventeen-year-old Polish Jew shot and killed a German diplomat in Paris named Ernst vom Rath. In response, Goebbels organized a massive pogrom for the night of November 9 in which Nazi members set synagogues on fire, plundered Jewish shops and houses, murdered almost a hundred Jews, arrested and tortured countless others. Because of the broken glass of Jewish shops, the pogrom became known, semi-ironically, as Kristallnacht. *Hertha Nathorff, whose maiden name was Einstein (she was a relative of Albert Einstein as well as the Hollywood film producer Carl Laemmle), had studied medicine and worked as a gynecologist in a maternity hospital. She married a* Geheimrat *and medical colleague from Berlin; both were working as physicians in the capital when* Kristallnacht *took place.*

November 1938

Deep, deep night. With a trembling hand I will try to write down the events of today, events that have engraved themselves in my heart in a script of flames. I want to write them for my child so that one day he will be able to read how [the Nazis] have reduced us to nothing, driven us into the ground. I want to record everything the way I experienced it. At midnight, alone and trembling at my desk, groaning like a wounded animal, I need to write to keep myself from screaming into the silent night.

Yesterday in Paris someone was killed. A Polish Jew shot an official of the German embassy. Now the German Jews must atone for this act. Even yesterday people were asking: "How could the man gain access to the inner offices? In no embassy is it possible simply to walk in off the street." And they say: "This is a second Reichstag fire. The man was hired by the Nazis themselves. Herr. v[om] R[ath]—in any case gravely ill—was on their blacklist . . ."

This morning my maid told me, "Last night they must have again started making all sorts of trouble. In the fur store next to us all the windows were shattered and everything stolen." I was only partly listening—we're already used to such things. A short while later I started on my way to the clinic.

[69]

Strange, so much broken glass on the streets! In the beautiful, fashionable clothing store all the windows have been smashed and the glass cabinets are empty. The same is true of the next store and Etam's across the street, the elegant hosiery shop. What have they done now? I ask myself. Just then I hear a well-dressed lady say to her husband as they walk by: "Serves them right, the damned pack of Jews. Revenge is sweet!"

Slowly I begin to realize what has happened and take a good look around me. Broken glass, broken glass everywhere. Demolished stores, insofar as there are still Jewish stores left on the Kaiser Avenue. Disgusted, I turn around and return home. I hear a few passers-by make some nasty comments, but most people are walking hesitantly and silently through the streets.

When I arrived home, my maid said to me: "Herr Doctor [Hertha Nathorff's husband] has already left. He had to rush off to a patient who had a heart attack." That's right, the telephone numbers are lying there in a list for my husband's house calls. So many of them today. I'm beside myself with worry until he comes home, and on top of that extremely nervous about everything I have to do this morning. The telephone never stops ringing. Again and again people ask urgently if the doctor is available. I try to reach him at his patients' apartments. Six or seven phone calls before I reach him and can say: "You must go at once to this address and that one—heart attack." "But I can't leave here yet. If it's so urgent, ask one of my colleagues," answers my husband. I try to reach one. Impossible! He too has no time. And that's how the morning is spent. I had a quick lunch alone with my son who tells me: "Mommy, did you know that the synagogue in the Prinzregenten Street is burning? I saw it on my way home, there's nothing but broken glass on the streets. People say that the Nazis have done all that." I'm hardly listening. I have my ears cocked for the sound of my husband's footsteps. In the meantime it's already three o'clock. The first patients are already arriving for his afternoon session. I have to reconcile them to waiting a bit. These are new patients who don't know me. One says to me: "Did you know that our synagogues are on fire? Who knows what still might happen today?" I have no time for conversation. Someone is ringing the doorbell. My sister has come. How pale she looks today, I say to myself. She's probably not yet over the departure of her brothers and sisters, or perhaps [the Nazis] have been harassing her husband during his science tours, I think to myself. But I have no time to speak with her. The telephone and the doorbell occupy me completely. My sister says: "Doesn't this awful traffic stop even today?" But I have no time to answer questions. Then my husband arrives—exhausted, run down. "I can't eat anything, just a quick cup of coffee." He greets my sister in haste and she asks "Can I see you alone a moment?" Thinking that she has a medical problem to discuss with him, I hurry out of the room. After a few seconds my husband returns and says to me, "You don't need to be alarmed, but they've taken Otto away." "Taken him away? How? Why?" I ask. "Oh," says my husband, "there seems to be some police action underway again. A number of my patients have been arrested. That's why there have been so many heart attacks. They even arrested all the men at a wedding." I ask my husband to call the brother of my brother-in-law immediately. His wife answers the phone and says, "Today he's not receiving patients. He took a trip with his friends to the Grunewald. Come over right away."

But my husband insists on seeing his patients! Then he accompanies my sister to her sister-in-law's. Their son opens the door and says: "They've taken daddy away." They tell me that by telephone, since I've stayed home. I ask my husband not to return, gather everything he needs for his evening calls, meet him on the street and go with him to his patients, sad and in despair. What should we do, what should we do? I ask him not to come home. "Spend the night with friends, just recently someone told me there's always room for you with us." But my husband? He thinks only of his patients. Of the men and women who had a heart attack today because their relatives were summarily hauled off by the police. And no one knows where. Later, in the evening, we read in the newspaper that the police action is over. And my husband insisted he wanted to go home. "Don't you realize yet that their newspapers are full of lies?" I ask him. But I can't keep him from doing his duty. It's nine o'clock at night. I at least go home to look after my son. My elderly cook has already gone to bed. I'm completely alone in the apartment, which is so silent it scares me.

Out of habit I lock the vestibule to our apartment. I sit by the radio listening to the news and waiting for my husband to return home.

Nine-thirty in the evening. Two short, sharp rings of the doorbell. I go to the door. "Who's there?" "Open up! The Police!" Trembling, I open the door, knowing what they want. "Where is Herr Doctor?" "He's not at home," I say. "What do you mean? The porter's wife says she saw him come home." "He was here, but he was called out again." They go toward the first door. Locked. The second door. Locked. "These are our offices where we see patients," I explain. "Ever since we were robbed, I always lock them in the evening when I'm here alone." They go to the next door. "Please don't shake it," I say. "My child is sleeping in there." "We know that Jewish trick." And, holding a revolver under my nose, one of them says: "Another word and a bullet will be in your brain. Where have you hidden your husband?" My knees are shaking. Just stay calm, stay calm, I tell myself. "I'm not lying. My husband isn't at home. But shoot my child first, then me. And don't miss." And I open the door to the bedroom of my sleeping child. The two young policemen are already preparing to leave. Finally they seem to believe me. But in this instant I hear someone opening the door of our apartment. My husband comes in. Unlucky soul—he arrives at the very moment I think he has been saved. And just as he stands there, they take him away. "You can thank God your wife doesn't have a bullet in her head." The young kid dares to repeat this, and he dares to use the name of God. And they leave with my husband. I run out onto the street after them. "Where are you going with my husband, what's happening to him?"

They shove me away, brutally. "Tomorrow morning, at Alexander Square, you can ask for him." I watch how they climb into a car and drive off into the night with my husband. Our porter stands in the entry way, takes my arm and says: "If I'd suspected this, I would have walked over hot coals to hide our dear Herr Doctor. It's a long way from Herr von Bredow [arrested and murdered by the Nazis in 1934] and our Herr Doctor! They go from one level of crime to the next. The way it's going, it won't end well." But my feet can hardly carry me upstairs. What now? I try to telephone some of my friends and colleagues. Always the same answer: "Not in!" In feverish haste I rummage through my husband's desk. I can't find anything that could be held against him. Every noise startles me. I have to be ready for them to come in at any moment and search the apartment. It occurs to me that a small sidearm from my husband's army days is in the kitchen. I take it out of a closet where I had kept it along with other valuables as a memento. Jews are no longer permitted to bear weapons, punishable by execution. I had intended to bring the gun to the police the next day. But what should I do with it until then? I hurry through the streets with the little gun, in a quandry. I'm not allowed to throw it away. But if it's found in our apartment it could be used against us. I must return home, something could happen to my boy. Around midnight a woman came to me. Stealthily and quietly. She had seen the light shining in my empty room. She makes tea for me in silence, then asks if she can do anything else. I hold her hand, not saying anything. "No one can do anything for me." Then I point to the gun. "Take this until tomorrow morning." Now it's three in the morning. Still completely dressed, I sit in my oh so empty apartment. They didn't come back. From the adjacent room I hear the even breathing of my child. And where may his father be? I want to lie down, turn off the light, just the way they turned off in me a holy burning light—my belief in the goodness of man.

November 11, 1938

I sent my son to school. "Be careful," I said. "Daddy has already gone out, he had to leave early to see some patients." Then I made some coffee and cake— for my husband, whose whereabouts I still didn't know. My old housekeeper, Frau H., came early this morning. Now she will live with me. "If people call, tell them Herr Doctor isn't in." I don't want to tell the truth, but I don't want to lie either. My sister and her little niece (who watched the Nazis shut down the Jewish vacation home in Lehnitz, who saw them steal all the supplies and confiscate everything else for a division of the National Socialist Party) pick me up and we drive to police headquarters. On the way I buy some bananas, hoping we will be allowed to give them to our husbands. At the police station we're not even allowed inside. "Go home. You'll receive written notice, your husband isn't with us any longer," says the officer at the window. Written notice! That is what Frau von Bredow received four years ago when she was asked to pick up the urn with her husband's ashes. This thought runs through my head but I don't dare say what I'm thinking. At this moment a woman, one of the directors of the Jewish League of Women, catches sight of me. She must have been trying to get information about the fate of thousands of arrested men. "You too?" she says to me. "But there's really no point in staying here. Drive home, there's nothing you can find out here. We will try to get information through our organization. But the fact is, the men are no longer here." And she helps me back into the car.

At home again. The telephone is ringing off the hook. "Where is Herr Doctor? Who is covering for him?" I don't know how to answer. Before, when my husband was sick, I was allowed to take his place. [As a Jew] I am no longer permitted to do this. I call the Chamber of Physicians. They give me the name of a replacement who tells me, "If the Chamber of Physicians says so, I have to do it, but please spare me your patients."

My house has become an insane asylum. People come and go, eat here, ask if they or their friends can sleep here. My house is suddenly a safe haven. Now that my husband has been arrested, [the Nazis] won't come back. The wife of an Aryan colleague goes through our library once again. There still might be one book that [the Nazis] find offensive if they search our house. My boy comes home from school. "Isn't Daddy home yet? So where is he?" I don't reply. I can't lie to my child. In the evening I called my girlfriend in my hometown [in southern Germany]. She sobs desperately on the phone. Her husband has been taken away. They have even pulled my old father from his bed, despite his heart problems, and put him in prison. Both of us are incapable of speaking on the phone. The line goes dead. At least my husband's gun is out of the house. The porter turned it over to the police this morning. [. . .]

Monday, November 14, 1938

I was so tired. Around one o'clock a man called me to say, "Your husband sends his greetings, he's alive, I spoke him with him this morning before I was let go." The news shook me up. I lied down on the sofa for a few minutes. My boy was still in school. The cook was in the kitchen, my housekeeper had gone out for an hour to do some errands. Shortly before two the doorbell rang. I opened myself. A slim, blond man was standing at the door and asked if I was the doctor's wife.

"I come as your friend. Can anyone see me? I'm a government official, with the police, if you must know. I've come to help your husband."

The man has already got his foot in the door. I let him in.

"Give me your word of honor that you'll keep everything I tell you a secret.

Only then can I help you. I'm with the government, and you know that they'll have my hide if someone sees me here and finds out I've tried to help you."

"You want to help us?" I ask incredulously. "Then tell me where my husband is."

"Your husband? In Tegel, in jail, locked up. Accused of breaking Law 218 [against abortion]. But I know the man who denounced him, and I know he did it out of jealousy to get even with the girl. This girl is the friend of my fiancée, who was once your husband's patient and who asked me to help him. I was able to get hold of the denunciation, here it is."

And with that he pulled a letter from his pocket which he neither showed me nor let me read. That would be against government rules, he assured me.

"My husband, breaking Law 218? It's not possible," I say. "I would put my hand in fire I'm so sure of it."

"But Frau Doctor, don't be silly. Jews are always guilty. Just think for a minute of Dr. G. How long has he been in prison? Your husband wouldn't even survive the prison time necessary for the investigation. We have to act fast, pay the guy off and get him to shut up or retract his denunciation."

I turn ice cold. "My husband is innocent," I say. And I don't have even a penny," I say truthfully.

"What about abroad?"

"We have nothing there either!"

"Well, where is all your money?" His voice is getting louder and louder, the man more and more aggressive. "Just be quick about it. I have to be back in the office at three. And here is the denunciation that I'm going to hand over to the authorities."

I become frightened. If only my housekeeper would come back! I stand up. I try to reach the telephone, the telephone, next to my pocketbook with all the money I withdrew from the bank a few hours earlier. Suddenly the thought comes to me. Would he do it? If I could just call out for help? The window was only a few steps away, but he must have read my thoughts.

"Do you really think I would let myself fall into your hands?" I hear him say. "You don't seem to know that we have a secret order to shoot any Jew on the spot." And again I see a shiny revolver pointed at me. I open my handbag.

"Here, take what I got from the bank this morning, a fact you probably already know. It should be enough. If not, my name is in the telephone book. Go away, you don't have to be afraid of me. I'll keep your secret just as I promised. I keep my word, even with a blackmailer."

He took the money, all the money, and left. I hear the door close. Then I fainted. My housekeeper found me lying on the ground, next to the door of my office.

"Who was that strange-looking man running down the stairs when I came home? Was he here?" she asked me. I just shook my head. She brought me to bed, and I asked her to call a doctor friend of mine.

But now I'm afraid of every move I make. Will he come back, will he follow me secretly out of fear that I might report him? That same evening I went to a lawyer and put everything down in writing. He advises me against filing a complaint with the police. First my husband should come back home safely. Then he'll see what might be done. [. . .]

November 24, 1938

Always new reasons to be afraid or worried. I run from one government office to the next. For hours I wait at the Emigration Information Center to get a certificate allowing me to apply for a passport. I'm not successful, although I have the feeling that the friendly official wants to help me. "A passport can be issued only if you state exactly where you are emigrating," he says, and I can't do that. I ask friends what I should do. Just book passage anywhere, someone tells me. I send telegraphs all over the world. I get wild offers. A visa for Chile for 3000 German marks, issued by an Austrian Nazi. This is how they profit from our plight. I'm at my wits' end. My money is all gone.

One of my husband's patients, who has come here from England for a conference, sends his secretary to ask if he can do anything for me. "Save my child!" I don't know what else to ask for. In the meantime, after hours of negotiations in a travel agency, I've been offered passage to Cuba in February. This is the only legal passage I can still book. I cable America and plead with my friends to deposit the show money that is required for emigration to Cuba.

November 30, 1938

The money for Cuba is supposed to be deposited from America. Now I can go back to the emigration office and finally apply for a passport. [. . .]

December 5, 1938

At the police station I hand in my passport application. And at the various tax offices I hand in our so-called "Certificates of Clean Tax Records."* An elderly, devoted official said to me, "Frau Doctor, do you really want to leave? In that case I'll have to apply some pressure." Back to police headquarters. I brought all my papers with me, including the certificate proving we had booked passage to Cuba. I receive no information about my husband and when he might be released. Back again to the American consulate. And again in vain! I'm almost fainting from hunger and cold. Two o'clock in the afternoon. I've been on my feet since seven this morning, and at three I have to be

---

* Before emigrating, each person had to obtain a certificate from the German Tax Office proving that no back taxes were due and, especially, that the special "tax for fleeing Germany" or Emigration Tax had been paid.

at the lawyer's. I don't have time, not even with our car, to drive home and back again. But where can I get something to drink? Just a glass of tea or a sip of water! Where is there no sign [prohibiting Jews] so that I dare enter? Zuntz's Coffee Shop on Potsdam Square. I rush across the street, almost running into a car. I've jaywalked. The traffic officer on the corner warns me: "Watch out, Miss, the next time that will cost you a few marks." I shudder. If he only knew who he was talking to, he would have arrested me as a Jew and I would have been locked up. And right now I need to stay free so I can take care of my husband and child.

I walked quickly into the coffee shop.

"Miss," I say at the counter, "a cup of coffee, quickly. I'm in a hurry, I have a train to catch."

It's a bald lie, and I'm ashamed. But how else should I explain why I gulp down my coffee at the counter instead of sitting down at a table? Someone could see me and recognize me. Even in such a big city as Berlin I am so well-known. Everywhere there are patients of mine. And how easily could one of them have me, the Jew, turned out of the shop. [. . .]

December 15, 1938

Today I went to the Tax Office to pay the "Retribution of German Jews" for the murder committed in Paris by a Polish youth. To get our money, they have people murdered! While paying the money I noticed to my horror that I was short approximately 1000 marks—one thousand—since I had only withdrawn the amount that a tax official (mistakenly, at it turned out) had told me I needed. What now? I had no more money with me. "Frau Doctor, we know you," said the official. "Pay the rest when your husband gets back. But then you'll also have to pay the interest. I'll give you a receipt. We have to take the money from you. We officials have no say in the matter and have to follow regulations." But I raced back to the bank and managed to withdraw the thousand marks from my account so that I could toss them into the state money bags, according to official decree. I drove back to the Tax Office with the rest of the stipulated amount. Again the offices were overflowing. How many thousands, indeed, hundreds of thousand of marks have Jews turned over to the German State today?

December 16, 1938

My husband came back. Suddenly, surprisingly—but in what condition? They shaved off his beard, which is growing back in patches, and turning gray. That doesn't matter. My hair is also showing the first signs of gray. And it's not my age that has taken away its color. But my husband has come back, and the main thing is, he's alive, he's here!

"I'm fine, I was fine [in prison]. And now don't ask any more questions," he said.

Of course I know that before being released the men must sign a document promising to say nothing, and so I don't ask anything. But I can't help noticing his raw, battered hands that have turned blue from the cold. These once so polished, manicured hands that his patients so loved. Hands that could do no harm, they used to say. And now I'd like to weep when I look at his hands. But I see more. His face has also changed. Closed and hard. But the main thing is, he's alive.

I know how many men were tortured to death behind those walls, physically and spiritually tortured to death.

Our son is overjoyed. Little, brave boy! I have watched how he suffered in silence during the weeks of frustrated waiting for his daddy to come home. Now we're back together again, and I can even laugh at the state of my husband's coat, which was completely ruined by the disinfectant in the concentration camp, his now fully useless suit, his leather gloves that have shrunk to the size of a child's hands. Today we will all sleep at home once again and, hopefully, never need to be afraid again. [. . .]

December 24, 1938

Christmas Eve! The last one in our house. No tree, no shimmering candles. Even my old cook has refused to have a little tree in her room. And the Christmas presents seem to give her little joy this time, unlike in former years. She also knows that this will be the last Christmas for her after thirteen years of service in our house.

Tomorrow we have guests again. Guests for a Christmas meal—I've invited some lonely people who would otherwise be without anyone. I have no idea what I will serve them to eat; I haven't had time to think about it.

New Year's Eve 1938

The year is over. It has taken everything from me that made my life cheerful and happy. The last months have completely transformed me. I no longer recognize myself. It's no surprise if others don't recognize me either. I just count the days before we can get out of this hell.

Many people go in and out of our house every day. Jews as well as Aryans with the right view of things. All of them have just one wish and aren't afraid to say it out loud:

"Let's get out of this country."

Annemarie Wolfram }

From the Eyes of a Child

Wolfram emigrated to the Netherlands in 1939 and later to the United States. The following is an excerpt from her unpublished manuscript written for the Harvard Essay Contest "My Life in Germany Before and After January 30, 1933."

This tenth of November (1938) was the most horrible day of my life. In the morning I went to school. Mom took me to the streetcar like every morning. I was late for the first time. But my teacher was not even in the classroom yet. The children were sitting in their seats so quietly, not making a sound at all. I already thought that was strange. Then our teacher came. She looked like she had been crying hard. "Children, you have to go home immediately. Our teachers have been arrested. Walk quietly in the streets, always in pairs, and as fast as possible." Because I was the biggest girl in our class and one was left over, I had to walk by myself. How horrible I felt. Everybody looked at us with such malicious joy and I heard awful noises—stones smashing the windows of our synagogues. I ran faster and faster. And all the time I couldn't stop wondering whether I would still be able to see my parents again.

At home Mom took me in her arms. My heart was beating so fast that I had to sit down in a chair. Then the doorbell rang. It was one of Dad's colleagues. "Can we still flee? They are arresting people from the streets completely at random." I looked at this man. His whole body was trembling. It looked so strange that it nearly made me laugh, although what I really felt like was crying.

Dad put on his coat to go with him. But in the meantime the doorbell was ringing again. Two men were asking for Dad. The colleague disappeared through the back door. He was so nervous that he could not get into his coat. But that night they took him away, too. That horrible night—I will never forget it.

We did not take off our clothes. Looting and shouting hordes roamed through the streets. We went to the window and looked out, but did not turn on the lights. Cars were whizzing past. Gestapo officers jumped out shouting,

"Are you Jewish? Identify yourself." People who couldn't prove that they were not Jewish were taken away in chains. So many Jews were wandering aimlessly through the streets. They did not dare to go home, for the officers had lists of the names and addresses of all Jews. They went from one house to the next and arrested every Jew. Sick people were taken from their beds, old people from old-age homes. They were rounded up like cattle. Suddenly our doorbell rang. It was our neighbor. We knew he was a Nazi. Yet he had always been friendly and nice to us. Now he was asking us if we wanted to come to his place for the night. He said he wasn't waging a war against women and children, that he wanted to protect us. This man was full of anger and disgust about all the looting he had seen on the streets. By the way, he later asked about Dad every day. But he, too, was afraid.

Our Dad had to leave with the two officers. He was only allowed to take two handkerchiefs. Mom was asking the officers where he would be taken, and why. But to all these questions they only replied, "We don't know." After three weeks we heard from Daddy for the first time. He was in a concentration camp with many others. I don't like to remember this time any more. My Mom, who had always been a very cheerful person, had changed completely. If only she could have cried. Many women came to her. She asked them for advice. They were like sisters to one another.

In the mornings Mom would go to the Gestapo. I wanted so much to go with her because I did not like at all to leave her alone. "That's not a place for you," was all Mom would say. I had gotten into the habit of listening at the door when the other women came who were in the same situation as Mom. I heard awful things then. At first in their desperation the women had gone to the Gestapo. There they had been thrown down the stairs. They did not give in, but instead returned again and again. I can well imagine the way they looked standing there—an endless line in a narrow corridor. Nobody dared to speak. And when somehow they made only the slightest noise, some stupid young rascal would come and scream, "If it isn't absolutely quiet here immediately, I'll throw this whole god-damned Jewish circus down the stairs!" Then the women would creep close to one another like frightened hens. They did not speak any longer, but looking at their faces one could see they were praying that they would succeed in helping their husbands. Some of them also had fits and cried and screamed. The others were helping whenever they could. They were all like sisters.

Sometimes I asked Mom to walk with me through the streets in the evening. But it always hurt me so much to hear her say, "I cannot understand at all that everything is continuing so quietly. Everything is running its course as usual although thousands of good, innocent people were torn away from their families just like that and are now being tortured to death."

At that time the horrible cold started. Daily we received news of the death of friends. We tried to keep it a secret from Mom. But she always found out in the end. At night I slept next to Mom in Dad's bed. Lying under his covers I felt as if Dad were holding me in his good warm arms. I used to pretend for Mom's sake that I had fallen asleep. But still I would notice that she was rolling around in her bed weeping softly to herself and unable to sleep. Mom used to call me her little "faith in God." And I did have faith in God. But sometimes I was terribly afraid.

We got a postcard from Dad. It was so courageous. But the handwriting was shaky. I can still say it by heart. "My dearest wife, my dearest child, don't be sad. Where there are so many of us, I must be, too. Be courageous. Whatever God is deciding for us, may it be for the best. Your Daddy." I used to recite it to Mom whenever she became too desperate.

On December 17 we had an appointment at the American Consulate to apply for our visa. That was Mom's last resort. She had filed a petition with the Gestapo asking that Dad be allowed to apply for the important documents after all. But as early as December 5 we heard that only men who already had their visas would be released. And then the awful time running from one hostile office to the next started. At the Gestapo they said, "Just bring us the visa, then your husband will be released immediately." "But that's impossible," Mom would say, "My husband has to undergo a physical examination before he can get a visa." "Then get him a notarized invitation from an interim country. Your husband must be able to leave the country immediately." Mom worked so hard to get this invitation. Invitations from Belgium, Denmark, France, and England reached us. But no consulate wanted to notarize these invitations. A few of the women said they thought that Mom's particular Gestapo officer was unusually nice and friendly. When Mom heard this she laughed full of bitterness, "I call that the friendliness of a cannibal. It's written all over his face how overjoyed he is. As if he were thinking: 'How appetizing she is looking. How good she will taste.'" And Mommy was right. One time the guy said to her, "We know each other very well by now, don't we. I can see you are wearing a different blouse today. You really look very attractive in it." Once, when Mom cried, he comforted her by saying, "A little bit of drilling will be good for your old man. By the way, I just noticed in the documents that he is ten years older than you. He is much too old for you anyhow." That she had to swallow all this silently must have been very difficult for Mom.

Then came December 15, By begging and pleading, Mom had succeeded in getting through to the American consul. Most of the time the women were turned away at the barrier. Mom asked him to write a letter to the Gestapo stating that unless Dad was released in time for our appointment at the American consulate, the emigration of all three of us would be in danger.

Later, when we had recaptured our sense of happiness, Mom described the conversation with the consul. "Dear Madam, you must make a written application." But Mom replied, "I need this letter immediately. If I write to you, it will take three days for the application to reach you. The answer will take at least three more days. I, however, am worried about every minute lost. It could mean my husband's death. I cannot go away from you like this. Mr. Consul, you must help me." The consul understood her desperation. "What do you want me to write?" And then Mom dictated the letter to the Gestapo. The Gestapo officer said, "You'll have him back by Christmas."

Mom, however, could not believe that. At that time she was not able to believe anything anymore. On December 17, Mom and I had to go alone to the appointment. The consul was so good to us. He recognized Mom immediately. "Was our letter successful? Your husband can come any day, as soon as he is released. You don't need another appointment." The consul wanted to help us. I would have liked to hug him. And all of a sudden I felt a strong belief in me that we would be saved.

Every evening from now on I prayed for the country that was to be our new home.

Prisoners who had not been allowed to leave the camps by December 23, could not expect to be released until after January 10. We knew that. Every day the cold became worse. We saw so many friends come back with heavily bandaged hands. Some had had their fingers amputated. We talked to a dentist. All he had left of his hands were two stumps. He would never again be able to work in his profession. Mom knew all that. She knew even more. Nobody dared to say it outright. But we had found out anyhow behind people's backs that our Daddy had been lying in the sick bay with a flu for the last two weeks. That was another worry for Mom. Friends, who had returned, had said, "Everything else is bearable—just don't get sick there."

December 23, Friday evening, the seventh Friday without Dad. The evening before Christmas. People were practicing Christmas songs in our house. Bright sounds came into our apartment: "O merry, O blessed Christmas season full of grace." It was snowing outside. Very slowly the snowflakes were falling to the ground and Mom's tears were falling just as slowly. It hurt me so much to see her cry. She usually was so courageous. Maybe it was good for her.

It was the second to the last evening of Hanukkah, our festival of lights. How much had I always looked forward to that day, when times were normal. Nobody had lit the menorah for us this year. No light was burning for us. However, I had still given Mommy a present. My letter was lying in front of her. Maybe it had made her cry. But at first she had smiled. Her sweet mother's smile as in the old days. That had been my present. I had written her a letter:

"Dear Mom, I have such strong faith in God. Don't you see how beautiful the blossoms of our azaleas are? They are blooming for the celebration of

Dad's return. How sweetly our little birds are singing today. They had been silent for so long. They know that Daddy is coming back soon. The birds and the flowers are purer and better than we are. They are closer to God. That's why they already know that Dad is coming back soon. I have such strong faith in God. Your friend, Eva."

But nobody came. How intensely Mommy was listening for the phone. Many women were finally relieved from their worries. Our loved ones had been brought to the concentration camp Oranienburg-Sachsenhausen. When they were released, the Jewish relief agency in Berlin took care of them. They returned with their heads shaven like prisoners. Their coats had been disinfected. Since most of them were made from bark, they did not survive the disinfection process and were hanging down in rags. Their hats looked like pancakes. The aid committee in Berlin had already given most of them new hats. And then the women would receive phone calls, "Long-distance call from Berlin. Reverse charges. Are you willing to accept the call?" How happy the women were to do that when they could hear their husband's voices again.

Until ten p.m. we sat next to the phone, but no call came. And then we went to bed. Neither of us could fall asleep.

Around eleven p.m. we heard the piercing sound of the telephone. But that was only a call from Hamburg. The long-distance company sounded much louder. Mom was very tired when she went to the phone. I will never forget her scream, "My husband, my good husband." Then the receiver fell out of her hand. "Mom, what's the matter with you?" But her face was glowing and radiant. "Eva, Eva, get ready. That was Daddy on the phone. He'll be with us very soon. He is already in Hamburg."

Later Mom told me that the two most beautiful moments in her life were, when I was born and when our Dad was finally standing before us unharmed. His face had become so small and thin. His fingers were frost-bitten. But he had kept his former sweet sense of humor. "Fed by the government for six weeks," he said, "and even the haircut was free." [. . .]

VIENNA: TO THE WEST STATION

With the Anschluss *of Austria in March 1938, Austrian Jews were suddenly subjected to German legislation and could be sent to German concentration camps like Dachau and Buchenwald. This interview, like the
one with the farmer from south Germany, is from the collection* We
Escaped *(1941). None of the contributors to that volume are named, no
doubt in order to protect relatives still living in Germany.*

My story is really not extraordinary or sensational. It is just what happened to many average people.

I was born of Jewish parents in Vienna and lived there all my life until I
came to America. I was an accountant by profession, and earned a modest but
perfectly adequate salary. My wife was a teacher of retarded children. We
lived in one of the big community apartment houses on the outskirts of the
city.

They were wonderful places to live, those apartment houses. We had a very
stimulating common life—always something was going on, with lectures,
sewing circles, and discussion groups. We were teachers, white-collar workers, and some artists.

The place was built around a central court, planted with grass and trees
and with benches to sit on. There the children could play without being
watched by their mothers, who didn't have to fear that they'd run out into the
street. We had a garden on the roof too and each person had his little chair up
there.

It was a quiet, very well-balanced life. I was taking piano lessons and came
home every afternoon about three o'clock and practiced until six. We had a
very small and very charming apartment—a good architect who was a friend
of mine had done the interior, and it was full of convenient devices such as a
built-in compartment for the bedding during the daytime, with special holes
in it for airing. That apartment became like a part of us. When we left, we left
it standing with the curtains at the windows, and the furniture just as it was.

Since our working hours were not too long, we had time for living. We
went to the theater nearly every week—and Vienna at that time had a great

theater and a great opera. Many of those actors are now here in America. Sundays we sometimes went to museums, and there were always concerts. Both of us had jobs which guaranteed us a pension, so that we could afford to travel in vacations. Especially we liked to go mountain climbing, often through the Dolomites; and once we made a walking trip through them and on into Italy, even to Venice. Another time there was open-air opera in the stadium in Verona, and the last year before the end we went to Switzerland, to the Matterhorn. But every year we spent the last week in the same place— Salzburg, for the festival. We were both great admirers of Toscanini, and I can remember how we stood for hours in front of the concert hall waiting for him to come out so that I could take a picture of him.

It seems strange now that we had planned to visit America, to see the World's Fair which we had heard was going to be held in '39! Unfortunately—no, I should rather say thank God—it turned out very differently.

The collapse of Austria came to us as a great shock. Of course we felt the danger and uncertainty in the air; all of us were worried about the political situation. It was because of the unsettled state of Europe that many of us felt that we could not take the responsibility of bringing children into that world. That was a general feeling among the young people. But we did not expect the end to come so suddenly.

You remember that Chancellor Schuschnigg intended to hold a plebiscite in Austria about the *Anschluss* with Germany. This seemed to me encouraging, and we were all excited about the possible results. Then, on the Friday evening before it was to take place, as we were sitting and listening to music on the radio, the announcement came suddenly that the chancellor was going to make a speech to us. Immediately his voice followed, and you could tell from his tone that he was unusually strained and excited. Everybody knows that speech now—how he had "tried to find peace" for the country, and was now resigning to spare Austria violence and bloodshed. We were stunned. When he ended, the station started to play music again, and what they were playing was actually Haydn's *Kaiserquartett*, which contains the melody of the Austrian national anthem. . . .

My friends advised me to flee to Czechoslovakia, but I did not want to. The next Tuesday police came and searched the apartment. Then they came again and arrested me.

We had a janitor whom I had recommended for the job myself. This man was the first to hang up a swastika after that Friday evening. Now, as I was being led downstairs by the police, his wife came running after us and whispered something in the officer's ear. She told him that I had rented an extra room on the corridor and put a refugee friend of ours—a German girl—into it. The officer said at once to me, "Why did you not report that you had this room also?" and went back to search it. Fortunately a cousin of ours had seen the woman speaking to the officer and guessed that she was reporting the refugee girl's room. She quickly ran to that room and removed an anti-Nazi book which was there. So when the police got in, they found nothing incriminating.

When my wife saw me being led away, she was terribly upset, and the guards said to her quite kindly:

"Don't worry—he'll be back in two days."

But when I was brought before a Prussian officer at the police station and questioned by him, I knew the worst was coming. I was given no reason for my arrest, and I had no chance to ask. You don't ask a Prussian officer anything.

A group of ten of us were put into a cell in the city prison, and we remained there for some time. But on March 31 it was announced that we would have no supper that night, and we began to hope that this might mean we were to be released and sent home. About 9:30 in the evening the guards came and led us out—and put us into police wagons. These were still the Viennese police, who were very nice to us. I asked one of them. "Where are they taking us?"

"To the West station," he said.

Then I knew what to expect. It is the station from which the trains leave for Dachau.

At the station, the SS men took us over. At once the whole treatment of prisoners changed. Each of us received a kick or a blow as he climbed into the train. In front of each compartment stood an armed guard. He did nothing but threaten us if we should try to get out. But there was a special group of SS men in each train, known as the *Schlagkommando*. These were four or five huge men whose only job was to go up and down, from car to car, and beat up or terrorize the prisoners.

Our group was brought before the head of the *Schlagkommando* for questioning. I watched his questions and his reactions to different answers—I had a chance to do so because I was sixth in line—and noticed that he followed a certain policy. The first man said he was a non-Jew, a writer by profession. He was let go unharmed. The second man said he was a Jew, quite a wealthy businessman. For a moment nothing happened to him. The third said he was a non-Jew, an unemployed worker. Immediately the officer turned to the rich Jew and called him names, asked him if he wasn't ashamed to have money when there were unemployed Aryans, and finally in a rage hit him in the face. The Jew was wearing glasses, which broke, and his injured eye began right away to swell up from the violent blow.

It appeared that they were going to be much harder on Jewish white-collar workers and the rich middle class than on the workers or unemployed. I thought as fast as I could, and when he called my name I stood to attention as stiffly as possible, in the military way. He said:

"Jew or Aryan?"

"Jew," I said.

"Profession?"

"Unemployed—was formerly in a metal factory."

He believed me, and I was left alone.

The trip to Dachau lasted twelve or fourteen hours. Again and again we could hear the sound of blows in the nearby compartments, blows given with gloves, not bare hands. When we got out of the train again, we got more kicks and shoves. They had, however, bandaged the head of the man whose eye had been struck, and who was all bloody from it.

As we came into the enclosure of Dachau, we were greeted with loud jeers and whistles. A double row of guards lined up, and as our names were read and we went forward to answer questions, we had to go along between the guards, who tripped and kicked us as we walked past. After the questioning we had to go back through that awful line a second time. We still had nothing to eat or drink, of course. At six we were dressed in prison clothes, our heads were shaved, and we each got a number. In addition to the number, each man had a colored triangle sewn on his clothing. The political prisoners and the Jews had red triangles. Ordinary criminals had green. Those who had "refused work" had black. (This meant, for example, a man who had protested when he had been torn away from his profession to dig ditches or build roads.) There was also a pacifist religious sect, the *Bibelforscher*, who would have been released immediately if they had been willing to recant, but who would not give up their principle—they had purple. Finally there was a small group of homosexuals who had pink. The Jews had a yellow triangle sewn on top of the red triangle so as to form a six-pointed Jewish star.

The concentration camp of Dachau is very efficient. It is impossible to escape—those who tried were just committing suicide. In the center there are the barracks. These are surrounded by a large open space, a big ditch, another strip of open ground, a series of machine-gun stations, an electric fence and a wire fence with sentries between the two, and the SS camps.

Inside the camp we were governed by certain prisoners selected by, and under the supervision of, the SS men. Of course they chose the most brutal ones, for they wanted the overseers to be very severe. There was one in each of the barracks, and one for each common room. The advantage of being such an overseer was that he didn't have to do other work; so they were anxious to keep their jobs, and they knew that the more brutal they were the better their superior liked it. One day one of the prisoners hanged himself in the common room. The overseer's comment was nothing but "Take that fellow away. The beds are badly made."

Those beds were a continual source of torture. We had straw sacks which had to be shaken a certain way, and shaped square, and there must not be a single wrinkle in the cover. That is pretty difficult with a straw sack. If the beds were not perfect, we were severely punished. I was lucky in having a bed in a dark corner. If the beds in the center of the room seemed all right at morning inspection, the overseer might not look at the ones along the wall so closely.

Of course there was a lot of corruption among the overseers, but you always had to bribe not only the overseer of your room, but the overseer of work as well. We were allowed a certain amount of money which we often used to buy food at the canteen, which was quite good.

The work is hard physical labor. The first day, after having been led to a fake "medical examination" (the doctor did not really examine us at all), we were sent out to work in the afternoon. *"An die Arbeit—marsch—marsch!"* On that first day the SS men were in charge of our work, not a regular overseer. I had a wheelbarrow filled with stones which I was to wheel over rough ground and dump. That would not have been so bad, if we had not been forced to do all the work at a run—actually running. After many trips to and fro, I fainted. With cold water and kicks they brought me to, and I got up again. My life was saved that day by my fellow prisoner who was taking turns at running the barrow with me—a man who had formerly been the mayor of Vienna. He took the barrow two or three times in succession, and that gave me a chance to recover.

We soon learned that the type of work one was assigned to was very important. Work inside the camp was better because, after all, the overseer was himself a prisoner. Outside the camp we were guarded by SS men, who were ready to shoot us on the slightest pretext. Also they put young men in charge of us who had been trained into a kind of sadism. They loved to ask the prisoners questions, and then give them answers which had been learned by heart. For example:

"What were you?"

"A doctor," the prisoner might say.

"Aha—you mean an abortionist!"

Or again:

"What were you?"

"A merchant."

"Aha—one of those who cheat the people!"

They had obviously been taught these phrases—I heard them again and again, and they were always the same.

On some days, when we were working, we could see in the distance the two towers of the Frauenkirche of Munich, or the line of mountains on the horizon. And that was a sign of rain—a bad sign. Rainy days were our worst, because we only had one suit of clothing and it quickly became soaked. It was made of some pulp material, and absorbed water so that it became very heavy on one's limbs and dragged one down. The only way to dry the suit at night was to keep it on, so we went to bed with the wet clothes sticking to us. One time I had a job digging in a muddy ditch, where I had to stand in water up to my knees all the day. At another period I worked for three months on a farm, where we had to draw our own plow—six men harnessed together. But I became hardened.

One gets used to everything; that is, one simply becomes an animal. All one thinks of is eating, sleeping, and saving one's life. One becomes crafty, like an animal, at these things. To newcomers we always said, "If you stand it for the first eight days, then you can stand it." But the first eight days were usually made exceptionally hard, because the newcomers were put as a rule under the most feared and hated overseer—Sterzer. He was not a political prisoner, but an actual criminal. When angry he would hit a man so that he fell down dead. I myself was never in his charge, probably because our group when it arrived was too large to be all put under him.

And yet not all were brutal. Once when I collapsed at a job, the SS guard led me over to a corner and said, "Lie down here, but if I whistle jump up immediately—it will mean an inspection is coming." They were always nicer when they were alone, and always became more brutal when a superior officer was present.

One day Himmler himself came to visit the camp. We were all carefully prepared. They said to one man, a hat manufacturer from Vienna:

"When he asks you in what profession you were, tell him, and then when he asks why you are here, say, *'Wegen unsozialem Benehmen gegen nicht-jüdische Angestellte.'*." ("Because of unsocial behavior toward my non-Jewish employees.")

When Himmler finally did arrive, the hat manufacturer thought perhaps that he could attract Himmler's attention and get into some kind of conversation with him if he did *not* give the required answer. You know, one gets all kinds of ideas at a time like that. So when he was asked his profession, and he had answered "Hat manufacturer," Himmler asked, "Why are you here?" and he answered:

"I don't know."

"So?" said Himmler. "Put this man in solitary confinement until he remembers why he's here."

As the man was dragged away, he shouted back the required statement: *"Wegen unsozialem Benehmen gegen nicht-jüdische Angestellte."*

But Himmler called back:

"Too late!"

Solitary confinement meant standing upright all day in a cell too small to lie down in. At night one was put in a cell where it was possible to lie down, but the first thing the next morning one would be put back in the small cell, so that the prisoner stood over twelve hours a day. During this period he would be fed only three times a week.

I was in Dachau six months—until September. Then I was sent to another camp—Buchenwald. Dachau had at least been clean. Buchenwald was the filthiest place I have ever seen, and it was in a state of utter confusion. One would have said such a place was impossible in Germany, which has such a love of order.

There were about 10,000 prisoners there, of which only 2000 were Jews. There were 300 of us crowded into one room. We had no regular toilet, although there were some just for show, and we had to go to a latrine outdoors in all weathers throughout the winter. We were not allowed to drink any water—supposedly to prevent typhoid. If caught doing so, the smallest punishment was twenty-five strokes with a wet ox-tail. When they beat prisoners, they usually hit them over the kidneys, so that men went out of there crippled for life. These floggings were performed to music. Once when a man was hanged, they forced his two best friends to do it. Of course we were all brought out to watch.

Here we had no canteen, and although the food we got was all right in quality, we were suffering from intense hunger. People died continually. At my table there were twenty-one at the beginning of one week and only thirteen left at the end of it. There was a group who did nothing but carry out and bury the corpses. Later on a typhoid epidemic did break out, in spite of the restrictions about the water. We were unable to wash decently—in our room the water was run for ten minutes every morning for 300 people. I am ashamed to say that from September 24 to the middle of January I was unable to wash my feet once.

I will not talk at length about Buchenwald. After November 10 the Jews in the camp were not allowed to buy any supplies, medicine, or bandages, and were not allowed to ask for a doctor, and of course were not allowed in the hospital. But Aryan prisoners smuggled supplies in to the Jews, often under great danger to themselves, and once we had the supplies we could manage more or less, since there were plenty of doctors among the prisoners themselves. There was also a great deal of bribery and corruption of the overseers—more than in Dachau. It was also sometimes possible to escape from Buchenwald, because it was so disorganized. But if anyone had come to us and asked whether we preferred six months in Dachau, or one month in Buchenwald, we would all have chosen Dachau.

One thing happened that is rather interesting. We were supposed to sing when working, and often sang a famous concentration camp song called the Song of Estherwegen—the name of a camp in the north, where it was composed. One day when we were exercising and singing this song, the commander protested, saying we ought to have our own song—a Buchenwald song. He then offered a prize of ten marks for an original composition! That night two of the men got together and wrote one, and from then on we sang it very often. We never could quite understand why we were allowed to, and even encouraged, since the words were defiant. I shall never forget them.

Eh' der Tag erwacht
Und die Sonne lacht
Die Kolonnen zieh'n
Zu des Tages Müh'n
Hinein in den grauenden Morgen—
Und der Wald ist schwarz und der Himmel rot
Und wir tragen im Brotsack ein Stückchen Brot
Und im Herzen, im Herzen die Sorgen.

Und das Blut ist heiss und das Mädel fern
Und der Wind singt leis: und ich hab sie so gern,
Wenn treu nur, wenn treu nur sie mir bliebe.
Doch die Steine sind hart, aber fest unser Schritt
Und wir tragen Pickel und Spaten mit
Und im Herzen, im Herzen die Liebe.
Und die Nacht ist so kurz und der Tag ist so lang!
Und wir singen ein Lied, das die Heimat sang:
Wir lassen den Mut uns nicht rauben!
Halt Dich fest Kamerad und verlier' nicht den Mut
Und trage den Willen zum Leben im Blut
Und im Herzen, im Herzen den Glauben.

Refrain:

Oh Buchenwald, ich kann Dich nicht vergessen,
Weil Du mein Schicksal bist.
Wer Dich verliess, der kann es erst vermessen,
Wie wundervoll die Freiheit ist.
Doch Buchenwald, wir jammern nicht und klagen
Und was auch unser Zukunft sei,
Wir wollen trotzdem ja zum Leben sagen,
Denn einmal kommt der Tag und wir sind frei!
(Wir wollen ja zum Leben sagen,
Denn einmal kommt der Tag und wir sind frei!)

(Literal translation)

Before the day wakes
And the sun smiles
The columns file forth
Into the toil of the day
Into the gray morning
And the forest is dark and the sky is red
And we carry in our breadsacks a morsel of bread
And in our hearts, in our hearts, we carry sorrow.

And blood is hot and the girl far away
And the wind sings softly—I love her so much,
If only, if only she stays faithful.

The stones are hard, but firm our tread
And we carry along our picks and our spades
And in our hearts, in our hearts, we carry love.
And the nights are so short and the day is so long!
And we sing a song that our homeland sang:
We will not let them take our courage!
Hold fast, comrade, and lose not your courage
And carry the will to live in your blood
And in your heart, in your heart, carry faith.

Refrain:

Oh Buchenwald, I cannot forget you,
For you are my fate.
Only he who has left you can measure
How wonderful freedom is.
But Buchenwald, we do not wail or complain
And whatever our future may be
We will yet say yes to life
For one day comes the day when we are free!
We will say yes to life,
Then one day comes the day when we are free!

I was in Buchenwald for four months, working from dawn to dark, mostly at breaking stones, with a half hour to eat at noon and one hour in the evening.

Then in January 1939, releases began. One was sent home as suddenly and with as little explanation as when one was arrested. One morning at six o'clock I was called to the gate house—I didn't know if it was for a punishment or not. They told me I was to be released. I didn't dare believe it, since it had happened that men had been told this and then deceived. They threw me my old clothes—completely crumpled and shapeless—and once more closely shaved my head. I had lost thirty pounds. At seven that evening we were let out and taken by bus to a nearby big city, where we were fed by a Jewish community. I telegraphed my wife, and when I got off the train at the Viennese station the next morning, she was there.

She will tell in her own words what had happened to her in the meantime.

As soon as my husband was arrested, I started going from one office to another to find out when he would come back and why he had been taken. It was lucky that I was a blonde, since that made it possible for me to go out on the street without being recognized as a Jewess. Our Jewish friends barely dared to go out anymore—there had been such a marked change of atmosphere in the city as soon as the Nazis had taken command. Everything was so different— they put in German officials in many places and already in the very first days you noticed the new Prussian tone.

Wherever I went, they all said at first that he would be back in a few days. But when I asked on what charge he had been arrested, they didn't give me any answer. When I said, *"Why? why?"* they would shrug their shoulders. There had been no decree explaining the arrests, and nobody could give me any reasons. It all seemed so disorganized.

I did find out in which prison he was, while he was still in Vienna, and I was allowed to bring him his laundry there. But I was never allowed to see him. And one day when I came with the laundry, they wouldn't accept things for him any more. They said, "Go home—he'll probably be there." Of course he was not. The next day they would only say that he was gone. It grew black before my eyes.

For weeks nobody told me where he was.

The official who told me that he was gone tried to back away when I asked more questions, and tried to close the door. I caught hold of his coat to stop him, but he only repeated that my husband just wasn't there. It was another official who told me much later that he had been taken to Dachau.

The Viennese guards were very nice and tried to comfort me. One even whispered in my ear the name of some high official to whom one might appeal. I was so excited and confused I didn't catch the name.

Then came the days of waiting in line, in long queues of women who didn't know where their husbands or sons or brothers were. I think there was no office where I didn't go. But one day came a card from Dachau—a printed card signed by my husband. It said:

"It's all right with me—am healthy—send me money."

Everyone, we soon found out, got the same cards—they were just a form, but we sent the money anyhow. He did actually get some of it. And for us it was the only comfort. After all, it was the only thing one could do for him. Once every fourteen days he was allowed to write, and we were allowed to answer. But there were certain very exact requirements about writing. Our cards could only be sixteen lines—not a word more, and they had to be in German script. It was a terrible thing to write those cards. I wanted to let him know certain things such as the fact that we were writing to America for an affidavit, so that he could leave as soon as they released him. But I was afraid to write such things for the censor to see, so we had to find ways of hinting at them. I always let two or three people read those "works of art" before sending them, for fear I might have let something slip that would hurt him. He thought up a way of disguising things by using his nickname, and speaking of himself as of a third person. I answered the same way. Once he wrote:

"Watch out for little N——, he is very hungry."

So I knew he was not getting enough to eat.

But at other times the censor would cross out a whole card, so one had no idea what had been on it.

At the beginning I always thought I might find some way to see him. A young man came to me who said he had pull with a high official, and that he would get me in. He said he didn't want money for it, but of course I gave him some. I didn't see him again. The loss of money wasn't the worst, but the fact that because I thought I was going to reach my husband that way, I stopped all other attempts for a while and so missed the one chance I would have had to see him. The women were allowed one visit to the men before they were taken to the camp, and of course my husband wondered why I didn't come.

There were many of these "scavengers," as we called them—men who got money from people for pretending that they could give them special information or privileges. I was taken in a second time, together with my husband's brother. I remember the man who fooled us—he was a big blond fellow. He got 1500 marks (about 600 dollars) out of me. We suspected he wasn't telling the truth, but you see we never wanted to think that we had left a stone unturned.

In the first shock and confusion I had not registered on the lists of those applying for admission on the quota to America. So we were not among the first to get on the lists. But the affidavit from my sister in America came soon, and I was able to buy a ticket from a German ship company. We think now that was possibly the reason why he was finally released from Buchenwald.

In the meantime the persecution in Vienna was increasing. A group of boys—about ten to sixteen years old—came one day from house to house and broke in, abusing and beating up people. This was instigated by some Nazi leader, of course. Finally a Jewish worker who was living in our house stood up to them and asked them very quietly if it wouldn't be more sensible if he just "opened the downstairs door and let them out now?" He actually got them to leave.

A big sign was put up on our apartment house saying that all Jews not living in the house were forbidden to enter. This meant that my own brother could not visit me in my home. At another time it was decreed that everybody going out must leave his key with the janitor so that anyone of the Nazi group could go upstairs in your absence and plunder your rooms.

And all this time I was wondering not only whether my husband would be able to hold out in Dachau with his body, but whether his mind would stand it? Many came back broken completely—they just weren't men anymore.

The day before he was released, I was at one of the offices asking about him and begging for his release. The official said no, there was no chance—he could not be freed for a long time. He said that to me with all the papers about my husband lying there on his desk before him—the camp record and all the inside information about the case. He must have known about the coming release. It always seemed to me the most sadistic act of all that he sent me home with that complete denial. That same day my husband's brother came to say goodbye to me. He was terribly upset because he was going away and leaving me when we still did not know what was going to happen. I think the worst thing of all one must go through is the separation of families and friends. The other things one can adapt oneself to, although they are hard the first days.

And then came the telegram from my husband:

"Expect me at West Station," at a certain hour the next morning.

It took hours before we could really grasp it. I called up his brother, who burst into tears at the news. At that time we were all expecting the outbreak of war (it was the time of the Czechoslovakian crisis) and now we were terribly afraid that it might break out before my husband arrived, and that we should not be able to leave, or he might not even be let free.

Of course that train the next morning was late. Finally it pulled in. A lot of people got out, and then I saw something yellow—a yellow piece of skin and bones covered with pus-filled boils and with a shaven head. Our little niece who had come with us to meet him screamed and ran away from him.

But as we started to leave the station an Aryan friend of ours burst out of the crowd, ran up to my husband, and threw his arms around him and kissed him. "I'll come to see you," he whispered to him, and disappeared into the crowd again. My husband was deeply touched. It was very dangerous for an Aryan to do a thing like that.

The Gestapo asked us when we were going to leave, but because all papers were not yet in order we were unable to leave on the date set. For one month we had to wait in Vienna, in constant fear.

But the people—the people of Vienna—were often very good to us. Everyone could tell my husband had been in a concentration camp because of his haircut. Once he went to get a ticket for a friend of ours from London to Southampton. The official told him that he was doing something illegal, since it meant sending money out of Germany, and as you know there were severe restrictions about that. My husband said he had not realized he was trying anything illegal, and assured the man he would not ask for the ticket in that case. The official looked at him and said:

"I'll give it to you because of your shaven head. . . ."

It was generally known that the Jews who had been let out of concentration camps were emigrating. A man sitting next to my husband in a trolley glanced at his head and said to him, "You lucky man—you can leave."

We lived now in a different part of town, where there were fewer Jewish families. But still we used to meet secretly—our old group of friends—the non-Jews too. That talk about Jew-hating is not true—it did not come naturally to the people, but was injected from outside. People who were Aryans kept taking risks for us, and I remember one evening when we were all together, one young Aryan woman came in who had not seen my husband since he got out of the camp, and she almost knelt down before him—you can't imagine it.

At last the papers came through. We took the train through Germany to Hamburg. I must say that all the way we were treated decently by the German people. In February 1939, we got on the ship at Hamburg and sailed for America.

We never want to go back. Not because we're not grateful to Europe—it has beautiful things in it just as America has. But even if it were possible some day, we wouldn't return. It is like a hospital room where you've experienced something so terrible that you never want to see it again.

CHAPTER FOUR

Heightening Persecution

The Trial
of a Shipping Magnate

Arnold Bernstein (1888–1971) was born in Breslau as the son of a grain and alcohol dealer. When his father's firm went bankrupt, he founded a new wholesale business in Hamburg, later building up an extremely successful freight shipping company. In the 1930s, after the stock market crash of 1929, he rebuilt his fortune and turned to the passenger trade, acquiring the Red Star Line and starting his own Arnold Bernstein Line. Although not religious, he also founded the Palestine Shipping Company, the first to be staffed only by Jewish workers. He was arrested in 1937, imprisoned, fined, and forced to turn over his company to the Nazis in exchange for his freedom. He emigrated to New York where he started another shipping company, but with only modest results.

At the end of 1936 I was ready. Notes, calculations, memoranda filled two big briefcases. It was tremendous and difficult work which I had to do chiefly by myself because I dared not make even my loyal friends acquainted with my plans. I had booked passage for myself and family on the *Queen Mary*, sailing in early February. Before that, in January, I went to Switzerland as usual. From there I could send uncensored letters and cables to [a business associate] in preparation for our negotiations. I returned to Hamburg on January 21, to celebrate my birthday on the 23rd, and to tie up loose ends before leaving Germany. Then came the fateful 25th of January, 1937. I was in Berlin with Li [my wife]. From there I intended to go alone to Stockholm. We stayed as usual at the Hotel Esplanade. Our guests for lunch were Lebrecht, the president of the Deutsche Orient Bank, and our friend Ziemke, ambassador of Afghanistan. The waiter had just brought caviar and vodka when a telephone operator came to our table and said, "Mr. Bernstein, a gentleman is in the lobby and wishes to speak to you."

"Tell him I have no time now," I answered, "and ask him if he could come back in an hour." The boy left, but came back immediately and said, "The gentleman insists and says it is of the greatest importance." I excused myself and went to the lobby where a man presented himself, showing a shield which identified him as a member of the Gestapo, and told me that he had the order to bring me back to Hamburg. I felt weak in my knees and had to sit down. "Does that mean that I am under arrest?" I asked. "All I know," he answered, "is that I have an order to bring you to Hamburg." "I have guests for lunch," I said. "You don't object that I finish?" "Not at all, but please don't mind if I sit at a neighboring table." Followed by him, I went back to our table, sat down, lifted my glass and said, "Prosit! This may be my last vodka for a long time," and told them what had happened. Their faces turned white. I could not tell what the Gestapo wanted, but we all knew it could only be the worst.

We finished our lunch, hardly talking at all. Then Li and I said goodbye to our friends and went to our room, accompanied by the Gestapo officer. We took our luggage, drove by taxi to the station, and boarded the train to Hamburg. I had a first-class compartment and changed my watchdog's second-class ticket because I did not want to sit among other passengers. Of course we did not talk very much. My guard told me that he was a higher official and the Gestapo deferred to my position and sent him instead of the usual way of making an arrest. He had the grace to leave me alone with Li for a short time. My poor darling! I can still see her beloved face, so white and frightened. We did not know how much danger and suffering lay before us. I was, of course, deeply shocked. That these pigs dared to arrest me was a menacing sign, but I told Li not to worry. I said that I had a clear conscience and was sure that the whole matter would be cleared up immediately.

In Hamburg two SS men waited for us. My guard passed me on to them and I had to say goodbye to Li. Without paying attention to the spectators, I took her in my arms, kissed her, and said, "Don't worry. It will all be cleared up." Then I had to leave her standing there alone, despair in her face. The two SS men took me to an open car with the SS flag on the right fender. During the drive, which lasted only five minutes, not a word was spoken. We turned toward the harbor, went across a toll bridge and stopped in front of a building which I later found to be headquarters of the *Zollfahndungsstelle,* a special Gestapo organization to apprehend violators of the strict foreign-exchange regulations. Foreign-exchange violations and crimes against German blood (sexual relationships with gentiles) were used by the Nazis to rob and destroy the Jews.

I was brought into an office, and from there into a smaller room, furnished with a desk and chair, with a small window set into the door; the main window was protected by iron bars. Here I was left alone. I heard what was said in the office outside. Three times the telephone rang and I heard one of the guards say, "No, we don't know anything," and the last time, very brutally, "Stop molesting us if you know what is good for you," and then, talking to the others, "There she was again," and everybody laughed. I was sure it was my Li and I could imagine how desperately my darling suffered. All my life I had "carried her on my hands," had guarded and protected her, and now I was helpless. The knowledge of my helplessness fell like a stone on my heart. It was cold in the room. I did not know what was going on, and I ran around like a caged tiger, shaken by fear and fury.

Nobody who has not gone through such an experience can understand my feelings. Suddenly it struck me that I was a defenseless prisoner. I was no longer the respected Arnold Bernstein, proud of my record, strong and safe. Suddenly I felt that I was in the hands of ruthless enemies who would not respect either law or human rights and that all my decent life and my merits would be of no help. A deep despair seized me. What a fool I had been that, relying on my good conscience, I had disregarded all the warnings of my friends. I had heard rumors of Jews being arrested without warning during the night and dragged away, never to be heard of again. However, nobody in a higher position had, up to now, been arrested, thereby giving me a warning. I was the first. I did not know what my staff, when questioned, had told them, but was sure it could not have been the reason for my arrest.

Later I heard that the Nazis, on the day of my arrest, had no reason whatever for seizing me. They had invented a reason to justify such an arrest, called *Verdunklungsgefahr* (danger that, when free, the suspect could destroy evidence). Under this pretext people, Jews without exception, were held for any length of time, until the Nazis decided what to do with them. Finally the door opened and I was taken one flight up into an office where I found a Mr. Heil and his secretary sitting in front of a typewriter. Heil began to question me; his questions and my answers were immediately recorded. I cannot remember all he asked me, only that he concentrated on the Palestine Shipping Company and that I told him that this company was approved by the Berlin authorities in cooperation with the Deutsche Werke Kiel. I had to sign the protocol, then I was brought back to my cell and again left alone. After about an hour they led me out. I had to empty my pockets; they put everything, with the exception of my handkerchief, into a paper bag: my new alligator wallet, the Christmas gift of Li, with a hundred and fifty marks, gold wrist watch and notebook. I never saw these again. Then they took me to a hallway, where I saw my chief accountant Wolf, my secretary Gibbarra, and Dr. Gottschalk, the lawyer for the Palestine Shipping Company—all standing with their faces to the wall. I had to do the same. Now I understood that while I waited, they had been questioned. Then an SS sergeant came and ordered us, yelling at us as if we were vermin, to follow. Again we were put in a car, talk strictly forbidden, and driven to a night police guard house. All the human rabble picked up by the police during the night were brought there—criminals, drunkards, whores. There we were locked up in separate cells.

In my cell was a cot, a wooden table, and a chair. Unfortunately, one of the window panes in the iron-barred window was broken, and the ice-cold winter air came in. I lay down on the hard planks and covered myself as well as possible, but I was shivering. Naturally I could not sleep. Since my fateful lunch in Berlin I had had nothing to eat or drink. Every minute seemed like an hour. I was tormented by the darkest forebodings and it was a relief when I was called to get up. Together with my colleagues, I was driven to the main police station, Grosse Bleichen, and again locked up alone in a cell. There I waited for hours. At noon a guard brought a fish dish and a bowl of coffee (thin, dark water). The fish smelled horrible, but I forced myself to eat, knowing that I would need all my physical and mental strength to survive the coming days. Shortly after, I was taken out. They took a picture for the list of criminals. I was fingerprinted and then brought into a courtyard, where I saw Wolf again, Dr. Gottschalk, and my secretary, Gibarra. Talking was, of course, impossible because we were guarded by SS men. We were handcuffed to each other, I to Dr. Gottschalk. Two days before we had been together at a party, where I had told him an off-color joke, ending: "Now we are united for all our lives," and I just wanted to whisper to him these words, when I suddenly thought: "Better not," because he was so tense that I was afraid he would break out in hysterical laughter and who could know how the SS men would react. [. . .]

My only fear was of being beaten. I had a hot temper, was a proud man, and I was afraid that I would attack the offender with all the consequences to be expected during the Nazi regime. However, my person was internationally well known, my fate of great interest, especially to my colleagues in the shipping business, and I heard later that an order was given by high officials not to make a martyr of me. Physically I did not suffer. The food which was given me was sufficient. I got newspapers and books sent by Li, and I read many hours; but mentally it was harder to bear from day to day. Stumme [one of my lawyers] came two or three times weekly, but the short time of his visit always went too fast and waiting for him was getting on my nerves. Negotiations to free me went on continuously and, according to what Stumme told me, I was filled with wild hopes one moment and, the next, plunged into despair. One day Stumme brought his associate, Dr. Labowsky, who normally handled all my business. Labowsky asked me, full of joy, "Do you know what I have here in my pocket?" When I looked at him questioningly, he took a check out of his pocket. "Here is thirty thousand dollars, your ransom. In a couple of days you will be free."

"Not so fast," said Stumme, and then he told me that the Nazis demanded that I transfer all the shares of the Arnold Bernstein Line and the Red Star Line to the trustee, Boeger, as a condition of my release. I was dumbfounded. Up to then I had still hoped that some arrangement could be made whereby I did not lose the fruit of twenty-five years' hard work. Stumme, seeing my dejection, explained, "You must know that, from the start, the whole purpose of the action against you was to eliminate Jewish influence in this great successful enterprise." A thousand German sailors under a Jewish owner was more than the Nazis could swallow. Kollmar negotiated with the Goering ministry for Boeger to take over, and immediately started sales negotiations with prospective German buyers. The new owners would take over the mortgage obligations of the Red Star Line, Chemical Bank would agree to supply a million of their blocked marks as additional working capital, and would give favorable long-term conditions to repay mortgage and new loan. The Red Star would take over the assets of the Arnold Bernstein Line. The name Arnold Bernstein was to vanish, and the Erie, now itself in bankruptcy, would only get a small compensation.

When I protested, Stumme said, "Mr. Bernstein, you must understand that it is the only chance you have to get out." He hesitated a moment and then added, "alive." Labowsky said that he was sure that I, with my intimate knowledge of the business and my relations with the automobile trade, and also aided by the influence of Chemical Bank, would be able to make an arrangement under which I would act as general representative abroad. However, the most important thing was to get me out. We talked back and forth, but what could I do? Finally I had to give my consent. A long imprisonment would break me, I would lose contact with the business, and who knows what might happen under a maniac like Hitler? After Stumme and Labowsky had left, I needed time to digest the new situation. All kinds of thoughts rushed through my mind, chiefly dictated by fury and thirst for revenge. If these German crooks thought that they could get away with their infamy, they would soon become aware of their mistake,

I was the soul of my business. Even backed by the mighty New York Central, Sudman was not able to take it away from me. Now I would be backed by the Moore-McCormack Line. Fighting against the German Red Star Line, I would make such inroads in their business that this wonderful business, wonderful under my management, would soon become a failure. Then, when the line could not pay the installments due Chemical Bank, Chemical Bank would foreclose and take over the vessels. All my energy returned. I saw myself already free and in full battle again and, not even thinking of sleep, I lay awake through the night full of plans of what I would do when I did get out. During the whole time in prison I was in permanent touch with Boeger. Primarily he wanted information, and I sent him long memoranda. Sometimes he came in person to talk to me. Now he came again. He told me that he first intended to refuse to accept my shares, but then he thought that this would not help me—the authorities would just appoint another trustee. He told me, with great pride, how splendidly the line worked under him and that 1937 was a great year for profits. You damned fool, I thought bitterly, don't you understand that I needed six years to save the line from the consequences of the 1929 crash and that you are now earning the fruits of my efforts?

When he was president of the Hapag, they could only prevent a catastrophe by offering their shareholders a quota of ten percent of their investment, and the government had to give substantial financial aid to avoid a complete breakdown. Of course I did not let him know what I thought, and especially not what I intended to do after my release. I agreed with him that the Red Star could easily be sold, and that with the new financial arrangement with Chemical Bank and taking over the Arnold Bernstein Line without repaying the mortgage held by the Erie, a financial success was as good as guaranteed.

Well, it was not to be. One day Stumme came to visit me. He was an older man, a little on the chubby side, his face emanating dignity and benevolence. His personal charm, combined with his high ability and reliability, had earned him the respect and liking of the authorities, and the trust of his clients. Today I saw immediately that he was deeply disturbed and asked him what was the matter. What I heard from him hit me like a thunderbolt. In all the ups and downs of the negotiations with the Nazis, the basis was always that no deal could be consummated without the cooperation of Chemical Bank, and from the start the bank had insisted on the condition that I, in compensation for giving up my shares, would gain my freedom. Now, Stumme told me, after all points were cleared by Kollmar, he had sent a long cable to New York, repeating the whole arrangement and the request for my freedom as a condition. Stumme told me that Chemical had cabled Kollmar that he had to drop the condition of my release, not to endanger the arrangement favorable to them. Kollmar, instead of getting in touch with Stumme immediately, had simply informed the Goering Ministry accordingly.

Stumme went to Berlin the next day and was amazed when Goering's assistant told him that he regretted it, but that under these circumstances there was no economical excuse for his office to include my person in the deal, and he had therefore given a free hand to the court in Hamburg to go ahead with the prosecution. He had just spoken to the general attorney. The attorney was also astonished, and said that now he had to hurry to finish the indictment. He had already stopped it, expecting that a deal would be made. We sat as if we were attending a funeral. There was not much to say. Kollmar, when pressing me to release the shares as the price of my freedom, had repeated again and again that he acted with the full authorization of Chemical Bank. I now suspected foul play, but what could I do? Stumme tried to console me, but I was too deeply depressed to pay much attention. After my hopes were so high, relief from my predicament so near and sure, the breakdown of all my hopes hit me like a thunderbolt.

Alone again, I felt sick, every limb felt cramped, my breath and heart were racing and I was sweating. I did not know what was in store for me—only that there would be danger, humiliation, and bitterness, separation from my beloved ones, inability to protect them, the end of all my hopes and perhaps, even my life. Then I cooled off, and my old will power came back. I would fight. I would not ask for pity and clemency. I would be honest, keep my dignity, and use my brain and experience to prove my innocence. I would make it clear to friend and enemy that I knew that any claim against me was unjustified and any judgment against me a crime committed by criminals.

[After seven months in prison, Arnold Berstein is finally indicted for illegal currency transactions and brought before a Sondergericht *(Special Court) in a trial that lasted six weeks and was followed by the international press.]*

Finally the trial came to an end, and the summations of the prosecutor and the defendants began. According to [the prosecutor] Jauch, I was the scum of the human race, a man who took advantage of everything to further his selfish interest, typical of a Jew, to make money, and that I had caused heavy damage to the German economy. Then my lawyers held their defense speech, first Stumme and then Bucerius. One has to keep in mind that a lawyer at this time, defending a Jew, ran a grave risk, endangering his career and even his freedom. [. . .]

Stumme was an honest and liberal man, as well as a first-class and highly respected lawyer. Nevertheless, it soon became clear that he was handicapped because he simply was afraid of defending a Jew, and therefore confined himself to defending my actions from a legal standpoint instead of ridiculing the whole indictment. Only once did he mention that I was a man who, maybe in his eagerness to build a great German shipping line, had overstepped his authority, but never out of selfishness. Maybe he was right not to antagonize the judges, in the conviction that they acted under orders. Anyway, his speech lacked color and left me with a feeling of disappointment. Then Bucerius continued my defense, and he really stuck his neck out. He described my life as an uninterrupted proof of my patriotism and eagerness to serve my country and my compatriots. He mentioned my outstanding war record and how in 1919, when many thousand went hungry in Hamburg, I had opened a public kitchen where everybody could get a nourishing, warm lunch and where daily more than a thousand people were fed, the expenses paid out of my pocket. He told how, beginning with nothing, I had built up a big passenger and freight line extending the German flag service to Belgium and Holland, bringing in during those years more than twenty million dollars for Germany and creating employment for more than a thousand German sailors. He mentioned that my honesty, responsibility, and ability had earned me respect at home and abroad, and made me an asset to Germany's reputation and economy.

The speech of this extremely clever and courageous man was as if a clear, fresh wind had blown into a thick, evil atmosphere. However, it was all wasted. The judges heard it with noncommittal cold faces, while Jauch smiled ironically. Then [the presiding judge] Moeller asked for a recess because it was noon. It was Friday and everybody expected that the trial would start again at two p.m., when I then would have the last word for my defense. However, they apparently did not want to give me the opportunity to be heard by the people in the big court room, and especially the foreign correspondents. They delayed the opening until five p.m., when everybody had gone, and I had to speak to an empty room.

Knowing that the whole trial was a farce, and that nothing I said would have any effect, I made it short. First I asked for clemency for the members of my staff, taking responsibility for whomever could be blamed, even if I had nothing to do with the technical, financial details. I said that I had always had only the success of my line in mind, that I fought a desperate fight to bring the line through the Depression, and that I was happy and proud when I finally succeeded. I asked my judges to consider the spirit in which I ran my enterprise, and that I never had had the intention of violating the law and regulations, and I never felt that I did. I also mentioned that I was proud that I was able to strengthen the position of the German Merchant Marine and give employment to more than thousand sailors. I said that I had already suffered under the long imprisonment, that in my willingness to save the line I had given up my shares, the fruit of more than twenty years of struggle, worry, and hard work. And that was all.

The judgment was given on January 25. The period before was a torture of waiting for me. Then came the moment when I stood before the judges, my whole body cramped with tension. One thing I was firmly resolved: whatever the judgment would be, I would not give them the satisfaction to see me show fear or despair. I read later in the Nazi papers that Bernstein heard the judgment without showing any trace of feeling in his cold face. It was bad enough. In Germany there is a difference between *Gefaengnis* (jail for minor crimes) and *Zuchthaus* (house of correction for heavy crimes). I was sentenced to two and a half years of *Zuchthaus*, the nine months during which I was already a prisoner to be deducted. I was deeply shocked. This was much worse than I had feared—and against this judgment of the Special Court no appeal was possible. While Moeller was still reading the justification of the judgment (I remember especially when he said, "That Bernstein had such an outstanding war record cannot be counted in his favor; on the contrary, a man devoted to his country was doubly a criminal when he committed treason", the door was suddenly flung open. Li ran in , stopped in front of Moeller, hit the desk with her fist, and cried, "You cannot do this to such a man. That is criminal!"

She was beside herself—my Li—the shy girl, always ladylike. Now she looked like a fury, her eyes afire in her white face. When she said to Moeller, "One day you and your children will pay for what you have just done," two guards jumped at her, took her by her arms, and pulled her back. I thought my heart would break. I went to her, told the guards to let her go, that I would calm her, and they did so. I took her in my arms and whispered, "Hold fast, my darling. This is not the end. Don't give them this satisfaction. We shall talk later." She cried bitterly, but did not resist when I led her to the door. I went back to my place. Everybody was silent. Moeller was white in the face. Finally he said, "One must excuse Mrs. Bernstein. It is understandable that she lost control" and, addressing the press, "I expect, gentlemen, that you will not mention this in your papers."

AN INVITATION FROM THE GESTAPO

Alice Salomon (1872–1948) was a pioneer figure in the German women's movement, an international authority on social work who founded the first women's professional school in Germany. Originally Jewish, Salomon converted to Protestantism and became a member of the "Fighting" or "Confessing" Church (Bekennende Kirche) which opposed the Nazis. She was forced to emigrate in 1937. The following is the last chapter of her memoirs, written in English in New York, which she was never able to publish.

The secret police summoned me in May 1937 to appear the following morning for a "report on my trips abroad." After four hours of questioning, I was ordered to leave Germany within three weeks.

It might seem strange that I should not have expected this from the beginning of Nazi rule. However, so far, people who were in danger had either left of their own accord or disappeared suddenly into a concentration camp. This was before the bestial pogrom in the fall of 1938, and before the mass deportations. To be expelled and expatriated was still a mark of particular distinction, although it was meant as humiliation.

"For what crime? What have you done? Were you a citizen?" my friends abroad wanted to know. My German friends knew that there need not be any such excuses for Nazi actions; they asked merely what charges were made and whether the secret police had any material evidence on which to base their order—the recording of a telephone conversation, the photostat of a letter, an "Open Letter" by Thomas Mann or Einstein, or anything else.

They had nothing, except the reproach of my frequent and lengthy sojourns abroad. Of course, though I had never been in party politics, I represented everything the Nazis detested. I was of Jewish "race"; I belonged to the fighting Protestant Church; I was a progressive woman, internationally minded and therefore of pacifist tendencies. Undoubtedly they believed I would do less harm outside the country than within. They were mistaken.

The son of one of my friends warned me of the danger of writing many letters on behalf of people who wanted to emigrate. I said, "If it's no longer possible to do even that, I would rather not live." But I did not expect trouble.

The Nazis wanted non-Aryans to get out—my activities should have been welcome. They had never searched or raided my home. When the summons came, I never even considered the possibility of being in danger.

Individual mishaps have become rather irrelevant since the recent Holocaust. I was, after all, not deported like my youngest sister, my brother's younger son, and so many of my friends. It would not be worthwhile to mention my inquisition by the secret police but for the futility of matters into which they pried, the stupidity of their accusations and judgment, may contribute to the unsavory picture of totalitarianism.

The iron gate of the huge red-brick police building in central Berlin was locked behind me as I passed through, and I was asked to produce the summons. In a bare, anonymous office room a young official questioned me and noted down my answers, while an older one who pretended to be at work on some files acted as watchdog and interrupted curtly several times. I was reminded of novels about Czarist Russia that I had read in my young days, portrayals of distrust and suspicion in an atmosphere where even spies were spied upon. Incredibly, I now found in real life, in my own country, the same system with a secret police whose members were no less distrusted, watched, and controlled by their own superiors from the highest ranks down.

I was questioned extensively about my various trips, their dates and routes, and the friends and places I visited. "How did you make that acquaintance?" was a favorite question. How does friendship begin? Sometimes with a glance, sometimes with an accord in the course of a conversation, sometimes through interest or cooperation in a common cause . . . I explained each case.

Apparently the names of my titled friends disturbed them, for these they took down when I produced letters of invitation. I had been collecting these "alibis" for years. Everyone did this during the Nazi regime, to protect themselves against possible charges of having spent money abroad. We were allowed to accept hospitality and railroad tickets from foreign friends, but no money even for the smallest expenses. The usual joke, when we commented on this ruling, was to say, "All right; but what about tips?"

They pounced on the name of an American hostess, a Mrs. Johnson, after I had given the address of Mrs. Emilia Johnston, a Scottish friend.

"You just told me that Johnston was in Scotland," the officer said, warily.

"Johnson," I replied, "is a common name in Anglo-Saxon countries."

The fact that I had spent every summer in Engelsberg was also suspicious in their eyes. Why go to the same place for so many consecutive summers, if not for some intrigue or underground work—even if it is only a quiet mountain valley?

"With whom did you talk there?" I answered that I had gone for a rest and lived very quietly.

"Do you mean to suggest that you never talked with anyone?"

"No, I do not. In a hotel you eventually talk to people."

"Then give us the names."

I mentioned the family of the proprietor, whom I had known all my life, the Cattanis. The absence of any Jewish name was rather disappointing. Quite obviously they were out to discover my connection with some Jewish plot or underground activity.

A trip I had made the winter before to the United States was my greatest offense. This had occurred about the time when Mayor La Guardia and Bishop Mundelein had commented on Hitler in terms that were far from complimentary. Evidently the secret police traced these remarks to my influence, which, however flattering, sadly overestimated my importance. The watchdog interfered curtly: "Do not keep asking her *where* she went, but *why* she traveled."

The significance attached to my innocent movements seemed so ridiculous that I burst out, "Why do you ask me all these things? So far as I know, it is not forbidden to travel. To whom should I apply for permission next time I plan to go abroad?"

I was already contemplating another trip without dreaming what sort of final journey lay before me. It was only later I realized that these subalterns had received orders to throw me out of Germany, and that it was left to them to find some warrant for the action. Toward the end of four hours of cross-examination I had arrived at a stage of exhaustion where I would have admitted anything. I began to understand how under pressure people will sometimes admit things they have never done.

For a long interval I was sent out into a corridor closed by iron bars. They called me in again and inquired about the organizations to which I belonged. This time my inquisitor attempted to imitate Hitler's famous "hypnotic glance." I had to admit that my organizations were all very mild, harmless groups concerned with women's activities and social work. His attention focused on the International Council of Women. Probably he assumed it was a Communist or Jewish organization in conspiracy against the Nazi government. He noted the names and addresses of all board members of the council and also of the International Committee of Schools of Social Work, of which I was chairman. Then he demanded, again with the hypnotic glare: "Fraeulein Doktor, did you meet any emigrants?"

Although the whole of Nazi policy had been framed to force all nonconformists, pacifists, republican politicians, Jews, and many Christians to emigrate, yet the Nazis behaved as if all emigrants were criminals. Mere contact with one of them made a German a leper.

I admitted having met quite a few, among others Dr. Weiss, former vice-president of the Berlin police, at the home of the Hon. Mrs. Franklin, who had offered him refuge. The Franklins were old friends of mine and I had visited them for many years. The watchdog was most anxious to know what Dr.

Weiss was doing in London. I informed him that he was the representative of a stationery firm. I might have added that a certain former cabinet minister represented a company making electric bulbs, and another, a Catholic, sold oil and incense to churches, and that all three had accidentally met in a motion picture studio where each was trying to place an order. I also named some very distinguished professors, several of them world famous. He expressed surprise when I explained that some of them had called on me in the United States. Apparently he considered such visits improbable unless we were agents of an underground organization. What had we talked about?

I answered, "Mostly about America. The United States is a very interesting country, and people who have recently arrived there are in the habit of discussing its institutions and customs."

"So you had scientific discussions?"

"Yes."

"But people must have asked you about Germany as well."

"Certainly. Some wanted to hear about mutual friends."

Then he asked, somewhat comprehensively, what the American people talked about and whether the general feeling was favorable to Germany. My answers were correspondingly vague.

Meanwhile I had repeated my request to make a telephone call to my housekeeper, who would be waiting for me with a friend I had asked to lunch. But my inquisitors seemed to fear that I would call for help. Although I explained exactly why I wished to telephone, it was not permitted.

After a long time—it was then after three o'clock—I was called into another room where a rather vulgar man asked me: "Miss Salomon, what had you in mind when you traveled abroad?"

"In mind? I traveled, as I have done frequently all my life."

"Do you intend to remain in Germany?"

"Certainly."

"That is impossible. You must leave this country within three weeks."

After a moment of shock, I said: "It seems pretty short notice!"

"Why so? What have you got to do here?"

"For example, to dissolve a home."

I did not add: "to say goodbye to life-long friends whom I shall never see again"; nor "to find a refuge"; nor "to go over the papers accumulated by a scholar and author and teacher during forty years, to decide what would best serve me in my profession in new and alien surroundings"; nor "to liquidate funds that have been entrusted to me."

He was quite uninterested in my personal reactions and demanded: "By which frontier station will you leave Germany, and where will you live?"

"I cannot possibly decide at a moment's notice. I may go to Switzerland, via Basel. But I can't tell."

Ironically, that very morning I had received word from my local police station that my routine application for a new passport (the old one having expired) had been granted, "as nothing unfavorable was known against me."

He continued: "Your passport has expired. When you get the new one come back to this room and tell me what day you will leave Germany and by which frontier station."

That was all.

I drove home. My friend and housekeeper were upset over the long delay, and both broke down when I told them the verdict. "I accept it," I said, "and you must do the same for my sake."

That night I decided to ask my British friends, the Franklins, if they would take me in for a time. I wrote to American friends for an affidavit so I could get an immigration visa for the United States, where an exile is allowed to work for a living. Two days later I told the secret police that I would leave by Bentheim, Holland, and was informed that I should have to travel without a passport until I claimed it at the frontier. I then asked to have the order of expulsion in writing. This infuriated the official. He jumped to his feet. "That can't be done under any circumstances! We never give anything in writing."

I said, "This is an enforced emigration."

"It is an order to emigrate," he corrected, "so as to avoid the concentration camp."

That was my sentence. They might have saved themselves and me the trouble of endless questioning. The order for expatriation had gone through, and it was a stupid order. So long as I lived in Germany I was powerless. In sending me away the Nazis loosened my tongue. Inadvertently, they gave me, after empty dreary years, a new lease on life; the need to work again and the freedom to do it. I have always considered this one of life's greatest gifts.

To have been marked by the Gestapo provides an insight into human nature beyond anything the psychologists can teach. It is a supreme test of friendship, loyalty, and courage, for any communication with a marked individual may endanger the others.

Immediately after the inquisition at Gestapo headquarters, I telephoned a friend who was a lawyer. Curt was a bachelor in his early forties and had frequently been my guest—a pleasant asset to small dinner parties and a good conversationalist. I told him that I had to see him and he came at once. I explained what had happened and asked him to advise me how to liquidate my German life. It was not easy: I needed an exit permit, for which in turn I needed proof that all my taxes, besides the emigration tax, had been paid, and none of these papers were granted without a certificate of "good behavior." I also had to give up the lease on my home, dispose of my books and furniture, and get a permit for the things I wished to take with me. My pension from the Berlin municipality, as former director of my college, and a life annuity on capital I had donated for the purchase of a dormitory would stop; but a fraction of my remaining funds could perhaps be transferred before my bank accounts were blocked. All this in three weeks.

Curt was dumbfounded. There was no regulation whatever that justified the expulsion of a citizen, in this case an aged woman with a record of public usefulness. People still thought in terms of the law. He considered my request for a moment. Then he said: "Alice, I am going to do it for you, and I am not going to take any money from you on the one condition that you follow my advice and that you don't let others meddle who think you could get a more favorable arrangement in some roundabout way. And I beg you not to talk about it. Keep the whole affair as secret as you can. Who knows what else these gangsters will do to you if it is discussed." He faithfully took care of everything.

One of the astonishing things about Nazi Germany was the speed with which news traveled in spite of fear, spying, and intimidation. Curt was so upset that he did himself what he had warned me not to do. He told a few people and soon everybody knew. Since I have been blessed with the kind of innocence that never anticipates disloyalty or disappointment in human relations, I did not realize then how great was the service I had asked of him, and that it might prove very inconvenient for his law office. Before my summons I had promised to dine at the home of very dear friends. Now I went to say goodbye. My heart was pounding, my hands were jittery, and when I told them, I spilled their best Bordeaux over my best dress. Only later it dawned on me that I might have been traced to their house.

Soon there were incidents that made me understand the situation. I noticed that the telephone never rang unless someone was calling from a public booth. A very intimate friend of mine, a prominent citizen of eighty years, rang up and said, "How are you, my dear friend?" "I am all right." He said, "People are telling so many stories nowadays. There are rumors about everyone." I told him, "Everything you may have heard is true. I shall come and explain." It turned out that someone had mentioned my case at a party the night before. He would not believe it but did not dare to reassure himself by telephone. Early in the morning he had come to my apartment. The elevator was out of order, so he had climbed four flights of stairs. He rang, but I did not hear the bell and my housekeeper had gone to early mass. This alarmed him still more. About noon he had gone to a public telephone to call.

Some people dared to come, but mostly after dark. A friend and former student of mine who was known for her courage came every day in her car, parking it ostentatiously in front of my house. Meaning to take my thoughts off my problem and to let me have a last glimpse to remember, she urged me to drive out to the lake district and see the beauty of spring. I told her, "The banks of the Hudson are beautiful too."

Paul, the great banker, came with his brother Frederick. They wanted to try to have the order canceled, but I explained that life in Germany would be impossible for me after this. I mentioned that the money I had earned during the lecture tour in the United States had been turned over to the Nazi government in exchange for worthless German marks. Max Warburg, in whose lovely home in Hamburg I had spent a day on my return from the States, had promptly had his bank exchange it for me. Paul volunteered to talk to Dr. Schacht or one of his aides, pointing out that it would be unspeakable to withhold money earned on a trip for which they turned me out of Germany. He actually succeeded in getting these few hundred dollars transferred at a better rate. These and a good many others were and remained my steadfast friends. There were some with whom I had worked for forty years, and from whom I have never heard again.

I could not possibly say goodbye to the great number of people who meant much to me, so I decided to send them a letter of farewell, explaining that I would have left Germany, never to come back, by the time they received it.

Several people warned me not to send it through the mail for it would endanger every addressee. I was advised to employ the method of the Confessional Church—to have them delivered by car, with a second person along to drop them into the mailboxes, ready to drive on before the letters were discovered. A friend promised to do it for me, and I asked my secretary to sort the letters in the order of their delivery and to accompany him. The next morning she declared: "P put the letters in order, but I will not drive in the car. According to the map I saw, the car will have to take so many turns it can't fail to draw attention." But the young man did it anyway.

I had told Curt that I wanted to get out as soon as possible, and it was settled that I would leave on June 12, two and a half weeks after the order. My friends were distressed that I had to go alone, without money and without a passport. Ursula, who had been secretary for the non-Aryan Christian Refugee Committee, welcomed the opportunity to visit an aunt in England and it was arranged that she would go on the same train. Of course she had to buy her ticket somewhere else, travel in another car, and board the train at another station. When we had passed the frontier, where the secret police gave me my passport, I asked her into my compartment. We looked out on Dutch houses covered with crimson ramblers, on gardens in bloom and cherry trees bending under the weight of their fruit. I said, "Look at this. Isn't God's world beautiful everywhere?" In amazement she told me, "We were all convinced you would collapse the minute we passed the frontier."

I waited in England for my visa, encouraged by the kindness of my English and Scottish friends. In September 1937 I arrived in New York for my new lease on life.

It has not all been bliss. It is hard work to lecture for a living, and I have always been physically frail. Also, it has been said so often that I hesitate to repeat it, the refugee loses caste. I lost many former friends, and sometimes when I see them at a public function I think of Henry George who said,

"These people once gave a banquet for me." A few of my old friends have been guardian angels and, as I have always been lucky, I have found new ones, and a church where people tell me that they have missed me when I have not been well enough to attend services for a few weeks.

It took me four years to start a home, and I am now rather proud of having learned in my seventieth year how to cook from a cookbook. A home acquires an aura that the most luxurious hotel suite can never have. It is made up of the people who go in and out. So I could be happy if the thought of this most cruel of wars, the suffering it inflicted, and its aftermath, would not intrude.

The germs of aggressive nationalism have long been latent in the German organism, as they have been at times in other nations. The only hope for a cure of Germany's delirium lies in the potential growth of her moral forces, and a rediscovery of the basic law of human relations: the law of interdependence. Or as it was expressed two thousand years ago: the law of human brotherhood.

WAITING

Born in Breslau, Elisabeth Freund (1898–1982) studied economics in Breslau and in Berlin, where she lived in the house of her uncle, the Nobel Prize winner Fritz Haber. After the emigration of her three children, she was forced by the Nazis to work in a large laundry and in an armaments plant. She and her husband succeeded in emigrating to Cuba just before Himmler suspended all emigration from Germany in October 1941.

We were so sure that we would now [May 1941] receive the visas for the United States, but we still have not heard anything about them. Our brothers and sisters in America write that we should inquire of the American Consul, that they had taken care of everything, that our affidavits* were at the consulate and were proper and adequate. Even a bank deposit was made for us, and a certification by the shipping line was sent, stating that the tickets were already paid for. Our waiting number, which we had applied for in November 1938, should have come long ago. But it seems like a disaster; we still do not have the summons to the consulate. If we only knew why we are not making any progress! Unfortunately, at the consulate no information is given about the state of matters pertaining to emigration. We are completely at a loss. What if some day America really enters into a war with Germany— everything does seem threatening enough—and then all contacts to foreign countries are barred and we have not received our visas in time! It is simply inconceivable. Then we will not be able to see our children ever again.

It is really enough to drive one to despair. We've already done so many things in order to get away from Germany. We have filed applications for entry permits to Switzerland, Denmark, and Sweden. It was all in vain, though in all these countries we had good connections. In the spring of 1939, from an agent we obtained an entry permit for Mexico for 3000 marks. But we never received the visa, because the Mexican consulate asked us to present passports that would entitle us to return to Germany, and the German authorities did not issue such passports to Jews. Then, in August 1939 we did actually get the permit for England. But it came too late, only ten days before the outbreak of war, and in this short time we were not able to take care of all the formalities with the German authorities. In the spring of 1940 we received the entry permit for Portugal. We immediately got everything ready and applied for our passports. Then came the invasion of Holland, Belgium, and France by the German troops. A stream of refugees poured to Portugal, and the Portuguese government recalled by wire all of the issued permits. As it happened, we were lucky that we had not given up our apartment and not yet sold our furniture. It was also good that in December 1940 we had not already paid for our Panamanian visas, for we noticed that the visas offered us did not at all entitle us to land in Panama. Things can again work out for us in such a way that we will no longer be able to leave.

We are convinced that in reality America wants to help and is receiving the European refugees in the most generous manner. But they do not know there how difficult the situation is; otherwise they would permit these poor and tortured people to get there quickly, while it is still possible. They could lock them up in a camp there until the situation of every individual is clarified, and the relief committees could bear the costs for it. But we had better get away from here, and as quickly as possible; otherwise we will meet the same fate as the unfortunate people who were deported from Stettin to Poland, or as the Jews from Baden, who were sent to France and who are being held captive there in the Pyrenees.

[On June 22, 1941, Germany attacks the Soviet Union. Shortly thereafter Elisabeth Freund collapses doing forced labor at the steam press.]

·I was sick for over three weeks and lay in bed practically the whole time. Our old Hedwig looked in on me every few days and tended to me in a touching way. She is an Aryan woman who has been with our family for more than forty years. As a young girl she was a domestic at my parents'. She knows every member of the family, and practically knows more about all of them than I. She also saw my children growing up and worries about them. Her husband works for the postal service and her son is already married. She never lost touch with us and says again and again that she will never forget that without my parents' help her boy would have probably died many years ago from a serious illness. She is such an upright, faithful human being; I can discuss everything with her and confide everything to her.

How she continues to stick by us amid the greatest difficulties is touching. For the risks that she takes upon herself for our sake are actually so great that I myself should dissuade her from coming to us. At the postal authorities all employees, thus also her husband, have just had to declare under oath once again that they no longer have any connections with Jews. Naturally, this declaration also applies to the acquaintanceships of the wife. If it comes out that she visits us, her husband will lose his position and therewith his livelihood. She herself is in a terrible conflict between fear and conviction. On the one hand, she explained to me that it was all the same to her whether a false declaration under oath was made or not: "One is being virtually trained to commit perjury. What things my husband has to constantly swear to, every week something else! One can no longer have any respect for it." On the other hand, she is terribly afraid that she could be caught. She told her Nazi sister-in-law, who asked about us schemingly, that she did not know where we have emigrated. She is very proud of this diplomatic answer. Early in the morning she scurries into the house and is constantly worried that she could be seen, perhaps through the window or when she leaves. When the doorbell rings, she hides. And in spite of this fear and nervous strain she still comes and hauls food, which I cannot even take because I know that she is depriving herself of it, and that it endangers us both. It is admirable how this simple woman has the courage that so many of the "educated" people do not summon. In such a time of distress the true essence of a person proves itself. Unfortunately, we were mistaken about some of our so-called friends. That much the more one must acknowledge old Hedwig's behavior.

She urges us all the time finally to emigrate. As if that were not our most fervent wish. The bystanders, the Aryans here, and probably people abroad can probably not understand at all why we are still here. They don't know that it does not at all depend on us, but rather that unfortunately we simply do not get admission to any other country. There are no more visas for the United States. My husband has made one last attempt and asked our relatives in America by wire for the entry visas for Cuba. That is the only possibility that still exists. No other country gives an entry permit to German Jews any longer, or is still reachable in any way.

Hopefully, we will succeed this time. The difficulties are already piling up again. The costs for such a visa are very high. large sums of money have to be deposited for us. I hope that my brother-in-law will raise the money for us. The United States has introduced an exchange embargo and, besides, the rush for these Cuban visas is very great at the moment, so that three to four weeks are necessary for transfer of the deposits. At best we can expect the visas by the middle of August. Hopefully, nothing unexpected will again interfere. After our failures we have become very pessimistic about all matters concerning emigration.

[Elisabeth Freund now has to work in an armaments plant.]

It is fortunate for me that I have landed here. Here the heat is not so terrible. When I hear how things still are in the laundry, then I have to be most content that I'm no longer there. No doubt the work is difficult everywhere. The worst thing is the situation of our boy workers. We have a large number, starting at the age of fourteen. I often talk with them when I meet them on the way. My own son is also almost fourteen now. I wonder if he is already as tall as these boys here. I hope that he will not be so embittered and serious. After all, he has it good in his English school. He has the chance to learn something and is growing up as an equal in a big group of comrades. For him it is bad only that he has to be separated from his parents.

The poor Jewish boys here in the factory! The worst thing is not the difficult work, it is the hopelessness. There is one fellow, Kurt, a tall and lanky boy in breeches that are much too short; his arms stick way out of his sleeves. Even the young people do not get ration coupons for clothes! Kurt worked for a year in a training center of the Jewish community, is very interested in technology, and wanted so much to become an electrical engineer. "Then isn't it actually quite interesting for you here, isn't there a great deal to learn?" I ask him. "Oh, that's what you think. Only the Aryan boys are apprentices; they are shown things. We Jewish boys are not allowed to learn anything here. At best we are allowed to work at a machine once in a while, and then we're shown the operation that's needed for that one machine. But that's really all. That's just it—we're supposed to remain unskilled workers." [. . .]

The poor fellows. Everything is hopeless for them. No diligence, no energy, no matter how great, helps any; they can learn nothing. They have a terrible youth. Under these conditions, how long will the educational level of the Jews, which until now was always so high, be maintained at all? The door to every possibility is closed to them. They are not allowed to attend either the theater or concerts. Museums, libraries, even the zoo are forbidden to them. The few Jewish schools still existing suffer from an insufficient number of teachers and insufficient teaching materials. In general, there is only one secondary school for Jewish children left in Berlin, and it, too, will probably not exist much longer. The good school buildings have long since been seized by the party.

I'm always hearing so much about all these hardships because I am friends with a Jewish school teacher. The financial means of the community for all its purposes are becoming more and more tight, the need greater and greater, the difficulties and the pressure more and more insurmountable. This summer, for example, one of the greatest problems was what to do with the school children during the vacation. In almost all families the parents are working in the factories; thus the children were unsupervised at home. Where was one to put them, these poor, overly nervous children, who after these last years with their terrible experiences needed a holiday rest especially badly? In earlier years the Jewish school administration had organized excursions for the children to the forest, with immense difficulty, for the Gestapo had declared that the children are allowed on the streetcars or city trains or subways only in small groups of no more than six. Just imagine how hard it is under these conditions to take even only a hundred children anywhere with supervision. Quite apart is the problem of finding a suitable and undisturbed place for

playing, where the children will not be assaulted and beaten up by some ruf-
fians.

This year, however, the Gestapo has also strictly forbidden these excursions
to the forest. What was left! The parks are also forbidden. Many of the Jewish
day nurseries do not even have a yard, let alone a garden, and if they have one,
the children are not allowed to play in it—because of the neighbors, who
complain about the noise. Finally, the Jewish community hit upon the solution of transforming every free spot in the Jewish cemeteries into playgrounds
with sand boxes for the smaller children. And the bigger children, class by
class, had the duty to clear the graves and paths of weeds, and to maintain
them in good condition. In this way the children were occupied and out in the
fresh air, and at the same time the graves were kept in order, which curiously
enough the Gestapo had suddenly demanded and for which otherwise, naturally, there would not have been workers or the financial means. This is what
things have come to now: In Germany the cemeteries are not only the final
resting place for the old people, but also the only spot where Jewish children
can play.

*[In September 1941, Jewish women between the ages of eighteen and forty-five are
forbidden to emigrate.]*

The Gestapo has permitted me to leave Germany, in spite of the prohibition! We do not even dare to believe it yet. It came about like this: My husband
met an old acquaintance quite by chance on the street, an executive in one of
the major banks of Berlin, with whom he had worked together a great deal,
especially at the time of the uprisings in Upper Silesia after the First World
War. At that time, my husband was a senior member of the board of the Upper
Silesian Iron Industry Corporation and, in constant danger of his life, he successfully saw to the provision of Upper Silesia with the financial means to pay
salaries. Without that, in addition to the bloody uprisings by the Poles, there
would have also been unrest among the workers. His clever negotiations with
the English and French occupation authorities prevented much misfortune at
that time, and have always been recognized. This gentleman, then, asked
quite innocently, in a friendly manner, how we were doing, and was absolutely flabbergasted when he heard what difficulties we were having. "But
really, that just can't be! These measures are not meant for someone like you!"
How often have we and a thousand other Jews heard these words already.
"These measures are surely not aimed at you!" At whom, then? And if they
really were not directed against "especially meritorious people"—who has
the right to determine whether a man in a "high position" has greater merit
than a simple worker, a hardworking merchant, or an academic? [. . .]
Well, at any rate, this gentleman was very sympathetic. He asked for exact
details and was going to discuss the matter with the management of his com-

pany. There they had the necessary connections to the Gestapo and would somehow fix things up for us. When my husband told me about this meeting I was so pessimistic and so tired from work that I scarcely listened. After all, we had experienced so many disappointments already; why should it turn out otherwise this time? We were also very afraid and not at all so pleased by the well-meaning offer, for after all, one does not know what could happen if something like that were passed on to the wrong place.

But the miracle happened. Things turned out well. The general on Kurfürstenstrasse* said to the bank that an exception will be made for me. We also do not have to pay anything. The Gestapo man who negotiated the matter, to be sure, would like to have a bed from us when we leave—that's all. And we will leave him this bed with the greatest pleasure. All these things are so scarce and cannot be bought in the normal way.

But we have nothing in writing on this decision. In principle, the Gestapo does not provide anything written in such cases. My husband immediately went to the emigration office of the Jewish Aid Society. He was congratulated there, but no one wants to take the responsibility for placing our names on a departure list. One cannot blame them for that; after all, everything is punishable by immediate deportation to a concentration camp.

There are still so many difficulties to overcome. No, I still will not believe it, otherwise there will again be a greater disappointment. We also must not talk to anyone about it. The one office of the Gestapo may have allowed it, but perhaps another one will put us in a camp for it. I must also continue to do my work in the factory, for how can I explain to the employment office for Jews that my work record can be closed for good. Without papers no one will believe me. But without termination of the work record we cannot be assigned to a departing group. We are still a long way from that.

I must go on with my work in the factory. My hours just fly by. My thoughts fly even faster. Even if I don't quite believe it yet, still, just in case, I must consider how to organize things best. A year and a half ago we were permitted to take along quite a few things as personal and household belongings for Portugal. The permission is still valid. But at that time one could still pay the transportation costs with paper marks. Now, every emigrant is allowed to take along only two small suitcases, and from the German border on one must pay in gold marks or dollars. That determines the size of our luggage. Only the most necessary things can be taken along. We will have to part with our whole household. That is bitter, especially for a woman. But I won't make it hard for myself. Three years ago I had to separate from my children—that was hard. Furniture—that's nothing to get excited about.

---

* The Department for Jewish Matters, directed by Adolf Eichmann, was located at 116 Kurfürstenstrasse.

The main thing is that we get out of Germany alive. I will give the things away to good friends; at least I will get pleasure from that. If only we were at that stage already! After all our experiences, we can give up our apartment and furniture only at the very last moment. It can happen to us again, as it did the other times, that once more at the last moment we can't get away. The best thing is to let the business of emigration simply happen, as if it did not concern us at all, as if we were acting in a film. Otherwise the tension is too difficult to bear. We still have a great deal before us: parting from our friends, leaving our old homeland.

Hitler said of the German Jews: "They are all gypsies, who feel just as well in Paris as in Budapest, London, or New York." We loved Germany as much as one can love only one's own country. We detest Hitler's Germany and everything associated with it. But we must leave the country whose language we speak, with whose songs and poems we grew up, and whose forests and mountains we have crisscrossed. For many generations, our families did their utmost for this country, and we are leaving behind their graves in this soil. Our children can grow into another future. My husband and I are no longer young enough. We are going to a foreign country, and much there will be alien and difficult for us. But once we are outside, when we are received in another country in which we are allowed to live with our children undisturbed, then, happy and grateful, we will take pains to work for this new land faithfully, as our parents and ancestors did for Germany.

Our emigration agent brings the news that there are now a number of cases in which exceptions have been made to the emigration prohibition for women. Unfortunately, not many. I also know of such a case in which the Gestapo demanded 5000 marks for it. In the main, such a permit was given if there was a gynecological certificate of infertility.

I am still working in the factory. My husband, however, now has assurance from the Aid Society that we will be put on the next departure list. However, the next groups are not leaving for three weeks. If we could only speed up our leaving. We are growing more and more frustrated.

Since last week we have been wearing the Yellow Star.* The effect on the population is different from what the Nazis expected. Berlin still has perhaps 80,000 Jews. In some sections of town one sees the Yellow Stars in very large numbers. People of whom one would not have thought on the basis of their appearance that they are Jews are wearing the Star. The population in its majority disapproves of this defamation. Until now, all measures against the Jews occurred in the dark. Now no one can ignore them.

Naturally, there are different kinds of experiences. What I hear from other people, I experience myself: I am greeted on the street with special politeness

---

* German Jews were required to wear the Yellow Star as of September 19, 1941.

by complete strangers, and in the streetcar ostentatiously a seat is freed for me, although those wearing a star are allowed to sit only if no Aryan is still standing. But sometimes guttersnipes call out abusive words after me. And occasionally Jews are said to have been beaten up. Someone tells me of an experience in the city train. A mother saw that her little girl was sitting beside a Jew: "Lieschen, sit down on the other bench, you don't need to sit beside a Jew." At that, an Aryan worker stood up, staying: "And I don't need to sit next to Lieschen!"

The Yellow Stars are not popular. That is a failure of the party, and then there are the failures on the eastern front. As the usual diversion, there now follows a terrible wave of anti-Semitic propaganda. In all parts of the city more than two hundred meetings are held at which the Jewish question is discussed. In the stairwells, early in the morning, there are fliers in which people are openly called upon to carry out pogroms. In the news that a soldier fell in battle, they say that the Jews are guilty of his death!

A former janitor of ours who is an army guard in a concentration camp in Poland sent his wife to us. We should see to it that we get away as soon as possible. She said that he could not bear the thought that the same could happen to us as to those poor people. Didn't we know what was in store for us? That sounds horrible. What in the world are they doing with the camp inmates? The Nazis just cannot be killing them by the thousands! That is just inconceivable—German people doing this to their fellow citizens, with whom they had fought side by side in 1914. And what is happening with the women and children? In Berlin one knows nothing about their fate. The janitor's letter to his wife does not mention any details. The army mail is probably strictly censored.

Almost every store along the entire Kurfürstendamm now has a sign: "No entrance to Jews" or "No sales to Jews." When one walks along the streets one sees "Jew," "Jew," "Jew" on every house, every windowpane, every store. It is difficult to explain that the Nazis, these fanatical Jew-haters, cover their own city completely with this word, whereas there are so few Jews left in Germany. One cannot look anywhere without coming across this "Jew." And it is not just, say, the luxury shops or cigar stores that are forbidden to Jews in the entire city; now the bakeries, the butcher, and vegetable shops are showing these signs. And no coal-ration cards were distributed to Jews for the winter. Where will it all end!

And I am still working at the factory. Until now I haven't dared to ask for my discharge there. Perhaps in the factory they know that for my age group emigration is barred. If that is the case, then there will be further inquiries and I have nothing to show from the Gestapo. All these things are so difficult. If we do anything wrong now, then everything can be put at risk.

A few days ago I asked the foreman in the propeller department to be allowed to go home an hour earlier because of emigration matters. He became furious and accused me of wanting only to avoid work; he knew very well that there was no longer any emigration and he would not let me do whatever I liked with him. I won't get anywhere with this man.

Then I am told that I am no longer listed with the propeller department, but have been transferred to the petroleum department. Now I must try it. I present my passport with the visas to my new foreman and ask him for a short leave. After five endless hours the foreman calls for me: "Here are your papers. You are dismissed. Go to the employment office and have your work record canceled."

For the last time I am taken by the Aryan escort to the factory exit. "Is it really true, are you getting away? Where is Cuba anyway? And there is really no war there?" He looks around cautiously: "Then I wish you luck. Then you are better off than all of us here."

I have actually been dismissed! Now I just have to go to the employment office. There they make things difficult for me. For people under forty-five there is no cancellation of the work record. Don't I really know that yet? Nothing helps. I have to go to the Gestapo on Kurfürstenstrasse. That is hardly pleasant, but it is the only possible way. The building of the Jewish Fraternal Society is completely empty. Besides me there does not seem to be another Jew there. I am directed into the former festival hall, along the side walls of which a few niches are fixed up as offices. An official listens to my case, but is not informed. He is very cold and quite obviously does not believe me. But he will ask his highest superior. I am told to wait. However, I may not wait by the wall, but must place myself exactly in the middle of the big hall under the huge chandelier, with strict instructions not to move from the spot. I must remain standing exactly in the middle of the inlaid floor. I had heard tell about this sadism, but had considered everything an exaggeration. But no, it was really done that way. During the three-quarters of an hour that I wait there, I am atoning for all my sins, as one says. It is difficult to stand in the middle of such a huge empty room without swaying, without getting "claustrophobic." But this is now the test: Will the Gestapo stand by the authorization in granted?

I wait. I wait. Finally the man returns. Everything is all right. He calls the employment office and gives the necessary instructions. Now I am free! No, not yet, not by a long shot! I know a young girl who was all ready to depart when the prohibition to leave the country came. She was to go one day later. And now she is working in the factory again; only her parents were able to leave. Only when we are across the border, only then will I be free.

Now there comes a great nervous strain. What if in the last moment we cannot get away for some reason! In the final week, my husband pays out all we own as the Reich emigration tax,* as the tax to the Jewish community "for the promotion of the emigration of Jews" (which the community, incidentally, does not receive, but which goes to a blocked account!), and for our ship tickets. The price of these ship tickets is determined by the value of the assets still left us. In a certain respect, I approve of that, for how else should people without assets raise the money for the crossing. In our case, for the tickets we must pay everything that is still left in hard cash after payment of all other fees. Why is there such a great fuss being made with the calculations? Whatever we were not able to turn into money, for example, real estate and mortgages, upon our emigration becomes the property of the state anyway, since we will then be deprived of our citizenship, as "enemies of the state," and everything will be confiscated. In the end, not a penny will be left of our still sizable assets. But if we cannot get away now, we will have paid everything and at best will get a partial sum back in paper marks; we will then be completely penniless. [. . .]

Last week a large number of Jewish families in Berlin received notice to vacate their apartments—not from their landlords, to be sure, but rather on printed forms from the police. They were told not to look around for other apartments. They would be notified about what will happen with them. They were told that all their possessions were confiscated. They could regard only a limited number of things as their own, in the case of a woman, for example, two dresses, three shirts, pants, stockings, etc., and one coat.

The agitation is indescribable. What will happen with these people now? Will they be sent to the province, to barracks, or to Poland? And who has received such notices, anyway? Apparently at first the so-called "previously convicted," that is, people who had not properly observed the blackout rules, or were not at home at eight o'clock, or at whose place something had been found during a house search. Bad news keeps coming from all directions. One can hardly keep up with it anymore. A number of our acquaintances are summoned before the Gestapo and punished, partly with a fine, partly with prison, because in the telephone book they are not listed with the compulsory middle names "Sara" and "Israel." Yet none of us has owned a telephone for more than a year. Despite that, they should have immediately applied for a name change in the telephone book. A good friend of ours receives the notification that his nephew, who was in prison for two years for allegedly having had sexual relations with an Aryan, was transferred from there to a labor camp, where he "died" after two weeks.

I go to the post office to make a call from a telephone booth there. I am scarcely in the booth when a woman rips open the door and drags me out

---

* This tax was originally introduced in 1931 for all emigrants leaving with more than 200,000 marks (at 25 percent). In May 1941, for Jews it was set at 80 percent.

screeching: "We Aryans have to wait. The Jews are always in the booths. Out with the Jews! Out! Out with all Jews from Germany!" Is is such a terrible scene that I don't know how I got out onto the dark street again. I was afraid she would rip the clothes from my body.

My husband receives a summons to appear at the Gestapo on Alexanderplatz. That is always very unpleasant. The halls leading to the offices have heavy iron bars at their entrance. Once they have closed behind you, you are never sure whether you will be let out again. Both of us had already been summoned more than once, either alone or together. It was always a question of whether we were finally emigrating. This time my husband can fortunately take along our passports with the exit permits. The official really does ask again why we are still there. When my husband presents the passports, the Gestapo official takes a slip of paper with writing on it from our file and tears it up. My husband asks very politely what this paper meant. "That was your expulsion to Poland," is his answer. "I'm glad that you are getting out of it!" He is glad! So, Gestapo men are sometimes also human beings.

That is on Thursday, and on Sunday we are supposed to go. Now everything is happening like clockwork. In the night between Thursday and Friday the Jews in Berlin are taken from their apartments for the first time. Everyone is allowed to take along only a small suitcase. The police come at night, around eleven. In the dark, just so that the population does not take sides. The poor people are taken to a transit center, the synagogue on Levetzowstrasse. The entire block there is closed off. The Jewish community had to provide nurses, doctors, and aides. In great haste provisions are prepared, for no one was allowed to take food along from home.

It is a terrible night, with rain and thunderstorms. The synagogue is not big enough. The people have to stand in the yard for hours in the rain. The scenes that took place there are supposed to have been indescribable. Families were separated, married couples were torn apart, children dragged away, parents left behind. Already during the arrests, in the apartments, people took their lives. There in the synagogue it goes on. Body searches take place, suitcases are ransacked. All must turn in their identification papers, birth certificates, passports, etc. Everything is taken from them that has monetary value, as well as soap, combs, shaving gear, scissors, brushes, everything that a civilized person needs in order to look clean and neat. They are supposed to become as neglected as the unfortunate Jews of the Polish ghettos, whose caricatures appear in the *Stürmer*.

It was only on the following two days that we heard these dreadful details from eyewitnesses. In the laundry people were picked up from the night shift by the police. So working in the factories does not protect one from deportation. A young girl whose mother was part of the transport ran from one Gestapo office to another in order to be deported together with her mother. Her request was turned down. "You are not going to Poland when *you* feel like it, but when it suits *us*." The fear, the panic everywhere simply cannot be described. Really, we have experienced so many horrible things already. But this, this cannot be compared to anything. It is like hunting helpless animals!

One morning I ride the streetcar crisscross through the city to find out about friends and acquaintances, whether they are still there or have already been hauled off. All of us know nothing of one another; after all, we don't have telephones! Not until the very early hours of Saturday are the poor people taken to the Grunewald Station, in barred police cars. This station is so out of the way that only few people can observe what is happening there. (That is why the hospital trains from the front also always arrive there.) The people are loaded into cattle cars. Word has it that the transports are heading to Poland. Nobody knows for sure.

Acquaintances come to our place. They know that we are supposed to leave. They ask us to convey their last greetings to their relatives abroad. We should please see to it that everything is done to procure them an entry visa. We should describe abroad what is happening here, what is awaiting them. Deportation to Poland, now, in the beginning of winter, that is death by freezing, that is starvation and typhus fever, epidemics, and a miserable death. Do the people abroad suspect what is happening here? Will it be possible for help to come before it is too late? Will it be possible to raise the high sums in dollars for the visas? After all, most of the relatives abroad have no money themselves.

A few of our friends have just received visas for Cuba. They are parents or old mothers. Parting from them is easier. We hope that soon they will be able to follow us. Hopefully, they will. It cannot be that now they may no longer be able to leave, after their children procured the visas after such problems. We have to hope that they will yet succeed!

A university friend of my husband says farewell to us. His sister in Breslau just took her own life as she was about to be deported. He himself is completely calm and composed. "I've never been a coward. Until now I have endured everything and coped with it. I have no possibility of getting out. As long as I can, I will put up with things here. I will not let them torture me. If it has to be, then I will know how to die." An old teacher, who lives with an even older sister and her ninety-year-old mother, comes to us. She, too, is admirably calm. "My sister and I would take this, too, upon ourselves. But our mother! We must not subject her to these tortures. She does not know anything about these deportations yet. When we get our notice to vacate the apartment, then we will sit down in the kitchen with mother and turn on the gas. That is the only act of love that we can still perform for our mother." We dare not contradict. These poor people have to decide that for themselves.

Our seventy-two-year-old friend F. asks us to write to his daughter in Bolivia that he is healthy and doing well. Perhaps she can speed up the visa for Bolivia, which was applied for over a year ago. "But don't alarm my daughter.

The poor girl cannot help me anyway." I have never seen this dear person be anything but cheerful and consistently friendly. Now, too, he speaks with us as if it were not a serious matter. "May things go well with you. I am really glad that at least you will be getting away. I am an old person. For me a few years more or less do not matter."

These terrible farewells. Don't cry, just don't cry. Once more I go through our house to take leave of the neighbors. One must not be cowardly. Perhaps they, too, have some sort of message. They can depend on us. We will pass it on immediately, as soon as we can write letters freely. If only it happens in time. I jot down addresses abroad; none of us say much, we just shake hands. Just no tears. One must not start that, otherwise one cannot stop. Who knows what will become of these people. In a situation like this, one can no longer say farewell in a conventional way. [. . .] What right do we have to leave this hell when the others have to endure it? Maybe we are only dreaming all of this. It is impossible that something so horrible exists on this earth.

For the last time we are sitting at our own table for a meal. Then we put on our coats, each one of us takes a knapsack and a small handbag, and we leave the house without looking back.

By city train we go to the Potsdam station. There, in the cellar of the station, the Jewish groups are assembled. After the examination of our papers we are let into the cellar. The door closes behind us. Thank God! The group is leaving today after all. Until the last moment we had been afraid that the journey would not be allowed. There are still many formalities with luggage and passports. We find out that last night the first groups also left Frankfurt am Main. Three hours pass until we are finally led in complete darkness through the unlit station to the train to Paris. A sealed car is designated for our group. We get in, the doors are closed, the train begins to move. We are riding to freedom.

Four days later the German government forbids departure for all Jews, and the army command discontinues the release of freight cars for the journey through France.

But the deportation of Jews to Poland goes on.

PART TWO

Passage

INTRODUCTION

Almost none of the people fleeing Hitler during the early years of the re-gime went directly to America. The overwhelming majority went across the border to a neighboring country—to France, Switzerland, Czechoslova-kia, and the Netherlands—where they could observe events in Germany, organize resistance groups, and, they believed, return home as soon as things settled down. Of the 65,000 Germans who left the country in 1933, 26,000 went to France, 15,000 to the Netherlands, 10,000 to Switzerland. By contrast, from 1933 to 1936 the annual number of Germans moving to the United States (not all of them for political reasons) hovered between 4000 and 6000, while a much larger number of U.S. residents *returned* to Germany. (In 1933–34 4,392 Germans immigrated to the United States, while 14,693 American residents emigrated to the Reich.) Notable exceptions were a handful of in-ternationally renowned scientists and scholars (such as Albert Einstein and the art historian Erwin Panofsky), who happened to be teaching in the United States when the Nazis excluded Jews from university employment in spring 1933 and who simply stayed on.

Quickly, many of these political exiles gathered together in Paris, Prague, Zurich, Amsterdam, and London in antifascist groups seeking to inform the foreign press of events in Germany and assist domestic resistance to the Nazis (see the accounts by Kantorowicz, Marcuse, Feuchtwanger, and Kesten). Having escaped arrest and imprisonment in Germany, many exiles initially led a comfortable life abroad that resembled an extended vacation; indeed, many of them took up residence in their vacation homes or checked into a hotel. Unlike the refugees who fled Germany after 1936, these early refugees often had access to personal savings, possessed legal identity papers, and could obtain residence permits (though usually not work permits) from govern-ments kindly disposed to their situation. In April 1933, for instance, the French interior minister encouraged the population to extend to the German refugees the same hospitality formerly offered to Italian, Spanish, and Russian citizens. Some of these exiles had an international network of professional contacts and friendships, which also aided them in adapting to their new lives.

These early advantages gradually disappeared, however, as Hitler remained in power, sending progressive waves of new refugees across Germany's borders. While internationally celebrated authors like Lion Feuchtwanger or Thomas Mann (both with foreign publishers and bank accounts that assured them a comfortable material existence) gave speeches on the meaning and moral purpose of exile, a grayer, more banal reality made itself felt for the majority of exiles, who grappled daily with the problems of finding food and lodgings, residence permits and work (see the contributions by Alfred Kantorowicz and Käte Frankenthal). This would prove to be the basic condition of life in transit for the hundreds of thousands of Germans who fled Hitler in response to escalating political and economic oppression after 1934: the Nuremberg Race Laws (September 1935), the *Anschluss* of Austria (March 1938) and *Kristallnacht* (November 1938). These people left home not as political exiles seeking temporary asylum but as emigrants and "racial" refugees. Unlike the early exiles, this latter group often arrived without legal papers or financial assets in countries that, plagued by political instability, unemployment and the growing number of refugees, had severely restricted entry visas and residence permits.

The individual odysseys that forced these people from Germany and eventually brought them to America are infinitely varied, as the contributions here attest. Nonetheless, one escape route did predominate because of the sheer number of German exiles who went to France. This itinerary led to Paris in the initial phase of Hitler's regime, then to Southern France when the Vichy government was installed, and finally across Fascist-controlled Spain to Portugal, where authorities there allowed the refugees to board ships leaving for America. When France fell to Germany in June 1940, an armistice was signed which stipulated that the French government had to "surrender on demand" all refugees from the Greater German Reich, including Austrians, Czechs and Poles. The Vichy government also closed all French borders, effectively trapping the refugees in a German-controlled state. Concerned individuals in New York formed the "Emergency Rescue Committee" and, in August 1940, sent a young Quaker and journalist named Varian Fry to Marseille with a list of prominent artists and intellectuals to be smuggled out of France. In the course of thirteen months, Fry and his assistants (among them Hans Sahl, and from New York, Hermann Kesten) managed to help some 2,000 refugees escape France across the Spanish border to Portugal and the United States, supplying them with forged documents, money, and transportation. To his credit, Fry realized that his initial mission—to save prominent artists such as

Matisse and Picasso—was not the most pressing problem, and directed his energies to the largely unknown Jewish refugees without legal papers, money, or high-level connections who came flocking to his hotel. These and other highly dramatic, often tragic cases of flight and escape from Europe to the United States form the basis of the following narratives.

CHAPTER ONE

Flight

LETTER TO ERNST TOLLER

Hermann Kesten was the literary director of Kiepenheuer Verlag in Germany until 1933, when he fled to Paris and quickly became active in the newly created section of German exile literature in the Dutch publishing house Allert de Lange. After being interned in France, Kesten managed to escape to New York in May 1940, where he played a key role with the Emergency Rescue Committee in helping prominent writers and artists to escape Nazi persecution.

Paris, Le Bon Hotel
42, rue Vaneau
23 March 1933

My dear friend Ernst Toller,

I'm in Paris, residing in the same hotel as Joseph Roth, on the same street as André Gide, five minutes from the Bon Marché, Zola's department store.

In Paris I feel as if I've been saved. Did you already hear that the SA came looking for you in your Berlin apartment early in the morning? They came to our apartment too. Suddenly the doorbell rang. The woman from the apartment below us was at the door, her husband is an editor somewhere—I know him by sight. Trembling, she whispered something about the police, the SA, a house search, and that because they were sure to come to us, we should go out the back stairway and get rid of any suspicious papers. Then she ran downstairs to her apartment. I was moved. What good souls there are in the world! Or rather, what evil souls? They took this poor editor away with them; he didn't return. I think often of him, of our friends, of other victims . . .

My dear friend, how are we to earn our living now? I brought a half-finished novel with me called *The Just One*. Shortly before leaving Germany I read the first chapter on a radio program, from six-thirty to seven o'clock. I went there with Toni [Hermann Kesten's wife], and the entire street was filled with SS. Every ten steps I had to show the letter with my contract from the radio proving that I was going to a reading. Then the *Führer* spoke to the German people from seven until forever. That such a creature has taken power is revolting. But that he should be loved by half the German people, that millions listen to his words in ecstasy, that they still believe in this abominable fairytale which truly exists and is named Hitler . . .

I spent only six weeks in the Third Reich, but that was an adequate lesson for a novelist, an instructive antechamber to Hell. Since 1914 we've seen enough. But this silent transition from law to lawlessness, neighbors who, in the blink of an eye, are transformed from philistines to henchmen. The police go hand in hand with the executioners in persecuting the innocent.

One thing that never fails to impress me: the way in which every revolt, every revolution, is not only staged by a very few people but also for a very few. The majority of the population understands nothing; they have neither a presentiment nor a sharp resentment. Every change in weather has a greater effect on them than this change in government. Doesn't the German people suspect that this new government is made up of Germany's gravediggers?

All day long authors came to the Kiepenheuer Press to say goodbye or exchange information. Everyone had stories about yet another person who had lost his convictions or his freedom over night. This one has suddenly seized the SA's point of view, that one was seized by the SA. For both the path leads to a place of perdition from which there is no return—a street leading to moral or physical death.

I'm enchanted by the city of Paris. I arrived with Toni, and because she wasn't yet familiar with the city, we spent the whole day visiting it together. What a dream exile is. You cross the border and immediately the terror becomes "foreign." In the same instant you begin to doubt the reality of the horror in Germany. Did we really understand it when we were at home? Write to me, dear friend, and above all, tell me what you're working on. Write soon.

With best wishes,
your
Hermann Kesten

PARIS-SWITZERLAND-PRAGUE

After her escape from Berlin in 1934, Käte Frankenthal worked with a refugee organization in Prague. She then moved to Paris, where a large German emigrant group was located, including many of her former Socialist colleagues.

Gradually, I got into that condition where you don't stand a chance anymore. If you can tell from the heels on someone's worn-out shoes that he's doing badly, he's surely lost. It wasn't the first time in my life I had an empty stomach. I had lived through the war and inflation in Weimar Germany. But it is one thing to be starving with the entire nation and quite another to be abandoned in a country where the others are leading normal lives. This is something one mustn't admit even to oneself. In the evenings I always had wine and tobacco. French wine is hardly any more expensive than coffee and I wasn't crazy about French tobacco, even the expensive kind. So I could just as well smoke cheap tobacco. Drinking wine and smoking recalled to my mind many pleasant evenings and gave me the illusion that life might yet be pleasant. Fortunately, I didn't owe money to anyone and it was nobody's business how I lived. Had I become a "welfare case," some young girl just out of college would no doubt have informed me that milk would give me more calories for my money—a fact I knew when she was still in diapers. But I just don't like drinking milk, so I drink wine.

I wasn't allowed to offer my services as a psychiatrist. But I could establish a counseling practice as long as I didn't call it "medicine" but "charlatanism." Being a charlatan was allowed, and I was willing to make this concession. I advertised in the following way: "*Psychodiagnostique moderne. Chirologie-Graphologie. Connaissez votre mentalité et vos aptitudes. Choix de profession, mariage, emploi de confiance.*" [Modern psycho-diagnostics. Chiro-graphology. Learn about your mental life and your aptitudes. Choice of career and marriage; confidential.]

This could turn into a modified sort of job and marriage counseling. I just had to look at the lines on someone's palm as I tried to get him to talk, and pretend that I was reading his answers in those lines. If a person didn't talk, I simply read nonsense from the hand. The minute they stepped into the room, I knew anyhow what sort of troubles were bothering the people who came to have their palms read. *Mundus vult decipi*! The world wants to be deceived. People don't spend a lot of money for something like that, but many are occasionally willing to treat themselves to a distracting amusement. In one particularly interesting case I did the Rorschach Test. But it wouldn't have fit my adopted role as a psychic to call it a scientific test. To the client, the reading of the image didn't seem very different from the reading of his palm and it cost the same. Whenever I was completely broke, I would go to a cafe with an acquaintance and start to read his palm. Inevitably, people gathered around who also wanted to have their palms read.

You become lonely unbelievably quickly when things are going so poorly. I kept my distance from the emigrant circles. When in need, people expect advice and help from their former government representatives and I had nothing left to give. They would hardly have believed I couldn't even help myself and would have felt further demoralized.

But loneliness draws people together as well. I saw some strange cases. A German came to me whom I knew quite well but with whom I had never socialized. He was a very well-known lawyer, a man in his late fifties with two grown children and a grandchild. He had just been told that his son, a young doctor, had committed suicide in Berlin. Why did he come to me? I wasn't close to the family and had hardly known the son. But at least I had known him. It was the need to speak with somebody who had been in Germany and knew all the misery he had gone through.

This need led to my being confided in concerning other family matters as well. The next day, the man's wife came to me and told me she had yet another source of grief besides her son. Her husband had just told her he was leaving her, that he had found another, younger woman without whom, he claimed, he couldn't live. Even the tragic news of their son hadn't changed his mind. They had had a harmonious marriage for thirty years. Ultimately they were able to save their marriage and found their way back together. I considered the whole thing an emigration psychosis, and it was not the only one I saw. The lawyer had been very busy, rarely at home, extremely wealthy. Both he and his wife had gone their separate ways and they had not realized how little they truly shared all this time. When they were forced to live together in a single room with worries over money and nothing to keep them occupied, things just didn't flow as easily. Under the pressures of emigration, long-standing marriages broke apart in a surprising number of cases, usually in a way that was tragic for one of the partners. I'm almost tempted to say that I know few emigrants whose family life remained completely intact. The young woman who was the source of the trouble in that marriage subsequently lived with other men and committed suicide a few years ago. She had tried to escape her loneliness by clinging to men, but she wasn't able to stand that kind of life after all. Such cases, too, I have often seen. The complete readjustment demanded by emigrant life requires a parallel readjustment of all one's habitual notions. You can call it "demoralization" or whatever you want. These are facts whose causes are easy to discover.

February 1934 was the time of great unrest in Paris. The two workers' parties were calling for a general strike; the Communist paper *L'Humanité* ran the headline: "Front unique à la base! Contre les chefs réformistes, saboteurs de l'action de classe!" [United Front among the ranks! Down with the reformist bosses, who sabotage class solidarity!] One could see the weakness of the "united front" even at this early stage, and the effect of French nationalism was clearly visible. I was never able to share the expectations which the French Popular Front would raise in the following years.

Also in February, the Austrian Socialists were defeated. I had had much closer personal ties with many Austrians than with the Germans. All these depressing events, together with the impossibility of earning a living, robbed me of my peace of mind. I wanted to leave, although I didn't know where. My passport had expired and the knowledge of being unable to leave increased my restlessness.

I went to the German consulate and demanded a passport. Because they turned down my request, I pressed on all the way to the consul who hardly ever received emigrants. But I was of the opinion that I had payed taxes in Germany long enough and that the consul should be there for me too. Finally, he gave me a passport that was valid for another six weeks, and only for returning to Germany! If one thing was certain, it was that I wouldn't be going back to Germany.

I still wasn't able to travel because I had no money. I was no longer in the mood to read palms. So I took all that was left of my "wealth." This consisted mainly of hiking boots, my backpack, and the emigrant's greatest treasure: lots of spare time! I planned to hike back to Prague in the next few weeks. Whether I would get there and how I would live once I arrived was still unclear. But hiking would do me good. I just couldn't stand all this sitting around in Paris any longer.

I didn't yet know what "thumbing a ride" meant; I learned it then. Now and then a car would stop and take me along for a stretch. The fact that you can get further in one hour in a car than you can in an entire day's journey on foot just about spoils all the fun of hiking. In Basel I crossed the border at night and nobody stopped me. I was, after all, unable to show my passport and I had to be careful not to wander onto German territory by mistake. I didn't encounter any difficulties.

It was the end of April [1934] and the weather was warm. Some nights were so warm that I could sleep outdoors. Otherwise, I stayed in small tourist hostels. It wasn't yet the time of year when many tourists were on the road.

People were taken aback when I showed up. I must have looked very disheveled and maybe they thought I was a madwoman.

I arrived in Zurich after about two weeks where I visited some friends. I hadn't considered staying in Zurich, because Switzerland was known as an expensive country and one could live in Prague much more cheaply. My most beautiful vacations had always been hiking trips through Switzerland. And now I had enjoyed myself as if I was on vacation, eating my bread and cheese as happily as if it was only the light lunch before a good dinner. In this way, I got over that dark mood which made it difficult for me to speak with anyone. I responded with a laugh to the same questions that had gotten on my nerves in Paris: "What sort of an idea is that?" "If I've got a lot of time and little money, I move through the world slowly and with no expenses. When things are reversed, I like taking an airplane in order to save my precious time. Is that so hard to understand?"

Here, when I was looking for nothing at all, I found an opportunity. I spent the happiest time of my emigration in Switzerland. The refugee group living in Switzerland was distinguished and intelligent and even now they didn't look as run down as the emigrants in Paris. They didn't engage in cliquish emigrant behavior, but instead had good contacts with the Swiss. Granted, almost all of them were living on borrowed money and they seemed to have gotten used to it. Of course, they had been welcomed as equals and as friends. The reasons why a group of German emigrants in Switzerland could do so well are eminently capitalistic. Switzerland is so expensive that the large mass of proletarian emigrants avoided it. Switzerland gave the visitors a friendly reception, but they were only a small group of cultivated people. Switzerland never experienced the real problems of emigration as Paris and Prague did. There was no way of getting a work permit here: in this regard the regulations were even more stringent than in other countries.

All Germans mentioned the name of one man [Dr. Hans Oprecht, Ed.], who was influential in many areas in Switzerland and who was considered the guardian angel of the emigrants. He always saw to it that they had something to do and received small incomes on the side. I had been urgently advised to call on him. Even if I planned to continue my journey the next day, my colleagues said it would be a friendly and polite gesture if for once someone went to visit him without asking for anything. I decided to be even more polite and not waste his time; I had developed an idiosyncrasy when it came to unsolicited visits.

But it seems I was destined to meet him anyway. One evening, at a friend's apartment, he walked in. I was told this was a rare event. He happened to be in the neighborhood and wanted to tell our host something. He didn't stay long. But we talked a little and he asked me to stop by his office the next day before continuing on my journey. I went there with my backpack, ready to leave Zurich right after my visit. But something happened that had not yet happened to me during my emigration. He tried fervently to persuade me to stay. He said the Swiss organizations didn't have as many experienced people as the big German ones did. There were always tasks that the overworked party officials couldn't finish. He didn't share the opinion that the only thing for the German emigrants to do was waste their time. In an international movement, these spare energies could be put to good use.

This was just the attitude I had sorely missed in Paris. There, the emigrants had been nicknamed the "at homers," a reflection of the emigrants' reception when they talked about how things were at home in Germany. To be sure, there was often something in their tone of voice that could be taken to mean that everything was better "at home." But after all our "success" in Germany, there was no reason for the French to take this seriously and get nervous when they heard the emigrants talking about how things were "at home."

The Swiss man, who was now a professional politician, had studied psychology. I'm sure he also often heard how things were "at home." But he wasn't surprised that people aren't easily separated from their past. (It is significant that the Socialist movement has generally counted few psychologists among its ranks.) It was agreed that I should stay with someone who worked in his office. It was a wonderful setting, in one of the pretty housing colonies in the countryside. After my life in Paris, I was in heaven.

During the first week I copied a book manuscript for an author. I had to make some money right away if I was to try my luck in Zurich. I could not have competed with a trained typist. But because I could type sitting at home on a beautiful balcony and nobody could watch how often I threw out pages filled with typos, it was a very suitable occupation. I needed a little more time to recover and to collect myself. Interesting writing assignments followed, which I didn't do just to pass time; they were published under the name of large organizations and thus exerted a broad influence. I was happy about things that had once bothered me, such as having to abandon my plans for the day when something urgent came up that needed immediate attention. Many Germans lived in the housing colony and I got to know a lot of Swiss. It was a happy occasion when friends invited me to their homes or suggested going for a walk, even when I had to say: "I don't have the time."

This kind of sunshine can't last during emigration. All the work I was doing was strictly illegal. The immigration officers would come into people's homes to check whether any emigrants were working there. Whenever the doorbell rang, I had to hide the material I was working on and put a half-finished private letter into the typewriter before opening the door. I couldn't say that someone was supporting me, because the condition for my residence permit was that I could support myself. Nor did I have money of my own to prove that I could live on my own. But obviously I was living on something. Naturally, I had to publish all my writings under a pseudonym. However,

Germans who knew my prose style and voice often surmised accurately which pieces I had written.

I had developed presentation material for an organization and was happy to be able to participate in this way in discussions where I was legally excluded. I had collected the material during several days of research at the library. In a small town, however, it's easy to put two and two together. After half a year I was expelled from Switzerland with the explanation that I couldn't account for my means of subsistence.

I found myself in a situation similar to the one I had been in in Dresden. Without a passport it was impossible for me to get into another country legally. I went to the German consulate in Zurich. The consul didn't even offer me a passport to Germany, but just laughed at me. . . . My plan was to travel to the various borders, except the German one, and each time tell the Swiss border guards that I was unable to honor their order of expulsion because no neighboring country would allow me to enter. In that way Switzerland could decide for itself how to solve my problem, which I was unable to solve. My friends were against this tactic and thought that the police might solve it simply by locking me up indefinitely. They were probably right. But still it would have been an interesting experiment.

Given the impossibility of my living legally anywhere in the world, I decided I might just as well stay illegally in Switzerland. I had found good friends here and that is the only real help that emigrants can find. First, I went to Geneva. In Zurich my high-German accent immediately marked me as a foreigner. In Geneva people speak French. I picked a name that sounded Swiss and registered as a Swiss in a hotel—passports were not asked for from Swiss guests. Even now I am grateful every day for the fact that in this country [the United States] people are not required to carry their passports.

I was angry with the government for having gotten me into such an unfortunate situation again, and so I decided to seek refuge in a state-run institution. I was able to get a position at a psychiatric hospital as a visiting intern doing research. The doctors there, led by an Italian, were decidedly hostile towards a German Jewess. I avoided all contact with them, for I couldn't afford any quarrels. They got a kick out of the fact that I didn't respond to their provocations, but I knew why I didn't react. However, the head doctor (who had hired me) and his wife were very kind to me and I made very pleasant acquaintances in their home. Of course, one of this doctor's first questions concerned my passport. I made some excuse or another, saying I didn't have it on me and that there was no great hurry anyway, because in Switzerland guests had to register with the police only after three months. I don't remember whether he later forgot the issue or whether he didn't come back to it out of kindness. I tend to think it was the latter. He was an intelligent man and must have noticed that I was in some sort of difficulty.

I was glad to take the opportunity to orient myself in my profession again.

Other than that, my life at this time was strangely split. The state institutions in Switzerland take good care of their doctors. I had a pleasant room, good food and service; all this was very middle class. Only when I went out did I become a proletarian once again, as in Paris. I often didn't even have ten cents for the streetcar.

I hadn't given up all hope that the "cleansing" of the immigration offices wasn't complete and that I might still find a consulate willing to issue me a passport. I went to Geneva to see whether I would have any more luck than I had had in Paris and Zurich. My tenacity was rewarded.

When the consulate official saw my name, he knew immediately who I was, and for once this was to my advantage. He started cursing the system and talking as if he himself was already a victim of the Nazis. By now, he will probably have become one. This was shortly after the bloodbath against the SA group headed by Ernst Roehm. "The pack of criminals! Murderers! It won't take long now! The system has suffered its first blow and will soon go to pieces!" That's what the consulate official believed on June 30, 1934, as did many emigrants who were already packing their suitcases in the hope of a quick return to Germany.*

Finally the official told me: "One has to vent one's feelings once in a while. After all, I know you won't get me into trouble." I was completely silent, said neither yes nor no, wondering whether the whole thing was a trap or whether I would get the passport I had been promised. I was told to return the follow- ing week and was handed my passport—valid for four years and for all coun- tries.

A few months later I advised some people who urgently needed passports to try their luck in Geneva; they told me later that they had to deal with some very unpleasant Nazi officials there who turned down their applications.

My passport didn't collect much dust before I needed it. The immigration police came to the hospital and demanded to see my papers. I wasn't even registered in Geneva and so their visit could only be the result of a denuncia- tion. I assumed that it came courtesy of the young doctors. I was ordered to appear at the police station with all my papers the next morning. I had no other choice but to leave Switzerland immediately.

I went to the village Annemasse, which lies near Geneva just over the French border. The issue of the passport had been solved by now, but I was again without financial means and thus unable to obtain a resident permit for France. Before leaving town I made a quick visit to a friend in Geneva who knew nothing of my situation. I only told her that from now on I would be living in Annemasse, and she said that her secretary lived there and came into

---

* June 30, 1934, was the date of the so-called "Night of the Long Knives" in which Roehm and his followers were murdered by the rival SS group.

the city by car every day. It might perhaps be convenient if she gave me a ride.

It was indeed convenient, because in this way nobody asked me any questions at the border, such as whether I intended to remain in France. The young woman who crossed the border every day was known to the guards, who suspected nothing. She suggested that we stop at her parents' house first, since they were well known in the village and might be able to help me find a place to stay. When we entered their house, several Communist papers immediately caught my eye. So I knew where I was. Both parents were teachers and to my great fortune the best kind of idealistic Communists. They knew immediately who I was and invited me to stay with them with such warmth that I accepted for a few days. In any case I didn't have much choice because I didn't have enough money to rent a room. With the help of these teachers, I found some students who needed tutoring in German. Among the many professions I have had in the past years, this was perhaps the most difficult. I had imagined that I knew my mother tongue well. To my surprise, I discovered I was only able to use it; teaching others was a different matter entirely.

Because I was now living in France, my Swiss friends were able to send me some writing assignments again, too. I was therefore soon able to pay for the room that had initially been put at my disposal so graciously. I had strayed into an interesting family, and I was very comfortable in their pretty little house. This was at the time of the Franco-Russian military pact. The Communist press was then fighting against the prolongation of mandatory military service in France. My Communists hosts supported this position. Even if France and Russia were allies in a war, they were against the militarization of a bourgeois state. When Stalin declared himself in favor of increased French militarization, this immediately became their position: "The French people demands militarization in defense of the Soviet Union and against the will of the French ruling class." I didn't always have the heart to argue with these fine and well-meaning people over the many contradictions in their political beliefs, which they held to like a religion.

I often went to Geneva on small country roads in order to work in the library there. All this had to be done with great care. I wasn't able to earn enough money in this way to make a living. But nor could I risk being thrown out of France where I lacked a residence permit. I had no other choice but to take up lodgings in a state-run psychiatric clinic once more. And I did in fact manage to find another one, this time in the canton of Zurich.

Unlike in Geneva, here I found a very pleasant group of colleagues. Once more I was working intensively on psychiatric matters and we spent pleasant, stimulating evenings together. The three months during which I didn't have to register with the police went by all too quickly. Before my departure could no longer be postponed, these three months had turned into five. I was especially pleased that the government which had expelled me would also give me money. While I was at the clinic, several doctors got the flu. I substituted for one after the other and did full-time medical work. The director explained to the employment board that he needed a substitute physician because of the many cases of illness. Because an immigrant had done this work without pay, he requested compensation for her. Upon my departure, I received 200 francs from him, which at that time was a great and unexpected fortune for me.

Now I had enough money to live for a while but again no place to go. Switzerland isn't a very big place after all, and I couldn't find any more state-run clinics. I suppose I could have set out hiking again. The head doctor and his assistant at the hospital were married and had become very attached to me. They suggested that we visit their parents' country house as a farewell trip. I gladly accepted, especially because the friend who had urged me to stay in Switzerland and who had loyally stood by me in all my hardship was out of the country at the time. While I stayed in this glorious house, friends arranged for a place for me to live in Zurich. I was safe there for a few weeks. Then, to my misfortune another emigrant moved in who brought the immigration officers into the house. I had to flee head over heels from my hideout.

I then adopted a French-sounding name, declared myself a widow, and stated that my residence was Geneva but that I had been born in Germany. This gave me an alibi for being Swiss but not speaking Swiss-German, and I rented a room. But as soon as other foreigners moved in and the police started watching the house, I had to leave again. This game repeated itself several times and got pretty tiring.

A friend of mine lived in a hotel run by people with whom I could speak openly about the political situation. They prepared a room in the attic for me where I stayed without registering with the police. But nobody in the house was allowed to know I was there, and I could leave the room only very cautiously, at night. I don't think I would have been able to stand this if I hadn't still had interesting writing assignments to keep me busy. A borrowed, silent typewriter was on the bed, and I sat on a stool and typed. There wasn't enough room for a table. Gradually my situation in Switzerland became untenable. No visa was required for Czechoslovakia, a passport was sufficient. I had just enough money left to make it there. So I left Switzerland for Prague, but with a heavy heart, for I had made good friends there and encountered many helpful people.

AMSTERDAM – PARIS

Deprived of their passports by German authorities, Marta Appel and her
daughters succeed in fleeing to Holland on a tourist boat in 1937.

We were strangers in Holland, the kind country which gave us shelter for a few months. Every kindness, every help was mixed with the desire to get rid of us. However, we were treated again as human beings.

How endless were the procedures before we were legalized, before we were allowed to stay for those few short months! How many difficulties we had to fight before we had in our hands again those precious little papers which the world calls passports!

And then long hours of waiting at the American consulate followed. Hours filled with disappointment, when we needed still another paper, still another proof from the dear fatherland that we were not scoundrels, but poor people looking for a new homeland, a little love and freedom. Nobody but a refugee knows what it means when those papers cannot be obtained. How sad and discouraging is the effort to make a consulate official believe that one is honest without a certificate from a government, especially when that government does not send one's papers, just to torment one even beyond the border.

Several weeks had passed since we had fled Germany. It had proved to be wrong that all anxiety and excitement would be over as soon as we had arrived in a foreign country. There were plenty of things which burdened our minds even then. In spite of that, it was not to be compared with the steady fear of every future day in which we had lived in Germany, and it was not to be compared with the disgraceful feeling of constant humiliation in the old homeland.

We had been in Amsterdam only a few days when we were summoned to the police headquarters. "We have a letter here from T——," the official explained to my husband, "which states that you are accused by the German authorities of having agitated against the German government in your sermons. An order is given to the German police to arrest you and your family whenever and wherever you are seen on German territory."

My husband explained why we had left the Reich, and that he had never mixed in any politics.

"I believe you," the Dutch official had answered. "Anyway this letter places you and your family in the category of political refugees. According to our constitution, Holland doesn't hand over political refugees. You may have shelter here for a few months, until your departure to another country.

Before we had left Arnheim, we had sent my parents and other relatives messages so that they would know we were safe in Holland. But weeks had passed and still we had not heard a word from any of them. They were afraid to communicate with us. We had no idea whether they had to suffer through our flight.

Only after nearly two months had passed, during which we were extremely disturbed about our family in Germany, did we get the first message. There was a Jewish meeting in Amsterdam with many delegates from Germany. They brought us the first news, the first letters from our beloved ones.

Our home and our whole fortune had been confiscated immediately. There was even a house investigation at my parents' home the day after we had left. Only through the Gestapo officials did the old folks learn that we had fled. Our card never reached them. It was a shocking blow to my father. He could not understand how we could leave the homeland. He was as offended as if it were a personal injury. For months and months he could not get over it, and we received no word from him. Everything that mother had overper- suaded me to let her store for me, all the treasured silver for my girls which we had bought for them during the years, she had to deliver to the Nazis on threat of being arrested if she hid anything that belonged to us.

Had it not been for all the difficulties which we had in getting immigration papers, all the sorrow we had about our family in Germany, we should have had an ideal time in Holland.

It was like a marvellous dream to be allowed to go everywhere. There was no sign in the museums that Jews were forbidden to enter. We could go into every café and restaurant if we wanted to. Nevertheless, when a waiter came to my table, my heart always began to beat loudly. I still expected that he would ask us to leave the place because we were Jews. I could not overcome the same feeling of fear whenever a policeman passed me on the street. "Will he arrest me?" I would think with a frightened feeling, and it took me years to overcome it.

We had not expected to stay very long in Holland. Our friend had prom- ised that everything would be prepared for an early departure. But it took much more time than we had thought before.

We were enrolled in the long list of all the homeless people. In the first years of Naziism we had visited the refugee committees in various countries, and with the greatest pity I had seen all those unhappy people standing in lines until their number was called, so that they could enter the offices to get advice or help. Now we were among them. Things which came to our ears in those hours of waiting were pitiful. People were there with no relatives anywhere in the world, with no country on earth to which they were able to go. Their certificate of residence in Holland expired, and there was no other land to go to.

"We still have the ocean," a man with two little children and a young wife said to us. He was one of a few who had managed to escape from a concentration camp in Germany. "Maybe I escaped only that we might die together in Holland," he said. Families which had left Germany together often had to separate in the country where they first found shelter, and then had to leave for different and far distant parts of the world.

I met a young couple whom I had known in the old homeland before they had been married. In the first year of Hitlerism they had gone to Spain. On one of the lovely Spanish islands they had opened a restaurant and had lived there for over two years in complete happiness. Their place flourished and they succeeded so well that they induced another young couple to come to work with them. The Spanish war put a quick end to their good fortune. Both men were arrested by Franco's troops. Their restaurant was blown to pieces. After a few terrible weeks, when the two women did not know whether they would ever see their husbands again, they were freed, but they had to leave the country as undesirable foreigners. With the small fortune they had earned, and a tiny baby girl, they fled to France, but they were not allowed to stay there. So they went to Belgium and then to Holland.

[. . .] Though we had such a nice time in Holland, a time when we slowly recovered from all the restlessness of the last years, we still had many troubles concerning our immigration.

"Everything is all right," the American consul told us after the medical examination was over, and we thought we should get our visas right away. But after a moment of hesitation, the consul ended, "I still need your certificates of good conduct for the last four years."

"But they won't send them," we protested unhappily. "We have tried everything without getting an answer."

"Try again," was the sole reply of the consul. Without it, America is closed to you."

What in the world should we do, we wondered in the greatest despair, when we stood again in the street. Where should we go if we could not enter the United States? There most of our family had lived for many decades. Letter after letter we sent to T——— to the police without getting any reply. Again my husband wrote asking for a certificate of good conduct, because we needed it for our immigration. Anxiously we awaited every delivery of mail which came.

Finally the police in T——— wrote, "We can't send you those papers, since you left Germany without permission of the state, and against the wishes of the German authorities."

That was a dreadful message. "Without it, America will be closed to you" those words still sounded in our ears.

Would the American consul really destroy all our hope when he saw the letter? Would there be no exception possible?

We had very little hope when we stood again before the American consul with nothing else in our hands but the refusal of the German police to give us a certificate of good conduct.

"Do you have the certificate this time?" the consul asked immediately.

"We got this answer," my husband said faintheartedly, and handed the letter to the consul. Carefully he studied the German answer.

Without looking at us, still studying each word, he finally said, "Didn't I tell you that you would get an answer? That's all I need. You may get your visa now, and leave for the United States as soon as you wish."

How was that possible? We did not quite understand; it was too much good luck. But we had learned in the long years in Germany never to ask an official for an explanation; so we did not ask here either.

We had what we needed, a visa for the United States, the future, the haven. The New World was finally open to us.

I had again the feeling that everything around me had changed suddenly. I had not noticed before that the day was so bright. Even the consul, who had always been so severe, had a smile on his face and his eyes looked friendly when we thanked him before we left his office. It was difficult to believe that really all our worries were over and we stood on the threshold of a new life. We were as though in a dream when we left the consul. Not until we had to go to the different offices to get all our papers, did we realize that all was real.

"Daddy, let us take the very first boat. I can't wait until we are there," my girl urged. She expressed only what was the wish of all of us.

We stood again in the street. We were still holding the papers in our hands. They were the most precious goods we possessed; they gave us the chance to step into a new life. This time we could not go home immediately. Our hearts were too full of bliss—we had to do something in our joy. "Let's go to a restaurant and have a nice meal, to celebrate this glorious day," was my husband's suggestion.

"Do you want to go to the cafeteria, or to the wine restaurant," the doorman asked us at the entrance of the large restaurant.

"To the wine restaurant, of course," we said at once. No other place would have been fit for that occasion.

"May we order what we like, Daddy, or do we first have to look at the prices?" the children asked.

"No prices today, children," my husband answered. "Today we are celebrating." I doubt that the place had ever seen people more happy and thankful for their fate than we were.

The last days in Holland passed quickly. We had been there over four months and the hospitality of the country had been provided us with all the necessary papers for our immigration. But that time was over, and, with thanks in our hearts, we left the friendly country on a Saturday evening.

Five days in Paris to see the World's Fair was a gift included with every boat ticket from the Netherlands to the United States during that summer.

We were glad to be able to show our girls the superb French capital. Five days in Paris would never be forgotten by them.

Once more I came near to my beloved home city.* I lived for some days in an atmosphere so similar to the one I had loved so much throughout my girlhood.

At six o'clock in the morning we arrived in Paris at the Gare du Nord. The sound of the French language made me feel very much at home. "Mommy, you speak almost like the Parisians," my girls said in admiration. For years and years I had not spoken French, but when I heard it again, it was as familiar to me as it had been twenty years before.

We did not rest very long in the hotel, because we were too eager to show the girls all the marvellous curiosities of Paris. No city has its peculiar vivacity. Always a large stream of people is in the streets. It is great fun to sit in an outdoor garden of one of the many cafés and watch the pulsing life. Nowhere have the women greater charm than in Paris. There is only one city in Europe which I think is more interesting than Paris, and that is Budapest.

From the Place de l'Opéra we walked down the elegant Rue de la Paix, and showed the girls the imposing Madeleine Cathedral. Many times my husband and I had been there and it was a pleasure to let the children see our favorite places.

One and a half days we spent at the World's Fair seeing the wonders of commerce and science from all over the world.

So quickly had the time passed that we were astonished when the day arrived for our departure. Sunny days and lovely memories had marked the end of our life in Europe.

---

* Appel was born in 1894 in Metz, then under German rule. Ed.

VERONA – BRUSSELS

From Essen, Germany, Hilda Branch fled to Verona, Italy, and then to Brussels in 1940. From Brussels she, her husband, and baby made their way to southern France, where they were interned by the French as "enemy aliens." She and her family escaped back to Brussels, where her German appearance made it possible for her to get a job until she was able to leave Europe.

On May 10, 1940, we were awakened at five in the morning by sirens and planes, and in a few hours we were rounded up by the Belgians. We had permits to live in Belgium but they interned us all anyway—my twenty-two-month-old daughter and my husband's aunt, who was over ninety. They kept the men between sixteen and sixty and let the rest of us go after a day. I was ready to immediately put on a rucksack, take the baby and try to get a train to southern France. My in-laws hesitated and I was the only who could drive. I finally fled by car to the coast near the French border. Later my parents-in-law and a cousin and her son caught up with us and we started driving toward France. We were stopped at the border because we were, after all, Germans. So there we were, and we saw the searchlights and the planes and we watched the French army marching north with their World War I equipment.

In the morning after we came to the border they confiscated all our possessions, including the car, and put us on a rickety old bus. They took us to an internment camp on the coast, somewhere between Boulogne and Calais. Of the hundreds of people there, there may have been about ten real Germans. The rest were refugees, being held as enemy aliens.

The men and women were separated but they let my mother-in-law bring her husband his insulin. He was a diabetic and she brought him some bread and the injection. She had been hoarding insulin for a long time for such an emergency and she also carried enough barbiturates to kill the whole family. My father-in-law was on the blacklist because he had refused to turn over his patents for making rubber to the Germans and his life had been in danger for some time.

The night before the French set us walking to Calais, my parents-in-law took a large dose of barbiturates. My mother-in-law offered some to me but I refused. I had my daughter and I thought I would try somehow to get out of the mess. My in-laws told me to tell their sons that they had had a good life and were not sorry to end together that way.

The next morning we were "liberated" by the German army. I left my parents-in-law unconscious but still alive. I remember putting some jewelry in their pockets just in case they made it, so they'd have something. And I had to run through the city of Calais, carrying my daughter, with the bullets flying over our heads. After that we began walking toward Brussels. There were two Austrian women, a seventeen-year-old girl, my cousin and her eight-year-old, and my daughter and I. We slept in stables and begged food from the peasants. We sometimes got food from the German army who came through on modern tanks. They thought we were Belgian refugees. I remember at the end of May I found an old-fashioned baby carriage from about 1890; I could put my daughter in the carriage with some cans of food we had acquired and keep on walking. We found a farm that had been taken over by refugees where we got some food, and stopped at every Red Cross station we could find. We even got a ride in a car that belonged to a German colonel. We could see the collapse of the French and Belgian forces. And though I was always expecting to be caught and put on a cattle car to Poland whenever I met a German officer, and though I kept trying to think who I would contact, what I could manage in such an emergency, it was not in their minds at the time. The army people were too busy to bother with catching Jews.

I bought a seat on a truck going to Brussels with some jewelry and finally got back to the city. There were no streetcars. The telephone lines had been cut by the English before they left. The German occupation had begun. My cousin's mother and mother-in-law had tried to get away. When they were stopped at the border, they bought a bottle of wine with their last bit of money and cut their wrists. The mother-in-law survived and told us the whole story.

I set up housekeeping in my parents-in-law's apartment and my cousin was in the one next to it. The Italian maid, who had left, came back and helped and I went looking for work because all the accounts were closed and we had no money.

I found a job with a German company. I had very good credentials and I was intelligent and spoke Italian, German, French, and English. When the man was ready to hire me I told him I was Jewish and he said, "I didn't hear you." I was later betrayed by a Belgian woman who had been my father-in-law's secretary. She had stolen some equipment from the factory and was working for the Germans, and she told the commandant. My employer, who had taken the risk of hiring me, had to get rid of me.

I still had advantages because I didn't look Jewish and nobody ever questioned me. When I heard that my husband had escaped from the internment camp and was in unoccupied France, I had the nerve to go to the adjutant of the commander of Belgium to ask for permission to go through to unoccupied France. As it turned out I used to go horseback riding with this man's son in Cologne and he gave me the permission. I got my daughter and my possessions on the train from Brussels to Paris in August 1940. But by the time I got to Nice, France had fallen and my husband was no longer there. He had gotten some false papers and was working. My brother-in-law was already in the United States and was trying to get us out of France. And we were constantly at the American consulate trying to get an emergency visa.

We had all kinds of passports. Fortunately my father had been honorary consul of Turkey and he had a better passport than most Jews had at that time. My father, however, didn't want to leave at all. He preferred to stay in France. He had rented his house in Cologne to the French consul and this gave him enough money to stay in Nice.

I hated the French more than the Germans. They began to denounce the Jews in Nice. The French were cooperating with the Gestapo and breaking the windows of Jewish shops. We heard Maurice Chevalier make pro-German remarks during a performance. The Germans, after all, had never promised us anything, but the French had promised a haven to the refugees. It was the country of *liberté, fraternité, égalité*, so it was worse for them to behave so badly.

On Varian Fry

Born in Dresden in 1902, Hans Sahl emigrated to Czechoslovakia in 1933, moving later to France and Morocco before emigrating to the United States. A poet and novelist, he was a major figure among exile writers in France and the United States; he worked with Varian Fry and the Emergency Rescue Committee in Marseille in the early 1940s, helping many German intellectuals and writers to escape. The following description of his initial encounter with Fry is from his memoir-novel The Few and the Many, *in which Sahl appears as Mr. Kobbe.*

"It began in a café on the Cannebière . . ." Kobbe said.

"You seem to have done a lot of sitting around in cafés," the girl with the artificial flower said.

"They became national foster homes for us," Kobbe said. "We lived in the café, slept in the café, wrote farewell letters in the café. Well, then, a friend came up to my table, a very witty person, and said to me in a low voice that a man was stopping at the Hôtel Splendide, a certain Mr. Fry, an American, who had heaps of dollars and a list of people who were supposed to be rescued. 'Your name is on the list. Call him up at once. He's waiting for you.' I said I wasn't in the mood for jokes, but then I telephoned the hotel anyhow and asked for the mysterious American. He answered at once. 'What did you say your name was? Oh yes, Kobbe. Come right over, I'll be waiting for you.' When I appeared at the hotel ten minutes later, two German officers were standing in the lobby. I walked past them to the elevator, rode up, and who should open his door but a friendly young man in shirt sleeves who welcomed me in, put his arm around my shoulders, tucked money into my pocket, drew me over to the window, and whispered out of one corner of his mouth, like a rather poor actor playing the part of a plotter: 'If you need more, come back again. Meanwhile I'll cable your name to Washington. We'll get you out of here. There are ways. You'll see—oh, there are ways. . . .'

"He poured me a glass of whisky. 'Incidentally, you need some decent clothes. You can't go around like that. We'll buy you a summer suit tomorrow.' I downed the whisky and said alternately. 'Thank you very much, sir,' and *'Danke vielmals,'* and *'Merci, monsieur.'* Imagine the situation: the borders closed; you're caught in a trap, might be arrested again at any moment; life is as good as over—and suddenly a young American in shirt sleeves is stuffing your pockets full of money, putting his arm around your shoulders, and whispering with the conspiratorial expression of a ham actor: 'Oh there are ways to get you out of here,' while, damn it all, the tears were streaming down my face, actual tears, big, round, and wet;' and that pleasant fellow, a Harvard man incidentally, takes a silk handkerchief from his jacket and says: 'Here, have this. Sorry it isn't cleaner.' You know, since that day I have loved America, because there these things are done so casually and yet with tact and practical common sense, and because in this country whenever you seem to have come up against a blank wall there is some man in shirt sleeves standing in front of you and saying: 'Oh, there are ways, you know. . . ."

"I stayed a good while longer in Marseilles because the visa from Washington didn't arrive, and then we formed a committee and smuggled people who were in immediate danger across the border, or hid them in monasteries; and then came the day when I myself was to cross the border, with a brand-new Danish passport that had been forged for us by one of the foremost specialists in that field; and in my suitcase were a great many little slips of paper with news from Occupied France—I hid them in toothpaste tubes and cans of shoe polish. Among other things I had the list drawn up by the Germans at the Hôtel Splendide, the names of the persons who were to be surrendered to them. When I arrived in Madrid I went, according to instructions, up to a porter wearing a certain number, gave him my suitcase, and said some password I've since forgotten. The porter nodded and took my suitcase over to a little horse-drawn carriage waiting by the station. I got into the carriage and was driven to a small pension on a quiet street. No one asked my name. I was given an ample supper, went to sleep, and next day the son of the household came and asked whether he could show me Madrid. We went first to the Prado, looked at the Goyas and Velásquezes, and then to the Cité Universitad, where we walked about among the ruins of the wrecked buildings. Neither of us had as yet said a word to one another, and I was on my guard against showing my emotion at the sight of these ruins in which a good many of my friends had been killed during the Civil War. In silence we rode home; in silence he took me to the railroad station next morning, and only when the train began to move did he say: 'Goodbye, friend, and when you're outside tell about what you've seen here. Help the poor Spanish people.' In silence I rode in a compartment filled with silent people toward the Portuguese border, while in the hills along the railroad embankment ragged children bobbed out of caves in the rock and stretched their hands out to us. In silence I handed my brand-new Danish passport embellished with the blue crown to the Spanish border official and walked, with my toothpaste tubes and shoe-polish cans full of secret notes, into spring in Portugal, where the almond trees were already in flower and where mountains of cake, tubs of whipped cream awaited me in the cafés of Lisbon, as well as my visa, which had at last arrived from Washington. . . ."

Ellen Schoenheimer }

FLEEING THROUGH OCCUPIED FRANCE

Written in English in 1941, this autobiographical report traces the struggle of a refugee family in France during the war. The author describes the plight of a mother who rescues her child, Pierre, after a German bomb attack of a refugee convoy south of Paris. Schoenheimer left her account untitled, and instead posted the following motto by Keats:
"Love is the ultimate human answer to the ultimate human question."

During the month of May, and through the first half of June 1940, the Paris police promised to issue me a travel permit, to evacuate my French-born child. To move from one's domicile without this travel permit would have meant to land in a "camp." Toward the 10th of June, the excitement grew, because the German troops were approaching Paris. In this atmosphere of panic you can travel without a *sauf-conduit*, the Paris police told me, and I packed all our clothes, papers, documents, both mothers and Pierre into the car, took along provisions for three days, and left our Paris apartment, where we had spent eight beautiful sunny years.

My sixty-year-old father was interned under terrible conditions in a camp, my husband had been "released" and drafted into the army. We had not heard from him yet and did not have his address.

Many apartment dwellers packed their belongings, took their pictures and their valuables. A frightening calm prevailed everywhere.

The wife of the superintendent was crying as she was helping us to fasten some mattresses on top of the car. I do not know who had invented this kind of protection against air raids! I only knew that every car had such a contraption, and that this seems retrospectively like a silly joke, based on the imagination of a child who had never experienced an attack from the air.

As I was coming down the stairs of our house, a delivery boy handed me a telegram which informed me of the death of a close relative in Vienna. I felt something akin to envy; he would be at peace now, he would not have to flee anymore, he would not have to answer the question: "Will we never come back, Mommy, and what will happen to my toys when the bombardment starts?"

The congestion began already on the streets of Paris which were crowded with refugees. The authorities had left only one road open for civilian traffic—the road to Chartres, familiar from many weekend excursions.

Nobody spoke in our car, in which I also took along some friends who lived in our house; the child was frightened too—the crowded streets, the cars, the bicycles, the pedestrians, the baby carriages occupied by the aged, the people who carried their last belongings on their backs, the dogs, the birdcages—a journey so ghastly that neither fiction nor screen can reproduce the full horror of its scope.

No one knew in which direction to travel. I wanted to go to La Baule. I did not succeed in obtaining a travel permit, but I had a residence permit for La Baule.

The exodus out of town proceeded with a speed of seven miles an hour, sometimes ten miles, and at the end of the day the distance covered amounted to hardly thirty-five miles. But one felt as tired and worn out as if one had travelled three hundred miles. This crawling along the road, this sight of the deserted suburbs, the wandering mothers in search for provisions for their children. All stores were closed, the owners having joined the march of the refugees. One shoe store was giving away its merchandise—the owner had been in Belgium in 1914, when the Germans arrived. He remembered the pillaging and figured that he would rather give his shoes to the Parisians.

In the evening a barn offered shelter for the night, straw could be had for a few francs. My mother and our companions rested in the barn, I stayed with my mother-in-law and the child in the car; the child slept until five o'clock in the morning when we continued our journey.

The road was even more crowded now, big peasant carts from the north were congesting the streets. Long wagons were loaded high with belongings and families. Infants were bundled next to rabbit and duck cages. Old people stared into vacancy—they had gone through the same experience during the last war.

There were also many soldiers on the streets, retreating troops, who were glad when the inhabitants shared their scant rations with them.

I did not make much headway—maybe twenty kilometers. Then we got stuck again, and then suddenly my car, like many others, abused by the ten kilometer speed, broke down. I got out for a few moments and noticed that many people watched the sky, where four planes, flying in formation, could be seen; they formed first a star, then a cross, etc.

Suddenly they dived quite low. Somebody cried "They are firing!" Everyone hurled themselves on the ground or in the ditches. I dragged Pierre from the car, lay down on top of him, with my abdomen on his back, my mother went on top of me, and my mother-in-law lay down on her back next to us, using a large bag as protection.

The attack was over in seconds, cries could be heard, mothers called for their children; a hot spray coming from the ditch hit me. Pierre said, *"j'ai une bombe dans ma nuque"* (I have a bomb in my neck) and looked frightened at the blood on the hands and the clothing of my mother.

We got up and all four of us walked toward a barn, with many others, who looked disturbed, or were crying or bleeding. Pierre was very quiet. His eyes seemed huge, without any trace of fear, very quiet, but his entire head was bluishly discolored, askew and distorted. Somebody made room for us on a mattress in a deep, basement-like dwelling. My mother-in-law, who was crying and moaning, also laid down on it; the child was very quiet and claimed he had no pain through the terrific loss of blood. I got two doctors from the road, from the military transports; they looked at the child and wanted to leave him there, while they gave orders to transport my mother-in-law, who bled profusely, in a military car to the hospital in Chartres. She was wounded in her hip. The bullet had entered through her handbag into her thigh and then out again through her buttocks. The impact of the bullet had been so strong, that it reached the child on the bottom of the ditch—there it remained, in the neck of the child.

My mother was crying bitterly, "do speak to the child," she said every minute, "he is dying." I thought so too, and spoke to him of his father, who would soon come on furlough, and also of the war, which would end soon; and he smiled all the time and bled. Then he wanted to go to the bathroom and a man in this crowded room which smelled of blood gave him a handkerchief; into this handkerchief the child had a tremendous bowel movement—the doctors told me later that this might have helped the child to survive. A nurse tried to send out a few people, so that there would be more air for the wounded, but nobody left of course; everyone was scared of new air raids. We took the child and carried him fifty steps to a neighboring inn. A man with a terrible headwound was lying in one room, another one's arm was ripped open. I put Pierre on the bed, cut the shirt open and bandaged the neck temporarily. "You have to get the child into a hospital," she told me, "maybe there is still hope." This idea had not occurred to me, the sight of that head did not leave any hope, I was all confused, and I had to respond to his smile all the time; I let the nurse call a soldier, who wanted to try to get us into a military convoy, en route to the hospital in Chartres.

Hardly forty-five minutes had elapsed since the accident when the child and I were loaded on a crowded truck. First I had to inform my mother that we were being transported to Chartres, they did not want to take me along with the child, because I was not wounded. I was forced to leave my mother behind. I advised her to take the small room for the night, Pierre's blood-soaked clothing was still lying around there. It provided shelter for her and four others for the night, while the constant bombardment continued.

The truck was completely overcrowded with people and sealed off from light and air. It brought us in two hours to a military ambulance where I joined a young man whose arm had been torn off, and a woman with an abdominal wound. A little later my completely frantic mother-in-law arrived too. She had been taken to the ambulance by a private car.

Pierre was conscious throughout the entire trip. Night had fallen and the car just crawled along the road which was congested with refugees. We all travelled of course without lights, the car had to stop often suddenly, and with each impact the bleeding increased and the child began to vomit. We drove approximately forty miles from the place of the accident to the hospital in Chartres in about four hours.

We got out and entered a completely darkened hall, filled with about three hundred completely blackened lifeless figures, who were spread out partly on the floor and partly on stretchers. From time to time a voice called for a drink of water, occasionally cries emerged from the little chamber which served as an operating room and which differed from all the other rooms because it had access to light. The cries frightened Pierre. I asked the only present nurse—she was over seventy years old and assisted the surgeon behind the open door—to take the child first, since he was the only one amongst the many, who had remained fully conscious, and they granted my plea. The physician, who was surprised that I was not wounded, gave me a white coat, and with the words "we need you very badly," he pulled me into the little chamber, where Pierre was already quietly sleeping under a chlorethyl mask.

I stayed only a few minutes, I just couldn't, I ran [back] to my mother-in-law and told her that she would be taken care of soon. Then I bent down and cut open the clothing on the many blackened bodies, undressed those who were closest to the little operating room, in order to help those two inside—a very young, inexperienced surgeon in French army uniform and a little old Catholic nurse, who crossed herself with the words "Friday the thirteenth, what a misfortune," when she saw Pierre.

It was twenty-five minutes later when the nurse came out in order to ask me "the child, is he baptized?" No, I said, without understanding what the question meant. She told me then that the child had already lost too much blood, that the doctor had to make a long cut under the ear, because he did not find the bullet from the back of the neck, and that the situation was very grave and serious, and the child was too weak. I did not feel anything. I did not understand anything, the hopelessness of her words, I only saw the rows of those blackened lifeless people, the head of my child, so terrifyingly blue and askew and his wonderful, unchanged eyes.

After an operation which had lasted forty minutes, the doctor came out with the child in his arms and told me that the child would not wake up from the anesthesia until eleven o'clock the next morning, that I should look for a bed, and that the child was weak and there was little hope. I carried the child to the third floor, which had not been occupied yet. The first and second floors were full of casualties left to their own devices, no help of any kind as the town had been evacuated. The beds had remained and they were filled with human beings crying out for water and help. I went down into the hall again. I was hoping I would find the child's overcoat or trousers, but it was impossible to find his things in the blood-stained heap. And while I searched, watches, papers, and money came tumbling out of the pockets, so that I had to give up the search.

My mother-in-law was taken care of quickly, she lay down on the bed next to Pierre's. She was talking incoherently and kept asking for the child, whom she could of course not recognize behind the huge bandage. The room filled quickly and those who were conscious took me for a nurse because of my white coat and begged for water or for the doctor, others asked for urinals. I could find only one for a ward with sixty people. Then there were women who asked me to look for their children, they continued to describe the children's clothing to me, they could not understand that nobody was dressed in blue or pink any more, that the beds were filled only with blackened bodies, which looked like crumpled carbon paper. Human beings who were attacked with "fire bombs" when they were on a Red Cross train from Paris to Chartres.

Suddenly I swerved, or the floor under me, I was not astonished. Six hours amidst these horrors, my knees caved in. I thought I was dizzy, but a terrible roar made me realize that the motions were due to the impact from bombs. I could already hear the planes and the alarm of the sirens.

My mother-in-law jumped with the rapidity of a wounded animal, out of her bed and ran down the stairs. I wrapped the child into a blanket and also ran down the three flights of stairs and then into the cellar, which was furnished with easy chairs and beds; two soldiers stood guard. Not many people were downstairs—most of the patients could not leave their beds unassisted.

When I heard the all-clear signal again, I carried Pierre upstairs, then twice down again. I left him downstairs at the third alarm—I could not take the stairs anymore, in my fear, and with the weight of the big seven-year-old boy in my arms. Mother ran unassisted again and again down to the cellar and then for a short while into bed again. That is how the first night passed, and when the morning dawned, the evacuation began under bombardment. I asked the Catholic sister to give me some clothing for the child, and she gave me a small yellow sweater, which I had to cut open. I could not pull it over the head with the huge bandage. That was all that the child wore. My mother-in-law had only her coat—no shoes, no stockings.

"Soldiers don't take the near-dead!" the soldier told me, as he carried the child from the cellar up to the corner of the hall. Patients were being transported by ambulances to the railroad station from there, but the child was grouped together with the aged and the dying, whom one did not intend to evacuate. I begged the exhausted physician—he had operated and applied dressings from nine o'clock in the evening all through the night—to see to it that a French child of a member of the armed forces should be evacuated. He hinted that the decision was up to the military authorities and that it was not worthwhile anymore to transport the child. I rushed down to the cellar and asked another soldier to help me. I made it clear to him that every attempt must be made. The newspapers had published only the week before that France did not have enough children. I nearly yelled, trying to explain to him "a child—and France" senselessly, as if all depended upon this one man. And then I succeeded in being evacuated from the castle with my mother-in-law and the child in my lap.

A soldier put the child, clad only in the small sweater and the huge bandage, on a bench in a compartment, while my mother-in-law looked out of the window and said "everything is on fire." I calmed her down by saying that we were by a railroad station and she was seeing the smoke from a locomotive. But Chartres was aflame and huge Nazi planes circled over the location of so many beautiful weekend excursions of the past.

Once aboard, we immediately received water, chocolate for the children, and a warm meal for all who were able to eat.

The train consisted of thirty-six cars, and only one car carried wounded soldiers. All the others were filled with women and children.

It was ten o'clock Saturday morning, and mother and our friends from Paris had arrived in Chartres at the same time. The town was in flames and they were urged to continue their flight. The cathedral was spared.

Around eleven o'clock, as the doctor had predicted, Pierre made an attempt to move and woke up slowly. Mother got up every second, raised her hands searchingly to the baggage rack, looked for her pocketbook, wanted to dress her feet, looked for a comb, looked for the things we had loaded into the car, and forgot that so much had happened meanwhile. Two physicians made the rounds during the day, they looked at Pierre and said there was nothing to be done, and that it was impossible to make a prediction. Head injuries heal either by themselves—or they don't, no medical help is possible; I should send a soldier for a doctor only if the child turned blue, and the child turned blue twice.

The night was quiet. The wounded were too weak to notice the bombardment of the ambulance train, and I was resting on the floor of the compartment. I did not know where we were heading, the military did not know it either. I just wondered how I managed not to lose my mind—the deranged old woman, the half-dead child, how to get word to my husband, the papers abandoned in the car, the lost money and the lost jewelry, some which had been entrusted to me by friends! The whole misery of that long train ride to an unknown destination.

In the morning I carried Pierre to the first car, an operating room. Three doctors discussed his case, "too much loss of blood," "too weak," "there is nothing to be done." They tried to give him some nourishment—first champagne, then an egg, but they could not get his mouth open. I looked for a

French word for "rectal feeding." I succeeded to get my meaning across and was told there was little hope, that he was already too weak for anything, we would be unloaded as soon as possible with other serious cases; Bordeaux, selected first, did not accept trains any more, but on Sunday at two o'clock we were unloaded in the Department Charente Maritime in La Rochelle.

The ambulance ride from the train to the Hospice St. Louis lasted fifteen minutes. A young doctor took the child in his arms, made a few entries on the tag from Chartres and told me "Sundays and Wednesdays clinic hours two to six o'clock." I followed him, I felt my world had collapsed when I heard I could not stay with the child. I saw mother being led into a different wing of the immense building and followed the nurse, who carried Pierre now. Because of lack of space he was put in the "ward" between children with minor childhood diseases which must be endured. The nurses gasped under their big sister coifs when they saw Pierre and they crossed themselves. Word was carried from mouth to mouth, from floor to floor, "Gunned down by the Krauts, even the children!" Those were the first civilian casualties these religious people, who lived removed from worldly strife, saw, and many of them could not hold back their tears.

I sat on my chair at the bed of the child, the clock marked seven when the nurse asked me to leave the ward. I begged her to make an exception and to let me stay, but she did not yield. I thought of the soldier, whom I succeeded in softening up and evacuating the child. I gathered fresh courage that these nurses would not send me away. And indeed, after many discussions with the head nurses, I succeeded in spending the night in the easy chair next to the child's bed. I did not sleep.

Despite my exhaustion I was compelled to think of the morning, of the fear to leave the child at the hospital and to look for a refugee center. No rooms were available in either hotels or boarding houses any more, only mass lodgings which offered straw beds and a bowl of soup. There I would have to wait helplessly for the visiting hours. Pierre slept like dead. Two days and two nights had passed since the operation, he did not have any liquids, he did not pass his water, he did not even moan, only this gruesome turning blue, and no other sign of life.

Like all French hospitals, the day began shortly after six, because the night nurses had to take the morning temperatures of the patients. The nurse came in bright and early and was amazed to find me there. She was followed by another stern and efficient nurse, who must have been, judging by the papers in her hands, connected with the office. She asked me immediately, somewhat severely and annoyingly at finding me there, if I could work. If I were willing, they would let me stay together with the child.

I do not know if there are many moments in one's life when one feels that all the problems are solved and all the worries have disappeared, one has found a magic solution, and everything will end well. I felt almost happy, I could have embraced the nurse. I stammered, "Anything you want me to do, I will do to your satisfaction"—when I said goodbye to her five weeks later, she told me, "I will never forget your terror when you were told about the visiting hours, and you were supposed to have been sent away, or your happiness when I offered you work, and I also remember your eagerness to learn dressings. You succeeded in making us forget that you did not always belong here." This was said with so much love and expressed in such beautiful French that this moment will always stand out in my memory, amidst this entire unfortunate period.

In the office, where I had to report after the sleepless night, I received white uniforms, which came in very handy, because my own dress was spotted with blood, and they also gave me a long printed form which informed me that I was now a "temporary nurse, voluntary, of course" and my reimbursement was to amount, after the deduction for lodging and food, to four hundred fifty francs.

This hospital consisted of five hundred beds in peacetime, and it had many separate pavilions, each surrounded by a garden. The whole area functioned like a little town, it had its own pharmacies, its own slaughter house, own laundries, a wonderful big kitchen, and of course a church and a mortuary with many biers.

The first day I worked only with "garments," that is, I changed diapers in the infants' ward and in the evening I helped to put a new casualty into traction. This performance induced the dressing nurse to claim me, and from the next day on until I left, with the exception of one day, I changed dressings in the children's ward. Children who were wounded by bullets or incendiary bombs—fleeing from Paris via Chartres, and who had now reached La Rochelle too. Most of them were alone, many had parents who were casualties in other wards of the same hospital, or impossible to locate.

It was fortunate that the younger children had identity disks, or their full names were embroidered on their underwear. Michael, the boy in the bed next to Pierre's, a charming eighteen-month-old, answered the question "Where is your mother?" with "*bum la haut*" (bombs up there), that is, an eighteen-month-old already could remember that something came crashing down from above. Those who did not see these children, this patience in bearing agony and the painful dressings, the head wounds packed with yards and yards of gauze, do not know what this war meant, and cannot understand that such an experience haunts a person all her life.

Not one's personal experience with one's own child, no, the hall in Chartres, the wards of La Rochelle, and more poignant than anything else, the country roads filled with refugees, this will remain forever in my memory.

I do not wish to go into details about the hospital and about Pierre's condition. The condition was still unchanged—there was no hope and the weakness did not improve. One day followed the other, fourteen hours of work, mostly on my feet, dressings, poultices, packings for sixty youngsters.

The food was quite good, we had starches and fruits, occasionally meat, sometimes butter, which we gave to the children, also sweets which we could buy through the hospital; the mainstay of our nutrition was bread, the wonderful French bread which was still available then; I myself ate daily 750 grams, that is how hungry we felt, not on account of the hard physical work, but also because of the nervous strain.

After ten days Pierre began to take tiny quantities of fluid from a teaspoon. But the progress was very slow. In addition the German army occupied La Rochelle, and the English proceeded to bomb day and night the oil stores in La Palisse, so that the Germans could not make use of it. The children who had experienced planes, alarms, and bombs were very restless. The trips back and forth, from bed to cellar, did not contribute to fast recoveries; the doctors ordered dressings and packings, but spoke little beyond that.

I asked after two weeks if the child would ever be able to move his head again, and the doctor replied, "You ask too many questions. I do not even know if the child will live." If one knows these Catholic hospitals, one understands that this reply was not prompted by lack of compassion. It is their faith that makes them so outspoken. The doctor told me from the beginning: "There is no more hope." That meant since he did not see any hope for the child, he as a human could not do anything. The decision was up to God, the doctors could only assist the patients by easing their pain, but not more, help must come from God. This attitude results in lack of action in severe cases, contrary to other hospitals, where an attempt is made to influence the condition by injections, blood transfusions or oxygen.

But a turn came all the same. Maybe it all sounds slightly exaggerated on paper—but after all these weeks, my nerves were overwrought. On account of the illness of another nurse, I was transferred to the ward for severe infectious diseases. I was not happy about it because it meant that I would only be able to see Pierre at night, after I had changed my clothes, because it was not permitted to go from one ward, especially from the infectious ward, into another ward. There I took care for five days of a very intelligent nine-year-old girl. Her condition was deteriorated and she consisted only of skin, bones, and gorgeous blond curls which fell out the moment one touched her head. There was little that could be done for her. Her completely weakened body accepted a few drops of liquid from a teaspoon. I tried frequently moistening her hot, completely cracked lips, and a smile appeared then in her eyes, which did not seem of this world any more, and I was rewarded with the same response when I talked of her little brother Marcel, whom she loved dearly.

The parents were permitted to visit her daily. They had already bought her burial dress and spoke only about death. The doctor prescribed "remedies" and one morning toward eleven o'clock, there was foam on her lips, and I, who had never met such a situation before, called the head nurse, who folded the hands of the little girl, and asked me if I wanted to help her. Not knowing what that implied, I answered in the affirmative. Then I had to wash the body, to dress her, to put a thin chain with a cross around the neck and a bow on the hair, to wrap the body in a sheet and to lay it out in the mortuary. Then I had to call the parents. I do not know how I accomplished all this. I had only one thought—today it is this little girl's turn, tomorrow it might be my son's—and this gave me the strength to face the ordeal.

Two hours later I got back from the chapel. They had saved lunch for me. I could not get my food down, and a nurse came and told me that I should eat, I could rejoice, the surgeon had made the rounds, there was a sudden turn in my child's condition *"l'enfant est sauvé,"* she said, adding "by a miracle," and crossed herself.

I begged for an hour's rest. I was then at the end of my rope. I fell on my bed and slept for the first time for a full hour without interruptions of any kind and without alarms. Then I went to Pierre and began to work his ward, relaxed and happier.

"Will you come *now* to mass this Sunday?" asked the nurse with whom I had laid out little Huguette, "now that your child has been given back to you?" "Even if I do not come" was my reply to her, "I do believe in miracles." "One has to be thankful" she said, and she did succeed. A few Sundays later, when Pierre was permitted to get up for a few hours, he joined her in the chapel. The large image of the Madonna looked down on the big black coifs of the sisters, on the even bigger bandaged heads of the little French children—and on a little Jewish boy.

All this happened in June and July 1940, and was written down a year later in Yonkers, New York, as a memento for my mother with the motto: "God in France",* and for my son in the hope that these forgotten days will be his first and only war experience, until such time in the future, when he will read this tale, which was written down for him by his mother.

---

* To live "like God in France" is an idiomatic German expression meaning to enjoy a life of plenty.

CHAPTER TWO

On the Meaning of Exile

THE GRANDEUR AND MISERY OF EXILE

Lion Feuchtwanger was probably the most widely read German author to go into exile. His novels had sold millions of copies in German and been translated into more than twenty languages. In 1933 he fled Germany with his wife to their vacation home in Sanary sur Mer in the south of France, where he continued writing, notably the novel trilogy Exile, The Oppermans, *and* Success. *He was interned in the camp Les Milles in the summer of 1940 but escaped through the daring intervention of his wife and an American consulate official, first to Marseille, then across Spain to Lisbon. President Roosevelt himself ordered the visas and affidavits allowing the Feuchtwangers to emigrate to America. This essay was written in France in 1938 for the German exile journal* Das Wort, *as an exhortation to the exile community.*

During the [First World] War and the two decades after it, revolutions took place in many countries. These cataclysms had driven thousands of people from their homes and into flight. There were therefore emigrants from many nations.

But the German emigration was more fragmented than any other.

Among the German exiles were many who had had to flee because of their political beliefs, and there was the mass of people who had seen themselves forced into leaving their homeland only because they or their parents were listed as Jews in the town registers. There were many Jews and gentiles who had left voluntarily because they simply couldn't breathe the air of the Third Reich any longer; and there were others who would have given everything to be able to stay in Germany if one had allowed them to earn their living in some way. There were those whose beliefs, those whose birth certificate or some other coincidence had driven from Germany. There were emigrants by choice and emigrants by necessity.

Among the one hundred and fifty thousand people hounded out of Germany were not only people of every political stripe, but also of every social class and every personal character. Now, whether they liked it or not, they all had the same label stamped on their foreheads, they were all sitting in the same boat. They were emigrants first of all and only after that were they the people they really were. Many resisted such a superficial classification, but to no avail. The group had been formed, they belonged to it, the connection proved unbreakable.

For both kinds of emigrants, leaving Germany meant renouncing their positions and their fortunes. For the jobs had to be given up, the money left behind. How else would the governing party satisfy the promises it had made to its members before taking control of the state? And so most of the German emigrants lived in poverty. There were doctors and lawyers who now sold ties door to door, did secretarial work, or tried—illegally, hounded by the police—to make use of their professional training. There were women with a university education who earned their keep as sales clerks, cleaning ladies, and masseuses.

Wherever these gloomy guests arrived, they were unwanted. Land and work were divided among the nations, among political and social cliques. As a result of the unplanned production and senseless distribution of wealth, a great portion of the population of the planet went hungry despite warehouses filled with food, and many machines stood idle despite the willingness of workers to work and the people's hunger for commodities. Countries in which new, competent workers would have been welcome, no longer existed. Instead the foreign newcomers who wanted bread and work were looked at with suspicious eyes.

They weren't allowed to work, and barely allowed to breathe. One asked for their "papers," for identification. They didn't have them, or what they had didn't suffice. Many had fled without being able to take their papers with them, their passports gradually expired and weren't renewed by the officials of the Third Reich. And so these exiles had a hard time of proving that they were who they were. In many countries that was a good enough reason to keep them out. It happened that people without any identification papers were secretly transported at night over the border of a neighboring country by the police, only to be brought back just as secretly by the police of the neighboring country the next night.

Only a very few were prepared to deal with the suffering they had to endure. For it is the case that suffering makes the strong man stronger, but the weak man weaker. Old German has two words for the exile who has been driven out: the word *Recke* [strong combatant], which means nothing other than the person driven out and despised; and the word *Elend* [misery], which again signifies the man without a country, one who has been driven from the land. In this way the wisdom of the German language designates the two defining poles of the exile experience. Among the German emigrants the majority were *Elende*, and not too many were *Recken*. For one's beliefs and principles are easier to give up than one's daily bread and butter, and when it's a matter of bailing out a sinking ship, morality will be the first to go. Many of the emigrants went to pot. Their bad qualities, hidden and protected in prosperity, came to the fore, their good qualities reversed themselves. The cautious man became cowardly, the daring one criminal, the thrifty one miserly, generosity turned into con artistry. Most of them became egocentric, lost their judgment and sense of measure, couldn't distinguish any longer between what was allowed and forbidden, used their misery [*Elend*] to justify every excess and caprice. They also took to complaining and bickering. Thrust from secure into uncertain living conditions, they became nervous, at once impudent and servile, quick to quarrel, demanding, know-it-alls. They were like fruit that has been ripped too soon from the tree, not ripe, but dry and bitter.

The more bitter their hope for return or at least for secure living conditions became, the deeper they let themselves fall. Many were ashamed to be emigrants, they sought anxiously to hide it, naturally in vain. Others, precisely because they had nothing but their identity as emigrants, made an arrogant show of it and developed increasingly higher expectations from it. Wasn't Hannibal once an emigrant, Dante, Victor Hugo, Richard Wagner, Lenin, Masaryk? They forgot that the little White Russian Maximov also belonged among the emigrants, the one who stood as a bouncer and pimp in front of the nightclub Koltshak in Montmartre; and Mr. Rosenbaum, who tried to pass off imitation silk ties as pure silk, and Mr. Zarnke, who went around offering himself as a spy to the German police.

They weren't loved, these German emigrants, and therefore they had to find company among themselves, among fellow foreigners. Then their misery and despair boiled over into petty, ridiculous squabbles; they rubbed each other the wrong way. Without knowing it they saw their own image in someone else and cursed in the latter's pettiness their own inadequacies. All of them wanted the same thing: passports, work permits, money, a new homeland, most of all the return to one's old, liberated homeland. But the reasons for wanting these things and the ways they wanted to achieve them were very different; what one exile found magnificent, the other found disgusting. In this way, through their constant proximity to one another, even those who shared the same fate and the same goals, wore each other down, caused each other mutual disappointments. There was hatred, sometimes mortal enmity among the emigrants. And more or less in good faith, each emigrant suspected the other of being lazy or betraying the common cause.

Yes, exile wore people down, made them petty and miserable. But exile also made some hard and great, made them *reckenhaft*. The sedentary life of someone who never leaves home demands and fosters other virtues than does the fate of the nomad, the free spirit. In the age of the machine, however, the age where the machine makes the great majority of farmers superfluous, the virtues of the free spirit are at least as valuable for society as those fostered by a sedentary lifestyle, and more appropriate for someone who has to fight each day for his life. The emigrant had fewer privileges than other people, but he also lost many of their limitations, obligations, and prejudices. He became more flexible, agile, quicker, stronger. *"Walzender Stein wird nicht moosig,"* one can read in the old Sebastian Franck—a rolling stone doesn't grow any moss—which apparently struck this German writer as an advantage.

For many, exile made their world smaller, but to the better ones it gave breadth and elasticity; it gave them a sense for the grand, the essential in life, and taught them not to waste time with trivialities. Individuals who had been thrust from New York to Moscow and from Stockholm to Cape Town were forced, if they wanted to survive, to reflect more deeply about a greater variety of issues than those who spent their whole life in a Berlin office. Many of these emigrants became inwardly more mature, discovered new strengths, became younger. Nietzsche's exhortation to "die in order to become," which transforms human beings from gloomy into joyful guests of this earth, became their touchstone.

Many people inside and outside the borders of the Third Reich have pinned their hopes on these emigrants. These exiles, they believed, have been called and chosen to drive out the barbarians who took over their homeland.

RESISTING AMERICA

Ludwig Marcuse (1894–1971) was born in Berlin and earned a reputation as a versatile essayist, biographer, and philosopher before fleeing to France in 1933 and later, rather unwillingly, to America. In recalling his own departure, he remembers those writers and friends who didn't make it, including the great Austrian novelist Joseph Roth.

It would be a terrible understatement to say we emigrated to America unwillingly. Nothing attracted me less. I would have preferred emigrating anywhere, just not to the New World, which struck me less as new than as uncanny. I simply wanted to get as far away from Europe as possible. After the Munich Agreement I was convinced that the German Thousand Year Reich would be nothing to brag about, but rather (at least for the duration of our lives) a simple matter of fact. As far away as possible—but why in God's name to the United States? Because (*pace* the most clever existentialists) we do not choose opportunity, opportunity chooses us. It puts the tracks in front of us on which we then travel—toward *its* goal. Neither Alaska nor Tierra del Fuego nor Panama had said to me: please climb aboard. But America had, in the form of an affidavit offered by the Institute for Social Research at Columbia University.* My first reaction, in the spring of 1938, had been: *nein, jamais*, never (at that time I didn't even know this last word). But I left for Marseille because of the gratitude I felt to the American consul; my file was put into the bureaucratic machine, and I myself forgot it completely.

What did I have against the States? My conception of the country, which was very vague. In school I had hardly ever heard that distant, not very powerful realm mentioned; after all, it hadn't even fought against Germany in the war. We studied lots of Greek and Latin and a bit of French in school, we had a "bonne" and a "mademoiselle" at home, but no "Miss." We were on intimate terms with Pericles and Augustus, we knew about the French because of

---

* Originally a group of young Frankfurt-based philosophers and critics who came to America and were funded privately. Members included Max Horkheimer, Theodor Adorno, Leo Löwenthal, Erich Fromm, Herbert Marcuse, and others.

Sedan and the Moulin Rouge. But the countries where English was spoken were only interested in making money. What did we, the sons of high government officials and the affluent, the pupils of a humanistic "Gymnasium," what did we have to do with the "buy me" countries? Even as a child I longed to visit the Champs Élysées; Trafalgar Square and Washington were as distant from my mind as Valparaiso . . . I hardly knew their names. I hardly knew anything about Pitt, never mind Jefferson. When, as a student, I saw the title of a book comparing the ideas of 1789 and 1776, I learned to my astonishment that there had been something like a French Revolution on the other side of the ocean. Young people today have no idea that, fifty years ago, educated Europeans lived in a world whose center was Paris. New York and the colonial territory surrounding it were further away than Africa, which our Kaiser had made famous for us. The valedictorian of our high school class wanted to go to Cameroon . . . The foundation for my conception of America? The image of skyscrapers lining sunless chasms in which untold numbers of people crawled about looking for dollars.

Then, after the Munich Agreement, I had one burning desire: better to go to pot in that dreary anthill than in the Germanic hell. I would have given everything, everything, in order to escape that fate. Ernst Weiss, Walter Hasenclever, and Walter Benjamin had the same thoughts six months later in half-occupied France. And because by that time they couldn't flee anywhere else, they fled into death.* So after the Munich Agreement I went every day to the American consulate in Paris. All my wishes vanished when compared to the one single wish for a visa. At that time Mephisto could have had my soul for that price. We were issued one for February 1939, valid for one month. In the middle of the month we received devastating news: we were missing a document, our marriage certificate in Frankfurt. How ever would we, as Germans who had been stripped of their citizenship, be able to get this within a week? "When can we get the next visa?" we inquired. "That is uncertain. But you have to give up your quota number for emigration." So we had lost our battle with Hitler. For it was very clear that he was about to swallow France.

In any case (in order to have all our papers), I wrote to the Frankfurt Registry. In less than a week I had what I needed. The American consul had to sit down, visibly alarmed. His first sentence was: "You Germans are unbeatable. You work like a fine-tuned machine. Have you really lost your citizenship?" he asked incredulously. "The German bureaucratic apparatus is the Thousand Year Reich," he added. Was that supposed to comfort us? Then he said, sadly: "But you're too late. I've already sent your quota number to the American consulate in Berlin."

I adapt easily to bad news because I take it for granted. My wife Sascha

---

*   All three German writers committed suicide in response to the Nazi occupation.

doesn't, her imagination for evil is less active than mine. She went back to the consul and insisted there must be another way out. He reflected: our number probably arrived in Berlin on Friday. No one was working on Saturday and Sunday. The consulate was closed on Monday because of Washington's birthday. Now it was noon Tuesday. "If you wish, I can make a call to Berlin on my lunch hour." My wife asked me if we should risk the money for a phone call to Berlin. I said no. She told the consul yes. Berlin answered back: "We were just about to give the number to someone else." Since that day we celebrate Washington's birthday every year . . . for very personal reasons.

One morning in March 1939, a few hours before we left for America, our friend Joseph Roth came to see us in the Rue de Constantinople. He sat there, his hat still on, balancing a thin little cane between his fingers, his coat slung lightly over his shoulder—everything to keep us from thinking he meant to stay. And so, after two minutes, he said the little phrase he always said when he found himself forced to enter someone's apartment: "Let's go down to the bistro." In the bistro he stared deep into the glass of some garish colored liquid.

The best conversations between old friends always begin: "Do you remember, twenty years ago?" "I really tricked you that time," said Roth with cynical warmth. "Right from the beginning, with a big fat lie. I had someone tell you I wanted to meet you because I liked your last book. I hadn't even read it. And when I read it, I was disappointed. I was simply curious about you." "The first time we met, I told an even bigger lie," I responded. Only slowly did he look up from his glass. The wet color was now swimming in his eyes, which looked me up and down like the eyes of a teacher completely satisfied with one of his pupils—but who still needs to check things over once more. He thought back and then said, surprised: "Even back then you were such a sentimental stickler for truth!"

"This is what happened," I explained. "You had the illusion of being a great graphologist and asked me to bring you some handwriting samples. I came with a bunch of letters by famous writers. Every one of your interpretations was dead wrong—but they were so imaginative, so witty, so gracious, you were so sure of yourself and your girlfriend from Vienna was so pleased with her tender psychic that I swore to both of you: 'You must have seen these samples before, otherwise it's impossible.'" Roth was already sinking into his private, toxic-looking little ocean. The thin blond goatee he had grown in the last decade was dripping with the fluid as if he had already drowned. Two months later he had.* And a few months after that, all of Europe.

At the St. Lazare station I should have taken leave solemnly from the Old

---

* The Austrian novelist Joseph Roth fled to France in 1933; ravaged by alcoholism and despair for the future of Austria, he died on May 27, 1939.

World. But in fact the grand emotional hour was a mass of bothersome details: one of our bags was missing, I was looking for my passport and already thought it was lost, friends were clambering up our window, the train to Calais was overcrowded, I was sweating and got jostled by the passengers fighting their way through the narrow corridor, my teeth were aching from a chocolate that Françoise had popped in my mouth, and the noise was so deafening I couldn't even have wanted to hear the "harmony of the spheres" . . . That was the grand hour of the grand leave-taking.

The emotion of that hour came to me only much later. I can still feel it from time to time; I know it by an indescribable twitch in my soul.

Alfred Kantorowicz }

An Ordinary Day
in the Life of an Emigrant

Born in Berlin in 1899 and involved in Communist politics at an early age, Alfred Kantorowicz fled to Paris in 1933 where he was active in exile resistance circles. He later fought in the Spanish Civil War before emigrating to the United States.

On September 27, 1935, the German emigrant Alfred Kantorowicz, thirty-six years and forty-six days old, a writer by profession, residing in Paris since late March 1933, found the following entries in his notebook:

that at two o'clock a meeting with three friends was to take place in his hotel room in order to discuss the vague plan of starting a journal;

that at four o'clock a member of the executive committee of the Association for the Protection of German Writers* was to arrive to prepare for the next meeting of the association, dedicated to the theme of "Freedom and Freedoms";

that he had to correct the speech he had given at the fiftieth anniversary of Victor Hugo's death;

that on behalf of a German publisher in Paris he was supposed to write a letter to a well-known German writer, asking him to write the introduction for an anti-Fascist book;

that he should try to convince another German writer, who had just come to Paris, to hold a lecture for the "Association";

that he had to answer the letter of a young German emigrant in desperate straits;

---

* The *Schutzverband Deutscher Schriftsteller* (SDS), founded in 1908 as a writers union, was refounded in exile in 1933 by German writers in Paris; Honorary Chair was Heinrich Mann, President Rudolf Leonhard, Vice-President Egon Erwin Kisch, Secretary Alfred Kantorowicz. The highpoint of SDS activities was its organization of the conference of "International Writers for the Protection of Culture" in Paris in 1935, its antifascist stance in the Spanish Civil War, and the 1937 exhibition "German Books in Paris, 1837–1937," organized in opposition to the exhibition of Nazi Germany in the Paris World's Fair.

that he had to make two telephone calls to find out how his wife could obtain valid travel documents after the German embassy had, without explanation, refused to renew her expired passport;

that today was the deadline for an article he had promised to write for a book edited by Maxim Gorki and Mikhail Koltzov called *Ein Tag in aller Welt* (*An Ordinary Day*).

His evenings were free. Which gave him the opportunity to work on a book—a novel—that was now at page 122.

The day began promisingly. For the last week his plucky and charming young wife had gotten some copying work in an office. Yesterday they had paid her an advance. She left ten francs on the table as she went out. "For last night," he joked cynically while jumping out of bed with a guilty conscience (it was already after nine).

Today he doesn't need a shave, he thought. At nine-thirty he bought two packs of Naja cigarettes in the tobacco shop across the street: forty cigarettes, his daily ration, which cost seven francs. With the remaining three francs he immediately bought a quart of milk and some bread. Since there was sugar and powdered chocolate at home, as well as some Quaker Oats, the material foundations for his day were in place. He had no excuse. Unfortunately, he had forgotten to save a franc for the two telephone calls. And that made him, as he remembered around ten o'clock when it was time to put through his calls, rather nervous. He already owed his landlady so much that he should have paid the small sum for the calls right away. This was an area where she proved to be completely humorless. A man should never be so broke that he can't toss fifty centimes on the table for a phone call (especially because most of the other hotels charged fifty-seven centimes or even a franc for the connection). So first he knocked on the door of his friend Hans, who lived in the same hotel, a well-known, even internationally known German writer who had already published more than thirty books.* His timid inquiry whether Hans could somehow come up with a franc was met with a roar of mocking laughter. On the other hand he had to give up three cigarettes and leave it up to his friend to borrow some tea leaves for breakfast.

Luckily, when he went into the concierge's room to make the calls (desperation having spurred him on), the concierge had gone out to do some errands. He couldn't get through. The line went dead twice—that was typical of the phones in Paris—and after asking for the connection four times, he was told that Mrs. V. had already left for the day, and that Mr. D. couldn't give him any helpful information, although three days earlier he had made a solemn

---

* The friend here is Johannes R. Becher, a well-known German Expressionist who later assumed a leading role in cultural affairs in East Germany.

promise to do so. The most annoying part was that now, because of the problems with the phone, he had to pay for four calls. Of course the concierge had come back in the middle of his last conversation, was puttering about the room, in a foul mood, complaining about the rising cost of living, the high gas bill, and the crushing taxes everyone had to pay. She used the opportunity to rub in the fact that her last telephone bill had been for three hundred and fifty francs. Her guests, she maintained, were constantly making calls in her absence that they never paid for.

Out of anger and guilt he lied to her and said he had made two calls. He knew very well that she would be charged for four. But was it his fault if the Parisian telephone never worked? That it was also not the concierge's fault he also knew. And he also admitted that she actually did have to contend with intolerably high taxes and the loss of American tourists who no longer came to Paris. But because every day and evening he saw her eating six-course meals with her husband, daughter, son-in-law and houseboys, he couldn't exactly muster an overwhelming sense of pity for her reduced profit margin.

It was the first time he had lied to her. As he walked up the stairs, he was disgusted with himself. In his room, which measured eight feet by eleven, he saw a printed announcement above his bed from June 8 stating that the Hamburg Communist Fiete Schulze had been executed.* He had hung the announcement up as a reminder. On the day of its publication he had made an entry in his diary, a diary he used only in extraordinary circumstances: "Measured against this event, the fact of whether and why my nerves are shot to pieces is of no consequence. I will keep going."

Now it was already 10:30. He wrote the two letters for the introduction to the antifascist book and the lecture for the German writers in Paris. He was interrupted twice. First came Harry, the laundry man, himself an emigrant and in impoverished circumstances, bearing the unpaid bill. Then his friend and hotel neighbor Hans came with a host of ill tidings he had found in his mail. It's impossible to describe this conversation and many of the subsequent details. There's a tremendous amount of material in one day, and if one were truly faithful in rendering it, a rather thick book would be the result.

Just answering the despairing letter from a young German emigrant from the Saar who was in a camp in southern France, would provide material for reflections that, if one wished to do justice to the actual situation, would have to be extensive. The correspondent, whom he doesn't know personally, is a young worker who had read an article by him and gotten his address through

---

* Born in Hamburg in 1894, Schulze was a member of several Communist parties, a leader in the Hamburg Workers uprising in October 1923 and had been sentenced to death during the Weimar Republic. He emigrated to the Soviet Union, returned to Germany in 1932, was arrested in April 1933 and, despite international protest, executed on June 6, 1935.

the journal. ". . . I can't even remember the last day I had a full meal . . . On top of that this damned loneliness. I haven't been able to do any work since the beginning of August, I suffer from anxiety and restlessness, I simply can't put my thoughts in order . . . We haven't found any work. It's impossible since there's no industry here and we're not allowed to go anywhere else. Now everyone is wondering what will happen to us." And so on. And yet this letter possesses a strength, a revolutionary willingness for self-sacrifice, that moves him.

But how should he answer? Make a few nice rhetorical sentences. The only thing he can say will be rhetorical because he can't provide the young man with work, he can't even send him a pack of cigarettes. However, he decides to have the Association of German Writers send him a small package of books, articles, and political tracts that he can pull together. In any event he will write at once, because receiving a letter will no doubt mean something for the young man. He recounts to him the difficulties of life in Paris, all while trying to appear confident in the future. While writing he wins back some of his own confidence, without which it is hard to fight, and harder still to hang on.

Now it is almost twelve o'clock. He turns to the Victor Hugo article. Before he actually starts working seriously, he dozes off for a good half hour. Desolate and wild daydreams. They beg description, encompassing as they do all the wishes a German emigrant can have: to be invited to a nice lunch and to lead a battalion in a decisive battle; to have a great book hit and to do illegal work in Germany. Somewhere a fantasy of sun, ocean, and tan young women lying next to him in the sand rises up magically, but in the next vision he imagines the reconstruction [of postwar Germany] after victory.

Today his fantasies are relatively precise. The map of Berlin is spread out before him, he redraws the city in his mind. The Horst-Wessel Square will be renamed Liebknecht Square, there will be a Thälmann Square, a Workers Square, a Farmers Square, the Castle Square must be renamed the Red Army Square. Will there also be an Intellectuals Square? Perhaps the square that is now called Breitenbach, where the artists' colony is located? It was once known as the "Red Block." John Scheer Street, Lütgen Street, Hüttig Avenue, of course. Perhaps also an Egon Erwin Kisch Street or a Heinrich Mann Street? All around Berlin, in a huge radius, will rise well-planned communities on the lakes, from Sakrow to Grünheide and beyond, small cities in the country, each with fifty thousand inhabitants and wonderful train, subway, and bus connections. He calculates that the subway system will need a good three hundred kilometers of underground tunnels, and that the train lines will require over two thousand kilometers of railway in and around Berlin: It will be the most comfortable, quick, and beautiful transport system in the world. For this he needs an equation to calculate the circumference, otherwise he can't determine exactly the connecting links. (His dreams are notable for their pedantic attention to detail while remaining generally possible.)

What is the value of π? He ponders this for five minutes. Now he has it: 3.14 . . . and so on. The circumference is two R times π, so with a radius of thirty kilometers that would make approximately one hundred ninety kilometers. Plenty of work for everyone. But the suburban lake colonies— equipped with schools, hospitals, union offices, sport fields, swimming pools, forest and lake walks, gardens, etc.—will be called Berlin-Marx, Berlin-Engels, Berlin-Lenin, Berlin-Stalin, Berlin-Liebknecht, Berlin-Luxemburg, Berlin-Thälmann. I'll live in Berlin-Thälmann.*

Rubbish. Now it was actually one o'clock. His friends were supposed to arrive at 2:30. He starts working on the Hugo article. He has to rewrite only a little. While working he becomes absorbed, indeed fascinated, by the similarities between the life of this great emigrant, who spent twenty years in exile fighting injustice in his own country, and the present situation. What a wealth of stirring connections!

Suddenly it is three o'clock. His friends arrive. Their discussion leads to no concrete result. They merely ascertain that at present there are no funds for starting a German literary journal for emigrants. Plans and hope still remain. In the meanwhile they will make do with a small newsletter which they themselves will write and print. Then his friend from the Association came. Information was gathered. Someone called to find out the address of [Aldous] Huxley. In the end he has an extra hour to finish his revisions of the Hugo article. His wife arrives at 7:30. They eat cheese sandwiches.

At eight he starts working on his book, the title of which is still unclear and whose story condenses the retreat and reformation of the revolutionary workers' movement in Germany, in the decisive thirty-six hours between the evening of March 4 and the morning of March 6, 1933.

Until nine o'clock he dozes off, doodles, and corrects the last chapter. Then he begins to write.

By two in the morning he has written four pages. He rereads them and is not dissatisfied. They are the positive result of an ordinary day in the life of an emigrant.

---

* After the war, East Germany indeed renamed many places after leading figures of the anti-Fascist Left such as Thälmann, Liebknecht, and Luxemburg. Since the fall of the Berlin Wall, many of these names have since been changed back to their pre-1933 status.

CHAPTER THREE

On the Brink

THE ILL-FATED STEAMSHIP *ST. LOUIS*

Originally from Poland, Max Korman had fled to Germany after World War I but, like many other Polish Jews, was deported by Germany to the Polish border in late October 1938. Korman obtained a Cuban entry permit and booked passage with the Hapag Steamship Company on the ill-fated St. Louis, *whose journey is described here.*

On Saturday, May 13, 1939, I and hundreds of other passengers strained the facilities of the Hapag Steamship Company at Hamburg's main railway station. We were about to embark on the *St. Louis*, and were being processed all afternoon. Toward evening we boarded waiting buses and these took us in about half an hour to our ship.

We boarded the *St. Louis* in a spirit of gaiety, delighted with the sense of relief from the tensions brought on by preparations for the voyage. Most of us explored the ship at once, running up and down staircases, gazing down gangways, and inspecting admiringly the interiors of the halls and dining rooms.

Exactly at eight in the evening, as the ship began to move slowly from its moorings, a grand vision possessed each of us: sixteen days in a luxurious floating hotel; sixteen days of freedom from burdens and sorrow; sixteen days to be climaxed in Havana by the embrace of loved ones, by the chance to send for wives, children, and parents who remained behind. A new chapter was to begin for us all.

In the days following our departure we became absorbed in the routine, the sights, the activities of our ocean journey. Because the *St. Louis* carried more than her usual number of passengers on this voyage, meals were arranged in two shifts to accommodate all one thousand of us. The food was excellent, and ample enough to satisfy the heartiest of appetites; those convinced that they had to eat everything soon discovered the discomfort of overstuffing stomachs unaccustomed to ocean voyages.

Our diversions were many. We could sun ourselves on deck, walk the promenade deck (six times around was the equivalent of one kilometer), or amuse ourselves on the sports deck playing ping-pong, volleyball, ringtoss, or miniature golf. In the evening the program alternated among three activities: movies in one hall, dancing in another, and concerts in still a third. The ladies really came into their own with all these diversions, for they could show off their entire wardrobes, from formal wear to playsuits and swimsuits. Most of them literally transformed themselves, stepping out of their skins, so to speak. They behaved as if they were truly on a pleasure cruise, seemingly forgetting that they were really well-dressed beggars; after all, each of us had only four dollars in his pocket.

The truly beautiful and sublime was nature, yes, only nature. Looking into the ocean we saw the ship splitting the water to create in its wake foam-laden waves that rhythmically chased one another. We saw the watery play of colors: greens, bright greens, blues, dark blues, and the rainbow sparkle as the sun's rays hit the ocean's watery spray. We saw the dolphins trying to overtake the faster swimming *St. Louis* by jumping up out of the water again and again. We saw the smaller flying fish rising suddenly, flying seemingly long stretches only to disappear again. We saw the sun rise and set. And we saw the incredibly beautiful cloud formations. It was a wonder to see all this and at the same time to feel one's aloneness in the ocean's enormous spaciousness.

Daily we tracked our journey west. At twelve noon tiny flags on a large map located the ship's position, helping us to see how each day brought the American continent and our goal closer. One foggy and rainy morning, accompanied by sea gulls, we passed the Azores. Land came into view. We could see steep, boulder-laden slopes and a valley snugly protecting a town and its red-roofed houses. As we continued to travel west the weather became warm enough for us to go swimming in the ship's pool. That day was especially wonderful! Thanks to fine sailing weather we arrived two days early. On Saturday at 4 a.m. we awoke to see Havana, and a few minutes later realized that in fact the ship had dropped anchor in the port. Preparations for disembarking began at once with the screening of all passengers.

The next step was never taken. Everything became quiet. Then we saw a decree from the Cuban police, but at first we did not know what it meant. The most diverse rumors began to circulate. First it was said that the Cubans do not work the Saturday before Pentacost, forcing us to wait until Monday before we could disembark. Then, some told us that because the arrival was two days early the port was not ready for the *St. Louis;* other ships, especially an English one and a French, had to discharge their immigrants first. We were bewildered.

Relatives and friends soon began arriving. They came in small motorboats, circling around the giant ship, calling, screaming, waving, and in other such ways trying to relate themselves to their loved ones aboard the *St. Louis*. Many wept, and no wonder: wife and child above, at the railing of the ocean liner; husband and father down below, in the motor launch. It was a dramatic reunion: months of hope and labor and joyful anticipations consummated as loved ones did in fact see one another, but from a distance. From below they soothed us with *mañana, mañana,* a call we were to hear again and again during the days that followed.

The wildest rumors circulated. The government had issued an injunction against landing. The Cuban president was hopefully being persuaded to change the injunction. Committees were working for us round the clock; five hundred telegrams had been sent to Cuban officialdom. We would in fact land if only we would remain calm.

We tried to influence our fate, but the odds became overwhelming. We formed a committee to represent our interests and negotiate for us; and its members tried everything possible, cabling everywhere, listening for even the feeblest response. But no encouraging sound was to be heard. Each of us became more and more tense and as our nerves began to fray we asked ourselves this question: with legal entry permits in hand, why had we journeyed for fourteen days across the ocean? to sit for three days in the port of Havana and to observe from a ship's railings the customs of the natives? One passenger, whose wife and two children were also on the ship, answered by slashing his wrists and jumping overboard. (A sailor leaped after him and saved his life.) We received news bulletins: the Joint* in New York and Havana had entered negotiations with the Cuban government; in fact, the representative from New York, accompanied by an American senator, had flown to Havana. The Cuban Parliament had been called into special session. American Jews had posted a five-hundred-dollar bond for each passenger. The boats with the relatives and friends continued to come, morning, noon, and night. They waved and screamed! "You are sure to embark." "The situation is favorable for us." "The parliament has voted and a majority is with us." "Now it's up to the president only." "Yes, yes." "Sure, sure." "Tomorrow, tomorrow."

Those words, those soothing words, well meant as they were, had the opposite effect on us. Continual disappointment had immunized us. We had learned to believe nothing. So we called back to them. "*Mañana, mañana;* it looks very good for us; keep calm." Finally, we did not even want to see the boats. The unrest increased. People cursed and wept. Many broke down. We were in a witches' brew, it seemed. On Thursday we heard that the ship would have to leave the harbor early Friday morning, and we feared the worst. The passengers organized young people to stand uninterrupted two-hour watches to prevent the feared effects of frustration—collapses and suicides. Concern about many of the women was especially intense; they now knew that on the morrow they would leave their men behind in Havana, perhaps forever.

---

* The Joint Distribution Committee, an international Jewish agency created by the Jewish community to deal with refugee problems.

Thus, we kept watch that whole night, and no doubt prevented many an extreme act of desperation.

Friday morning, around ten-thirty, the gentlemen from the American Joint came aboard, gathered us in the social hall, and declared, "The Cuban government refuses to continue negotiations so long as the ship remains in Cuban waters. The captain is therefore forced to leave port immediately for the waters outside the three-mile limit. At that point the government's terms for further negotiations will have been met." The leader of the delegation then asked, "Do you want to trust me?" When all said yes, he declared, "I promise you that you shall not return to Germany." He promised further to inform us every two hours about the developments in the negotiations. In the meantime, he asked us to remain calm. Then his group, and the police guarding us, disembarked.

The ship turned, and slowly, very slowly, left the port, accompanied by the many small boats, and also by autos driving along the harbor front. The harbor front itself was crowded with people, who, as in the preceding days, could not approach the ship. They yelled, and waved, and wept; for in spite of promises that we would return to Havana, many had begun to abandon hope of ever seeing their loved ones again. And in that mood we left the port, seeing Havana in all its glorious panorama: the dome of the capitol, the skyscrapers, the attractive landscaping, the palms.

Our frightful pleasure cruise into the blue had begun once again, and with it came an awful feeling of despair. At first, when the ship stopped after a few hours of travel, all sighed with relief: the coast of Havana was still in view. But then, even as the first dispatches came, imploring us to be courageous and patient, the *St. Louis* suddenly resumed its journey at full speed. The next morning, seemingly moving toward Cuba, we found ourselves looking at the coast of Florida: Miami's skyscrapers, beaches, the bridge to Key West. All these wonderful facilities seemed within a swimmer's reach. As the yachts and other luxury boats greeted us, you can well imagine the feeling that dominated me. Here lived our uncle; this was the land to which I was supposed to come. And here I was so near, but oh so far.

I was not alone. The moment of truth had arrived. What rotten merchandise we must be if no one is prepared to accept us. The slaves must have been better: at least people paid for them, but here and now, when many wanted to pay for each of us, we are still rejected. Are we really so bad and so rotten? Are we really humanity's vermin and thus to be treated as lepers? Or has mankind ceased being human? Has it decided to imitate the natural elements and join with them in a war of annihilation against all the weaker and helpless forms of life? If yes, then man stands revealed. You have no capacity for understanding. You have no ideals. You have no noble purposes. Man, you are lower than the beasts; for they fight only when driven by hunger, by nature's survival demands, which leave them no choice. You, man, use your ability to reason, to kill, to destroy. And what a hero you are, man. You battle against the weakest. Among your kind are great scientists: they specialize in studying the most complex, difficult problems. You do everything to help them because you claim that their research will yield the best of all possible results for your kind. But with us Jews, man, you preach one thing and practice the opposite: you destroy what you do not comprehend or do not want to comprehend. Man, you are a lie.

The cruise along the Florida coast lasted until noon, when suddenly the ship turned and with full speed sailed in a northerly direction. The captain explained his new course by telling us that technical reasons required him to leave the Florida coast for a waiting station that offered cooler weather and was about equidistant from Havana. Haiti, and New York. Our tense and fearful mood instantly worsened. The despair became intolerable. In Havana we had not jumped overboard. What should we do now? The evening brought a reassuring message: everything was not yet lost. Santa Domingo offered haven if American Jews would pay five hundred dollars for each adult and three hundred dollars for each child. A straw, but in the meantime the ship continued to travel in a northerly direction, away from Santa Domingo!

Still another cable arrived that evening: landing permission secured from Cuba's Isle of Pines, south of Havana. Relief! Passengers kissed one another, laughed, danced, and believed: they were free at last from the torture of uncertainty. As if to reinforce the message, the *St. Louis* changed course and drifted; apparently the captain was awaiting orders from Hapag Hamburg for his return trip to Havana. By our calculations we could not arrive there before Wednesday morning.

When we arose the following morning, however, we wondered why the ship was moving so slowly. Our wonder turned to alarm as the *St. Louis* changed course again and steamed with full force in the direction of Europe. Something was wrong. Obviously. Fearfully, we awaited an explanation. It came when the captain told us that efforts were still being made to change the mind of the Cuban government, that in fact that government now had at its disposal deposits of five hundred dollars for each of the *St. Louis* passengers. He had no choice, however, but to continue sailing northward toward the cooler waiting station. That station would be reached by Saturday afternoon. Any change of course could come only upon orders from Hapag Hamburg. As we clutched our straw of hope, groups of pessimists argued with groups of optimists. On one point all agreed: the news about landing on the Isle of Pines was a delusion or an impossibility, for the island didn't have accommodations for a thousand people.

These were truly the days when our despair reached its lowest ebb, for the weather also turned against us. Rain, fog, and storms unleashed themselves against our already overtaxed nervous systems. Seasickness was accompanied by silence from the world beyond. Instead of coming hourly, or three times a day, the bulletins now came only once each day. They told us nothing new, but still we yearned for them, like dying patients begging for morphine to dull their pain. Many prayed. Many fasted.

Finally, even we insisted upon knowing the full truth. When we discovered that our passenger committee had protected us from some important information and that one of our New York negotiators had been convinced all along that settlement with Cuba was impossible, the most intense point of our despair arrived. We abandoned faith in our committee and organized a general assembly of all passengers to hear all the latest cable messages. Then, to remind the world again of our fate, we decided to telegraph Roosevelt, the King of England (who was then visiting Washington), the American press and radio, and Jewish agencies in New York and Paris. We begged them to transfer us to another ship, which could be rented and which could await a favorable settlement of our fate.

Into this cauldron of emotions came a cable from a representative of the Joint in New York, trying to instruct the captain to sail into New York Harbor, drop anchor at Bedloe's Island, and wait there while Congress acted on petitions to provide landing arrangements in the United States. As well intentioned as the sender of this telegram had been, his cable worsened our mood because of its futility. We knew that Hapag Hamburg alone could affect the captain's course; we also knew that Hapag Hamburg would not act upon such vague expectations.

Fortunately, the captain now began to play a more direct role in our affairs. We trusted his word, for he had been marvelous in every way, and had worked day and night on our behalf. He now reminded us about the promise that had been made to us: we would not be returned to Germany. He also told us that negotiations were continuing and that the point of no return would not be reached until Sunday noon.

That slight glimmer of home did not prevent depression. There were some nervous breakdowns. Some wished the ship would sink. But somehow most still hoped for something, although we were all fed up with suffering, the ship, the people, the ocean: this horrible feeling of sailing about on the high seas searching for a harbor that might in fact not exist.

Finally, on Saturday afternoon, as cables came to the *St. Louis* from European capitals and institutions, we realized that the critical stage of the negotiations had moved from the New World back to the Old World, from which we had come. Within thirty-six hours (we heard from Paris) we would have news of our fate. But, having been disappointed so often, we had lost our ability to really believe anything. And we did not believe. The thirty-six hours passed slowly, and with their passage the *St. Louis* came closer and closer to Hamburg, Germany, its home port. The thirty-sixth hour came and went without word from Paris. This we had expected. We were beyond despair.

The cable finally arrived: England, Holland, Belgium, and France had declared themselves ready to accept us *all*. The wording was critical, since much doubt and confusion reigned. Fights broke out as people, disagreed over the conditions of acceptance: passengers with affidavits only; men only; no women and children—they had to return to Germany. But it was *all* of us who had really been accepted by these countries. We would land in Antwerp and from there be distributed to the host nations.

And so it came to pass in the glare of worldwide publicity.

One last word. We left Hamburg on May 13. We learned of our fate, our harbor, on June 13.

Two Letters to Hermann Kesten

*Stefan Zweig—novelist, playwright, biographer, translator, and "good
European"—was reluctant to leave Europe and wary of the United States,
though he had traveled there often and, near the end of his life, was planning
to emigrate to New York. Spiritually broken by Hitler's successive political
and military triumphs, he and his wife committed suicide in Petropolis
(Brazil) on February 23, 1942. Like the death of so many writers in
exile—Joseph Roth, Walter Benjamin, Ernst Toller—Stefan Zweig's suicide had an enormous resonance for the entire German emigration.*

Rosemount
Lyncombe Hill, Bath, England
24 January 1940

My dear friend,

I thank you from the bottom of my heart for your kind letter. We now need
to break apart the iron band encircling us. In this last year we have lost not
only our friends, but also our belief in mankind. In a recently published book,
I found this wonderful sentence: "The nineteenth century was in despair because it had lost its belief in God, our century because it has lost its belief in
humanity."

Your trip to South America isn't possible, at present. I've thought the matter over and seen too many difficulties. Even a trip to Paris is terribly dangerous now. I haven't attempted it yet although I would badly need it.
Incidentally, we must stay here because we would never return to Europe
if we left now. And we must stay, even if it's a losing battle. Here we can
fulfill our duty, simply by being here. America would swallow us whole. I
also believe that spring will bring the end of all this. Let's hope it's the end
we want.

Here I'm leading the life of a hermit, though in a lovely setting. I have
completely withdrawn myself from London, tired, after all these years, of
being regarded as an "alien enemy" as well as of seeing how they reject every

offer I make to be of use. But after due reflection, I'm content not to be forced to dip my pen in other peoples' inkwells. I'm looking after my own work—the best way for all of us to save what can be saved from our bankruptcy.

Your old friend,
Stefan Zweig

Petropolis (Brazil), 15 January 1942

My dear friend,

Thank you for your letter. Perhaps in the meanwhile you will have received mine, for when the war broke out the mail deliveries were all mixed up for a while. I only fear that its content will have been made obsolete by the recent events. The expansion of the war, no matter how welcome it must be to us from a political point of view, stands in a poor relation to the possibility of distributing our books. The international transport and payment network will so thoroughly collapse in the near future that the courage of [exile authors] with their plans for a new publishing house will have to transform itself into patience while they wait for the mysterious "afterwards" (which I'm actually curious to experience).

I have little news to report about myself. I've written a novella in my favorite, unlucky format—too long for a newspaper or magazine, too short for a book, too abstract for a broad public, and too marginal in its theme.* But as you know, mothers have the tenderest feelings for their weak but gifted children. Since I'm not up to working on my Balzac, and a novel of mine is stuck in the middle, I'm now working on my Montaigne, which will be a *pendant* to my Erasmus book. Naturally, it won't be a concrete, systematic biography reflecting all the material facts. Of his problems I'm particularly interested in one which confronts us today as urgently and perilously as it did then: how can I remain free, how do I maintain the clarity of my mind in a heartless, fanatical age?

My autobiography has long been finished, and I could almost say, in a variation on Pirandello: "Three manuscripts are searching for a good translator."

I hear from my friends now and again. Here my only visitor at the moment is Michel de Montaigne, who died three hundred and fifty years ago, but still it's good company together with Balzac, Shakespeare, and similar old comrades.

---

* Zweig's last story was called "Schachnovelle" or "The Chess Story."

All my best wishes to your wife and all my friends, and thus above all to you yourself.

Yours truly,
Stefan Zweig

THE LAST DAY IN EUROPE

*Hans Natonek (1892–1963), born in Prague and a brilliant writer of po-
etry, stories and essays in Weimar Germany, fled Germany for Prague, then
Paris and the United States. Unlike many exiles, he never recovered his
former intellectual vitality and fought unsuccessfully with the "problems of
being a bilingual writer" (this the title of an essay he wrote in 1944). In
America he was a frequent contributor to the* Aufbau, *which published the
following piece on April 4, 1941.*

We sat in a circle and each of us told our story about the first day here and
the last one back there. Every exile has a first and a last day. Their
experiences don't have to be special, and mostly they're not. There are people
who arrive here as if they had taken an hour's train ride from Berlin to Stettin
or from Vienna to Budapest. And then there are people who leave Europe the
way they leave a theater after a bad movie—it's gone, not worth talking
about. They've changed continents like a set of clothes, and for them that's
that. Their new life completely absorbs them. And yet, to leave Europe is an
extraordinary and perhaps definitive experience if one lives through it in full
consciousness.

"One shouldn't look back," someone says. "Europe is over. Finished, done
with. The ones who can't forget it and are always turning to look back remind
me of Lot's wife who looked back at Sodom. She turns into a pillar of salt. We
need to put a line through it, forget it. That was my last day in Europe."

Another said: "For me the last day in Europe was the sum of all the last days
in Europe. I felt a strange doubleness, an indescribable sense of being torn in
two, like not being able to get away fast enough from a loved one. As if I was
kissing the dust that fell from my shoes . . . *Panic plus the pain of departure*,
that was the emotional situation of many travelers headed for America. For
weeks we had been swept along in the awful maelstrom of an entire continent
being evacuated and which emptied out into the port cities of southern
France. As if we were in an overfilled lifeboat that couldn't get away from the
sinking ship, or rather, from the sinking shore. Panic encourages more the use
of your elbows than your altruism. All of us were only one of many, but there

were too many of us in the same lifeboat, and almost every one was "booked up." The last Europeans, we were soldiers of flight; but were we always "good soldiers"?

"Every army has good and bad soldiers," one of the listeners observed.

"On the day of my departure for America," the other continued, "an unforgettable day of painful gaiety, I remembered an awful event that became linked with my last impression of Europe. In late summer a young man had arrived in Lisbon, one of the first, if not the first, to succeed in illegally crossing the Pyrenees from southern France into Spain. He was a loner, always quiet and shy. He'd worked out every detail of his plan, stubborn and alone in his room in Perpignan. He had studied the special maps of passes in the mountains, he'd gotten letters of introduction to the former Social Democratic mayors of the towns along the border, and, to make doubly sure, had had an experienced forger change the age listed in his passport from twenty-one to seventeen. This way the Spaniards wouldn't send him back because of his eligibility for military service. You couldn't have prepared yourself better than this young Austrian had. (We were such amateurs and improvisers, later.) With all the energy of his twenty-one years he threw himself over the burning Pyrenee wall, the first one to venture into uncertain territory. Three times he tried to cross at night, three times he got lost, went hungry and thirsty, slept outdoors on stones in the mountains, determined to die rather than let himself be locked up. A solitary wanderer, a boy in shorts, apparently calmly contemplating the landscape, in reality trying to contain the panting breath of a runner—this is how he walked into the Spanish border town. They let him continue walking, further and further, to his destination, to Lisbon, where he arrived overjoyed, breathless, sunburned, a bit wild. And this is when something incomprehensible occurred. For some trifling reason—perhaps the change of age in his passport—he got into an argument with the authorities and went into a rage. The police were called and as they brought him to the prison, he threw himself off the third-floor landing with the same stubborn and peculiar intensity as if the railing had been the Spanish border.

I can't explain why, in the moment when I was boarding the American ship, I suddenly found myself thinking of this European marathon runner who collapsed at the finish line. I felt only that there is a dangerous limit beyond which we cannot absorb such destructive experiences. I had to think of him and all those who hadn't been (or had not yet been) able to finish the long race out of Europe, who collapsed along the way; all those comrades of flight we left behind in their graves or in great need. In front of me stood one of the most beautiful historical settings in all of Europe, Baroque and Gothic monuments, but it was as if the ship were already sailing down the Tejo, as if they were disappearing like unreal ruins in the setting sun. In this light I had seen the towers of Prague, the gay, gracious Viennese landscape of a forgotten era, the Luxembourg Garden of a deserted Paris—my entire, abundant life in

Europe. Everything was magically present and everything disappeared like a ghost in this last European moment. It was too much. I stumbled, as if Europe were pulling me down—I too a marathon runner. Then I felt the hand of a woman next to me. "You have to pull yourself together," she said laughing. "When you get on board, you'll be on American soil." Her voice almost seemed festive. I climbed slowly up the steep gangway—it was more than a border—and although it was securely fastened, I felt it floating up and down beneath my feet. Up above, at the entrance to the ship, I turned around one last time. My eyes went black and I couldn't see anything. Neither the woman who remained below on the pier, tiny and helpless, nor the friends who had succumbed along the way, nor the beloved cities, that together was Europe and beloved. We left behind too much. And what was near, even before the ship was loosed from its moorings, was already so far away. I had the feeling that this last gaze was putting out the light of Europe. Truly, you can turn to stone if you look back.

With a broad smile a gray-haired, bespectacled steward asked the man sunk in his thoughts: "How do you do?" He was already in America.

You have to have been here a while and breathed the air of America. Then you can begin to feel the unforgettable moments of the last day in Europe coming back.

Josef Thon }

SEDER ON A REFUGEE SHIP

This letter appeared in the Aufbau *on 16 May 1941.*

My dear friend,

You're wrong to say we could celebrate Seder again next year on the deck of a refugee ship. There's little probability that refugee ships will still be able to sail, and it's absolutely out of the question that the emigrants who have spent this year's Seder on a refugee ship will ever again be able to board a ship in this capacity.

Yes, it was a deeply moving experience that we had on the deck of the oh-so-tiny steamer called *Guiné*. There we were, two hundred of us, pressed together from all the lands of the Earth: the man to my left had been released from a "work" camp in Germany ten days before; the woman to my left, a week earlier, had witnessed the rage of the new rulers in Paris. Across from us sat the eighty-five-year-old wanderer from Poland who for all of us came to represent the image of Ahasuerus during our fourteen-day voyage from Lisbon to America. With his deep, wise eyes he witnessed the murder of his brothers in Warsaw.

On this holy evening there were no more Eastern and Western Jews, no more German- and Yiddish-speaking refugees. Bent over the Hagadah which a friend of ours had saved from Antwerp and whose three-hundred-year-old, yellowed pages recounted the story of our wandering ancestors, we listened to the words of Scripture. In the middle of the ocean, thousands of miles from Europe, racing to the rescuing shores of the New World, we translated the ancient story. We too had been made into the slaves of a modern Pharaoh . . . we too had to work for him as slaves . . . we too had to leave everything, everything behind . . . this Pharaoh too will be vanquished . . . we too will once more know the "time of our freedom." And as a hundred tormented hearts sobbed out loud, as we looked inside ourselves, vowing not to forget those languishing in death, we saw the true image of the

New World: the Statue of Liberty, the symbol that the "time of our freedom" was approaching.

And for this reason, for this image, we will no longer celebrate Seder as refugees . . .

Yours,
Josef Thon

PART THREE

New Worlds

INTRODUCTION

Like virtually every immigrant group in America, the Germans who came to the United States as a result of National Socialism tended to cluster together for mutual support and the preservation of their identities in a foreign environment. The great majority arrived in the port of New York and, being used to city life, eventually settled in this most European of American cities, which they helped make even more European and cosmopolitan. They settled on the Upper West Side of Manhattan, in Washington Heights, Riverdale in the Bronx and in the Forest Hills section of Queens, infusing New York's intellectual and cultural life with new energy, talent, and enthusiasm. A small group of well-known writers, directors, actors, and musicians also settled in the Los Angeles area, forming a storied community of German exiles that included Thomas and Heinrich Mann, Marlene Dietrich and Peter Lorre, Otto Preminger, Arnold Schoenberg, Lion Feuchtwanger, Theodor Adorno, Franz Werfel, and many others, but which for this reason was atypical of the exile experience. Many exiles chose not to settle in either of these centers, moving to smaller cities or even small towns and rural environments where they could find work and assimilate more easily, or simply remain true to their former identities (see for instance the account by Carl Zuckmayer, a famous playwright who obtained a lucrative Hollywood contract but gave it up for the life of a farmer in the Vermont woods with his wife Alice Herdan). Refugee relief organizations, concerned about the reaction of professional groups to the sudden influx of highly skilled doctors, dentists, lawyers and businessmen, also urged the new arrivals to avoid the established exile centers. The Emergency Committee in Aid of Displaced Foreign Scholars helped place many refugee academics and their families in colleges throughout the nation.

As they did in the transit countries, the exiles who arrived early in the United States—before the heavy immigration of 1937–1940—had a comparatively easy time: not only because of a more hospitable environment, but also because they often had not experienced the most harrowing aspects of Hitler's persecution and arrived with less psychological trauma (see, for instance, the different tones of voice in the letters by Lessie Sachs and Hilde Walter). After several years, however, the differences between political exile and "racial" emigrant, so pronounced in a European context, tended to be effaced in America where both groups were similarly destitute, psychologically battered, and unknown in the eyes of Americans, who viewed them simply as German (or Jewish) refugees. Yet, as Hannah Arendt somewhat testily remarked, many of them were hardworking professionals who resented the term "refugee," preferred to call themselves "newcomers" or "immigrants," and accepted menial labor rather than handouts from relief organizations. In addition to losing their homes and fortunes, many also endured a devastating loss of professional and social status: licensed physicians worked as gardeners and housekeepers (Nathorff), high-level industrialists started businesses from scratch (Bernstein), talented creative writers became farmers (Zuckmayer and Herdan) or German teachers (Plant) or Hollywood underlings (Anders, Polgar, Brecht).

The transition to a new identity in America depended on many factors, especially age, personal flexibility, and one's command of English. Young people could enroll in public schools, learn the language, and assimilate quickly. Hannah Arendt, a student when she left Germany, became famous in this country; Peter Gay arrived as a high school student and rose to the pinnacle of academia. Yet the peculiar aspect of the German immigration— the high percentage of well-educated, successful professionals of middle- or advanced age—resulted in a highly differentiated situation for these older emigrants varying from successful if painful assimilation to a complete failure of integration. An interesting middle ground was occupied by scholars, scientists, artists, and writers who made their European outlook and training into the basis of their identity in America (see especially Arendt, Plant, Niederland, and Pachter). For writers who had had successful careers in Europe before emigration, the transition to English almost always proved impossible. Many of them, having never truly accepted American culture, returned to Europe (Thomas and Klaus Mann, Brecht, Ludwig Marcuse, Döblin, Zuckmayer) or stayed in America without reaching their European level of fame (Heinrich Mann, Feuchtwanger, Natonek, Sahl). Many died here, virtually unknown.

Soon after their arrival in America, "Hitler's exiles" would confront a new set of political and social issues: the division of Europe and the Cold War, McCarthyism, and—most closely related to their own situation—the arrival of Holocaust survivors who had been liberated from Nazi death camps (see the interview with William Niederland). Yet the interaction of the German exiles with postwar America is the subject of another book. The following selections focus instead on their first, immediate encounters with America: as "ordinary exiles" from Nazi Germany, not as the American citizens of European birth that so many of them were about to become.

CHAPTER ONE

Liberty . . . and Work in New York

THE SIGHT OF NEW YORK

Marta Appel arrives with her husband and children in New York in 1937.

I was awakened by the bright sunshine which came into our room. My body
still had the sensation left over from the slight rocking of the boat, so that it
was not until I had opened my eyes and had noticed the strange surroundings
that I remembered that we were in America.

After so many years of persecution in Germany, after so many months of
anxiety in Holland, it was the first day of real freedom for us. A marvelous
feeling of happiness and safety arose in my heart. Though America was still a
strange country, for the first time in years I felt at home once more.

The only shadow which darkened my thoughts was that now we had to
separate from our children. Our relatives had come to meet us on the boat and
the children would leave and have a home with them. Though I knew that in
this way my children would be spared the fate of the homeless, the thought of
being separated was hard and painful for all of us. "Children have become
letters," we used to say in Germany, and I had always pitied those poor parents
who lived from one letter to the other, letters which came from every corner of
the earth where their children had been scattered. At least this would be
spared us; we lived in the same country with them, and no censor would re-
strict our writing to meaningless words.

The four days which my relatives stayed in New York passed much too
quickly. With the startling impressions that enormous city made on us, we
hardly came to ourselves.

"Everything is larger, wider, more powerful and vivacious here," I thought
when we walked through the streets of Manhattan. London, Paris, Berlin,
each one had its special charm, but New York with its skyscrapers, with its
millions of lights when evening came, made an overwhelming impression on
us newcomers.

The children had gone. We had all been very brave. None of us had revealed how painful the moment of departure was. Now the real life would
begin, the first four days which had been spent with the girls and our relatives

lay like a dream behind us, but from now on it was reality which we had to face.

"Let us start right away," my husband suggested after the girls had left. "It is the best way to overcome any loneliness."

It was clear to us that without knowing the language we should always be strangers. As quickly as possible we wanted to become a part of the American people. This would be only a small sign of the thanks we felt—that we wished to learn to speak and to think with the people and for this country.

That very same evening, after the children had left us, we entered a night school in Brooklyn where we had rented a room not far from my brother's home.

It was on the second evening of our attendance in school that we were reminded again of all the fear we had endured in Nazi Germany. We had hardly entered the classroom when the teacher called my husband. Two men were waiting at the door, and with them my husband stepped out of the room.

"What does this mean?" I thought, and anxiously I watched the door, waiting for my husband's return. "After all, there are no Nazis here," I tried to calm myself, as time passed on and he did not come back.

It seemed to me an endless time before the door finally opened and I saw him again. But what was it? Five, six men were coming in with him. All were talking to him, and he seemed pale and disturbed. He was holding a letter in his hand, but he was not looking at it. His eyes were searching for me. I got up to meet him. "Will you read this letter?" he asked me. "I don't know what all these men want with me."

My English was too poor, and besides I was too excited to read. "Will they deport us?" I feared. What else could it be?

I could never explain how it happened that I thought of it, but on a sudden inspiration, I asked the men, "Are you reporters?" Eagerly they nodded their heads, and their smiling faces proved how glad they were that finally we had understood why they had come.

We laughed too when one of them said in very broken German, "No Nazis, only photographers to take your pictures for the newspapers."

While we were seated beside the principal and the teachers for our first snapshot in America, it slipped through my mind that such publicity would have been provided in Germany only for a king or someone very near to it.

"How much more must a humble person mean in this country," I said to my husband on our way home, "when reporters are interested in unknown people like us."

It was not only this little event which made me feel so. When in the next days we went to the different offices to apply for our first papers, we were treated so differently from the way we had been handled by German officials. Even in the times before Hitler a certain militaristic and haughty spirit made it unpleasant to deal with government officials. They always felt superior to civilians and seldom had they enough tact not to show it.

One of the most striking things for us was that no one asked us, "When will you leave again?" In Holland this had been the question which we had, without exception, to answer first. Instead we were asked in every office, by everyone we met in the street, "What can I do for you?"

"They don't want to get rid of us," we felt. They wished us to stay, to live with them. For years we had been considered as "unwanted people," as "wandering Jews." For the first time in years we were treated with equality, and the humiliating feeling of being considered inferior began to vanish.

It was shortly after our picture had been taken in the night school that we went to take our lunch in a small Chinese restaurant. We had been there several times before, and the waiter seemed to know us already. He smiled at us when we entered and as soon as we were seated he came and sat at our table and had a little talk with us.

"I saw your pictures in the papers," he began, and then he wanted to know how we liked America, and to hear about Hitler. However, our English was too poor for any conversation and with a rather disappointed look, he retreated.

"Can you imagine," my husband said as soon as he had gone, "a waiter in Germany or anywhere in Europe who would have dared to sit down for a conversation with a customer?"

"No," I admitted, "this would have been quite impossible as great as the class differences are in the old homeland." Quite often we were surprised by the frankness of the common people and their freedom from embarrassment—not even during the days of the young democracy in Germany had we experienced it. Yet it was also a constant source of pleasure to observe it.

I remember the day we had visited my cousin and she accompanied us to the subway. It was the station where she took her train every day. Daily she got her paper at the newsstand of that station and the man knew her well. That evening when she accompanied us, we bought a paper too, and on that occasion she introduced us to the man as refugees from Germany and told him that my husband was a minister and had a big temple. To our surprise the man came immediately from behind his stand, shook hands with us, and spoke to us without any feeling of servility. "Never," we told our cousin later, "would a simple man in Germany have dared to offer his hand first to a minister, and never would he have talked with this free feeling of equality."

That feeling of equality made it so easy to be at home in America, this was what made the country so dear to us. "To be poor in Europe," my husband often said to me, "is so much worse than being poor in America." Here in America it is the man and his deed which counts, in the old country it is the social background alone which makes you free.

Our stay in Brooklyn did not last long. We soon realized that the progress we made in a night school was far too slow for our wish to improve. Therefore we moved to Manhattan where we had the possibility of attending a day school. I think that no country in the world gives a newcomer such a marvelous chance to acquire its language as America. Every day from then on we went to school for six or eight hours. Our teachers were excellent. The proof that this beneficent work was fully appreciated by the immigrants, was that the classes were so crowded they had to be closed to further newcomers.

Instinctively we had done the right thing by going to school at once. It was not just because with the knowledge of English, our chance for the future grew so much better; we found that study was also the safest way to overcome the greatest danger of a refugee—the feeling of being a nuisance, of sitting around, killing time.

Soon we found that every restlessness, every dissatisfaction in refugee circles, grew out of the long waiting hours in the offices of the different committees. There the people stood waiting for endless hours, hoping for a job. Their only conversation was of the past. The disappointment which so many experienced when no job was available for them, when for weeks and months they had come to the office without any success, had resulted in a complete hopelessness for the future. The only way for them to escape the fright of the days to come was to live in the past. "Do you remember?" played the greatest part in their lives. An unknowing observer would have been astonished, had he listened to the conversation of these people who stood in long lines waiting for help. Their pale features were marked by sorrows and their eyes were dim from tears, while their lips spoke of Cannes and Nice, of all the famous places which they had once visited on the continent. And this unknowing observer would have wondered had he heard these poor people say, "You can take a room or a suite only in the Imperial; the Excelsior is not fashionable enough."

We had not loved our homeland less than all these people. Our hearts were just as sore as theirs, but we wanted to begin our new life without bitterness and resentment; we felt that we owed it to this country, which gave us shelter in our greatest need, to become Americans as soon as possible. Never was this possible as long as our thoughts were bound to the past. The stony way of a refugee is only rougher when it is paved with reminiscences of a better time.

Nonetheless, one of the hardest things to overcome was the loss of one's social position. As soon as we were settled in our little one-room apartment we went to visit the many people to whom we had recommendations from the most outstanding personalities in our homeland.

"Don't be too hopeful," my husband warned me when we were on the way to our first visit, "and don't forget what I have always told you, that we are 'nobodies' in a foreign land."

STARTING OVER

After serving two and a half years in prison, paying a $400,000 fine, and relinquishing control of his company, the shipping magnate Arnold Bernstein was released in July 1939 and arrived in New York on September 1, where he was met by his wife and two children. The next day he paid a visit to the office of his New York company whose assets had been seized by the Nazis; his former manager—a man named Eckert—had managed to salvage three thousand dollars and was still there.

The next morning I went to my old office, 17 Battery Place. My Red Star general agency had been taken over by Eckert, the Arnold Bernstein agency had been dropped, and Eckert and Company continued now working for the Holland-American Line as acting agents for the Red Star Line, because the Dutch wanted to make use of the close cooperation of the American car factories with my old organization. Eckert offered me a desk in my old office, where before I had been the boss. I began to look around to call on old friends. My first impression was not encouraging. Everybody was friendly, or rather polite, but nobody made any suggestions. For them I had been too much of a big shot in the past to offer me a small position which, of course, I would not have accepted. I went to Detroit, where in the past I had had many friends in the big factories—General Motors, Chrysler, Ford. They gave me a bang-up lunch; the press was also present and wrote a most flattering story about me. Everybody assured me of cooperation, but in reality everybody waited for me to make a suggestion as to how we could work together for our mutual benefit, as in the past. However, this past looked to me like a high mountain, where I used to be on top, while now I was at the bottom, looking up and wondering if I would ever be able to reach the top again.

I had only the three thousand dollars which Eckert had saved for me and I told Li that, if we did not spend more than three hundred dollars monthly we could live on that for ten months, and that I had to find something before this small fund was exhausted. During the first days, we did not even go out to eat. [My son] Ronny bought sandwiches in the drug store, which we ate in our hotel rooms. However, even the modest hotel was beyond our means. Ronny went back to college in Richmond. On East 68th Street, near Third Avenue, we found a small furnished apartment—two bedrooms, bath, sitting room and kitchen—where Li, [my daughter] Steffi, and I started our life in New York.

It was tough. The lack of capital was the greatest stumbling block. My experience told me that it was only a matter of time till prices for old tonnage would rise as a consequence of the war. Old vessels, like the so-called Hog-Islanders, eight thousand tons, were still offered for eighty to ninety thousand dollars. With a down payment of five thousand dollars one could buy such a vessel, the balance to be paid on delivery two or three months later. I knew I could borrow the five thousand dollars. However, and likewise on later occasions, I did not have the courage, because my only capital was my name and reputation, and any setback would have finished me for good. The effect of two and a half years in prison had, without doubt, also something to do with my hesitation. Three months later, these Hog-islanders were traded for between three and four hundred thousand dollars; in fact, vessels bought with a five-thousand-dollar down payment were sold with great profit before they were even delivered.

I was also not too lucky. I paid a visit to Isbrandsen, my competitor and opponent on many previous occasions. He asked me what my plans were. I told him that I intended to make use of my close relationship with the automobile export trade, and asked him if I could do something for him. He said I could. Isbrandsen was always an outsider and in permanent conflict with the regular lines. Now he lacked enough cargo for a sailing from New York to the Far East, and asked me if I could not influence some of the big car factories to grant him some cargo. Forty thousand cubic feet was what he needed. I rang up my old friend Krass, traffic manager of Chrysler. He happened to have a shipment ready for Bombay, but was at first reluctant because he had never before shipped with Isbrandsen. Finally he agreed to give me the forty thousand cubic feet. I told Isbrandsen that I could arrange it, but Chrysler paid commission to his regular shipping agent, and Isbrandsen, therefore, had to pay me a commission. The freight amounted to almost forty thousand dollars, and he agreed to pay me three thousand dollars (because it was a great advantage to him to get into business relations with Chrysler). One can imagine what this deal meant to me. However, ten days after delivery, the Chrysler employees went on strike, the shipping contract was cancelled, and that was that.

Just when I was trying to digest this setback another blow fell. Eckert came back from the office of the Holland-American Line. I saw that something was on his mind and when I asked him, he said, "Well, Mr. Bernstein, I am in an embarrassing situation. They asked me, 'Why does Bernstein hang around in your office?' Apparently, they are suspicious because they remember what a formidable competitor you were in the past." What he had in mind was quite obvious. I said, and I was sure he noticed the contempt for him, "Mr. Eckert, I don't have any intention of embarrassing you. Goodbye." I took my hat and left my old office. I went to the Bowling Green subway station sat down on one of the benches. I was furious and, at the same time, deeply depressed. [. . .]

What should I do? Now I had not even a desk, no place from which I could work, no money to rent even the smallest office. I had the feeling that all the big buildings around me were falling on top of me. All the great offices, all the wealth, everybody busy and I all alone without either business or money. While I sat there a man I knew, Walter DeLappe, a good freight agent, greeted me and sat down at my side. "How are you making out, Mr. Bernstein?" he asked me. "Well, nothing to brag about," I answered. He must have seen in my face that something depressed me. "I understand," he said, "that you are working with Eckert again." I knew that in the past he had been associated with Eckert, and when he pressed me with further questions, I finally told him what had just happened in Eckert's office. He swore. "This pig," he said, "Why do you think I separated from him? His stupidity is only surpassed by his selfishness—this is incredible, after you made him what he is now. Mr. Bernstein, will you do me the great honor of coming into my office? You will have your own room and secretary, and my whole staff will be at your service."

I looked at him. He was a good fellow and had a good reputation. What had I to lose? I was touched by his sympathy and eagerness to be of help. I thanked him and accepted. I stayed almost one year in his office, after which I had developed enough business to take my own office. Two years later I operated thirteen Liberty vessels, which I had chartered from the Maritime Commission. These ten-thousand-ton vessels carried coal and grain. I booked the cargo only through DeLappe, and he made more than a hundred and fifty thousand dollars in commissions. So I came into his office. I knew I had to build my own establishment, because I could not work forever as just Arnold Bernstein. I had no vessels, no regular service and therefore, chose the neutral name Arnold Bernstein Shipping Company, Incorporated, under which I worked until I was able to build up a regular line service again and changed my company's name to Arnold Bernstein Line Incorporated.

One month after I started in DeLappe's office, I had my first break. A Mr. Bernstein called on me. His office was in the same building, 17 Battery Place. He was a small broker—what his business was I never really found out. He told me he had two thousand tons cargo, to be shipped from Riga in the Baltic to New York. There was no regular service at that time from Riga to the United States. To ship the cargo to a bigger European port and reload there to a trans-Atlantic steamer was too expensive, and therefore he had to charter a small vessel. However, he had no connections with the shipping industry and would have to pay the whole charter in advance. Could I help him? I could.

On the strength of my name and reputation I could charter a small vessel without even making a deposit on it. I found such a vessel seeking return cargo from Riga to the United States. The only question was if this Mr. Bernstein was reliable and able to deliver the cargo because, if not, I was responsible for the charter money. I don't remember the details any more, only that he committed himself to paying me two thousand dollars commission and that the deal was consummated. Two thousand dollars commission was at this moment a fortune for me, representing six to seven months income for living expenses.

Arriving in New York

*After sending their son to England, Hertha Nathorff and her husband man-
age to emigrate from Germany in April 1939, spend a brief period in England where they are reunited with their child, and arrive together in New
York early in 1940.*

February 22, 1940

After exchanging greetings and embraces, which hardly improved my sense
of vertigo, after much deliberation about what to do with our luggage (we had
brought some gifts for friends from their children in England, which we gave
to them right away), we looked about, somewhat dejected, and then someone
asked: "So where are you planning to stay?" No one had thought of reserving
even a simple hotel room for us, no one had thought of our accommodations—probably for fear of being left with the bill! I couldn't believe my eyes.
I saw my husband grow pale, and he looked out at the ocean, at the ship by the
dock, to the horizon, thinking that we once had a homeland, a house, a place
of our own.

My friend Friedel whispered to me: "If I'd even dreamed that your relatives wouldn't take care of a room, I would have reserved one for you." My
cousin must have heard her. She had been like a sister to me, and during her
student years in Berlin our home and our heart were always open to her.
"*Well*," she said suddenly, "my husband won't be home this weekend, so you
and your boy can stay with me until then." In the meantime my husband's
childhood friend offered to put my husband up. We had to accept because we
didn't have the money for even a few nights in a hotel. This way we were
"safe" for at least two days and nights. After that, I thought to myself, I'll be
sure to find some job so that we can afford a furnished room. Thus our new
country divided us in the very first hours after our arrival—what a sad omen.
With great effort we shrugged off our disappointment. We'll soon be back
together, whispered my husband to me as we left each other. But I could read
in his eyes the sadness of his heart, just as he sensed my sorrow. I remained
silent and mechanically let everything wash over me, but I know that my

heart, once so quick to forgive and forget, will always start bleeding again when I hear the question: "So where are you planning to stay?"

February 25, 1940

The two days and nights with my cousin were dreary and full of torment. For the first time in my life I have felt what it means to be "tolerated." My food remained stuck in my throat, because my stomach was deprived of food and drink during our famished period in England and then on the boat. Now I have to learn how to eat again.

Thanks to an acquaintance we happened to run into, we have found accommodations in a "Shelter for the Homeless." A rabbi, Stephen Wise, originally from Europe, has opened a house for destitute immigrants.* The Congress House on 68th Street, near Central Park, will be our home for the next three to four weeks—for you can stay that long until you have found work and lodgings. We sleep in narrow dormitories, men and women separated, we take our meals in the canteen at small, nicely set tables, we frequent people from our own cultural circle. So many of our acquaintances are here, even an aunt with her daughter and son-in-law. Why didn't anyone think of sending us here right from the start? We would have been spared so much humiliation.

Today we took our first Sunday walk in New York, here in the nearby Central Park. How beautiful the park is: snow is everywhere, and it falls like powdered silver from the trees with their gleaming, icy pinecones. It is bitter cold and the people we meet have red, friendly, laughing faces. Joyful, laughing people—how long have we not seen such a sight! Like children in a fairytale, we march through the snow-covered ballroom with its column-like trees, searching for our way and using the skyscrapers to point us in the right direction. How fascinating this city is, how immense, how beautiful.

Will the city give us work and food? Early tomorrow morning I will start looking. I want to earn a new homeland for myself.

February 27, 1940

The hoop-jumping has begun again, by which I mean the trips I have to make to various organizations in order to get advice and assistance for our new life and, above all, to find work. For that is one thing I am sure of: I don't want to live off "charity"—I don't, my husband doesn't, not even my child. We stand in a long line, waiting until we finally can talk to someone and make our plight clear. Clear? But how? I myself, who studied in a high school where

---

* Rabbi Stephen S. Wise (1874–1949), born in Budapest, emigrated to New York in 1882 where he founded the Free Synagogue. His wife, Louise Wise, directed the Congress House, where more than 4,000 European refugees were welcomed.

ancient languages were taught, never learned English. And how far does my husband's knowledge of the language go? We'll find out. These counselors are partly true-born Americans who speak only English, partly emigrants who arrived a few years earlier than us, encountered fewer difficulties, and act as if they don't understand a word of German. Our situation is desperate. Our sponsor died shortly before our arrival. His will, no doubt very complicated, will take years to be settled. Much was left unclear. From the beginning his heirs, clearly interested in receiving their father's fortune—worth millions—while honoring his obligations, have been trying to keep the latter as small as possible and, understandably enough, to incur no new ones.

On top of that, in a personal meeting with him in Germany years ago, I once said I would never be a burden to him. At that time I still believed that, if we indeed had to emigrate, I would be able to bring a major portion of our savings and our belongings with us. How wrong I was. We arrived completely destitute. And the hope that we would at least get the container with all our belongings out of hock—furniture, household items, dishes, linen, clothing, pictures, carpets, precious collections of porcelain and glass, and last but not least two complete sets of medical tools—now appears illusory despite all my efforts to obtain a loan for the seventy-two dollars we still owe.

When I finally made this clear to the social worker, she said to me: "Furniture, housewares—what's the point? You're too attached to your fancy lifestyle and elegant apartment in Germany! You don't need them here. You want to be a doctor again? Get that crazy idea out of your head. We have enough doctors here, we don't want any more, and especially not any lady doctors. Your husband and you should take a job as domestic housekeepers. That way you'll have a roof over your heads, some food in your stomachs, and on top of it you'll have a salary and can start saving."

So this is the kind of assistance we could expect. Dumbfounded, I remained silent in the face of so little understanding and sympathy. Then I said, stuttering: "Fine, we'll take a job in someone's home as housekeepers. But only I will work, I can work enough for two; my husband has to study so he can get his doctor's license. Who knows, despite all the doctors you have here, maybe one day you'll be pleased to have me as a doctor as well."

I asked her to give me the name of an appropriate family, and tomorrow I'll start working.

March 7, 1940

I haven't written in my diary for a while, but have been gathering new "experiences." The other emigrant women and I all agree on one thing: if we had ever treated our servants in this way, they never would have been so faithful to us for years and even decades. I sometimes smile at the thought of what my dear servant Minna would say if she could see me now. How often she pushed me out of the kitchen saying, "This is no kind of work for you," whenever I tried to lend a hand. Today, no job is too heavy or too dirty for me. People often call me "dirty refugee," words I understand perfectly well. I work, I work for the modest daily bread we need. What pains me most is to have to stay away from home, even overnight, when in addition to the normal housework I have to take care of an old, sick woman, who calls me a dozen times a night, often just to bother me because she can't fall asleep.

Today I applied for a new position. When the "lady of the house" saw me, she could only utter the words "lousy Nazi spy" and slammed the door in my face. What should I answer when confronted with such small-minded prejudice?

March 11, 1940

Today I'm at home again. The baby I was taking care of, in addition to watching over four other children and doing all the housework, doesn't need me anymore. I start my next job the day after tomorrow. How wonderful it is to be free again, to be able to rest, although it won't be much of a rest. Our room needs sweeping, the laundry has to be done, I also have to shop and sew—and I'd also like to study some English in my spare time!

My son goes to school far away from here. He earns his bus fare and whatever else he needs by delivering packages after school. The poor boy—he's so quiet now, and recently he came home blue from the cold.

Silently, doggedly, my husband studies for the English exam he must pass in order to be admitted to the medical board exam. He works without ever letting a complaint cross his lips. But his eyes look serious and sad, and the lovely sparkle that greets me when I come home disappears quickly.

Our home: a miserable room I rented because I mistook the fire escape with the burglar bars for a balcony. One bed for the two of us, as narrow as the one in Berlin that each of us had, so roomy and comfortable. Our son sleeps on a small cot in a windowless alcove. The so-called kitchen is, as is typical here, a small room which they call a kitchenette. The bathroom, no matter how bad it looks, is ours alone. And when we close the door, this is our home, not a furnished room in someone else's apartment where we would constantly be with other people.

We only have two chairs, and they wobble, but I don't care. I'm hardly ever "at home," and so father and son can at least both sit at the small table for the "sumptuous" meals they prepare for themselves. With a few throw rugs from our suitcase I've tried to give the room a homey look. It's not much help. The smell of poverty which greets you as you climb the narrow stairwell fills the entire house. We don't have visitors—who could climb such stairs, who would visit such poor relatives or colleagues? Oh, I'm so ashamed, not for myself but for the others who let us live in such circumstances and won't loan us the few dollars it would take to rent a decent apartment. This room costs us eight dollars a week, which is much more than it's worth. (Why shouldn't the people here also profit from the misfortune of others?) But I earn only ten to fifteen dollars a week, from which I must pay for transportation, small shoe repairs, etc. Only then can we think of food and drink—on average we have one dollar per day to spend. Nowadays I often say "I've already eaten at work," and skip a meal. One can still train one's stomach.

April 2, 1940

From one job to the next. How hectic life is in this country. There's not even enough time to admire all the beautiful things in this fascinating city. The technology, the tall buildings, the bridges, tunnels, subway—I'm constantly amazed, but where is the time to take it all in? To go to a museum or, a special treat, to a movie or a concert—who has the time and the money?

My husband is more taciturn than ever. I sense how humiliated he feels because he has to live off my salary. I console him, saying he will soon be back in his old profession and then I'll have an easy life and will always be able to stay with him and our son, and can even study as well. What would he say if he knew that I secretly take his notes and attempt to study during the night when I can't fall asleep?

Today I received the first letter from my parents. They try to appear confident, to calm our worries about them in the old country, to encourage us not to give up. Dear, good parents, if only you knew . . . I'm going back to work. This time night duty—and I cry bitter, bitter tears. My husband mustn't see my tears. He is so peculiar, and I sense a glass wall between us—no, no, that mustn't be.

April 6, 1940

My mother has passed away. The news hits me hard. My poor father, now he's all alone. My son tries to console me, and asks me not to go to work today. How could I? We'd have less to eat then, and mother wouldn't have approved of that. She was a woman who lived only for others and put her own life last. I intend to be a daughter worthy of her dear mother. I'll go to work and bear my pain alone—even my husband can't understand me anymore. Where are we heading to?

May 10, 1940

The days pass in a constant flurry of work. How demeaning it is. Not the work in itself—I don't mind what I have to do to meet our modest living expenses. But the way one is treated. Impudent men who dare to put their arm around you—I can put up with them. But these women who want to be "ladies"—they are saucy, inconsiderate, with no sense of tact. Many of them look at you as if you were an animal or less than that—who knows?—and they have no understanding of our fate. How could they? What is happening over there—war, murder, immorality—is so far away, but I fear that even this "far away" will someday be quite close. I myself have no more confidence, no hope that things will ever be different. Hitler has now invaded Holland. I had predicted this and people laughed at me for such crazy ideas. All my hope is gone now. I pleaded with them, "Help us before it's too late, save my profession which means my life to me." Now they want to loan us the pitiful sum we needed to get our belongings sent over from Holland. Now, when it's too late. Everything is lost, I can tell, I'll never become a doctor again, and yet I want to fight for it even though I'm again without a job for the moment. I think I take care of people too well and work too hard; then they don't need me anymore. Besides, the people I'm sent to are not well off; otherwise they wouldn't ask for help from an immigrant organization, help that is cheap and hardworking, people they can count on. [. . .]

June 5, 1940

My husband has passed his language exam. I'm happy, but nonetheless, I can't keep up with him the way I used to. I have to go to work while he's been preparing for the exam with his colleagues.

It's my birthday today. My husband and son have tried to make me happy with a few small presents. I put on a good face—love can also sometimes pretend. We get little mail from Germany. I'm exhausted from worrying about our relatives and friends, as well as about our own lives. Day and night I think about what's going on over there, and here at night when the trolley rattles through the street I wake up from a half-sleep and think about the bombings we lived through in England. What's happening to the people over there? Are they still alive?

Our social circle here is composed almost entirely of immigrants, almost all of them people we knew earlier and who represent a piece of our homeland as we do to them. Many of us are of "mixed" marriage, as the nice Nazi term would have it—German women who emigrated with their Jewish husbands and who now, like me, support their husbands, work for them until they can get back into their profession or find another job. It takes a long time, very long. And the German husbands with their Jewish wives—they emigrated with and for their wives rather than divorce them and stay in Germany to serve their country. We remain faithful friends and try to give each other support. But the uncried tears can be heard in our voices when we speak about the old country.

I myself have just had some luck. I start tomorrow as a night nurse in a hospital. How will this job turn out? In any case, how thankful I am to my old and famous professor, who, as long as I was his assistant, had me do so many jobs that were not, strictly speaking, a doctor's business. "A woman must do everything," he said—he who actually was opposed to women doctors. And now this woman really does everything she is asked to.

My husband shakes his head and remains silent. Does he sense all my heart's sufferings, does he realize that wherever I go, men are courting me? In vain, because my heart belongs to him, even when it is sad and discouraged.

June 14, 1940

"Bronx Express"—that was the name of a play that was all the rage in Berlin. Only now do I know what the Bronx Express really is, because I take it everyday to work. The train whizzes from Manhattan to the Bronx. I commute evenings with a Swiss woman who is actually an actress; for the time being we are both night nurses in a hospital. It's hard work, and I don't have an easy time of it because I do lots of things that the others refuse to do. "You make it harder for us when you run to the patients at the first ring of the bell," one of the nurses tells me. Someone else yells at me because I rub down the patients on hot summer nights with a mixture of alcohol and water. And a doctor put me in my place for having dared to call him because of a child with appendicitis.

"How dare you make a diagnosis? I'm in charge of diagnoses," he hissed at me.

I stuttered a bit, then said: "I promise not to do it again, but the child doesn't have pneumonia as the charts say, it's a typical case of appendicitis."

"Get the kid ready for an operation and bring him into the operating room."

Of course I rushed to get the child to the operating room and wanted to go in and watch the operation. Again he put me in my place:

"Go back to your station. You'll be called when the operation is over and you can bring the child back. An operating room isn't for you. You wouldn't be able to stand it."

He's probably right—I wouldn't be able to stand it to have to watch someone else operate. I run away, my tears start flowing; just get away from here, don't think, do your job without thinking. How long has it been that I stood at the operating table myself? Just don't think about it. What's more, there's a doctor who shows up every night no matter where I am, and today he started a conversation. He's looking for a nurse for his office—would I be interested?

"Can I ask my husband what he thinks?"

I laugh, laugh up there on the roof garden where the night staff is allowed to go and rest during breaks. How beautiful these nights are, and the view from the tall building onto the shimmering lights of the city—it's almost a fairy tale. But down there, a few stories below, is work, sickness, suffering and pain. Here too.

[Hertha Nathorff takes several other jobs, including one with her child in a summer camp in the Catskills while her husband remains in New York.]

December 20, 1940

My husband has passed his [medical] exam—the whole thing, on the very first try. No one can believe it, and I myself have trouble grasping it. The exam is over, he's a doctor again, soon he'll have a praxis. I start dreaming, perhaps one day I too . . . No, I can't even write it down. I know only that now I will work even harder to earn some money, for we have nothing in our apartment, nothing with which to set up a new life. But we're going to make it, and there are only four more days until Christmas. I'll have the day off, my employers promised me they would get a replacement, how nice. I can't speak or write, I can only fold my hands in silence, happy that fate has proved so merciful to us after all.

December 25, 1940

Christmas. Yesterday evening a German-American acquaintance, one of the few we've made over here until now, brought us a wreath with lights. And so a light shines on us again after all the dark days. We sat quietly and peacefully at home, all three of us on the narrow bed, pressed close together as we tried to sing the old Christmas carols. Our thoughts strayed far and wide, back to our homeland. The unfortunate people we love and worry about, where might they be now? Are they too thinking about us? Yes, I can feel it, for there is a faithfulness which knows no dividing barriers or walls or oceans.

Christmas, peace on earth—where?

None of us wants to speak about our life back there. We know how much it would hurt, and today is Christmas, a holiday. We took a walk through Central Park. It is glorious in its winter splendor, and all the happy, laughing people on our way made my heart lighter. Perhaps one day we too will stroll through Central Park happy and laughing, sit quietly on a bench late in the evening and enjoy the sea of lights, the blinking lights of the skyscrapers all around us, and our hearts won't cringe in pain as they did today.

Hilde Walter }

Everything Is Always Different

Born in 1895 in Berlin, Hilde Walter went to France after Hitler came to power, and then emigrated to the United States. The following letter to a girlfriend in Europe was written 5 months after her arrival in New York.

New York, March 3, 1941

Everything is always different from the way we imagine it. Apparently you don't know that we were all imprisoned in Paris last May. On May 14 all the men who had been released after endless interrogations following the first internment in September were arrested a second time; on May 15 they arrested all women without small children. Public announcements on May 13. That's how we lost everything, because we could take only thirty kilos of possessions with us to the camp. The women were taken to the bicycle race-track in Paris for eight days: 200 meters from the Eiffel tower (heavy artillery close by). Three thousand women under a glass roof, on sacks of straw, with huge haystacks piled up in the middle of the arena. After two nights in this set-up with constant air-raid alarms, even the French thought it was too dangerous for us and took us to Gurs. In the end we were spared the dangerous and horrible flight from Paris in June. But we were so cut off from everything that we complained about the isolation more than about the hunger and the dirt.

The French planned to liberate the wives of men who had been mobilized three days before the cease-fire. Because we didn't want to hang around for the Nazi *Gauleiter*, we organized a special escape for the women who didn't want to fall into German hands and who had no soldier-husbands to show for themselves. Although I had an American visa in my pocket, I almost got locked up again for this in Marseille—*pour examiner ma situation*, to investigate my case. Those who went into a camp at that time are still stuck there. I fled to a hospital until I got up my nerve to go to Perpignan without a residence permit or the necessary travel papers. Because of difficulties at the border, it was weeks before I could get into Spain on foot. On the last day in Cerbères (that's the border town), eight officers of the German *Reichswehr*

[223]

with thirty soldiers arrived. On unoccupied territory! They rode up and down the street that we planned to take the following morning for our escape. When I left, they weren't actually at the border. But you could never know for sure ahead of time.

The worst time was between Gurs and the telegram from New York, telling us that our visas were waiting in Marseille. One month spent hiding in a village in the Pyrenees, because the governor in Pau had said that all emigrants were to be turned over to the Germans. During the cease-fire there was no way to find out what they had actually decided to do with us. At any rate, nobody got permission to leave without approval from Vichy, meaning from Wiesbaden.

I know, I should have answered your nice postcard last winter, but I did nothing that wasn't absolutely necessary. The house without heat, the terrible camps where the men were living, our general bitterness—it was an awful winter. And yet, now that it's over I wouldn't want to have missed this year's experiences. Well, I could have done without specific events. I just mean the sense of having been part of it. The year did, however, take its toll on my health. The doctors are constantly examining me: gallbladder, stomach, appendix, it's not clear yet what's wrong. I haven't gotten any prettier through it all either. The climate is hard to take; everyone who has been here a while looks very old. We are all going through a rough time. Unbelievably rough. The ones who are earning some money and have connections like O.N. get torn to pieces by all the demands for help. He has his parents here, his brothers and sisters arrived very late, and demands for help pour in from the four corners of the globe. Every one of us, having arrived without any belongings but considerable debts, has left behind six intimate friends who need to be saved. We are all trying to get them out, and that's how we spend our time. Whatever is to become of us *à la longue* is a very difficult question. Even those who are already settled don't have a firm position. I'm not optimistic . . .

As you can see, it's all very different. Carry on as we did in 1921? That would be possible here if we didn't have any worries. New York City is similar to Berlin in many ways, not least because there are so many people here whom we haven't seen since the old days in Germany. But our peace of mind is gone. Nobody has time. Really no time, not just the "gotta run" kind, as Tucholsky called it. Maybe we could understand and love this country if we weren't still attached back to Germany with a thousand strings. But that's how it was in Paris as well. There too I was always living and acting "backwards." We carry the worries of those we left behind from one country to the next, and so we remain strangers twice over. Once upon a time that kind of life had meaning.

Today it is nothing but a human obligation.

Of course funny things happen too. For example, a regular tea party of ladies who were saved has been nicknamed the "Club of Formerly Young Girls from Gurs." By the way, that pretty much sums things up: the French camps and the flight and all the waiting in the Pyrenees and in Lisbon have created the closest of personal bonds, which are very different from the old ones waiting for us here. We have, so to speak, two large families: the old one from back home, partly our true family, and the new one created in the past seven years. The first one works, labors, provides for its kin. The second one can't earn anything yet, lives off the Emergency Rescue Committee or friends, usually a combination of both, and is still looking. As a result competition runs rampant within this second "family," unless the friendships are very strong. Insofar as they are writers and journalists, they all have the same material, of course. From time to time, O.N. inquires after the various friends who arrived with me. What is so and so doing? And so and so? He's inevitably surprised when I say that I can't ask them that; I don't tell them and they don't tell me either. When it comes to anything other than work, people are really wonderfully good to each other. There is a lively exchange of hand-me-down dresses and coats. Everyone calls up everyone else and passes it on if the size doesn't fit.

In good times I would have wished for what I saw of the world in bad times. For seven years I longed for the Riviera and wasn't able to get there. Not to speak of the Pyrenees. And Spain and Lisbon. At least the time in Lisbon was free of the worst pressure. Despite the festering wound on my foot and a swollen arm from the hike and the rides at night. Spain is a nightmare. And before that the little details: in the camp where [Konrad] Heiden and [Norbert] Muehlen were interned, writing was forbidden before the Nazis got there. All the camps for the men were located in combat regions. Toward the end of July, I had news from [Hermann] Kesten in New York that the two of them had made it as far as Toulouse (Kesten's wife was with me in the village in the Pyrenees). Before that, nobody knew if the Nazis had caught them. And then our dangerous trips from the villages to Marseille, which could have gotten us all locked up again. And then an American consulate in a glorious Mediterranean landscape. And the real miracle of guest visas for people without a fixed domicile, without passports, comprising an army of unofficially demobilized worker-soldiers. And the two Americans with real dollars for the trip to Lisbon, after the Jewish organizations in France hadn't been allowed to give us a penny. And the rendezvous in the cafés, complete with the obligatory jumping up and running away as soon as a cop appeared because nobody had a residence permit. As I said, I was living in a hospital. Muehlen was staying in dingy sleeping quarters where he had to leave with all his things every morning and could only return at night, because the place had daytime "clients." Heiden was staying on the bathroom floor of some Polish friends. Now remember, these are a few dozen writers who have all experienced the same thing. Just to be safe, [Franz] Werfel stayed in the hotel where the Nazi search commission was located. [Walter] Mehring was locked up everywhere he went, now including Miami. And our ship. (We didn't all get away at the same time.) Mine—the last voyage of the Nea Hellas—arrived on October 13 with Werfel, Heinrich and Golo Mann, the Polgars, the Stampfers, Walter Victor and Maria Gleit, and 150 other rascals. To a very elaborate reception. All the poets, publishers, cultural and political associations you can imagine—it was moving. In Lisbon we all mourned for [Rudolf] Olden.* It really got to us. Especially because we had just made it to safety.

This is my first long chat letter. I know you like it, and I was very touched by yours. I'm glad you went to the country. You are all in my thoughts. I think of Europe too much, and much too little about where I am. I don't consider my five earlier lives as successful as you say. They were colorful. I hope the last one won't be gray; so far it very much looks like it will be.

Farewell, love to Heinz, write again.

---

* After being declared an enemy alien in England, Rudolf Olden received a visa for the United States but died when the refugee children's transport ship he was traveling on was torpedoed by the Germans (September 17, 1940).

Chapter Two

"The Privilege of Being Safe and Far Away"

Lessie Sachs }

ADVICE FROM THE MIDWEST

A poet and essayist, Lessie Sachs left Germany with her husband—a pia-
nist from Breslau named Josef Wagner—and her child in 1937. Many of
her articles appeared in Germany or in the Aufbau *in New York. The*
following light-hearted piece appeared in a Jewish newspaper in Berlin and
in the Aufbau *in the March 1, 1938, less than two weeks before the An-*
schluss *of Austria.*

St. Louis, early January 1938

My dear ladies and friends in Germany! If you plan on emigrating, don't
accept too much advice. For no matter how much you prepare for your new
lives, you'll get it wrong. I spent so much time worrying about the problem
"With or without furniture?"—and in the end we sold everything off. When
we arrived in New York that decision struck me as correct. Small, elegant
apartments and my huge pieces of furniture? Oh well, it's a good thing they're
gone. But when we came to our final destination, St. Louis (Midwest) . . .
Oh well, in St. Louis you can rent spacious quarters, bungalows and apartments, for quite affordable prices, all of them equipped with luxurious bath-
rooms and kitchens unknown in Germany. Yes, with very gracious,
harmonious, large rooms. And now where is my furniture? It's in Europe, in
the hands of brokers, or other people, or who knows where. In any case it's not
here where I want it.

Moral of the story: if you know in advance where you will settle, ask the
people there for information, no one else.

And now for those of you who are beautiful, attractive, and charming—
well then, for all of you—I'd like to discuss the clothing question. (Oh dear, in
hearing that you've probably gotten your hearts set on an evening dress.) Well,
in New York you can wear one, but in the smaller towns you won't need a long
formal dress. Sorry. And as a general rule, my charming and plucky friends:
don't ruin your finances for clothes. Attention, red warning signal, stop! The
American woman is so completely, so totally different in her way of dressing
that, in every case, you, in your European clothing, and no matter how cre-

atively you may have dressed beforehand, will wind up seeming European, that is, different from the American norm. Unfortunately. It has to do with something ephemeral, a je ne sais quoi. I suspect our hats, those jaunty little contraptions, of sitting somewhere on American heads where we're not used to seeing them. You also have to beware of the climate and temperature. The European woman is always dressed too warmly or not warmly enough. Acclimating oneself in general is a very strenuous business over here, in every sense of the term.

For a moment be serious and stop thinking about your *make up*.* Instead— and now I'm addressing the industrious and hardworking among you— listen to me and learn the language of the country you will emigrate to. Learn the language, and when you think you speak it perfectly—start over again. You're not perfect. Sorry. But you're not perfect. The foreigners who arrive here feel as if they are deaf and dumb. And oh yes, just try to use your new language on the telephone . . . Truly, social connections are of the greatest importance in America, and to cultivate these connections you have to be able to carry on a conversation. Can you do that? I can't. I stand around like a bump on a log, stuttering. I make a fool of myself. You have to know the language! And those of you who are honest and careful with your money and want to keep house and do the shopping: Do you know the words for, let's say, allspice, root vegetables, margarine? Or, say, Ajax, spot remover, Valerian? (With the mention of Valerian it occurs to me that the medicine chest you take with you should be as fully equipped as possible.) To be honest, at first you won't even recognize the stores. You run into a "drugstore" and that turns out not to be a pharmacy. And you can't ask the way to a pharmacy because you won't understand the answer. Oh, and if you happen to have a headache . . . Gradually, however, my dear housewives, you'll see that keeping house is only half as difficult as it is at home. Indeed. Here the trash cans are close by, the sink is next to the pantry, you will always, always, have an abundant supply of hot water, all the furniture is easy to move, and whatever is heavy has wheels attached to it. As for grocery shopping, here everything— from coffee to calf's liver—can be bought in one and the same grocery store, which naturally saves you an enormous amount of time. You rent furnished apartments with a *kitchenette*, that is, with some kind of stove in the corner, and you'll find everything you need, from washrags to window cleaner.

So far so good. But stay with me for just another minute, and pay close attention. At first, every trip to the store, every walk outdoors, every visit, every conversation, every encounter, every drive out of town will require an inhuman effort. Everything, and I mean everything, from the door handle to the traffic rules, is completely different from what we are used to in Europe.

---

*   Words in italics indicate the use of English terms in the original German text.

You will be prisoner to a maelstrom of impressions, and the pendulum of your emotions will swing to extremes—from feeling the greatest discomfort to being totally fascinated by something. But it's hard to keep your balance. And if on top of it you happen to be in St. Louis, that is, the Midwest, you'll find that people are incredibly willing to help out. The American in these parts takes it as a point of honor to welcome every newcomer. *Newcomer*—voilà! He has to be fitted in. Does he have proper lodgings? Does his little girl have enough dresses and booties? Does he have contacts? Which ones? Are they the right ones? The Americans telephone on your behalf . . . What are his plans? What kind of job should he be given? Which strings need to be pulled? He should watch out for colds. Does he still have money? Is St. Louis the right place? They will talk it over. If not, someone will write to his friends in New York or in Hollywood or wherever . . . *"A newcomer!"* says the American in the Midwest, stretching his arms out wide: *"Oh, come on!"* And in most cases they succeed in taking care of the *newcomer*. Now listen, you tell this to the serious heads of households, your husbands: If you don't have compelling professional reasons to be in New York, go somewhere else. America is enormous, it's a large part of the world, it's a blooming country and there's room . . . everywhere. Just don't stay in New York. And tell it to your friends.

The American in the West is punctual, reliable, adventurous, polite and cheerful. America! Toward evening the sky grows dark, and I ask myself when have I ever seen it looking so fateful? A strip of canary yellow at the horizon, aggressive, loud. Is something wrong? Oh dear, we have a different climate here, different weather conditions, a different sky, we're on a foreign continent, have you forgotten that? Nothing is wrong. We're in America . . .

Every Friday in America I go to temple and enjoy a beautiful, exhilarating, short hour of worship. It's true. It goes approximately like this. The liturgy is short but very solemn, full of sincere religious feeling. Here, however, the rabbi, who in Germany usually gives a sermon, to our great surprise doesn't give a sermon at all. He announces a topic for discussion, he talks about a book, an article, a current affair. And because our Rabbi Gordon is a man of integrity who thinks things through to the end, and who speaks with a very earnest and impressive voice, this service results in an hour of true spiritual and emotional edification. And the synagogue is always full.

America—St. Louis, Missouri. In St. Louis I happened to visit a school for deaf children, which is the admirable work of Dr. Max Goldstein. It's wonderful. Hygienic, airy, cheerful, equipped with the most beautiful toys, built according to the best methods, run by a distinguished staff that is patient, gentle, and cheerful. America is generous, very generous. I saw a private nursery school and noticed the same qualities, the same cheerful, gentle atmosphere. And yet in St. Louis I didn't see a single public playground, not one sandbox, not a single bench or path for walking—Americans don't take walks. I saw the Mississippi late in the evening, *downtown*—sinister, dirty, down and out, lonely, so godforsaken it would move a stone to pity. I saw Chinese children who spoke no English, Italians who were selling fruit, Americans who spoke German. What's that dialect now? Oh yes, his father was from Stuttgart. America! The *melting pot*.

The streetcars and city buses race past you. You don't know where to catch them or where to get off, how you should cross the street, how you should walk, stand or behave. On top of that a thick wave of heat and smog hangs over the city, we're in the middle of January and it should be winter. Have you gone crazy? The seasons are topsy-turvy and so are the clocks. As I write these lines you have long since gone to bed, my dear girlfriends in Germany, for in St. Louis we are seven hours ahead of you or . . . or behind. I don't know, I don't know anything anymore, I'm a newcomer, and everything that I was in Europe, everything I was worth or knew, doesn't count here. It doesn't count!

Start at the beginning, at the very beginning, start your life over again from the very beginning. Is that easy? There's no turning back. Between you and our homeland lies the Atlantic, day and night and night and day you must sail across the ocean, and you'll see nothing but sky and water, day and night. And then New York jumps out at you, fiery, shimmering, throwing sparks, a resounding colossus, a magnificent city, a majestic city, full of magic . . .

Start your life over, here you count for nothing. Do you dare to take the leap? *"Take it easy,"* say the Americans. "Oh yes, . . . take it easy."

Sibylle Ortmann }

"So Utterly Connected"

At her own request, Sibylle Ortmann (1918–1976) was sent from Berlin to England by her mother in 1933 at the age of fifteen. After a return to Germany in 1934–36, she went back to England and then emigrated to the United States in September 1937. After attending night school in New York for one semester, she entered Radcliffe in September 1939 and graduated summa cum laude at the head of her class. The following letters, written in English, are mainly addressed to her future husband Milton Crane, an American, and to Mary Rubinstein, an English woman who took Sibylle into her home in England in 1933.

To Milton Crane
Saturday night, October 29, 1938

. . . I am so glad I did not go to the party. Not only that I need a clear head this weekend and cannot afford to get drunk, but somehow the idea of parties and their artificial merriment is revolting to me today. Have you read those awful reports from Germany and what they are doing to the Polish Jews?* And to think that [Fritz] Lechner's [Ortmann's stepfather] father (seventy-six years old) and any number of our friends may be amongst them. All that is worse than murdering and killing.

. . . It's another anniversary today, you might call it an anti-climax to the one we celebrated on Sept. 9. It's five years today since that terribly grown-up kid that bore my name waved and wept goodbye to her crying mother on Bahnhof Charlottenburg. Don't you think that those $20 I had with me have carried me quite far? Of course, it was far more necessity and adventurous spirit than that "courage" that people have attributed it to. One thing is sure, it was probably the most decisive event in my life. . . .

To Milton Crane
Monday - 6 p.m. October 31, 1938

. . . Have you read the reports about the Polish Jews? One *can't* simply close one's eyes and look elsewhere.

---

* On October 26 – 28, Polish Jews living in Germany were expelled to the Polish border, where they were denied entry by Poland.

[233]

To Milton Crane
Thursday, November 3, 1938

. . . I have not "reproached" you at all, but if you want to call it that, I have
not done it for having neglected an ideological necessity of "talking politics"
for the sake of humanity. But you can't persuade me that those things that
occupy my mind really touch you in any way as personally as they do me,
which is natural. It's such an old experience that hearing of an accident will
stir you a million times more if you know the people involved, even if only
slightly, than if they mean nothing but names and figures to you. Just as you
say that, knowing you, you regard the goings-on in Europe as more than "a
deplorable thing," isn't it natural that to me they must mean a whole lot more
even than that? If seen logically, politically, from a high perspective, those few
1000 Jews, those hundreds of children that have been carried straight from
their schools in Germany and dropped somewhere in Poland, mean little
compared with China, compared with the tragedy of Hitlerism altogether.
And still, you have gradually grown accustomed to these horrors. Self-
preservation! But to think of those many individual tragedies that might have
included anyone of people I know (for instance, Lechner's parents), and to feel
that you yourself are safe and guarded—*should* make one happy—it makes
me ashamed and guilty and desperate at not being able to do anything about it.
There is far more to it. But I don't seem to be able to find any of the right words
for it. I will *tell* you one day. In the past week Heinrich [Löwenfeld] has had
about five letters from people who—beyond the point of despair—write
cold-bloodedly that they are going to kill themselves (not because they are
tired of living but because they simply have no alternative). And do you really
think one can go on enjoying things and feeling no remorse? You can try to
and succeed in putting disasters which you can't help out of your mind. But if
they come up, in spite of that, you can't give them a secondary place. And if I
mention them, it is not because I think: "Now you ought to be thinking about
them," but because I *am* thinking and worrying. Get that straight, and *do*
understand that it has nothing to do with us. Nothing, darling. It's just a little
punishment for your fooling around with little refugee girls.

I have written hurriedly and more than I wanted to on the subject. And I
think it must be quite confused and confusing. But try to understand! There
is hidden in me some guilty conscience of a political deserter. . . .

To Milton Crane
Wednesday, November 16, 1938

. . . The "Bremen" has come in with another heap of distressing mail, and we are all quite paralyzed by it.* It is all so terrible, there are no words for it, I'll have to show you some of those letters, *Hilfeschreie* [cries for help], and we unable to do anything about it. A singer whom we knew well: slain in a concentration camp. My aunt imploring us to send affidavits for her sister-in-law, who has had her house and all belongings burnt, her husband taken to some concentration camp, her eight-year-old child shipped to some country, Holland or England, probably to be sent on to one of the colonies. She herself is being looked after by another family in the most distressing circumstances: They live and sleep eight people in one room. And so on and so forth, one letter after another. People, strangers, call us from morning till night asking for affidavits. People are resorting to the strangest and extremest of measures, and one can't help them. Be happy that you are far away from all this. And if you find an undertone of reproach in some of the things I have said to you in this connection, it's merely a sort of envy that makes me talk this way, which perhaps you can by now understand.

Here is something I have wanted to ask you for the past two days: I want Lili [Faktor, Ortmann's closest friend in Berlin, who fled to Prague with her family in 1933] to apply, at least apply—what harm can it do?—for one of those refugee scholarships of which there has been so much in the papers. And this is what I want you to find out: . . . Would she be eligible, and what has she to do? And would the fact that she might already come over in the near future jeopardize those chances? But don't say that she is sure to come over. Darling, don't be angry at this commission, and at the businesslike form, but I have so little time and I can type so much faster than I shall ever learn to write by hand. And if you can't help 600,000 Jews, you can at least try to do whatever you can think of for those few that you know and that are your friends (don't misinterpret this "you," it was meant to refer to myself).

To Milton Crane
Sunday, December 4, 1938

. . . Whatever has been causing *me* to be depressed and distressed, these last few weeks, has been of quite a different order. It's the same thing that has given Lili Sachs a nervous breakdown and makes Carl Sachs weep continuously, that causes Fritz [Lechner] to be so irritable that we have quarreled fearfully in the last three days and still don't talk to one another. I don't know what it is that eats most on our nerves: I suppose it's being protected from and yet so utterly connected with a disaster, and at the same time one's impotence

---

* Reference here is to *Kristallnacht*, November 9 – 10.

to do something for those that are hit by it, which would be one's only justification for the privilege of being safe and far away. It's the old story again, and
I had promised that you should not hear it again.

To Mary Rubinstein
December 12, 1938

Dear Mrs. Rubinstein,
    . . . I have just paid a weekend visit to Cambridge and have seen the
Harvard-Radcliffe people and they have been quite encouraging. I hope to
save enough to pay for my first year's tuition, and I have been next to promised
that there will be a room-and-board job when I get admitted, which would
take care of the most essential items of my budget. For pocket money, whatever little I need, I hope to be able to depend on my family, and for the coming
years' tuition on scholarships. I have developed into quite an optimist—for
sheer necessity, I suppose, so as not to wonder too often at the sense and use of
all this hard work. Altogether, personally, I am quite happy. I have made very
good friends, or, to be more honest, I have made one very good friend, who has
made me like America and the fact that I have come here. He won a fine
fellowship to Harvard University (after he took his M.A. at Columbia) and is
studying for his doctorate in English, after which he will go back to Columbia
University to teach. We hope to get married then, but there are yet almost two
years to go.
    It sounds strange to be talking of oneself as being happy, while our minds
have been so occupied with the general and individual reports from Europe. It
is true, the general events are bad enough to rouse an entire world, but the
world and oneself get used to hearing and reading of those horrors, and one
realized it only when one day it hits one's own people and friends and the
whole catastrophe of the destruction of thousands of individual lives is
brought home to one to its full extent. I don't want to paint myself too black.
All I mean to say is that no reports from Spain nor China, nor of what we
knew was going on in Germany in the past five years, have had the effect on
us, have seemed to us half as distressing and disastrous as what we now gradually learn about the fate of our different friends and relatives who were still in
Germany, and who have either been killed or disappeared in some unknown
concentration camp or, as the seventy-years-old parents of my stepfather, they
have been taken right out of their beds and shipped to Poland (from where
they had come forty years ago), where they camped in the open air and had
nothing to eat for forty-eight hours. My stepfather's parents, fortunately, after
fifteen days in Polish asylums and camps, finally got to some of their relatives
who are taking care of them temporarily.

To Milton Crane
March 15, 1939

It is just as if the New York weather God were mourning Hitler's marching into Czechoslovakia, Prague. Of course, we all knew—since Austria's annexation just a year ago—that it would happen in just this way. And yet, that Prague should overnight have become like any other city in the Dritte Reich, comes as a sudden shock, pretty maddening to grasp. It must be like knowing someone one knows doomed for a long time, and then not being able to realize, one day, that he is dead. However, no silly flowery language. Police, soldiers, and civilians walk through the streets of Prague weeping and crying like children. As they did once before, when those fine democracies England and France delivered them to Hitler's knife. I didn't cry, but I walked and went downtown in a daze and realized only that I had somehow gotten to Wall Street, when I started looking for my office key. Lili left Prague just four weeks ago, think of it! Heinrich and Jela were coaxed into coming over by my mother. But there are too many left, in a way the creme of our emigrants, who have next to starved for the past five years but have made Prague the center of antifascist propaganda and action. And it's like a dead end for them, no country that will take them, the American quota—only hope—closed for the next five years. I sit here and I can't help brooding over what is going to happen to our friends, to Lili's friends, her brother, her father, her mother. And that a whole world should be looking on passively. It's a futile thing to repeat for the hundredst time and yet it is to me the great enigma of this time. Darling, darling, what a world to live and want to raise children in!

Last night, an elderly lady came to our door, whom we hardly recognized. The wife of a great German physician, a professor, almost sixty-five years old or so, whose son we know, who is also a doctor in Chicago, and who came over a few months ago and spent an evening at our house. Nice, educated people, very rich formerly, with a fine enormous house in Berlin. Well, the man has to take his state board exam—although people used to travel to him from all parts of the world for his treatments—and it takes him long, of course, because he is so old. . . . His wife now goes from house to house, from morning till night, selling stockings, making pennies on each pair. There are sadder cases than that, but I don't feel like reiterating to you even one tenth of what I come across every day, in the office, at our apartment. A girl that Lechner went to school with, the richest, most spoiled child of Stettin, selling butter and eggs, with a husband and child to live on that. They came to see us one day, all of them, and when they walked into our living room, the husband burst into tears at seeing people apparently settled in their own rooms, with something to call a home. (Incidentally, a physician, who is working for his state board, but is so worn out with worries, so hypernervous that he keeps on failing it.) Perhaps this will explain a little why it is so difficult for me to free myself of the conception of work, whatever kind, mind-killing and whatnot it may be, as a heaven-sent privilege to hold on to, making such extravagant desires as mine look blasphemous and monstrously ungrateful. Remind me, I haven't time nor quiet nor mind to do it now, tell you of my mother's second brother, and of her reaction when he wrote us that he had become a taxi driver in Johannesburg.

Some malicious sadism must have gotten hold of me today, to be plaguing you with this recitation of sad things. Sometimes I want so much to tell you what it is that weighs on me so, or that I am trying to cast off, and that makes me feel so different from your friends, that also makes me despair a little and wonder whether I shall ever be able to do things that I can only do well when I am completely detached from all this sadness. . . . I know, I torture you when I say things like this. . . . All we both can hope is that that dilemma, these scruples can be overcome completely, and that I will still do better than I now think I can. And perhaps, that the future will afford us something better than victory after victory of what has crushed so many of us, so much in us, and what might very well crush us completely one day.

. . . This thought of Czechoslovakia has been hammering on my mind all day. . . . And even now, I have a feeling that I am not fully aware of what is happening, that I can still stand it. I wonder which of the two thoughts is more paralyzing: the fact that Hitler is ruling Europe from the Rhine to the extreme East (with Russia not budging one way or another into the affairs of Europe—thereby freeing Hitler of his only possible obstacle in his Napoleonic march), or whether it is that of the individual lives, each of which one believes to know, that are caught in the trap.

To Milton Crane
March 16, 1939

Very little news since yesterday. By now it can be assumed that Lili's father, her brother, her friends, and various other people, who don't mean anything to you but the more to us, are in German concentration camps. Heinrich came over last night, and we talked and talked, and the more we talked the more aware did we become of what is actually happening, with all its implications. Tonight I shall see Lili on her first day-off, I am quite at a loss as to what to say to her to calm her down, comfort and encourage her. Heinrich has a patient who is willing to give an affidavit for some young Communist in Prague. This might do for either Lili's brother or for a journalist friend of hers who is among the first to be persecuted. But after all, what does an affidavit mean, these days, but three years on the consulate's waiting list? What a hope to live for! There is going to be a suicide wave. . . .

To Milton Crane
March 17, 1939

Lili thinks that her parents and brother, knowing that she is out and does not have to be cared for any longer, will commit suicide, as they have often planned to do in case of the occupation of Prague by the Germans. The same is true of Lili's best friend (a woman of thirty, to whom she is terribly attached) and the latter's friend (a former poet who turned political writer and is on top of the blacklist). Lili, incidentally, has the same strange way of talking about these things as I have, and it is only for split seconds that we ever grasp what is happening, that none of those people to whom we wrote last night, for whom we are asking for affidavits and guarantees, may be alive at this minute, that most certainly those that are alive are in concentration camps and will be very difficult, probably impossible, to locate. You should have seen Lili's bewildered, absent-minded look when she said, quietly last night: *Ich weiss es. Sie haben alle Selbstmord gemacht.* [I know it. They've all committed suicide.]

Klaus Mann }

My Last Day with Ernst Toller

Ernst Toller's suicide on May 22, 1939, in an Upper Westside New York hotel room came as a shock to many exiles who had admired in him a courageous, tireless figure of resistance to the Nazis. Klaus Mann, the son of Thomas Mann, fled Germany in 1933 and played an active role with his sister Erika in exile literary circles in the United States; he published this account of his last day with Toller in the Neue Weltbühne *in 1939. Mann himself would commit suicide ten years later.*

The meetings of the PEN Club in conjunction with the New York World's Fair had come to an end. The high point was a formal dinner in honor of the French writer Jules Romains, in the Plaza Hotel. Ernst Toller had introduced the German writers to the international circle of guests. Before saying our names, he recalled those who were no longer among us with a few simple and very moving words: "Many have fallen, many have become victims." He meant Erich Mühsam and Carl von Ossietzky and Kurt Tucholsky, and a hundred others. He meant the martyrs. He hadn't forgotten a single of his murdered friends. He stood next to the festively laid table and spoke in praise of them with a beautiful, powerful, moving voice.

As a conclusion to the PEN festivities, a group trip to Washington had been arranged. We had received handsome engraved invitations from the White House: "Mrs. Roosevelt requests the pleasure of the company of Mr. . . ." Then came our names, not written but engraved like the rest of the text. It made a very flattering impression.

We met, early in the morning after our dinner at the Plaza, at a designated spot in the large hall of Pennsylvania Station. The whole thing reminded me of a class trip. The friendly and efficient PEN secretaries behaved like the teachers whose task it was to keep a boisterous class from getting out of line. I remember that Ernst Toller was the first one I greeted that morning. His mood struck me as distinctly better than it had been in the last few weeks. Since the beginning of this year his depression, which descended upon him periodically like an illness, had taken on a truly disturbing intensity. But that morning he was smiling. His way of smiling is unforgettable. His beautiful eyes contained the shadow of a gentle sadness, while his mouth struggled movingly to keep a happy look. Even his shoulders, hunched forward somewhat asymmetrically, seemed to be asking forgiveness for his no longer being able, despite his best intentions, to find joy in anything.

During the trip to Washington I spoke little with him. Our group had been given its own car—an entire railway car full of writers from every country . . . For a while I saw Ernst Toller sitting with the Parisians, with Jules Romains and André Maurois who were making elegant, witty conversation in French. Both of them very refined, very distinguished, with the large rosettes of the Légion d'Honneur making them look like high diplomatic officials. Of the German authors in our group there were Alfred Döblin and Arnold Zweig, Annette Kolb and the playwright Bruckner, Prince Hubertus zu Löwenstein with Princess Helga. Austria was represented by Raoul Auernheimer, who had spent months in the Dachau concentration camp. We could hear the Scandinavian languages and much Spanish, for most of the South American countries were in attendance. The Italian Max Ascoli was there, and Ralph Bates, and my dear old friend from Denmark Karin Michaelis, and the Swiss writer Hermann Kesser whose Talleyrand drama I had seen the previous summer in Basel with Albert Bassermann as lead actor. Dorothy Thompson had traveled ahead of us with the night train to Washington. She was waiting for us at the White House.

Mrs. Roosevelt led us into the president's study, explaining: "He doesn't have time to have lunch with us—by the way, he rarely has lunch—but he would like to greet you." The president sat at his desk. We filed by, one after the other. Each of us was introduced and for a second he looked us intently in the eye as he shook our hand. His gaze struck me as very cordial and somewhat tired. His eyes were a deeper, more intense blue than I had imagined from pictures of him. He knew that many of us were exiles, refugees from Italy, Germany, or Spain. The men in power in our native countries would murder us if they could catch us. But he is the most powerful man of the most powerful country of the globe, and he finds it important to honor us with this friendly gesture. [. . .]

After lunch Mrs. Roosevelt showed us the White House, which architecturally is somewhere between an impressive little palace and a very comfortable private home. Toller was delighted with the simplicity and noble tact with which the *First Lady of the country* gave a guided tour to the international writers. Repeatedly he praised the nobility of our hostess and the atmosphere of the house. "We never had that in Germany!" cried Toller. "The representatives of the Weimar Republic never managed to find it, this good taste uniting truly democratic and aristocratic dignity . . ."

He seemed quite preoccupied by all this. The four of us—Dorothy Thompson, Annette Kolb, Toller, and I—went for a drive in the car, and he was talkative and lively. Dorothy showed us General Lee's house, up in the hills, and the graves of the soldiers who fell in the World War and the Spanish-American War and the Civil War. Toller seemed moved by the sight of the many white tombstones. He explained how moving he found it that here, under this earth, the enemy soldiers who had shot at each other were lying together so peacefully and that the city of Washington was giving the same honor to all of them, the sons of the South and the sons of the North. [. . .]

Miss Thompson, Toller, and I continued our conversation in the Mayflower Hotel while Annette Kolb rested in another room. Then, having split up from the group, we were reunited with the rest of our "class" in a beautiful private house: Mr. Eugene Meyer, the owner of the *Washington Post*, and Mrs. Agnes Meyer were hosting a reception for the PEN Club. Around seven o'clock the group broke up in order to catch a train. Toller and I were the only ones to stay for dinner. The conservative journalist Marc Sullivan had also been invited. Toller remained as animated as I had seen him all day. Mr. Sullivan spiced the conversation with little attacks against the New Deal, recalling nostalgically the times that he and Mr. Hoover had played some amusing and restorative game in the White House—a kind of table tennis, if I recall correctly. By the way, we were quite polite with the experienced, intelligent *gentleman*. A difference of political opinion in civilized company is no reason to jump at each other's throats . . .

"It's been a wonderful, full day," said Toller to me as we sat next to one another in his Pullman compartment. "It was a useful day. We've seen and learned a great deal."

He was still quite confident, although he mentioned his worries. In a friendly, open way he talked about what made him anxious and fearful. His difficult financial situation also played a role in our discussion, and we reflected how it might be improved. He seemed more concerned by his plans for the future than his worries. He spoke at length of a trip to Europe he had decided to take, of a collection of his essays and manifestoes that he wanted to publish in London, and of a new play he was working on.

Before we said good night to each other—I had a berth in another compartment—he called me back with a beseeching voice that suddenly verged on a sob: "If I could just fall asleep! No one who hasn't gone through it himself can know what it means not to be able to fall asleep."

But he couldn't sleep. The next morning, as we had breakfast in a cafeteria next to Pennsylvania Station, he looked awful. His face was gray, and dark shadows had etched themselves around his tragic eyes. "I laid awake the whole night," he told me. Then we spoke of the morning news. I noticed that Toller had trouble concentrating and that it hurt him when he forced a smile to his lips.

We parted at a subway station. Now, looking back, it seems to me as if he shook my hand longer than he normally did, as if he looked at me in a particularly comradely and yet strangely distant way as we said goodbye.

That was on May 12, 1939, ten days before Toller's death. I couldn't stay in New York at the time and didn't have the opportunity to see him again. The day in Washington was our last time together. While we were laughing and talking, in the White House or in the Mayflower Hotel or at Eugene Meyer's house, his heart had always been harboring that "other" thing, like a wound growing bigger and bigger—that dark impulse toward death which he fought and kept at bay but which finally, in his darkest hour, overwhelmed him. I find it almost unbearable to imagine how he must have been suffering in our midst, without our noticing it. And more tormenting than the pain we feel for a missing friend is the helpless question that remains with us, the living:

What do we know of one another?

ERNST TOLLER'S LAST DAY

*Hermann Kesten was in France when he received the news of Ernst Tol-
ler's suicide and wrote to Ludwig Marcuse asking for news. As previously
noted, Kesten would later emigrate to New York and become a key figure in
the Emergency Rescue Committee, helping numerous German writers to
escape Europe.*

New York City
June 15, 1939

Dear Hermann Kesten,

It was good of you to force me to write. If you hadn't, you would have had
to wait a long time for news. I don't know what I should write. I was about to
send you an account of Toller's last days when I received word of [Josef]
Roth's death. Then I gave up the idea of writing. Now at least I would like to
give a brief answer to your questions.

Christiane [Ernst Toller's wife] isn't in New York but in Hollywood. She
had her "Wilhelm Tell" premiere the day of Toller's funeral. It's possible I
may get a ride in a car going out West. If I happen to speak to Christiane, I'll
tell you what she plans to do with [her husband's] unpublished work.

Until then I'm staying out of things. And this is why. After Toller, completely alone, had reached the end of the line—in the end he had perhaps four
friends he could talk to—the funeral became a social event. Everyone claimed
to have been with him the last evening, everyone claimed to have done him the
last big favor, everyone used the occasion to push himself into the limelight. I
immediately withdrew. I haven't spoken or written or worried about what he
left behind. It's impossible to behave any other way if you want to avoid being
drawn into the circle of petty vanities. So I can only answer by saying that I'll
write to you after speaking with Christiane.

And now a few bare facts about his last days. On Friday, Saturday, and
Sunday he was packing his bags for England. On Saturday and Sunday,
Sascha [Marcuse's wife] spent the whole day helping him. On Sunday he gave
her some reviews and pictures of Christiane, saying, "It's better if the two of

you have this than people I don't know." Sunday evening he was with us. We spoke for an hour about suicide. He tended to confuse the reasons for suicide, was very much opposed to my overly rational approach to the phenomenon, and talked much about the will to life and so forth. He left around eleven o'clock, neither better nor worse than usual. At his request, one of our friends accompanied him to his hotel room and gave him a light sleeping potion. On Monday morning at ten, because I had to pass by his hotel, I sent a letter up to his room suggesting he visit the doctor he had most confidence in and speak openly with him. (He had four doctors in the end.) His secretary, Ilse Herzfeld, spent the entire morning in his room. As always in the morning, he was very depressed. She left at twelve and returned at one. It happened in between. Assuming one can speculate about what happened in the meantime, I would say this: looking at his packed bags, he suddenly asked himself, "What will have changed when I get to England?" He fought against the act [of suicide] to the very end. He called us up twice in the last week: "Come here right away, I can't be alone with myself." But he had been meditating the step for years. Indeed, longer than that. And this time the noose didn't give way.

My dear Kesten, let's not say anything about the feelings that move us. One of the few plans he had for the summer was to be with you. [. . .]

And now don't take it amiss if I say nothing about myself.

Best wishes to you and your dear wife from Sascha and yours truly

Marcuse

The only ones present at T[oller's] cremation were Toller's cousin, myself, and an interested American journalist friend. The cousin asked me if it's true that T[oller] used to give such expensive farewell gifts.

Please write me a few lines. I really need it.

CHAPTER THREE

Exiles, Enemies, or Emigrants?

Gottfried Bermann-Fischer and Thomas Mann ⎤

THE "ENEMY ALIEN" QUESTION

In 1940 more than a million of the five million registered foreigners in the United States were classified as "enemy aliens." Following Dorothy Thompson's initiative for the refugees, Gottfried Bermann-Fischer (Mann's publisher in Germany, and an exile himself) successfully enlisted the help of Mann and other well-known exiles to reverse this classification.

February 9, 1942

Herrn Dr. Thomas Mann
740 Amalfi Drive
Pacific Palisades, Calif.

Dear Herr Doktor Mann:

Can't anything be done to resolve the Enemy Alien problem?

The groups of German emigrants, both the politically active and the apolitical, have done nothing. It is truly depressing to see how these former politicians squander their time with fruitless attempts to be recognized as the future government, to build German resistance and to resolve the problem of postwar Germany's future, while disregarding this most immediate and pressing issue.

If this continues, we must fear that the willingness of the [American] government to recognize the loyalty of the majority of German emigrants—quite palpable at the beginning of the war—will give way to the influence of ultra-nationalists, who are everywhere.

The undifferentiated registering of all German emigrants as "Enemy Aliens" signifies a heavy moral blow to the emigrants, who had expected everything except the misperception and disregard of their principles and beliefs. For the moment the most troubling aspect is their widespread anxiety, because naturally no one believes the attorney general's reassuring explanations, and their fear grows that the registration requirement is only the beginning of more comprehensive measures. The undifferentiated internment and evacuation of certain areas on the West Coast, where the German emigrants are given the same treatment as the Japanese, encourages their fear of the worst. Until now the only voice that has been raised against this danger has come from Dorothy Thompson. I enclose the excerpt from the *New York Post* with this letter.

You are the only one, my dear Dr. Mann, who can assume leadership in this matter. It should be possible to appeal to the [American] government with a letter signed by the most celebrated emigrant figures or to send a representative committee to Washington. What the Austrians were able to achieve, should also be possible for the group of German scientists, poets, writers, etc. whose vital importance is recognized in America. And it should be possible to find a way to distinguish between Germans who are loyal to America and those who are not. We must put an end to the current situation, which threatens to become unbearable and dangerous. I would appreciate receiving from you a speedy reply.

Yours truly,

G. B. Fischer

Thomas Mann's reply:

February 13, 1942

1550 San Remo Drive
Pacific Palisades, CA

Dear Dr. Bermann:

You can well imagine that the enemy alien matter has also kept me continually occupied and depressed. . . . For weeks I have been asking myself what I might do and now have taken the most direct and perhaps most promising route to President Roosevelt. Enclosed please find a copy of the telegram signed by Toscanini, Borgese, Sforza, Bruno Frank, Bruno Walter, and myself. Let's hope for the best!

Yours,

Thomas Mann

OPEN LETTER TO
PRESIDENT ROOSEVELT

President Franklin D. Roosevelt
The White House
Washington D.C.

Mr. President:

We beg to draw your attention to a large group of natives of Germany and Italy who by present regulations are, erroneously, characterized and treated as "Aliens of Enemy Nationality."

We are referring to such persons who have fled their country and sought refuge in the United States because of totalitarian persecution, and who, for that very reason, have been deprived of their former citizenship.

Their situation is such as has never existed under any previous circumstances, and it cannot be deemed just to comprise them under the discrediting denomination of "Aliens of Enemy Nationality."

Many of those people, politicians, scientists, artists, writers, have been among the earliest and most farsighted adversaries of the governments against whom the United States are now at war. Many of them have sacrificed their situation, and their properties and have risked their lives by fighting and warning against those forces of evil, which at that time were minimized and compromised with by most of the governments of the world.

It is true that the "Application for a Certificate of Identification" provides such persons with an opportunity to make additional statements as for their political status. But as, so far, no official announcement to the contrary has been made, these victims of Nazi and Fascist oppression, these staunch and consistent defenders of democracy, would be subject to all the present and future restrictions meant for and directed against possible Fifth Columnists.

We, therefore, respectfully apply to you, Mr. President, who for all of us represent the spirit of all that is loyal, honest and decent in a world of falsehood and chaos, to utter or to sanction a word of authoritative discrimination, to the effect that a clear and practical line should be drawn between the potential enemies of American democracy on the one hand, and the victims and sworn foes of totalitarian evil on the other.

[Signed by]

G. A. Borgese	Thomas Mann
Albert Einstein	Arturo Toscanini
Bruno Frank	Bruno Walter

WE REFUGEES

Hannah Arendt was born in Königsberg in 1906, studied philosophy in Germany during the 1920s, and fled to Paris in 1933, where she worked in relief organizations helping Jews emigrate to Palestine and providing legal aid to anti-Fascists. She emigrated to New York in 1941, where she assumed a leading role among German exiles and became one of the most influential political and philosophical voices in postwar America.

In the first place, we don't like to be called "refugees." We ourselves call each other "newcomers" or "immigrants." Our newspapers are papers for "Americans of German language"; and as far as I know there is not and never was any club founded by Hitler-persecuted people whose name indicated that its members were refugees.

A refugee used to be a person driven to seek refuge because of some act committed or some political opinion held. Well, it is true we have had to seek refuge; but we committed no acts and most of us never dreamt of having any radical political opinion. With us the meaning of the term "refugee" has changed. Now "refugees" are those of us who have been so unfortunate as to arrive in a new country without means and have to be helped by Refugee Committees.

Before this war broke out we were even more sensitive about being called refugees. We did our best to prove to other people that we were just ordinary immigrants. We declared that we had departed of our own free will to countries of our choice, and we denied that our situation had anything to do with "so-called Jewish problems." Yes, we were "immigrants" or "newcomers" who had left our country because, one fine day, it no longer suited us to stay, or for purely economic reasons. We wanted to rebuild our lives, that was all. In order to rebuild one's life one has to be strong and an optimist. So we are very optimistic.

Our optimism, indeed, is admirable, even if we say so ourselves. The story of our struggle has finally become known. We lost our home, which means the familiarity of daily life. We lost our occupation, which means the confidence that we are of some use in this world. We lost our language, which means the naturalness of reactions, the simplicity of gestures, the unaffected expression of feelings. We left our relatives in the Polish ghettos and our best friends have been killed in concentration camps, and that means the rupture of our private lives.

Nevertheless, as soon as we were saved—and most of us had to be saved several times—we started our new lives and tried to follow as closely as possible all the good advice our saviors passed on to us. We were told to forget; and we forgot quicker than anybody ever could imagine. In a friendly way we were reminded that the new country would become a new home; and after four weeks in France or six weeks in America, we pretended to be Frenchmen or Americans. The more optimistic among us would even add that their whole former life had been passed in a kind of unconscious exile and only their new country now taught them what a home really looks like. It is true we sometimes raise objections when we are told to forget about our former work; and our former ideals are usually hard to throw over if our social standard is at stake. With the language, however, we find no difficulties: after a single year optimists are convinced they speak English as well as their mother tongue; and after two years they swear solemnly that they speak English better than any other language—their German is a language they hardly remember.

In order to forget more efficiently we rather avoid any allusion to concentration or internment camps we experienced in nearly all European countries—it might be interpreted as pessimism or lack of confidence in the new homeland. Besides, how often have we been told that nobody likes to listen to all that; hell is no longer a religious belief or a fantasy, but something as real as houses and stones and trees. Apparently nobody wants to know that contemporary history has created a new kind of human being—the kind that is put in concentration camps by its foes and in internment camps by its friends.

Even among ourselves we don't speak about this past. Instead we have found our own way of mastering an uncertain future. Since everybody plans and wishes and hopes, so do we. Apart from these general human attitudes, however, we try to clear up the future more scientifically. After so much bad luck we want a course as sure as a gun. Therefore, we leave the earth with all its uncertainties behind and we cast our eyes up to the sky. The stars tell us— rather than the newspapers—when Hitler will be defeated and when we shall become American citizens. We think the stars more reliable advisers than all our friends; we learn from the stars when we should have lunch with our benefactors and on what day we have the best chances of filling out one of these countless questionnaires which accompany our present lives. Sometimes we don't rely even on the stars but rather on the lines of our hand or the signs of our handwriting. Thus we learn less about political events but more about our own dear selves, even though somehow psychoanalysis has gone out of fashion. Those happier times are past when bored ladies and gentlemen of high society conversed about the genial misdemeanors of their early childhood. They don't want ghost stories any more; it is real experiences that make their flesh creep. There is no longer any need of bewitching the past; it is spellbound enough in reality. Thus, in spite of our outspoken optimism, we use all sorts of magical tricks to conjure up the spirits of the future.

I don't know which memories and which thoughts nightly dwell in our dreams. I dare not ask for information, since I, too, had rather be an optimist. But sometimes I imagine that at least nightly we think of our dead or we remember the poems we once loved. I could even understand how our friends of the West Coast, during the curfew, should have had such curious notions as to believe that we are not only "prospective citizens" but present "enemy aliens." In daylight, of course, we become only "technically" enemy aliens—all refugees know this. But when technical reasons prevented you from leaving your home during the dark hours, it certainly was not easy to avoid some dark speculations about the relation between technicality and reality.

No, there is something wrong with our optimism. There are those odd optimists among us who, having made a lot of optimistic speeches, go home and turn on the gas or make use of a skyscraper in quite an unexpected way. They seem to prove that our proclaimed cheerfulness is based on a dangerous readiness for death. Brought up in the conviction that life is the highest good and death the greatest dismay, we became witnesses and victims of worse terrors than death—without having been able to discover a higher ideal than life. Thus, although death lost its horror for us, we became neither willing nor capable to risk our lives for a cause. Instead of fighting—or thinking about how to become able to fight back—refugees have got used to wishing death to friends or relatives; if somebody dies, we cheerfully imagine all the trouble he has been saved. Finally many of us end by wishing that we too could be saved some trouble, and act accordingly.

Since 1938—since Hitler's invasion of Austria—we have seen how quickly eloquent optimism could change to speechless pessimism. As time went on, we got worse—even more optimistic and even more inclined to suicide. Austrian Jews under Schuschnigg were such a cheerful people—all impartial observers admired them. It was quite wonderful how deeply convinced they were that nothing could happen to them. But when German troops invaded the country and gentile neighbors started riots at Jewish homes, Austrian Jews began to commit suicide.

Unlike other suicides, our friends leave no explanation of their deed, no indictment, no charge against a world that had forced a desperate man to talk and to behave cheerfully to his very last day. Letters left by them are conventional, meaningless documents. Thus, funeral orations we make at their open graves are brief, embarrassed, and very hopeful. Nobody cares about motives, they seem to be clear to all of us.

*   *   *

I speak of unpopular facts; and it makes things worse that in order to prove my point I do not even dispose of the sole arguments which impress modern people—figures. Even those Jews who furiously deny the existence of the Jewish people give us a fair chance of survival as far as figures are concerned—how else could they prove that only a few Jews are criminals and that many Jews are being killed as good patriots in wartime? Through their effort to save the statistical life of the Jewish people we know that Jews had the lowest suicide rate among all civilized nations. I am quite sure those figures are no longer correct, but I cannot prove it with new figures, though I can certainly with new experiences. This might be sufficient for those skeptical souls who never were quite convinced that the measure of one's skull gives the exact idea of its content, or that statistics of crime show the exact level of national ethics. Anyhow, wherever European Jews are living today, they no longer behave according to statistical laws. Suicides occur not only among the panic-stricken people in Berlin and Vienna, in Bucharest or Paris, but in New York and Los Angeles, in Buenos Aires and Montevideo.

On the other hand there has been little reported about suicides in the ghettoes and concentration camps themselves. True, we had very few reports at all from Poland, but we have been fairly well informed about German and French concentration camps.

At the camp of Gurs, for instance, where I had the opportunity of spending some time, I heard only once about suicide, and that was the suggestion of a collective action, apparently a kind of protest in order to vex the French. When some of us remarked that we had been shipped there *"pour crever"* in any case, the general mood turned suddenly into a violent courage of life. The general opinion held that one had to be abnormally asocial and unconcerned about general events if one was still able to interpret the whole accident as personal and individual bad luck and, accordingly, ended one's life personally and individually. But the same people, as soon as they returned to their own individual lives, being faced with seemingly individual problems, changed once more to this insane optimism which is next door to despair.

We are the first nonreligious Jews persecuted—and we are the first ones who, not only in *extremis,* answer with suicide. Perhaps the philosophers are right who teach that suicide is the last and supreme guarantee of human freedom: not being free to create our lives or the world in which we live, we nevertheless are free to throw life away and to leave the world. Pious Jews, certainly, cannot realize this negative liberty; they perceive murder in suicide, that is, destruction of what man never is able to make, interference with the rights of the Creator. *Adonai nathan veadonai lakach* ("The Lord hath given and the Lord hath taken away"); and they would add: *baruch shem adonai* ("blessed be the name of the Lord"). For them suicide, like murder, means a blasphemous attack on creation as a whole. The man who kills himself asserts that life is not worth living and the world not worth sheltering him.

Yet our suicides are no mad rebels who hurl defiance at life and the world, who try to kill in themselves the whole universe. Theirs is a quiet and modest way of vanishing; they seem to apologize for the violent solution they have found for their personal problems. In their opinion, generally, political events had nothing to do with their individual fate; in good or bad times they would believe solely in their personality. Now they find some mysterious shortcomings in themselves which prevent them from getting along. Having felt entitled from their earliest childhood to a certain social standard, they are failures in their own eyes if this standard cannot be kept any longer. Their optimism is the vain attempt to keep head above water. Behind this front of cheerfulness, they constantly struggle with despair of themselves. Finally they die of a kind of selfishness.

If we are saved we feel humiliated, and if we are helped we feel degraded. We fight like madmen for private existences with individual destinies, since we are afraid of becoming part of that miserable lot of *schnorrers* whom we, many of us former philanthropists, remember only too well. Just as once we failed to understand that the so-called *schnorrer* was a symbol of Jewish destiny and not a *shlemihl,* so today we don't feel entitled to Jewish solidarity; we cannot realize that we by ourselves are not so much concerned as the whole Jewish people. Sometimes this lack of comprehension has been strongly supported by our protectors. Thus, I remember a director of a great charity concern in Paris who, whenever he received the card of a German-Jewish intellectual with the inevitable "Dr." on it, used to exclaim at the top of his voice, "Herr Doktor, Herr Doktor, Herr Schnorrer, Herr Schnorrer!"

The conclusion we drew from such unpleasant experiences was simple enough. To be a doctor of philosophy no longer satisfied us; and we learnt that in order to build a new life, one has first to improve on the old one. A nice little fairy tale has been invented to describe our behavior; a forlorn émigré dachshund, in his grief, begins to speak: "Once, when I was a St. Bernard . . ."

Our new friends, rather overwhelmed by so many stars and famous men, hardly understand that at the basis of all our descriptions of past splendors lies one human truth: once we were somebodies about whom people cared, we were loved by friends, and even known by landlords as paying our rent regularly. Once we could buy our food and ride in the subway without being told we were undesirable. We have become a little hysterical since newspapermen started detecting us and telling us publicly to stop being disagreeable when shopping for milk and bread. We wonder how it can be done; we already are so damnably careful in every moment of our daily lives to avoid anybody guessing who we are, what kind of passport we have, where our birth certificates were filled out—and that Hitler didn't like us. We try the best we can to fit into a world where you have to be sort of politically minded when you buy your food.

Under such circumstances St. Bernard grows bigger and bigger. I never can forget that young man who, when expected to accept a certain kind of work, sighed out, "You don't know to whom you speak; I was section-manager in Karstadt's [a great department store in Berlin]." But there is also the deep despair of that middle-aged man who, going through countless shifts of different committees in order to be saved, finally exclaimed, "And nobody here knows who I am!" Since nobody would treat him as a dignified human being, he began sending cables to great personalities and his big relations. He learnt quickly that in this mad world it is much easier to be accepted as a "great man" than as a human being.

The less we are free to decide who we are or to live as we like, the more we try to put up a front, to hide the facts, and to play roles. We were expelled from Germany because we were Jews. But having hardly crossed the French borderline, we were changed into "boches." We were even told that we had to accept this designation if we really were against Hitler's racial theories. During seven years we played the ridiculous role of trying to be Frenchmen—at least, prospective citizens; but at the beginning of the war we were interned as "boches" all the same. In the meantime, however, most of us had indeed become such loyal Frenchmen that we could not even criticize a French governmental order; thus we declared it was all right to be interned. We were the first *"prisonniers volontaires"* history has ever seen. After the Germans invaded the country, the French government had only to change the name of the firm; having been jailed because we were Germans, we were not freed because we were Jews.

It is the same story all over the world, repeated again and again. In Europe the Nazis confiscated our property; but in Brazil we have to pay thirty percent of our wealth, like the most loyal member of the *Bund der Auslandsdeutschen*. In Paris we could not leave our homes after eight o'clock because we were Jews; but in Los Angeles we are restricted because we are "enemy aliens." Our identity is changed so frequently that nobody can find out who we actually are.

Unfortunately, things don't look any better when we meet with Jews. French Jewry was absolutely convinced that all Jews coming from beyond the Rhine were what they called *Polaks*—what German Jewry called *Ostjuden*. But those Jews who really came from Eastern Europe could not agree with their French brethren and called us *Jaeckes*. The sons of these *Jaecke*-haters— the second generation born in France and already duly assimilated—shared the opinion of the French Jewish upper classes. Thus, in the very same family, you could be called a *Jaecke* by the father and a *Polak* by the son.

Since the outbreak of the war and the catastrophe that has befallen European Jewry, the mere fact of being a refugee has prevented our mingling with native Jewish society, some exceptions only proving the rule. These unwritten social laws, though never publicly admitted, have the great force of public opinion. And such a silent opinion and practice is more important for our daily lives than all official proclamations of hospitality and good will.

Man is a social animal and life is not easy for him when social ties are cut off. Moral standards are much easier kept in the texture of a society. Very few individuals have the strength to conserve their own integrity if their social, political and legal status is completely confused. Lacking the courage to fight for a change of our social and legal status, we have decided instead, so many of us, to try a change of identity. And this curious behavior makes matters much worse. The confusion in which we live is partly our own work.

Some day somebody will write the true story of this Jewish emigration from Germany; and he will have to start with a description of that Mr. Cohn from Berlin who had always been a 150 percent German, a German superpatriot. In 1933 that Mr. Cohn found refuge in Prague and very quickly became a convinced Czech patriot—as true and as loyal a Czech patriot as he had been a German one. Time went on and about 1937 the Czech government, already under some Nazi pressure, began to expel its Jewish refugees, disregarding the fact that they felt so strongly as prospective Czech citizens. Our Mr. Cohn then went to Vienna; to adjust oneself there a definite Austrian patriotism was required. The German invasion forced Mr. Cohn out that country. He arrived in Paris at a bad moment and he never did receive a regular residence permit. Having already acquired a great skill in wishful thinking, he refused to take mere administrative measures seriously, convinced that he would spend his future life in France. Therefore, he prepared his adjustment to the French nation by identifying himself with "our" ancestor Vercingetorix. I think I had better not dilate on the further adventures of Mr. Cohn. As long as Mr. Cohn can't make up his mind to be what he actually is, a Jew, nobody can foretell all the mad changes he will still have to go through.

A man who wants to lose his self discovers, indeed, the possibilities of human existence, which are infinite, as infinite as is creation. But the recovering of a new personality is as difficult—and as hopeless—as a new creation of the world. Whatever we do, whatever we pretend to be, we reveal nothing but our insane desire to be changed, not to be Jews. All our activities are directed to attain this aim: we don't want to be refugees, since we don't want to be Jews; we pretend to be English-speaking people, since German-speaking immigrants of recent years are marked as Jews; we don't call ourselves stateless, since the majority of stateless people in the world are Jews; we are willing to become loyal Hottentots, only to hide the fact that we are Jews. We don't succeed and we can't succeed; under the cover of our "optimism" you can easily detect the hopeless sadness of assimilationists.

With us from Germany the word assimilation received a "deep" philosophical meaning. You can hardly realize how serious we were about it. Assimilation did not mean the necessary adjustment to the country where we happened to be born and to the people whose language we happened to speak. We adjust in principle to everything and everybody. This attitude became quite clear to me once by the words of one of my compatriots who, apparently, knew how to express his feelings. Having just arrived in France, he founded one of these societies of adjustment in which German Jews asserted to each other that they were already Frenchmen. In his first speech he said: "We have been good Germans in Germany and therefore we shall be good Frenchmen in France." The public applauded enthusiastically and nobody laughed; we were happy to have learnt how to prove our loyalty.

If patriotism were a matter of routine or practice, we should be the most patriotic people in the world. Let us go back to our Mr. Cohn; he certainly has beaten all records. He is that ideal immigrant who always, and in every country into which a terrible fate has driven him, promptly sees and loves the native mountains. But since patriotism is not yet believed to be a matter of practice, it is hard to convince people of the sincerity of our repeated transformations. This struggle makes our own society so intolerant; we demand full affirmation without our own group because we are not in the position to obtain it from the natives. The natives, confronted with such strange beings as we are, become suspicious; from their point of view, as a rule, only a loyalty to our old countries is understandable. That makes life very bitter for us. We might overcome this suspicion if we would explain that, being Jews, our patriotism in our original countries had rather a peculiar aspect. Though it was indeed sincere and deep-rooted. We wrote big volumes to prove it; paid an entire bureaucracy to explore its antiquity and to explain it statistically. We had scholars write philosophical dissertations on the predestined harmony between Jews and Frenchmen, Jews and Germans, Jews and Hungarians, Jews and . . . Our so frequently suspected loyalty of today has a long history. It is the history of a hundred and fifty years of assimilated Jewry who performed an unprecedented feat: though proving all the time their non-Jewishness, they succeeded in remaining Jews all the same.

The desperate confusion of these Ulysses-wanderers who, unlike their great prototype, don't know who they are is easily explained by their perfect mania for refusing to keep their identity. This mania is much older than the last ten years which revealed the profound absurdity of our existence. We are like people with a fixed idea who can't help trying continually to disguise an imaginary stigma. Thus we are enthusiastically fond of every new possibility which, being new, seems able to work miracles. We are fascinated by every new nationality in the same way as a woman of tidy size is delighted with every new dress which promises to give her the desired waistline. But she likes the new dress only as long as she believes in its miraculous qualities, and she will throw it away as soon as she discovers that it does not change her stature—or, for that matter, her status.

One may be surprised that the apparent uselessness of all our odd disguises has not yet been able to discourage us. If it is true that men seldom learn from history, it is also true that they may learn from personal experiences which, as in our case, are repeated time and again. But before you can cast the first stone at us, remember that being a Jew does not give any legal status in this world. If we should start telling the truth that we are nothing but Jews, it would mean that we expose ourselves to the fate of human beings who, unprotected by any specific law or political convention, are nothing but human beings. I can hardly imagine an attitude more dangerous, since we actually live in a world in which human beings as such have ceased to exist for quite a while; since society has discovered discrimination as the great social weapon by which one may kill men without any bloodshed; since passports or birth certificates, and sometimes even income tax receipts, are no longer formal papers but matters of social distinction. It is true that most of us depend entirely upon social standards; we lose confidence in ourselves if society does not approve us; we are— and always were—ready to pay any price in order to be accepted by society. But it is equally true that the very few among us who have tried to get along without all these tricks and jokes of adjustment and assimilation have paid a much higher price than they could afford: they jeopardized the few chances even outlaws are given in a topsy-turvy world.

The attitude of these few whom, following Bernard Lazare, one may call "conscious pariahs," can as little be explained by recent events alone as the attitude of our Mr. Cohn who tried by every means to become an upstart. Both are sons of the nineteenth century which, not knowing legal or political outlaws, knew only too well social pariahs and their counterpart, social parvenus. Modern Jewish history, having started with court Jews and continuing with Jewish millionaires and philanthropists, is apt to forget about this other trend of Jewish tradition—the tradition of Heine, Rahel Varnhagen, Sholom Aleichem, of Bernard Lazare, Franz Kafka, or even Charlie Chaplin. It is the tradition of a minority of Jews who have not wanted to become upstarts, who preferred the status of "conscious pariah." All vaunted Jewish qualities—the "Jewish heart," humanity, humor, disinterested intelligence—are pariah qualities. All Jewish shortcomings—tactlessness, political stupidity, inferiority complexes, and money-grubbing—are characteristic of upstarts. There have always been Jews who did not think it worthwhile to change their humane attitude and their natural insight into reality for the narrowness of caste spirit or the essential unreality of financial transactions.

History has forced the status of outlaws upon both, upon pariahs and parvenus alike. The latter have not yet accepted the great wisdom of Balzac's "On *ne parvient pas deux fois*"; thus they don't understand the wild dreams of the former and feel humiliated in sharing their fate. Those few refugees who insist upon telling the truth, even to the point of "indecency," get in exchange for their unpopularity one priceless advantage: history is no longer a closed book to them and politics is no longer the privilege of gentiles. They know that the outlawing of the Jewish people in Europe has been followed closely by the outlawing of most European nations. Refugees driven from country to country represent the vanguard of their peoples—if they keep their identity. For the first time Jewish history is not separate but tied up with that of all other nations. The comity of European peoples went to pieces when, and because, it allowed its weakest member to be excluded and persecuted.

THE EXILED WRITER'S RELATION
TO HIS HOMELAND

Thomas Mann, born in 1875 in Lübeck and the recipient of the Nobel
Prize for Literature in 1929, was one of Germany's outstanding novelists
when the Nazis took power; on vacation in Switzerland at the time, Mann
decided not to return to Germany and accepted a position at Princeton in
1938, later settling in the Pacific Palisades for the duration of the war. His
public criticism of the Nazis as well as his international reputation made
him into one of the leading spokesmen for the German exile movement and
for the idea of a "better Germany" outside the nation's geographic borders.
This speech was delivered in California in October 1943 to a Writers' Con-
gress sponsored by the Hollywood Writers' Mobilization and the University
of California.

It was a splendid and generous decision on the part of the heads of this Congress that, in the course of the discussions of the problems of the writer in
wartime, the literary exiles should also have their say and should be invited to
express their opinions concerning the relation of the emigrant intellectuals to
their own country in this war and, looking into the future, after this war. But
I do not know whether to be pleased that this task has been assigned to me;
these are painful and complicated matters about which I am to write—
experiences which one can scarcely communicate in words to you who, in
these times, live with your own people, in complete harmony with them, in
unshakable faith in their cause, and are permitted to fight enthusiastically for
that case. This perfectly natural good fortune is denied us; not the enthusiasm,
only the battle is ours. We also battle; these times permit no one to retreat to an
ivory tower, to an existence of a peaceful cult of beauty. But it is our destiny to
carry on this battle against our own land and its cause of whose corruptness we
are convinced; against the land whose speech is the spiritual material in which
we work, against the land in whose culture we are rooted, whose tradition
we administer, and whose landscape and atmosphere should be our natural
shelter.

You will say to me: "We are all fighting for the same cause, the cause of humanity. There is no distinction between you and us." Certainly, but it is your good fortune to be able to identify yourselves more or less with the cause of your people, of your fighting forces, of your government, and when you see the emblem of American sovereignty, the Stars and Stripes, you are perhaps not naively patriotic enough that your heart beats with pride in your throat and that you break into loud hurrahs. You are critical people and you know that these colors must conceal many human weaknesses and inadequacies and perhaps even corruption and yet you look upon this emblem with a feeling of home, with sympathy and confidence, with calm pride and heartfelt hopes, while we————. You can scarcely conceive the feelings with which we look upon the present national emblem of Germany, the swastika. We do not look upon it, we look away. We would rather look at the ground or at the sky, for the sight of the symbol under which our people are fighting for their existence, or rather delude themselves that they are fighting for that existence, makes us physically ill. I speak as a German; the Italians may have similar feelings at the sight of their national fasces. You do not know how horribly strange, how detestable, how shocking it is for us to see the swastika-ornamented entrance to a German consulate or embassy. Here I have this experience only in the cinema; but when I lived in Zurich I often came into the neighborhood of the house of the German representative with the ominous flag upon it, and I confess that I always made a wide detour as one would about a den of iniquity, an outpost of murderous barbarism, extending into the realm of a friendly civilization under whose protection I lived.

Germany—a great name, a word which carries with it hundreds of homely and respected, pleasant and proud associations. And now, this word, a name of terror and of deadly wilderness, into which even our dreams do not dare to transport us. Whenever I read that some unhappy person has been "taken to Germany," as were recently the party leaders from Milan who had signed the anti-Fascist manifesto, or as was Romain Rolland, who is said to be in a German concentration camp, cold shudders run up and down my back. To be "taken to Germany" is the worst. To be sure, Mussolini has also been taken to Germany but I doubt whether even he is happy under Hitler's protection.

What an abnormal, morbid condition, abnormal and morbid for anyone, but especially for the writer, the bearer of a spiritual tradition, when his own country becomes the most hostile, the most sinister foreign land! And now I wish to think not only of us out here in exile, I finally wish to remember also those people who are still there, the German masses, and to think of the cruel compulsion which destiny has forced upon the German spirit. Believe me, for many there the fatherland has become as strange as it has for us; an "inner emigration" of millions is there awaiting the end just as we. They await the end, that is the end of the war, and there can be only one end. The people in Germany, in spite of their strangled isolation, are well aware of it, and yet they

long for it, in spite of their natural patriotism, in spite of their national conscious. The ever-present propaganda has deeply impressed upon their consciousness the pretended permanently destructive results of a German defeat,
so that in one part of their being they cannot avoid fearing that defeat more
than anything else in the world. And yet there is one thing which many of
them fear more than a German defeat, that is a German victory; some only
occasionally, at moments which they themselves regard as criminal, but others
with complete clarity and permanently although with pangs of conscience.
Imagine that you were forced with all your wishes and hopes to oppose an
American victory as a great misfortune for the entire world; if you can imagine that you can place yourself in the position of these people. This attitude has
become the destiny of uncounted Germans and it is my deep conviction that
this destiny is particularly and unimaginably tragic. I know that other nations
have been put into the position of wishing for the defeat of their government
for their own sake and for the sake of the general future. But I must insist that
in view of the all-too-great credulousness and innate loyalty of the German
character the dilemma in this case is especially acute, and I cannot resist a
feeling of deepest resentment against those who have forced the German love
of country into such a position.

These people have been deluded and seduced into crimes that cry to high
heaven. They have begun to atone for them and they will atone even more
severely; it cannot be otherwise; common morality or, if you wish, divine justice demands it. But we out here, who saw disaster coming, we, who, ahead of
our compatriots intoxicated by a fraudulent revolution, ahead of all the rest of
the world, were convinced that the Nazi rule could never bring anything except war, destruction, and catastrophe, we see no great difference between that
which these scoundrels have done to us and what they have done to our people
at home. We hate the destroyers and we long for the day which rids the world
of them. But with very few exceptions we are far from being victims of a
wretched emigrant hatred against our own land and we do not desire the
destruction of our people. We cannot completely deny their responsibility, for
somehow man is responsible for his being and doing; but misfortune is a
milder and more understanding word than guilt and we feel that it is more
appropriate to speak of misfortune and error than of crime.

To my own surprise I became conscious of the indestructibility of the bands
which link a man and particularly an intellectual to his home, to the mother
soil of his personal culture, when, soon after the outbreak of the war the British Broadcasting Corporation gave me an opportunity to speak to my fellow
countrymen with my own voice from time to time. It is no easy fate to be
completely severed from the spiritual and moral life of the nation into which
one has been born. Emigration in our days has assumed a much more radical
form than in earlier times. The exile of Victor Hugo, for example, was child's
play compared with ours. To be sure he sat as an outcast far from Paris on his

island in the ocean, but the spiritual link between him and France was never broken. What he wrote was printed in the French press; his books could be bought and read at home. Today exile is a total exile, just as war, politics, world, and life have become total. We are not only physically far from our country but we have been radically expelled from its life both in the purpose and, at least for the present, in the effects of our exile. Our books are outlawed, just as we ourselves are; they exist only in translations, in fact, since the conquest of the European continent, by the enemy, they exist only in English. We can count ourselves fortunate that it is still so, that that which we produce exists at all, for every writer will feel with us what it means to exist only as a literary shadow, to live only a translated and denatured life. The English broadcast gave me the only opportunity in these years to break the stupid ban, to exert a direct and original effect in German speech rhythm behind the backs of the dictators; and I have used this opportunity with the greatest satisfaction and have tried once a month to inform those people over there of their situation, to speak to them for their own good and to appeal to their consciences as impressively as possible.

This unfortunately weak and uncertain contact with the people at home I owe to the war; and it is true that without the war those of us who sought refuge in strange lands would have lost all but the most nebulous feeling for our land. Through the war, however, it has again come into more attainable proximity and we now live in hopes of an end of this estrangement. Did we therefore wish for this war? I know that this prejudice existed against us, that we were looked upon as warmongers in a time when the world was still trying to win peace by flattery from the Fascist dictators. We were given to understand that the world could not go to war *pour vos beaux yeux,* and I know that even today there still lurks a certain resentment in the regard of many for us, born of the feeling that people who wished the war are in some manner responsible for it. But it is not true that we wished the war. We only know that it would come without fail if the march of Fascism were not interrupted, and we knew it at a time when that was not only possible but easy. We knew that appeasement was the surest means of bringing about the war. Indeed we have suffered from the unwillingness of the world to grasp the fact that domestic and foreign policies are one and the same, and that the sort of policies which the Nazis carried on in their own land were already war even though at the time in domestic form. It required no prophetic gift to see that, one needed only to be a German.

Now that the war is here we support it with all our hearts and we stand firmly on the side of the nations who, for the honor of humanity, had to undertake the difficult and costly struggle. Their final victory is our most urgent prayer, not because we expect revenge against the land which exiled us, but because the defeat of Nazi Germany is the only means of bringing back our country into the community of civilized nations, of taking from the name

Germany the horror which now clings to it and of returning to us the spiritual fatherland.

It is an entirely different question whether we intend to take up again our former life in our fatherland after its liberation, no matter how that liberation may occur. This question can only be answered individually, and the answers would vary according to personal circumstances. If I ask myself I must say: No. The idea of returning to Germany, to be reinstated into my property, and to regard these ten years, or how many they may be, as a mere interlude, this thought is far from me and appears to me quite impossible. It is now too late for me, and I say to myself that at my age it is of no consequence in what place one completes the life's work which, on the whole, is already established and which in a certain sense is already history. I am not on the point of becoming an American citizen just as my grandchildren who were born here and are growing up here, and my attachment to this country has already progressed so far that it would be contrary to my sense of gratitude to part from it again. To spend a few months every year in Switzerland where I lived five memorable years would be sufficient for my character as a European. As for Germany, all my wishes would be fulfilled if it were again spiritually open to me and if my work, so closely linked to the German language, again had access there.

Many emigrants may have a similar view with regard to a return home. Many have taken root in the lands of their refuge, have built up a new life and will not wish to start over again. Others perhaps, especially younger ones, await nothing more longingly than the historic moment when the bells will call them back to their home. With the first airplane, with the first ship, with the first train, they will hasten home, anxious to serve as cultural or political leaders in the new Germany. Equipped with the experiences which they have collected in the years of their cosmopolitan life and which have broadened their horizons, they can indeed be very useful to their country; for what Germany needs most is fresh air from the outside, knowledge and understanding of a world in which it has long been alone.

But those who renounce the return home will also have their responsibility and their mission for Germany, for Europe, and for the world. In any case it is an advantage today and a historically appropriate position to be a citizen of two worlds. The world wishes to become unified. Humanity faces the alternative of lacerating itself in one destructive war after another and of seeing civilization perish, or of agreeing upon a form of life which is based upon the idea of union and cooperation, in which the entire world is regarded as the common home of all and in which all are granted a similar right to the enjoyment of its fruits. In such a world and in preparation for such a world it is of small importance to be a German, an American, or an Englishman, in short to be a national in spirit, experience, language, and feeling. The old word *Weltbürger* ["citizen of the world"] or cosmopolitan, which, for a time, appeared old-fashioned, will again become honorable, and it is a German word.

We are writers and we claim to be psychologists enough to recognize that this monstrous German attempt at world domination, which we now see ending catastrophically, is nothing but a distorted and unfortunate expression of that universalism innate in the German character which formerly had a much higher, purer, and nobler form and which won the sympathy and admiration of the world for this important people. Power politics destroyed this universalism and brought about its downfall, for whenever universalism becomes power politics then humanity must arise and defend its liberty. Let us trust that German universalism will find the way to its old place of honor, that it will forever renounce the wanton ambition of world conquest and again prove itself as world sympathy, world understanding, and spiritual enrichment.

How closely connected are liberty and peace, and how closely connected the liberty of Germany and peace of the world! We emigrants are deeply ashamed when we think of the sufferings and sacrifices which the world has had to undergo on account of the errors of Germany, but all the more inspiring is the thought that Germany's liberty will be the peace of the world.

CHAPTER FOUR

A German Colony
on the Pacific

Alfred Polgar }

LIFE ON THE PACIFIC

Known as the "master of the short form," the Austrian writer Alfred Polgar (1873–1955) was a prominent theater critic in Berlin during the Weimar Republic. He emigrated to California in 1940 where he had contact with many emigrant writers, actors, and directors. The following essay appeared in the Aufbau *on September 4, 1942.*

The *Aufbau* has asked me for a piece about "life on the Pacific," presumably with particular emphasis on emigrant life. I can assure you that life here—if one is in good health, if one's heart isn't troubled by worry about the fate of one's family, friends, and distant acquaintances, if the general and particular reasons to be worried, disappointed, or disheartened aren't overwhelming, if one has enough work, if hope has half-paralyzed the despair about what is happening and about what is not happening, if there's enough money at home and most probably will be there tomorrow—under these conditions life on the Pacific is altogether tolerable, even pleasant.

We Pacificists owe this above all to the local climate which, as everybody knows, is remarkable for its tenacity. When a weather condition settles in here, it settles in for a long time. At the moment, i.e., for the last few months, very hot weather has settled in. But the people in Hollywood have a trick to make the heat more bearable. They imagine how people in New York are suffering from the heat, and the air around them immediately feels a few degrees cooler. The flora and fauna do their part to give life on the Pacific its friendly colors. In California the roses bloom several times a year. Over and over they start at the very beginning and run through their cycle to the very end. It's as if they wanted to tell the exhausted and discouraged human beings around them: "You just have to want it, then life will start going again . . ."

In sum, one can say that the person who's doing badly here is doing badly better than he would in comparable circumstances in one of the big eastern cities. He lives here in decidedly more comfortably sad conditions than anywhere else. Misery is surrounded by blooming roses, and once in a while a hummingbird floats gently by.

Emigrant conversations on the Pacific, especially in Hollywood—once the necessary statements about the world war and the world suffering have been objectively uttered and the accumulated grounds for personal bitterness have been aired—tend naturally toward the film industry. Conversation lingers there for a long time and is particularly bitter. The criticisms about *pictures* diverge enormously and (particularly the criticisms of those who have only a nonprofessional relation to movies) are radically inflexible and definitive. There is hardly any middle ground between "fantastic" and "disgusting." With regard to "fantastic," I should point out that in picture matters "fantastic" is Hollywood's lowest form of praise. If for instance someone has done something that is common practice on the Pacific, such as writing the story for a film, everyone—family, friends, agents, and people at all levels of the film studio—are sure to find it "fantastic." The only one who doesn't think it's fantastic is the author, whose fantastic stories no one knows what to do with.

Now the European actors driven out by the Nazis have more work. They find employment in the many war films which are currently being produced. Marvelous irony of fate: to become known—indeed, to get star treatment—for playing the part of the bestial Nazis who destroyed us.

In the material lives of emigrants on the Pacific, as probably on all other coasts, the search for a job plays its usual exhausting, nerve-racking role. It is an amazing coincidence of the English language that the standard biblical work on human suffering is entitled *The Book of Job*.

About the intellectual and cultural life of emigrants here I should report that it appears for the moment in its simplest, by no ways worst form, that is, reading. Material distress, emotional cares, and the curfew all lead one to take refuge in a book. But which of the profane writings should the distressed emigrant read? The books from back then take place in a world that no longer exists; they make certain moral assumptions, the ground for which has been swept away. And the books of today, vainly competing to be more up-to-date than contemporary events, will be tomorrow already hopelessly the books of yesterday. The only form to triumph is the fairy tale. Embedded in its thick layer of unreality, it is immune against all the vicissitudes of reality. With the fairytale the reader stands on firm ground. Truth, when it ages, becomes a lie, understanding turns to error. But time and academic research can't touch Peter Pan's tender, magical world; and our doubts, with their pain, are assuaged by Alice's experiences in Wonderland.

LETTER FROM THE
L.A. PUBLIC LIBRARY

1347 N. Citrus Dr., Hollywood
April 20, 1942

Dear [Hermann] Kesten,
   I'm sitting here in the Hollywood branch of the Los Angeles Public Library, poking around in books and magazines. This is what we have instead of a café in the afternoon. I commute here daily from three to five o'clock with virtually astronomical precision, in this way filling out my day a little bit. For what is one to do in this desert of drugstores and rooms masquerading as houses? To top things off, all of my potential acquaintances have become *Körffjuden* [curfew Jews] and can only move within a radius of five miles. We've also been advised to make our telephone calls in English. Well, New York's advantages are probably not overwhelming either. Here one experiences what exile really is. With regard to charity too. For soon, when I lose my unemployment money in three weeks, I will have reached that point. Oh well.
   The restless talk about Klatzkin refers merely to a few comments I made several months ago. You can also find them in my book *Robinson in France*. My constant, inner struggle with the figure of Christ, which continues and also found expression in volume two of *1918*.* *That's all.* How are you doing, Kesten? What is your lovely wife up to? *Ah quelle vie!*

Yours,
[Alfred] Döblin

---

* Reference here is to Döblin's conversion to Catholicism. Klatzkin was the editor of a Jewish Encyclopedia published in Berlin. *Robinson in France* was published in 1949 under the title of *Schicksalsreise* (Fateful Journey). Döblin's novel trilogy *November 1918* appeared after the Second World War.

A Part of Myself

Carl Zuckmayer (1896–1977) was a well-known playwright during the Weimar Republic whose plainspoken opposition to National Socialism resulted in a ban on his plays in Germany after 1933. He escaped from Austria with his wife, Alice Herdan, to the United States, served in the American Military Government in Germany after the war, and eventually settled in Switzerland. This selection is taken from Zuckmayer's autobiography of the same title.

Friends awaited and embraced me in Hollywood. There were endless reunions. Albrecht Joseph, the companion of my years in Kiel, Berlin, and Henndorf, was here; so were Bruno Frank and his wife Liesel, and Marlene Dietrich with her warmhearted camaraderie. Remarque had rented a handsome bungalow in the park of the Beverly Hills Hotel, where I took a room. He and I sat up long nights, drinking rum or vodka, just as if we were still in one of our Berlin nightclubs. The German movie directors Ernst Lubitsch, William Dieterle, and Fritz Lang invited me to their houses and their parties, where I met more friends from Germany, Austria, Hungary, France, and England. These directors knew my plays and other writings, but they could not use them for the American "market." They needed, they indicated, seasoned Hollywood writers for their scripts.

I also met some Americans—powerful, omnipotent rulers of an empire with feet of clay. My agent and my friends introduced me to them. At first they were very obliging, for I was a new arrival wearing the label of a "successful writer." They counted on my adjusting, shifting gears, fitting into their production process and their style of work. I therefore received that well-known "seven-year-contract," which in my case began with the sizable initial salary of seven hundred and fifty dollars a week, but put the signatory totally at the mercy of the company, which for its part was entitled to dismiss him on a week's notice. One of the clauses in this contract stated: "I hereby declare and affirm that for the purpose of this contract the concept of so-called intellectual property does not exist." Which meant that whatever you wrote on assignment from the studio belonged to the producer like delivered goods; he could do whatever he pleased with it, use it, throw it away, have it rewritten or completely altered, without the author's having any say in it. I was shown the "Writers' Building," a spacious structure in which there were many large, well-furnished offices for the scriptwriters. Such an office was assigned to me too, with a surplus of all kinds of writing materials and a secretary in the reception room. There was nothing I could do with her except give her a friendly greeting and leave her bottles of Coca-Cola, since I was not yet capable of dictating so much as a letter in English. I was also not geared to working in an office, and stayed there solely to take care of my personal mail. As for the script that had been assigned to me, I toiled at it by night in my hotel room. From time to time the telephone in my office rang, and the voice of the studio boss's head secretary asked: "How is your work going?" "Very well," I said. "Thank you," she said. Otherwise, no one paid much attention to me, and experienced fellow exiles told me that the main thing was to be seen there—lunching, for example, in the restaurant where the celebrities ate. For the rest, there was no point in overexerting myself, they said.

In Hollywood too there were many invitations at the beginning, but in contrast to New York, life was very expensive. In order to count for anything you had to live in a top-class hotel or have your own showy home. To prove yourself, you had to frequent the expensive restaurants of the movie industry's upper crust. Moreover, if you wanted to "belong" permanently, you had to begin issuing invitations yourself. You had to act as if you were rich and happy—nowhere have I ever heard the word "happy" so often as in that anteroom to hell called Hollywood. And because nobody was, everyone drifted into drinking even when he was in no mood for it, and ended up in a morass of joyless, humorless, and dreary nightlife.

Some weeks after "happiness" had come to me in the form of a contract and a weekly paycheck, I happened to be attending a Sunday afternoon party at Max Reinhardt's house. Almost the entire German colony was present. "I'm not staying here long," I remarked. "This is no life for me." Those words provoked roars of laughter. Everybody, I was told, had said the same thing after three weeks, everybody in this room, but they were all still here—some of them had been for many years. The check . . . Where else in America could you drift through life so comfortably?

There was some truth to that, but it did not console me, for I had seen that what was being drifted through could not be called life. Word spread like wildfire through the "colony" when one of these studio serfs had his check increased or reduced. You were ranked by the size of this check. I didn't think that funny. Max Reinhardt too did not join in the laughter. He had become acquainted with Hollywood's tough side, just as the first wave of refugees had early encountered the tough side of Switzerland. Something had happened to him that must not be allowed to happen in Hollywood: his movie *A Midsummer Night's Dream,* done in the lavish style of Reinhardt's baroque period, had netted less money than the studio had expected. The industry had dropped him, for if a man's work does not bring in a profit, he himself is regarded as worthless, however great an artist he may be in his field. On Broadway too Reinhardt's rigorous directing, with its concern solely for quality, had not accorded with the laws of the box office. Now he was running a drama school in Hollywood and occasionally giving performances with the more talented of his students. But these performances were attended only by connoisseurs, professionals, and Europeans. He himself did not know, and probably never learned, that his school and its performances were being secretly financed, in a most discreet and tactful way, by Gert von Gontard, a highly intelligent, cultivated, and sensitive lover of the arts and humanity, whom I later was to count among my best friends. But Reinhardt knew that Hollywood was no Garden of Allah. A few years earlier he had been the idol of international society and the theater world. Now, in his late sixties, he was once more embroiled in the struggle for status and livelihood.

In spite of the check, in spite of the presence of so many friends, Hollywood did not make me "happy." Never have I been so wrapped in the mists of depression as in this land of eternal spring, in whose irrigated gardens, with their chlorinated swimming pools and dream castles perched on the slopes of canyons, short-lived pleasure is at home, while in the depths sprawls a dreary, murderous wasteland: the city of Los Angeles, one of the ugliest and most brutal metropolises in the world.

[. . .] In the midst of my serfdom to the Hollywood check and still under contract, I had to go to New York to straighten out our legal status with the immigration authorities. We would have to leave the United States once more in order to re-enter on a legal visa. In our haste we had come on visitors' visas, and I had no right to accept paid work in America. In Hollywood exceptions were made, but with limits. Now for the first time we became acquainted with the tough side of New York. We went from office to office and stood in line at consulates. We encountered nasty police officials who treated us like criminals as they took our fingerprints, who shouted at us, cursed the "goddamn foreigners," did not attempt to conceal their admiration of the "strong man" Hitler and their contempt for the people he had exiled. That sort of thing existed in America too. The recommendations I had from people such as Thomas Mann and Hemingway, Dorothy Thompson and Marlene Dietrich, Thornton Wilder and Albert Einstein, made no impression on such officials. They did not even know most of these names, except for Marlene Dietrich. Here I was a smudge in an opaque mass, already halfway a "nothing." This was a period of rushing around and agonizing uncertainty. At last we were able to arrange to immigrate via Cuba. That too was a gamble; up to the last moment we did not know whether we would make it or be stranded penniless in Havana, at that time a favorite resort for rich American tourists and a city of refugees.

[After obtaining their visas in Cuba, Zuckmayer and his wife return to California.]

[. . .] My wife went on to San Francisco, where we had friends and life would be more economical than if she were with me in Hollywood. I moved back into my hotel room and chrome-plated desk in the Writers' Building. I wanted to finish the work I had taken on, cash a few more checks, and then — where to? Everything was uncertain. The one thing I knew for certain was that I did not want to stay there. Desperately I searched for a gap between the bars, like a newly captive bird. Then the supreme power, in other words the studio itself, came to my aid.

I was working on material that seriously interested me: a filming of Arnold Zweig's novel *The Cast of Sergeant Grischa*. It was the story of a Russian peasant soldier in the First World War who is falsely accused of espionage or sabotage, and although no one believes he is guilty and he wins the hearts of those who guard him, he is torn between the millstones of a divided bureaucracy.

In the midst of this work I was called to a projection room and without explanation shown a thoroughly ludicrous old Don Juan movie-strip from the days of the silents. Then the mighty Hal Wallis invited me into his office. Offering me a cigar and a glass of whisky, he told me to forget about Grischa. The studio had decided to drop the subject for political reasons. The Russians were currently engaged in their war against Finland, and this little country stood very high in American eyes because she punctually paid her war debts; the music of Sibelius monopolized the airwaves. At such a time it did not seem wise to bring out a movie whose hero was a likable Russian.

Instead I was to write a Don Juan script for Errol Flynn, romantic, melodramatic, with plenty of duels and love scenes, in a Renaissance setting: Medicean Florence. . . . I objected that the Don Juan legend applied to Spain and not to Florence. That didn't matter at all, Wallis assured me. The Medici (he meant the Borgias) were a fascinating bunch. The climax would be an affair between Don Juan and the famous lovely poisoner. This was a prime subject for a European writer, wasn't it? Yes or no? Would I let him know my decision in the morning. With a second cigar and a second glass of whisky, I was dismissed.

That evening I met the director Fritz Lang and told him what had happened. I said I had decided to turn down the project. I had been going along beautifully on *Sergeant Grischa* and could not abruptly switch to such trivial childishness. After all, I said, it was perfectly clear that they did not want a kind of poetic Don Juan done in ballad style, or a Mozartean Don Juan, or a fable, but some typical movie nonsense, and I had neither the talent nor the urge for that sort of thing. Fritz Lang, who wished me well, was horrified. In Hollywood you never said "no" to anything, no matter what was asked of you, he advised me. To refuse an assignment was to be fired. And how could I ask for anything better than this offer? It would keep me occupied for years; that kind of expensive costume spectacular went slowly, so that I could count on staying on for the length of my contract, which provided for an increase in the weekly check from year to year. I ought to rent a nice house and hire a Filipino couple as domestics, buy a car on installments, bring my family here, and be "happy." Besides, I would have a three-month holiday every year during which I could do my own writing. For God's sake be reasonable and say yes, Lang urged me; otherwise I was finished in Hollywood.

But I wanted to be finished. I knew that I could live comfortably here, but at the expense of my inner independence and my productivity. All around me I saw examples to prove that three months of holiday after nine months of apathy could never lead to any true and untrammeled work, to the completion of anything of substance. I felt I would perish in this golden cage, and now at last I had a glimpse of a gap between the bars. Next morning I refused the Don Juan assignment. On Monday I found the famous dismissal slip on my resplendent desk, the specter that haunted all the serfs in Hollywood. It contained a curt notice that my services were terminated as of the end of the current week. For me it was a release. I cashed my last check and went on a spree.

My wife too was glad that I had cut loose from Hollywood before it had swallowed me up or sapped my vitality. We had crossed the ocean to be free. We had no idea how we would win our freedom. But anything was better than submitting voluntarily to a sated, living death. Not for that had we escaped the Nazis' death camps.

It was Christmas week. I saw Hollywood one more time in all its horror. Artificial Christmas trees with electric candles in all imaginable colors, chiefly pink, orange, and silvery blue, stood in front of the houses. I had been invited to a party given in the Beverly Hills Hotel. A slide had been covered with artificial snow and men in bathing trunks, women in silk jerseys, skied down it directly into the cocktail tent. Huge crimson poinsettias bloomed in all the gardens. The sight of all this nauseated me. I said goodbye to my friends and went to San Francisco to join my wife.

Anyone acquainted with Hollywood knows (and it should be apparent to all) that this is an entirely subjective account, the personal experience, impressions, and decisions of an individual with whom the climate there did not agree. Let no generalization, no verdict, be drawn from my remarks. That would be unfair. This weird combination of artificial and artistic fragments, or business and imagination, of pointless motion, real activity, and high ambition, saw many others through the hardest years of their lives. Many magnificent productions—some that can safely be called works of art—were and are being created there. At this period I am discussing anything decent had to emerge from an obstinate battle with the monstrous industry; today the good things stem from the daring independent producers. But to achieve this takes conviction, takes total devotion to the medium, to the good and the bad sides of the production system. You have to be obsessed by the craft, or else, if you want to live a peaceful and relatively human life there, you have to practise resignation and be content with subsidiary technical contributions. Neither of these attitudes was possible for me.

We spent Christmas in San Francisco. That was the saddest, most forlorn Christmas of our lives. My wife had rented cheap quarters, set up a crèche, decorated a few pine branches with candles. On Christmas Eve we sat in an Italian basement restaurant and tried not to talk about home. Then we returned to New York.

Exiled from Our Era

Already in 1923, Brecht was fifth on the blacklist of the Nazi Party. He went into exile in Switzerland in 1933, moving later to Denmark and, in 1939, to the United States, where he lived in New York and California. An avowed Marxist, Brecht was interrogated by the House Committee on Un-American Activities on October 30, 1947; he left for Paris the next day and later settled in East Germany, where he died in 1956. The following are excerpts from his diary of the period, Bertolt Brecht Journals, 1934–1955.

july 22, 1941

feuchtwanger lives in santa monica, in a big, mexican-style house. his personality is unchanged, but in appearance he has aged. he is working for the theatre here on a play about a german astrologer and charlatan. his advice is to stay here, where it is cheaper than in NY, and where there are more opportunities for earning.

august 1, 1941

almost nowhere has my life ever been harder than here in this mausoleum of *easy going*. the house is too pretty, and here my profession is gold-digging, the lucky ones pan big nuggets the size of your fist out of the mud and people talk about them for a while; when i walk, i walk on clouds like a polio victim. and i miss grete, here especially. it is as if they had taken away my guide as soon as i entered the desert.

august 9, 1941

i feel as if i had been exiled from our era, this is tahiti in the form of a big city; at this very moment i am looking out on to a little garden with a lawn, shrubs with red blossom, a palm tree and white garden furniture, and a male voice is singing something sentimental to piano accompaniment—it's not a wireless. they have nature here, indeed, because everything is so artificial, they even have an exaggerated feeling for nature, which becomes alienated. from diet-

erle's house you can see the san fernando valley; an incessant, brilliantly il
minated stream of cars thunders through nature; but they tell you that all t
greenery is wrested from the desert by irrigation systems. scratch the surface
little and the desert shows through: stop paying the water bills and everythin
stops blooming. the butchery 15,000 kilometres away, which is deciding ou
fate right across europe at its broadest point, is only an echo in the hubbub o
the art market here.

[august 1941]

walter benjamin has poisoned himself in some little spanish border town. the
guardia civil had stopped the little group he belonged to. when the others went
to tell him the next morning that they were being allowed to carry on, they
found him dead. i read the last article he sent to the institute for social research, günther stern* gave it to me, commenting that it is complex and obscure, i think he also used the word "beautiful." the little treatise deals with
historical research, and could have been written after reading my CAESAR
(which b. could not make much of when he read it in svendborg). b. rejects the
notion of history as a continuum, the notion of progress as a mighty enterprise
undertaken by cool, clear heads, the notion of work as the source of morality,
of the workforce as protégés of technology, etc. he makes fun of the common
remark about its being astonishing that fascism should "still be possible in this
century" (as if it were not the fruit of every century). in short the little treatise
is clear and presents complex issues simply (despite its metaphors and its ju-
daisms) and it is frightening to think how few people there are who are prepared even to misunderstand such a piece.

october 25, 1941

evening at döblin's. little rented house for $60 a month that they have to leave,
now that he has been *fired* along with 8 others who got *picture-writer* contracts
when they arrived from france, including heinrich mann). he has nothing and
nowhere to go, but still shows his old berlin sense of humor. what business
could he start? to sit medical examinations he would have to study for a year,
to work as a healer he would have to speak english (i can hardly hypnotise a
man to ask him for the word that i want to say to him). it might be possible to
screw something out of the film industry if you could set up a brothel for
elderly ladies, for that would help tame the censorship which is largely in
the hands of these ladies. i suggest to him he should modernise half a dozen
classics.

---

* Real name of Günther Anders.

november 14, 1941

it is difficult for refugees to avoid either indulging in wild abuse of the "americans," or "talking with their paychecks in the mouths" as kortner puts it when
he is having a go at those who earn well and talk well of the USA. in general
their criticism is directed at certain highly capitalistic features, like the very
advanced commercialization of art, the smugness of the middle classes, the
treatment of culture as a commodity rather than a utility, the formalistic character of democracy (the economic basis for which—namely competition between independent producers—has got lost somewhere). so homolka throws
out bruno frank because he gets to his feet and shouts, "i will not permit the
president to be criticized here," kortner shows up lang as the source of an
anti-semitic remark, nünberg hates lorre, etc.

january 21, 1942

odd, i can't breath in this climate. the air is totally odorless, morning and
evening, in both house and garden. there are no seasons here. it has been part
of my morning routine to lean out of the window and breathe in fresh air; i
have cut this out of my routine here. there is neither smoke nor the smell of
grass to be had. the plants seem to me like the twigs we used to plant in the
sand as children. after ten minutes their leaves were dangling limply. you keep
wondering if they might cut off the water, even here, and what then? occasionally, especially in the car going to beverley hills, i get something like a
whiff of landscape, which "really" seems attractive; gentle lines of hills, lemon
thickets, a californian oak, even one or other of the filling stations can actually
be rather amusing; but all this lies behind plate glass, and i involuntarily look
at each hill or lemon tree for a little price tag. you look for these price tags on
people too. not being happy in my surroundings is not something i like, especially in these circumstances. i get great store by my status, the distinguished
status of refugee, and it is quite unseemly to be so servile and keen to please
refugees as the surroundings here are. but it is probably just the conditions of
work that are making me impatient. custom here requires that you try to
"sell" everything, from a shrug of the shoulders to an idea, ie, you have always
to be on the look-out for a customer, so you are constantly either a buyer or a
seller, you sell your piss, as it were, to the urinal. opportunism is regarded as
the greatest virtue, politeness becomes cowardice.

april 18, 1942

this country blows my *UI NOVEL* to smithereens. it is impossible to show up the
sale of opinions here, where it is nakedly practiced. the comedy of those who
think they are leading but are in effect being led, the don-quixotry of a con-

sciousness which labors under the delusion that it is determining social existence—all that only applies to europe.

april 20, 1942

[Hanns] eisler here. he has a grant from the rockefeller foundation (subject: film music) "15 ways of describing rain" (film-clip of rain, accompanied by taut music). perhaps after all my tui novel is not totally . . . eisler is his old self in wit and wisdom.

april 21, 1942

i sent a piece about hitler to READER'S DIGEST (sales 3.5 million) for their series "my most unforgettable character." it came back very promptly. feucht-wanger tells me thomas mann and werfel, who has been very successful here, had their contributions sent back too. the magazine submits readers' contri-butions to half a dozen experts. one checks whether the thing is brown, a second whether it stinks, a third that there are no solid lumps in it, etc. that is how strictly it is checked to see that it is real shit before they accept it. (expert on suspense, expert on characterization, expert on "truth of life," etc)

july 11, 1942

kortner cannot get any part. eisler recounts that the people at RKO laughed out loud when the screen test was shown: he rolled his eyes. real acting is frowned upon here and only accepted from negroes. stars don't act parts, they step into "situations." their films form sort of comics (a novel of adventure in installments), which show a fellow in tight corners. (even the accounts of the story in the press say things like: gable hates garbo, but as a reporter . . . etc.) but his very unemployment forces kortner to act much more, even in private life, than he ever did on the stage. i watch him with a mixture of amusement and horror as he recounts a simple tale of inconsequential events with a plethora of expression and gesture.

october 19, 1942

interesting how a person falls apart if one function is closed down. the ego becomes formless if it is no longer addressed, approached, ordered around. alienation of the self sets in.

during the work i was occasionally hard put to it to avoid getting involved in solving their grubby little problems, like finding those slick, smart "*lines*" and the transitions from one pointless situation to another, and writing gush in general, all of which i left to others. that kind of thing can seriously damage your handwriting, at least that's how i felt.

november 5, 1942

winge went to the *us employment service* to find out about openings in the *defence industry*. the official in the industrial division, a thin, quiet man in spectacles with a rather worn collar looked at his card, said to him, *"you're a refugee? see, our defence industry is owned by big money, got me? and big money doesn't like people who don't like hitler, got me? and big money doesn't like a certain racial minority either, got me? and so they are not taking people like you."* winge got him.

november 15, 1942

high hopes of the second front in africa. though the political arrangements are a little surprising.

work with feuchtwanger in the morning on JOAN OF ARC FROM VITRY, occasionally pop into the studio. when lang sets up a fight between the gestapo commissar and the heroine's fiancé something that almost looks like art emerges, and the work has the dignity and the respectability of craftsmanship. it is technically not uninteresting to see the precision and elegance with which a jackboot deals a kick, first to the chest and then in the ribs of a man on the ground. naturally this fight is inserted here, and not at the nobler point we had suggested, when the kitchen staff of a restaurant prevents the gestapo from capturing an underground cell . . .

october 30, 1947

morning in *washington* before the *un-american activities committee*. after two hollywood writers (lester cole and ring lardner jr) had answered the question whether they belonged to the communist party by saying that the question was unconstitutional, i was called to the witness stand, followed by the lawyers for the nineteen, bob kenny and bartley c crum, who were not permitted to intervene in any way. about eighty pressmen, two radio stations, a newsreel cameraman, photographers, in the public galleries theater people from broadway as friendly observers. as had been agreed with the other eighteen and their lawyers i, as a foreigner, answer the question with "no," which also happens to be the truth. for the prosecution stripling reads from DIE MASSNAHME and has me give an account of the plot. i refer them to the japanese model, define its content as dedication to an idea, and reject the interpretation that the subject is disciplinary murder by pointing out that it is a question of self-extinction. i admit that the basis of my plays is marxist and state that plays, especially with an historical content, cannot be written intelligently in any other framework. the hearing is excessively polite and ends without an indictment; i benefit from having had almost nothing to do with hollywood, from never having participated in american politics and from the fact that my predecessors refused to give evidence.—the eighteen are very pleased with my statements as are the lawyers. i leave washington immediately, along with losey and hambleton, who had come over. in the evening i listen to parts of my hearing on the radio with helli and the budzislawskys.

october 31, 1947

in the morning i meet laughton who is already going around in his galileo beard and is pleased that it isn't going to take any special courage to play galileo, there being, as he says, no *headlines* about me. in the afternoon i take off for paris.

CHAPTER FIVE

New Lives

Alice Herdan }

A Second Childhood

The wife of the German poet and dramatist Carl Zuckmayer, Alice Herdan
describes the somewhat unusual experience of living off the land on a farm
in Vermont, far from the masses of other German emigrants clustered in
New York—an experience of strangeness that she likens to a "second child-
hood."

So there was the house in which I was supposed to live, and around the house the meadows, and around the meadows the forests full of brush that hadn't been cleared away.

There was the pond from which dead trees rose like the limbs of the drowned.

There a brook ran steeply down into a forest where raccoons climbed on trees, snorting porcupines scratched and pushed their way through the undergrowth, while sometimes a lynx would crouch on rocks with gleaming eyes and piercing cries.

Wild cats hissed there and rabbits scampered about freely, skunks shuffled by while a bear sat in the scrub eating raspberries. In the fall cranes flew over the woods to the pond. In the summer hummingbirds hovered in front of the windows, the music of unfamiliar birds rose from the trees, and in the barn huge spiders with heavy bodies sat in their webs.

At night the moon hung above this landscape with its strange animals like a reclining crescent.

There were wooded mountains with fir trees, spruces, pines, beeches, birches, elms, and maples. In the woods there were weasels, martens, and foxes. It was a landscape that resembled the one I was long accustomed to down to the smallest detail, and yet it was completely foreign and strange.

It was as if one had strayed into an enchanted, haunted forest where every shape and form had been transfigured, and above which even the moon hung at a different angle. The sky too no longer seemed to border the earth in an arch like a glass bell. It was as if the sky and the earth had become parallel planes intersecting somewhere in the invisible, in infinity.

This brought on a feeling of expansiveness and boundlessness that I had never known before.

In optics the law of refraction states that "the size of the image on the retina depends only on the angle of vision." Now it seemed as though the angle of vision had shifted and with it the images on the retina.

We could no longer rely on what we had learned; everything was completely new and completely different.

Many immigrants have experienced this condition as a second childhood and have called it that.

You had to learn to see, hear, feel, smell, taste all over again. You had to get used to the vast open space, to the distribution of objects within this space, and only very gradually did you find your balance in the unfamiliar dimensions. The forest, the meadow, the house all smelled different.

Everything tasted different, for the soil was sweet and produced sweet plants and fruit. People mixed sweet and sour and the taste was strange to us. We had to learn to speak and know hundreds of practical terms for our everyday life. We learned the common language but the language didn't seem common to us.

Everything was completely different and completely foreign.

In late fall a loneliness settled around the house that came from outside and that condensed almost to the point of visibility. Later, with the first snowfall, a quiet descended, a quiet full of movement, rising and falling, that rang in our ears.

It had happened on a Saturday night. At noon on Sunday, Finnish friends called us from the nearest university town.

"What will happen now?" said the woman in a worried voice, "and what will you do?"

"What we always do," I responded innocently. "Keep the house warm, cook, tidy up, slowly prepare for winter."

"If they let you," she said, and I suddenly noticed that she was speaking English even though we always spoke German with each other.

"Has something happened?" I asked.

"But haven't you heard about Pearl Harbor?" she asked with astonishment.

"No," I said, "we haven't turned on the radio since the day before yesterday. What is Pearl Harbor?"

"The war," she said.

From that moment on we had the radio going day and night, with few interruptions.

Sometimes the radio is an eerie instrument. So there we were, sitting in our farm house that stood in the woods like the island of Robinson Crusoe, and suddenly we could hear the droning noise of masses of people gathered together in a large room. One could hear the shuffling of feet, people clearing their throats in a group as they waited for something.

In our imagination we could hear and see Washington waiting more clearly than a film might have shown it. For a moment there followed total, deadly silence, and then he began to speak: "Mister President."

It had been a long and warm late autumn and we had had only a few cold days, even though it was the beginning of December.

But now, in the days of the Japanese declaration of war, a gruesome cold seeped into the house and it became impossible to tell whether it was the cold from outside or the cold of despair which put us in a constant state of trembling.

We waited three days and nights for a decision about Germany to be reached.

Monday, Tuesday, Wednesday. . . .

We sat, caught in the cold and damp grotto of a mountain, and heard time trickling by.

"When I resurface to the light," I thought, "one hundred years will have passed. All those I once knew will be dead and everything will have changed."

On Thursday the German declaration of war rang out.

On Thursday afternoon we realized we had no more food in the house and lacked everything from salt to bread. We decided that Zuck [Carl Zuckmayer] should go to the local store and buy the most urgent things there. The trip to and from the general store, the only store in town, took an hour and a half.

I can remember that afternoon down to the smallest detail.

I was sitting in the living room in front of the open door of a closet where I had hung a spring coat that needed hemming. It was a senseless occupation, for I wouldn't be able to use the coat for the next six months, and I don't know why I had picked up precisely this coat. Outside a storm was howling and screeching as if someone were pulling a silk ribbon through one's teeth.

Zuck had filled the stove in the living room to the brim with large pieces of wood and had built a big fire in the fireplace.

Still, the cold came through the walls in invisible billows, freezing one's fingertips and toes.

Zuck was now standing in front of me with the wood-bin on his back and a knapsack in his hand.

"You mustn't let the fire die down," he said. "I can't make it back in less than two hours."

I kept on sitting there, sewing, and suddenly I had the strangely painless sensation of a large lump of ice lodged behind my forehead, right above the bridge of my nose. When Zuck left, I sat down by the fire to warm my fingers.

"Now it's over," I thought, "now we are completely cut off from Europe. No more letters, no more news. Now it's all over. We left Germany, we didn't belong there anymore. We've come to America, but we're not American. Will they mistrust us here because we come from such a plague-ridden country? Will they lock us away in camps as they did in France, or will they deport us as they did in England? This is the end. Emigration and immigration are final like death and birth. I have not yet been reborn."

I sat there, dull and numb, waiting for the touch of the witch's wand to turn me to stone, or that of the magician to teach me to fly. When Zuck got home, the fires had gone out and the house was freezing cold.

Zuck, who had no sense of humor when his fires weren't tended to, was mild as a sage this time and got his fires going again after just a little scolding.

"What are they saying in town?" I asked him.

"They aren't saying anything," he replied. "They're not talking about the war."

"Maybe because we're foreigners," I said.

"I don't know," Zuck said pensively. "My feeling is that even when we aren't around and might be listening in—the war isn't something people talk about."

That same evening, when Zuck turned on the water in the sink, a small trickle of black, slimy liquid came out and then the water stopped running. An ominous bubbling, hissing noise was coming from the water tank in the kitchen.

"There's no more water in the tank," Zuck said. "I have to turn off the stove in the kitchen or else the tank will explode."

I went to the telephone and called the landlord in town.

"There's no more water in the pipes," I said, "and the tank is about to explode. Please send someone over or come up to the farm right away to find out what might have happened."

"I'll come by tomorrow," he replied calmly. "I know. The pipes are frozen. They freeze easily at twenty-five below."

We spent half the night working.

Zuck carried glowing embers outside from the fire in the kitchen and fetched buckets of water from the pond, which was frozen over with a thin layer of ice that he first had to hack open.

I boiled water in a tea kettle over the open fire and melted ice cubes from the freezer for drinking water.

When the landlord arrived the next morning with a plumber, they brought candles and torches and warmed up the pipes so relentlessly that one of the pipes in the bathroom burst. A torrent of water came gushing out right above our library in the middle of the living room.

All these catastrophes taught me always to watch the stove and fire and—come what may—never to forget to take care of the small, immediate tasks.

On Saturday morning I woke up early, bothered by a glaring, hot light that seemed to come from the bedroom walls.

It was even more quiet than usual, and then I heard for the first time that silence full of movement which seemed to rise and fall in the room with no regular rhythm in the interval of a cuckoo's call, often repeating either the high or the low note.

It was still very cold, but snow had fallen during the night, the first snow.

Snowed in like this, the house seemed to be even more remote and more distant from other human habitation.

In this white loneliness I could hear the comforting sounds of morning.

I heard Zuck getting up, putting wood on the fires, going to the kitchen to prepare breakfast. We had a gentlemen's agreement that he would be the breakfast cook and I the lunch and dinner cook, as well as the dishwasher.

I heard the clatter of the dishes, smelled the hot, slowly percolating coffee and started feeling warm, sheltered, and safe.

Then suddenly I heard steps coming toward the house. That was unusual and somewhat odd, because hardly anybody visited the house during the fall and winter months after our summer guests and friends had left.

I got up, went to the window and saw two men coming up the steep hill.

One of them was wearing a dark uniform and didn't look familiar; the other was the district sheriff.

At first I was paralyzed with fear.

"They're coming to get him," I thought. "We've put 5,000 kilometers between us and the country of deportations, and now it's happening to him again here."

I threw on a bathrobe, ran down the stairs and stopped at the door to the living room.

I couldn't make out what the men were saying, but their voices sounded calm and measured.

"Here are our immigration papers," I heard Zuck say. The conversation lasted barely ten minutes.

"You can find out about all the regulations through the newspapers," I heard the sheriff say loudly.

Then they said goodbye and I watched them go back down the hill.

I went to Zuck in the kitchen.

"They couldn't make it up the hill in the car," he said, "they had to leave it on the main road. There's too much snow and ice in the driveway."

"What did they want and what will happen now?" I asked.

"I think nothing at all." he said, "They just wanted to see our papers."

That day, a snow fall started that seemed never to end, and the snow rose in front of our windows like flood waters.

We could barely sleep that night.

The beams were squeaking and groaning, and sometimes one could hear small explosions in the rafters that sounded like bullets hitting the house. We were later told that in old houses this was caused by the large wooden nails, which popped loose during such weather.

On the following day when I opened the kitchen door to step outside—it opened inward—I suddenly found myself standing up to my hips in snow. After Zuck had dug me out and I was back in the kitchen, I said: "We have two cans of food left. Do you think you can make it to town?" "I'll try," he said. He tried to go on skis and sank into the snow so that he had to take them off and carry them and could only use them again on the last stretch, on the larger road. Three hours later he returned, weighed down like a mule, soaked to the bone, and exhausted. After a couple of whiskies, he said: "That was quite an expedition. This time around it went okay. But I have to have snow tires, otherwise we can't make it."

"And we need supplies," I said, "not just for two days at a time. We have to set up camp here as if we were in a refuge in the Alps. If this keeps up, we could be snowed in for a week at a time. If only the snow plow would come and clear a path.

During that night the snow plow did come.

We had fallen asleep late, kept awake in this third night of snow by an added noise: the sound of compacted masses of snow sliding from the roof and thudding to the ground, piling up in front of the ground-floor windows like solid mounds of ice. Just when we had finally fallen asleep, we were woken up by an earthquake.

The walls were trembling, the windows rattling, the house seemed to be shaking down to its very foundation.

At the same time we could hear the whining sound of a running motor, like an airplane in a tailspin, and headlights lit up the inside of the house.

It was the snow plow.

It was two in the morning.

We quickly pulled on our clothes and coats and went down to the kitchen.

The snow plow had come right up to the kitchen door and cleared a broad, smooth path.

Now it turned away from the kitchen door, humming and grumbling, its back coming to a standstill at our kitchen door. It looked like a tired bug that had eaten too much.

Zuck went and got some beer from the basement and the drivers came into the kitchen.

There were three of them. They cleaned off the crust of snow from their coats and gloves, and hung up their wool hats. Then we all sat around the warm kitchen stove, they clapped their hands to get the blood moving, and they drank beer from the bottle.

And they started talking: "Lots of snow. It'll be a long winter. We're just coming from Hunger Mountain where all the farms are. The farms are first in line. Lots of snow. But it'll get worse yet. It took us two hours today to get from

Hunger Mountain to your place. It'll take even longer now. This is just the beginning of the winter. Eighteen years ago, now that was a winter. . . ."

And then came the stories of storms and disaster. And all of a sudden I felt like I belonged with this winter, these storms, these disasters.

The kitchen stove and the three plow men gave off a warmth that took away our feeling of being strangers in a foreign place and kindled a spark of hope.

When they climbed back onto their snow plow at 3:30 a.m., they waved and called out: "Good night. Let's hope it gets better by Christmas."

It was ten days before Christmas.

We had forgotten all about Christmas.

An Immigrant Family

Life Story of a Recent Immigrant — A Cook.
Interview done Febr. 14, 1945 — Archives of the YIVO Institute for
Jewish Culture

My daughter and I came over in 1934. She was twelve at the time. Some friends got me a job in St. Paul, Minnesota. I was a cook for this lady and we lived in her apartment. It was a lovely place overlooking the city. Then the lady was very kind, you would think we had known her all our life. She had four boys and wanted very much to adopt my daughter, and sent her to art school while we were there. Both she and I went to night school. They had a very nice International Institute with citizenship classes there, and I miss that here in Philadelphia. I had learned English in school, but couldn't really speak a word. My daughter hadn't learned any yet.

In 1933 we came to Philadelphia. I had some friends from Germany whom I had visited in Philadelphia before, and I liked it. I took a cooking job on the Main Line in a house with fifteen servants. I stayed there six years. It's somewhat hard to have to work for someone else when you are old, and to work hard, but I can adjust myself to anything. In my own household I had eight people, and I used to do the cooking because I liked it, although I had help. Here there were seventeen people to cook for and it was terribly hard the first week, but I got used to it. There were fifteen servants in the house, and I had only to do the cooking. I never would take any job in a household except cooking, that's the only thing that interests me. If I hadn't had my children to worry about, that job would have been ideal. I had a little home about fifteen-minutes walk from the main house, and my girl could go to school there. Of course I did have to work awfully long. I stayed at that job until 1941.

My boy is six now. I left him in Europe with his father and he stayed there for four years till his father died in 1938. He was always depressed in Germany. He was a sensitive boy, too sensitive. For a young boy he got no pleasure in life. He came over in 1938 and stayed with me. About two and a half years ago he first went to a mental hospital for a couple of months. But he got worse and worse. Friends helped me to get him into the Philadelphia State Hospital last summer. In the last four weeks he's gotten much worse. The bad thing is that he gets no treatment there, although the doctors who sent him there recommended that it was important to get insulin and electric shock treatments for him. Still, I have every confidence in the doctors there.

I worked at other cooking jobs, but a month or so ago my boy got worse and could not come home on weekends alone. Before that they had let him travel down by himself. They think that I have to come and get him every weekend, so I could not keep up with the cooking job and do that. Several weeks ago I started to work in a factory making cases for bullets. The first two weeks they trained me. It was very simple, and very monotonous. At first I worked on a reamer machine, but now I'm on an assembly line. I had an accident after I'd been there ten days, when I got my hair caught in the machine. Factory work is play after the work I had been doing. The hours are not so tiring as household work. There you work from seven in the morning until eight or nine o'clock in the evening, you are really never through. This job keeps me eight and a half hours, but with household I was never less than twelve or fourteen, and worked longer when there was company. Never had a chance to live any private life. It was just going and going with no stop. I just cut out an article here on a union of domestic workers. That would be good, if you could have shorter hours and have some life of your own. For instance, in the first place where I worked it was a tremendous house with thirteen people to serve and only five servants. My daughter worked with me there. We started at 7:20 with breakfast, then there were always luncheons, and dinner of thirteen people even if there weren't any guests. We never got through. If the hours could be shorter, it would be alright. Still, factory is awfully mechanical. I like to manage and plan things, work with my head. As a cook I always ordered and planned the meals, I wouldn't do it otherwise.

My daughter is twenty-three and she is going to graduate from Agnes Scott College in June. She has loved it there, she has really grown into the place. She wants to go to graduate school for a year, and then go back there and teach. They expect her to come back. She's now teaching eight hours of German for them. She has many friends down there. She got a scholarship there through the friends and was helped by them while she was going there. She has really loved it although it is very strict. There is no smoking for example, but the people and the faculty have a wonderful spirit. She is doing honors work this year without any classes.

In the summertime my daughter and I have always worked together. We always work as cook and waitress.

The people in the factory are pretty nice, although there are a few Irish people who don't seem to like the Germans and it was the same in domestic service. The other day we had some German silver for soldering, and one of the girls said, "Oh no, I don't like to use this, it's German." But on the whole they are nice and kind. When I had my accident, everybody was wonderful and the forelady called to see me every day. They have lots to talk about there though, besides foreigners. Today they had an election. A CIO man promised us wonderful things. I don't know if they were true but I think probably the union will win. The man told us about how he had raised the wages at Budd's Plant. It sounded good, and I think they will win. But somehow most of the people I've known have always been nice. It seems like a miracle to me that we have got along as we have. I never knew how it happened, but we've been very fortunate, in my getting jobs and in my daughter getting a scholarship. Nobody could have been nicer than the people I've worked for.

I don't know what I'll do from now on. It depends on how my son gets. For one sure thing I am never out of a job. So far I've always been lucky to find them. I may go back to cooking after the war, maybe if there are shorter hours.

An American Life

*Having passed his New York State Medical Examination, Hertha
Nathorff's husband sets up a practice on Central Park West. Slowly, she can
begin to develop her own career—though no longer as a physician.*

January 10, 1941

Our son's birthday. I managed to put together a few apples, a piece of cake,
and a small book as birthday presents. He thanked us excessively. You
shouldn't have done this, you shouldn't have bought anything for me, he said.
But still he was pleased, and that's all that matters.

We are going everywhere, looking for an appropriate office for my husband. I'm so discouraged, I've started studying in secret for the exam. My
husband says nothing. I've lost all my courage, the glass wall between us is
back, I sense it, and an awkward silence reigns.

February 15, 1941

We've found an office. Here, facing Central Park, as a tenant in a colleague's
office, for a few hours each day, at great expense. But it's a start, and I know
that patients will come. A few have already told us how much they've been
waiting for their old doctor (and for me).

May 9, 1941

Now I've passed the language exam, despite all my other work, the heavy
manual labor. If I weren't so determined, the work would have demoralized
me, but I want to make it through to the end, I want to! The struggle to earn
the money for our old belongings or, at least, for our medical instruments and
a few precious pieces from our old apartment—that struggle continues. No
one wants to give us the small sum it would take. Nonetheless, now we are
showered with invitations to tea, to dinner, now suddenly they all realize that
we're about to make it! Now! But enough trust to lend us the little bit of
money, no, that they didn't have. And invitations? I don't have time for them,

and even less desire to accept them. I say quite openly: "Now we can afford enough food to fill our stomachs, but this past year, that's when you should have invited us to dinner or at least given my boy an apple or a piece of bread." And then an awkward silence sets in, and I've succeeded once again in making myself unwelcome. My husband furrows his brow, he doesn't understand how I can say such things. But I can't help myself, something inside me is screaming to get out.

May 30, 1941

Memorial Day—the day of mourning for the dead of World War I. Concert in Central Park. How beautiful, and yet how sad.

September 1, 1941

Now a good portion of the year has passed and I've written nothing for a long time. My work was so exhausting, the people made it so hard for me. Again we spent the summer in a camp—I hope for the last time. Again we were the refugees who must put up with every prank, who have to work three times as hard for a third of the salary that a so-called American would get. Who or what exactly is an American? I often scratch my head over that. In the camp I was able to do some investigating, and I think I can say where the parents of every child originally came from. But most of the children don't know where they come from. "From somewhere in Europe," most of them respond— children of immigrants who once came to the New World as destitute as we were and who didn't even tell them why or how they came here.

September 18, 1941

All my earlier depression is back again. I'm trying to prepare for the [New York State Medical] examination. But my husband probably doesn't approve—even back in Germany it didn't quite sit well with him that his wife had a job and earned a living. He can't get rid of his upbringing as the upper-class son of a *Geheimrat,* the whole stuffy atmosphere. His pride, his stupid pride that he alone must provide for his family, torments him, but it also torments me. "Please help me," I pleaded with him a few times when I didn't completely understand something. "Everybody knows that," was his answer. I was ashamed of my ignorance, and so recently I ran outside late at evening, I stood at the edge of the water, by the Hudson, and the water beckoned to me . . . I took off my shoes, my light coat and hat, put everything including my purse on a nearby bench, and I walked further and further, closer and closer to the water. Suddenly a hand grabbed me, rough and firm. "What are you doing? Where are you going?" yelled a voice at me in German. Without resisting I let myself be led back and placed on the lonely bench, and

I cried helplessly. I didn't know what the man was yelling at me until he became very quiet and gentle, and he kissed me on both eyes.

"So young and pretty," he said. "And here in America. Here is where life really begins, there's plenty of time for dying . . ."

He accompanied me to my door. I was almost ashamed to show him the house we lived in. He wrote his telephone number on a piece of paper and made me promise I would call him tomorrow to tell him I was still alive. Justin is his name—Justin. I don't know anything about him except that he also came here from Germany.

October 13, 1941

Time races by, and I race with it, from one job to the next, while my husband has found his way back to his beloved profession. And from the time his small doctor's sign has been hanging outside the building at the corner of Central Park, the invitations keep flowing in. Now everyone knows, everyone keeps telling us we are about to make it, and I have to hold my tongue to keep from giving them the answer they deserve. Once I did say: You dragged the ship-wrecked onto land, but then omitted to give them oxygen to breathe. And the sins of omission weigh heavy. The invitations? No, I can't accept. Back then, when we arrived and had nothing to eat, you should have invited us then. Today when I have some free time I visit the friends who were faithful to us from the very beginning. My "new" friend Justin keeps asking me to call him, and I do it because I promised him that fateful night. I may be playing with fire, but it won't burn me, this fire, it warms my frozen soul.

And today is our anniversary. My husband was as tender and grateful and attentive as can be. In the evening we even went to the movies, how "upscale" we've become. But something was missing, perhaps it's the constant nagging worry about life "back there," the homesickness that is especially strong on such occasions. Just don't think about it, don't think of the past, I repeat to myself every day. But I can't manage it. And that's why my studying isn't going well, despite all my effort and longing for my old profession. I'm not progressing with my clandestine studies, it's as if my memory were impaired since the horrible experience back then when I saw a gun pointed at me in my own house. I still dream about the extortion attempt, and then I start crying and call out in my sleep. And that's the worst part—to have to spend the night in someone else's house, with strangers.

Recently I asked the wife of the elderly, paralyzed man I care for if I could have a screen that could be put in front of my bed—a miserable old couch. The woman almost laughed herself silly. She'd never had such a prudish nurse in her house, she said. But that's the way I am, that was how my mother raised me, and her lessons are still with me.

December 7, 1941

Japan has attacked [Pearl Harbor]! The war is getting bigger and bigger. Still more suffering, even more sadness and destruction, how pointless it all is, and here I am worrying about my own, small, insignificant fate. And yet how much more useful and better work I could do if I were back in my old profession. "You were always an above-average physician; don't you feel an obligation to be one again?" my former professor asked me in a letter. I was his assistant for many years. Me? Yes, I feel the obligation like a burning wound, but what about the others? And my husband? They don't feel it, and I'm going to pieces inside because of it, in silence; I've asked and begged and pleaded long enough.

In the meantime I've been studying with a colleague and friend of mine, but I'm slowing him down because often I have to cancel our meetings because I can't get off work. I don't want to be a burden to anyone. But recently they did it to me again. I had gone out with my husband to attend a medical lecture. In the elevator we met a colleague to whom I once referred many patients when we were both practicing in Berlin. She shook my husband's hand (no doubt thinking that he will send patients to her) with the words "Good evening, my dear colleague." And then she turned to me:

"Ach, you're here too. What are *you* doing here?"

Does she think that one can only be interested in a medical lecture when one has a license to practice? I pretended not to hear her insulting question and I stayed behind until she had entered the lecture hall at my husband's side. So alone, so abandoned—not even my husband takes pity and sticks up for me.

A small French woman, a dermatologist, visits us from time to time so that my husband can explain a few things about the state board exam. With the patience of an angel he tries to teach this dull-witted woman while I, busy with the laundry in the bathroom, turn on the water as loudly as possible. No, I don't want to hear anything, I don't want to learn anything if one forbids me.

February 9, 1942

So much has been happening every day, a thousand little things that mount up into an avalanche of suffering and problems. Not just in my case, but with all the other women in distress. A few days ago I went to a [refugee] organization* to complain that things couldn't go on this way. For the first time I felt some of my old fighting spirit. I explained: you send out women and girls to work with the words "Eat or be eaten," so they can earn a modest daily wage.

---

* The German Jewish Club of New York was founded in 1924 and then renamed the New World Club. Among its most important activities, starting in 1934, was the publication of the German-language newspaper *Aufbau*.

Without any training, without any experience, you send them to take care of sick people and babies, or to run an entire household. Tremendous pressure and tiny salaries, because everyone knows that until recently these women lived fancy lives in the old country and don't know how to do anything, and that people employ them only out of pity and in order to save them from financial ruin. But what a danger they are to invalids and children. Hasn't anyone thought of that? And why do most of them lose their jobs a few days later? Because they're not up to them. I am poor, I have no money to donate, but I'd like to do what I can to help out, I'd like to train these women, give them lessons, free of charge, naturally. If I just had a suitable room. I can't ask anyone to our "house." Please help me find a room, I said to the secretary, without knowing that my name was familiar to her from Berlin. "I'll have to think about it." That was her evasive, noncommittal answer. Oh, I would have liked to shake that lady by the shoulders as she puffed on her cigarette. The meeting was over and I started to leave.

Suddenly the woman called out to me. "Wait a second, aren't you so and so from Berlin? How would you like to hold a lecture for us sometime?"

Furious, I replied: "I didn't come here to hold a lecture, but to do something for the women. And besides, how do you know that I'm capable of holding a lecture?"

And with that I was out the door and into the elevator. When I got downstairs I told the operator I wanted to go back upstairs. He stared at me with a curious look but took me upstairs. Back into the lion's den. She was still standing by the window and I yelled out at her:

"I've thought it over. I'll hold a lecture, as you wish, and I've also got a topic: Women as Companions!"

"Fine," said the lady, "You'll be hearing from us."

And so now I'm waiting.

February 22, 1942

We arrived here two years ago. Despite all the problems, the constant struggle just to survive and live decently, our life here strikes me as "pleasant." Our lot is improving and we have each other. Never before have I felt the depth of my love for my husband as I do now. I've become such a part of him and he of me that we often express the same thoughts with the same words. If only he would loosen up a bit. In the first years of our marriage I was able to open him up, remove the bonds of his inner reserve. Now I miss his laughter, he has become so serious and quiet. It's true of my boy also; when he's at home and has finished his homework, he reads quietly in the corner, which he calls his room.

In the meantime I've held the lecture. The room was overcrowded. Women, intellectual women, who like me are doing brutal work as domestics, in factories, behind typewriters — they came because of their hunger for spiritual nourishment, for an evening in which they could forget their cares. But they also came to convince themselves that it was really me who was speaking, that I really was among the living and not, as many had thought, among the "victims" back home.

I myself felt how I was able to talk myself into a state of exaltation. Without a text I spoke of the responsibilities of women today to prove themselves, not only as the companions of men, no, but as companions to other women, and in the fight to survive in this, our new and novel life in America. I was rewarded with lots of applause, much too much. I saw tears in many eyes, and I went home as if in a trance and threw myself into my husband's arms.

"Oh please, don't ever leave me alone, I still want to do everything for you and for our child."

Why was I feeling, instead of joy, a horrible fear? My husband murmured the most tender and wonderful words of love, tried to console me and cheer me up.

"Your first success in America, after all the many private successes you've had in the two years you've sacrificed for me and Erich, as well as for those you've cared for."

Success? No, my heart doesn't want this kind of success, my heart cries out for only one thing.

After lengthy negotiations I've begun today the first course for women who want to become professional caretakers. The organization that sponsored my lecture has already informed me that on one or two evenings a week they will let me use a room in their holy chambers so I can teach women — without compensation, of course — but on one condition: I am supposed to solicit new members.

"I'm completely unsuited for that, and I won't force anyone, but if you can get new members through my courses, that's fine with me," I said gruffly, and with that we came to an agreement.

I'm happy as I haven't been in a long while, for now at least I can give back something, do something for people. May it be a good omen! I will gladly sacrifice the evenings when I could be earning money or secretly studying for my board exam; somehow I'll make up for it.

May 3, 1942

I've been unpacking our small suitcases because we moved out of the damp, dirty cave we were living in. Just two streets away, a small, clean, furnished apartment, two rooms. I have the feeling I'm living in a palace. Here I can breathe at least, here our friends can visit us. Everything is so bright, and the sun is shining. Despite my work I went out for an hour and took a walk in the nearby park. Everything is blooming and blossoming so early this year. How magnificent is this part of the gigantic city, where so much beauty and pomp reside right next to filth, ugliness, and poverty.

I walked by my husband's office and read his name on the small doctor's sign over and over. I wonder if my name, as it once did, will soon hang in the window next to his. My heart tightens and I don't know why I simply can't believe it anymore. And then all my heartache comes back, all the despair and a certain envy of my husband and all those who are practicing medicine again. Why didn't we come here a few years earlier when physicians were allowed to practice right after they passed the language examination?* Now they have to take the difficult medical board examination, and they arrive in misery and poverty. They are tortured beyond belief, for it is real torture, and more than a few have already committed suicide for this reason. [. . .]

July 20, 1942

We've rented our own apartment, a bit small, only three rooms, but we can combine our apartment and the office, just as we did in Berlin. The new arrangement will have advantages, but also some disadvantages. The most important thing is, I'll have a new job: as my husband's assistant . . . If only he knew how I felt, how conflicted my feelings are. The once independent physician, the director of a large obstetrics clinic and children's hospital, now a doctor's assistant. But at least I will be able to see patients, put in a word or two, indirectly make use of my training. Oh my husband, how rich you make me, how poor and small you make me!

August 20, 1942

The awful war continues. I'm now completely cut off from my friends back home. We only get grisly reports through the newspapers and radio. Occasionally a short letter is sent by way of a neutral country. But what news they send us! We should be happy and grateful we got out of the European hell when we did—as if we had left of our own free will! It's almost as if they reproach us for having left.

I'm still giving my courses. The women are so grateful, and I make sure they find work afterwards. My "job agency" is becoming well known. It's funny how fast word travels in this gigantic city. In the meanwhile they've elected me against my will as president of the so-called Women's Caucus. All my former students insisted on my accepting the position, and now we have regular evening meetings with music and other performances. There are so many immigrants here who are happy to perform for an audience, and so as

---

* Until 1935 successful completion of the language examination sufficed for German-speaking physicians with proper immigration visas to obtain certification from the New York State Medical Board.

often as possible I try to give them this opportunity. My coworker, the club secretary, is a very smart, very energetic woman who has a good sense for publicity. I have no understanding of this, basically I hate *publicity*, but in this country you've got to have it if you want to succeed. To have knowledge or ability isn't enough. I go along, inwardly resistant, for the sake of the women and out for gratitude for the organization that provides me with a room to teach. I also do it out of love for my husband. He is so proud of me, I feel it. He who is so unconcerned about reputation, the noise of the masses—he is happy and proud that his wife is becoming well known, that she is held in high esteem, indeed, is praised with love and gratitude. It is after all his name that is being honored—his and his son's name, and also mine, and that's the only thing that makes me proud. No inflated self-esteem but the knowledge that one belongs to an old and well-regarded family: that's what counts, today and always . . . [. . .]

For the last few weeks I've had my own program on the German radio, once a week. I have to ask myself if it's really me. How did it come about? A telephone call: they had heard about me and wanted to know if I could hold a lecture.

"Ah, hmm, I don't know if I can, and on the radio?"

I was completely confused. It happened that a former patient was with me. She pulled the receiver from my hand and said:

"The Frau Doktor is busy right now, please tell me what you want from her, I'm her secretary." Finally I heard her say: "Tomorrow she will be at your address punctually and will talk over all the other details." And with that she hung up. My maternal friend—for that is what she has come to mean to me—turned to me:

"Miss Doctor," she said, "you get asked to speak on the German radio station and you want to say no. Don't you know what a tremendous opportunity this can be for you? Please, go and see the man tomorrow and make an appointment, but just don't say "no'!"

How well this old woman knows me—I say "No thank you" so often for myself, thinking that others can do it much better, and thereby passing up so many opportunities. But this time I went, as agreed, and said yes. They wanted a medical talk, fifteen minutes long, so and so many words. Before I knew what had happened the very friendly but apparently very busy man had shown me the door.

And two days later, as promised, I held my radio talk. While I was speaking the man who introduced me, who was also the station's director, held up a piece of paper in front of the window between us. In large letters he had written:

"Very good. Can we announce you'll be speaking again next week?"

I could only nod my head, and so it continues. I've come into a whirlwind. Calls from people who heard me speak, letters with questions and requests to

speak about this or that topic, and again and again the comment, "Your wonderful voice . . ." After all, I did take voice lesson for so many years, I once
dreamed of being an opera singer. But then the First World War came, I was
still in school, and I made my decision: I want to help, really help. I want to
become a doctor—and that's how it went. But now? Today? Yes, I still want
to, after all this time. But as long as I have to work night shifts to pay for the
new instruments we need in our practice, it will be difficult to assimilate all the
new unnecessary information I need to pass the board exam.

December 2, 1942

In addition to my domestic work, helping out in my husband's growing practice, and part-time jobs—at the moment I'm working nights taking care of an
invalid—I now belong to a host of committees, association boards, etc., and
people are beginning to take heed of my opinion, just as they did in Germany.

The lectures for the radio station continue, bringing me into personal contact with many German Americans. Recently someone told me: "If you were
to walk down 86th St. in Yorkville (the German neighborhood in New York)
while your radio program is on the air, you would almost be able to hear your
voice on every floor." Yes, people like my program, as I know from the letters
and visits I receive from my listeners. And here perhaps is a mission for me, for
everyone keeps asking me: What made you come here? What's happening in
Germany? And in this way I come to know the inner conflicts of so many
people who love their old homeland and worry about the people over there,
but who have grown deep, deep roots here for decades and now ask themselves: where is my homeland?

I try to tell them in simple terms what happened over there—without
hatred, or bitterness, although they can hear the sadness in my voice and often
I have to break off in mid-sentence. I have such a longing as well as a knack for
being happy, for making others happy, but my task is to tell them of suffering
and criminality and all the misfortune that a single individual is hardly capable of withstanding.

For the moment I'm earning some extra money for Christmas gifts for my
loved ones. Woe is me if my husband were to find out. I think it would almost
constitute grounds for divorce if he knew *his* wife were doing this. What am
I doing? I play the piano and sing for an hour before my night shift begins, in
a small restaurant not far from my job. A few days ago I went to work a bit too
early and strolled about the neighborhood. I heard music, awful piano music,
coming from a small bar. An old black man stood in front of the door. He must
have noticed me shaking my head in disapproval for he asked me if I could
play piano. When I said yes, he replied:

"My grandson's playing. He stepped in to replace the piano player who got sick, but he's going to scare away all my customers. Could you play for them? The pay is good."

Fifty cents an hour, that's the good pay. But for me it's good enough, and without much thought I agree. So now when I go to my night job (very early, as my husband observes), I secretly pack my good black dress into my little suitcase and appear in evening wear for my guests, all blacks who listen to me very attentively. I think the tall, blond woman has caught their fancy. And now I've begun to sing some small German *Lieder*, some Advent and Christmas songs, and my clear soprano rings through the smoke-filled room and the sound of clinking glasses as it once did when I sang at home as a child in the choir. My black audience grows quiet and listens, and here and there someone hums along a melody that he's learned. But this evening they want to dance. Dancing—no, that's not for me. I'll sing for them, but dancing, with a man putting his arm around my waist, is out of the question.

Otherwise I get along great with my black friends, and they behave like gentlemen, or is that just my imagination? My mother-in-law from the "good family," she would have shrugged her shoulders and said, as she once did in Berlin: "Well, you and your husband just have plebeian tastes." How fortunate that I have them and that I've never paid much attention to titles, social status or a fat wallet, but only to people, people who are good. And there are good people everywhere in the world. It's just sad that the mass of evil people oppress and destroy the good ones. I think that's the source of all the suffering and misery in this world.

New Year's Eve, 1942

The year comes silently to an end. If this atrocious war and all the rest weren't going on, one could breathe a sigh of relief and look to the future in good spirits. In any case we owe many thanks for all the good things that have happened this year. My husband has regained some of his happiness, and our son is growing up with fewer cares. I alone am still afraid, and am still plagued by the old cares and doubts. I've achieved much and yet not what I long for most, the return to my profession. It has been and still is too difficult. Today I received a bouquet of violets from a woman who wished to thank me. I'll carry them into the new year with me, along with all my love.

July 2, 1944

It's so quiet this evening, quieter than usual because my husband has gone to a lecture. My heart is bursting so that it seems to have lost its ability to speak, or to write. How empty our home has become since our son left. He's a soldier in the army, at war.

And I pray, I pray day and night that the Lord will bring my boy back safe and sound and that he will put him somewhere where he won't have to kill other people.

So much new misfortune has beset our circle of friends. So many of us are of "mixed marriage," and all of us, Christians and Jews, are receiving such bad news, often through a third party. This one has died in battle, that one passed away, another has disappeared from his apartment, his city. And suffering doesn't come to a halt at the gates of America and its citizens. How long can it continue?

All around me men try to please me. My husband finds it amusing, but it makes me angry. I can only pretend not to notice it so as not to destroy old friendships.

August 3, 1944

Our son became an American citizen today. He was sworn into the army, and he now has a "fatherland" once more. If he needs one, he'll also have a passport as the free citizen of a free country. He told us this by telephone, bursting with pride. For the first time, after all the years of suffering and work, we have fled the New York summer heat and taken a vacation. We landed in Pine Hill, a small village in the nearby Catskills, the closest if not the highest mountains in New York State. The countryside is pleasant and the heat tolerable, the nights are even cool. We are staying in a small hotel called "Paradise," and that's how we feel. For the first time I have people waiting on me again, my bed is made for me. All these years I've done it for others, my husband and child had to do it for themselves at home in New York. I almost strike myself as a "high lady" [*gnädige Frau*], a term I could never put up with. It was too Prussian, too formal for me, just like the kiss of the hand that went with it, and today I tremble deep inside when my husband often kisses and strokes my hands during our evening walk. The once so finely manicured surgeon's hands— what a sight they are now—coarse, red, worn out, witnesses to the labor I've done for my loved ones. [. . .]

May 13, 1945

The historical events are so earth-shaking that individual experience has lost almost all significance. Roosevelt's death, the news reports from the various war fronts until the decisive date of May 8, have given each day a special contour. But we are sure of one thing now: there will be no more shooting or murdering, no more bombs will fall on cities and civilians—at least we have come this far. But peace, real peace? It will take many years. That is my gut feeling, and just as I was able to sense in advance the entire Hitler catastrophe, so I feel the future deep in my heart. They may all have laughed at me, even my dear husband, but in the end I was proved right, without being self-righteous. Today only one thing matters: my son will soon be coming home, safe and sound, and for that I thank Providence.

Today is Mother's Day as well as the anniversary of our engagement. On my desk stands a vase of magnificent, fragrant lilacs—almost as blue as the lilacs in the zoo back home, my "blue sky" of hope from years back. How many storm clouds have crossed the heavens since then, and even now there's a storm, and the wind has driven us from the park back home. We sat there in the living room and made plans until "our son is back home." He's grown up so fast. Often I wonder if I shouldn't have dedicated more time to him. I always had to put him second, my husband was the focus of all my thoughts and actions, and there were always other obligations and work that took me away from my child. To be sure, I always made it up to him when I had the time; but was it enough?

August 13, 1945

Finally Japan has conceded to the strength of a greater power—finally. My husband's eyes grew moist when we heard the news over the radio, and the telephone rang off the hook. People are looking for other people with whom they can share the news and be happy. Happy? I don't know. Too much suffering and worry have preceded it—one can't be truly happy anymore. Now slowly but surely we will learn what has happened everywhere, and what the warring countries look like now that it's over. If only I could be active and help others. I'm already dreaming and starting to make new plans again . . .

Richard Plant }

BEING GAY, BECOMING JEWISH

*Born in Frankfurt in 1911 as Richard Plaut, Richard Plant fled Germany
in 1933 because of his fear that the Nazis would persecute him as a homosexual. He lived for five years in Basel, completing a dissertation in German
literature while writing crime novels, children's stories, and film reviews.
But without a Swiss resident permit, he was eventually forced to emigrate
to New York, where he lived until his death in 1998. The following interview was conducted by Dorothea von Moltke in 1996.*

My father was a devout Socialist. Marx and Engels, no Bible. Head of the
Socialist Physicians League, deputy in the Frankfurt communal elec-
tions. A special doctor for the railway union. That was his life; he came back
from World War I with a bad knee injury and a devout hatred of war. He ran
a hospital in Turkey, and a hospital in the Ukraine, where they spoke nothing
but Yiddish. And he learned Yiddish, which for a German-Jewish doctor is
unheard of, and he began to appreciate the culture. He never believed Hitler
would make it. He believed in the role of the proletariat: the laborers would
not allow this. And he paid for it.

Did you have a self-understanding of being Jewish at the time?

That's exactly it. I didn't. I was never Bar Mitzvahed. I was never in a
synagogue until I came to New York. My father laid that down. Once the
Revolution comes, all these differences would go away. It was very difficult: in
New York I had to become Jewish. You were either Jewish or nothing; otherwise nobody would help you. I had picked up some Yiddish from my father's friend, a Mr. Gruenstein. But to this day I never solved that. If people
ask me now, I say I'm Jewish. But that's a way out so I won't have to explain.

After [my happy years in Switzerland], New York was trouble. A month
later my two friends came, so we had a little bit of a household on West 75th St.
and Riverside Drive, which was one of the émigré hangouts. I did nothing but
learn English. I went to two language schools, but they were no good. I knew
more than they did. And then I found a great help. Anne Hood, may she be
blessed, she's dead now. A Southern woman who taught all the intellectual
émigrés. And you know what we did? We read *The New Yorker* together; and

for five years twice a week I went to see her. And we became good friends. It was tough. I couldn't get used to America. I sat there on a bench on Riverside Drive, it was eighty degrees, I was in a flannel suit, and I thought, "Oh my God, what will I do here?"

Did you have any money?

I had enough money for one year, which I had saved in Switzerland.

But you knew nobody?

I had my uncle, who didn't want to have anything to do with me. Well, he had two sisters and six nephews and nieces who he had to give affidavits to. So he had his hands full. Besides, he knew I was gay and he hated gays. That changed when I became a professor at City College and when I won a prize from *Harper's*; I got a fellowship for the writing of my book.* Then I was "my nephew the novelist and a professor." In 1938 I was the needy emigrant and a nuisance. I was a little bit effeminate, which he hated. He was one of those. And he didn't believe the Nazis would last. He toyed with the idea of going back to Germany [until] my father's suicide became known, on *Kristallnacht*, in '38, through a letter that my sister mailed. Then his attitude changed a little bit.

So how did you begin to take root in New York? How did you begin to make your way?

That's a good question. Number one, in the language school I met a couple of people. And number two, Riverside Drive was peopled by gay people sometimes at night. And I sat there, thinking how I would get back to Switzerland. And a man with a dog came by. The dog of course wanted to make contact. It was a nice dog, a golden retriever, and they are very friendly. The man was a voice teacher, of course 72nd St. was a voice neighborhood. He talked to me and realized I was German; he wanted to learn German. So we became friends. He was my first lover. That lasted a year; it was a great help. I even met his mother, who was a dragon lady, but she was happy he found me because he had picked up quite a few bad boys and she realized I was a gentleman. I forget his name now. He had a circle of people interested in music. And of course anyone who speaks German and knows music—I have a good background in music—was interesting to them. So I found a circle of people whom I could go to before Erika's salon opened. They were all Americans.

That seems unusual to me.

Very unusual. My uncle always said to me: "Where did you meet all these people?" His wife, however, who was the one who made the relationship to Switzerland [allowing me to stay there], was a Warburg. She was much better. She realized that I had made my first contacts.

---

* Plant's autobiographical novel about his flight from Germany, *The Dragon in the Forest*, was published in 1948.

My first job was at Bloomingdale's. I sold books and men's pants. The book section doesn't exist anymore. Bloomingdale's was run by a committee with other department stores. The man in charge was called Ira Hirshman. He was a friend of my godfather Kurt Goldstein, a neurologist who got a job at Harvard and wrote a book with the simple title *The Brain*. After my father died, we got together sometimes. He was my father's best friend. He said, "It's too bad your father could never accept the fact that you are gay. I tried to tell him, I said 'Richard will make it, he's not bad looking, he's intelligent, and he can adjust himself to people and he likes people.'" My father worried that I would go under here. So he knew Ira Hirshman. And one day, imagine you are working at Bloomingdale's, you are a low, low, low Christmas replacement, the rest were fat Jewish women who all mothered me. And I come in in the morning and get ready and sell my stuff and someone says: "There's a telephone call for you from the office; Mr. Hirshman. My God, did you steal something?" Mr. Hirshman said: "I heard that you can read German and English quite well." I said, "Yes, I can." "Where did you learn it?" "In Switzerland." "So. Mr. Goldstein is your godfather?" "Yes." "Well, we are considering withdrawing all our ads from the German papers in America. If they print the Nazi news, we as Jewish merchants do not want to put our ads in there. We want you to go to the library. Stop selling whatever you're selling. I'll give you much more than you get now. Go and find out about papers in German, particularly in the Midwest." So that was my first job. I was jubilant.

So for work you depended on the Jewish community that you entered and for friendship it was the gay community?

Yes. Always at the edge, and in between everything. My two friends were delighted. By that time we had quite a nice home. One of them got a job teaching German in Maryland, the other got a job teaching German at Smith, in Northampton. And I stayed.

I'm wondering: you said earlier that you became a Jew in New York. When did this happen and how did this happen?

Well, I didn't become a Jew in New York if you mean that I believed in the Bible and would go to the synagogue and learn Hebrew. But I realized that my identity, if I wanted to have one, had to be Jewish or non-Jewish. I couldn't be non-Jewish. Also, I'm circumcised, so . . . But it's always been a problem. I went to one Jewish organization in the beginning because a job was open. And the woman—I'll call her Mrs. Greenberg: there was always a Mrs. Greenberg who was from Brooklyn, who chewed gum, was in her fifties, had bad teeth, and was sharp—she said: "You're not Jewish, you can't fool me, you don't even speak Yiddish." And she kicked me out. So when there was a questionnaire and it said "religion", I wrote "Jewish". That kept people from asking. Also, don't forget this was Hitler-time. If you were not Jewish, what were you doing in America? They were always afraid of spies and agitators. That goes back to World War I. But that happened to many people. When I worked at Friendship House,* people came there who were totally assimilated and had been baptized and suddenly they were Jewish. It was a conflict.

Did you experience anti-Semitism as well at the time?

Once in a while, yes. But not much.

So that didn't add to the conflict?

No. That wasn't the conflict. The anti-gay thing was much worse.

How did that manifest itself?

Well, among my colleagues at City College. Not directly; this is academe, not the Teamsters' Union. But one day there was a dean's reception, everybody came with his wife, and I had no wife. I never found out why my boss, the head of the German Department, who was born in Galicia and still spoke with a heavy accent, why he liked me and protected me. I don't know. I was everything he wasn't.

Maybe that's why.

Maybe that's why, yes. That's what I figured. When there were attacks on me, he said: "He's a good teacher, he speaks very good English for an émigré, he knows his stuff, and the students like him and we need that." He died in Israel at the age of ninety-two; and he held his hand over me.

Let's go back to 1939. Do you remember when the war broke out? Did it affect your life?

Yes. I was in Friendship House. I remember a friend of mine, with the name of Count Valentini, a real shubiak, came by and said: "Pearl Harbor has been bombed. Have you heard?" I hadn't heard. So I realized Friendship House would be finished. All the money would go to the war effort. Germany declared war on America, you know. Roosevelt didn't have to do it.

Did this change people's attitudes towards you as a German?

Yes, I became an enemy alien, suddenly.

How did that make itself felt?

I couldn't travel without permission. But, again the perversity of history. I met someone on a bus, I saw a face I knew, I said it can't be, so I got off when he got off. "Ernst Erich, is that you?" "Richard, is that you?" I said "Yes," and he said, "Thank God I found you." [. . .] He worked at NBC making anti-Nazi propaganda. Shortwave [broadcasts] to London [which the] BBC broadcast into Germany. They needed someone who knew German and knew enough English to translate into German. I said, "No problem." Typical New York. "We'll have to clear you with the FBI." "Great, I'm without a real job now." Oh no, I had a job as a secretary to an old, old, horrible guy. And so I went to the FBI headquarters downtown, trembling, but it was no problem. And of course my writings helped and the fact that I spoke comparatively

---

* An organization founded in 1938 by the American Council of Christians and Jews to help emigrant doctors, lawyers and academics prepare for their English examinations.

good English, for an émigré. They expected the real heavy accent. First he had to get Americans, [but] he couldn't get anybody. So I became a member of the staff of NBC till the end of the war. The best-paid job I ever had.

Did you like the job?

Yes. Except the hours. . . . I often was on the lobster shift, which is from five in the afternoon to four in the morning. No good. They sent us sheets from Washington with propaganda speeches, which were totally unusable. With no knowledge of what you had to do for propaganda. Hymns to Joe Stalin. . . . So we rewrote our stuff and we realized nobody was listening to it in Washington. I could have been writing Nazi propaganda and nobody would have known. So it was quite interesting and I got to know the war. I couldn't tell most of my friends what I was doing. It was confidential. So that took me to the end of the war. I had a job also for a short while at a magazine called *Tomorrow* where I edited the book section although I was a foreigner. And everybody there was nice to me.

What do you think were the important factors for you in becoming and feeling integrated?

The fact that I could work in an American environment, like a magazine, and then twenty-seven years at a college with Americans only. That gave me an identity, finally. I was a college professor. I never pretended that I was American. That makes no sense. And now the older I get, the more European I feel; that's inevitable.

So it was also a function of your age that you were able to feel more integrated?

Yes. By the way I began to have rather long-lasting relationships with some fellows, which helped to give me some security. It wasn't perfect, some of it was grotesque. One was an Italian hairdresser who made about five times as much as I made as a professor. And he worked on the upper East Side and told me incredible stories about the rich women.

How did you meet him?

At a party. He fell for me more than I fell for him. Finally we split up, he went with a Jewish lawyer who was much better for him than I. But it also helped me to feel sort of at home.

What was your perception of the gay movement in America when you came, even in the early years?

Oh, here it was terrible. It was all secret, secret, secret. It was all closets. It wasn't a closet, it was a safe. With four locks.

Could you try to compare it to Germany when you left?

In Germany it was much more open. Then the Nazis came and everything disappeared. And after the war, I don't know.

So you had to adjust to this phobia in America?

Yes. Well, it's much worse here still. On the one hand, there's a gay movement, gay newspapers, every major city has a gay organization, often run by lesbians, who are much better at that, much more organized and reliable. On the other hand, the backlash is gigantic.

And during the war years?

No. During the war years all this disappeared, because they needed everyone they could get for the army. They didn't even ask you whether you were gay for the army.

I'm also curious how you see the relationship between the existing Jewish community in America and the newly arrived émigrés.

Good question. The Jewish community was all Eastern European Jewish. Ninety percent. And of course they all hated each other. The Rumanians hate the Ukrainians, the Ukrainians hate the Russians, the Russians look down on the Poles, the Hungarians look down on everybody, and everybody hates the Germans. In Israel, they're called *Yekkes*. That means crazy. So to many of the American Jews, this was "deserved," because the German Jews had treated them badly. I remember one of those Mrs. Greenbergs saying: "My brother wanted to open a tailor shop in Frankfurt, but of course the Frankfurt Jews didn't want someone from Poland. Now they come here and want help. Ha, ha, ha." Not quite as bad.

But there was resentment.

Oh, was there ever! And many Jewish émigrés ran up against that when they applied for jobs, or when they applied for help from the Jewish Committee and it turned out they couldn't speak Yiddish. It was a real problem. Also, the Jewish population here had a real proletariat. There were Jewish bakers, there were Jewish plumbers, Jewish mechanics, Jewish factory workers, Jewish automobile persons, Jewish butchers, deli [owners, whereas] most of the Germans were just business people. They were not bakers. If you were a baker, there was no problem. But there were almost no Jewish bakers or Jewish butchers who came. So the classes were also in conflict. The German Jews were, I would say, petty bourgeois, and the [East European Jews] were proletarians. There were Jewish boxers here; there wasn't a single Jewish boxer in Germany.

That must have made the question of identifying with a Jewish community even—

Yes. Impossible. Well, I was lucky. I escaped into the academic world early, and nobody asked me to bake bread. Which I wish I could do. I took a course here in cooking, you know. Not that I ever became a good cook, but enough to make a simple meal. I couldn't afford to go out all the time. There were a few old, old aristocratic Jewish families here, like the Lehmans, the Morgenthaus, the Schlesingers, the Seligmans, the Kahns. They were millionaires. They were old German families that had come at the time of Lincoln. And they in turn looked down on the Eastern European Jews, and they all looked down on the new Germans.

CARING FOR THE SURVIVORS

Born in 1904 in East Prussia (now Poland), William Niederland was trained as a doctor and worked in several cities in Germany at the beginning of the 1930s. He fled to Italy in 1933, to England in 1939 where he was interned as an enemy alien, and after a brief wait in the Philippines managed to emigrate to San Francisco. He set up medical practice in New York, received a position as Professor of Psychiatry at New York University, and specialized in the treatment of Holocaust survivors. The following is an excerpt from an interview conducted in German.

My father was a rabbi. His first job was with the Jewish community in Schippenbeil. You won't know the town, which no longer belongs to Germany: Schippenbeil, near Königsberg, in East Prussia. It was a small community, perhaps one-hundred-twenty Jewish families. Then a few years later he went to Pfungstadt near Darmstadt, a somewhat larger Jewish community. And then in 1913 to the large Jewish community in Würzburg, which then had three thousand Jewish families.

My mother was a housewife, of course, a good German-Jewish housewife and a very good mother, but with very strong artistic gifts, especially in music. My father also had artistic abilities in drawing. He once drew a picture of Kaiser Wilhelm and named his second son Wilhelm. That's why I'm named William, Wilhelm: in honor of the Kaiser. Back in the good old days, in 1904 (for the Jews, in any case, they were good). There had always been anti-Semitism. Jews called it the "good old *Risches*." *Risches* is the Hebrew word for "mean spirit." So whenever someone called you a "smelly Jew" or "dirty Jew," that came under the heading of the good old *Risches*, the good old mean spirit. But there was no persecution.

I took my high school degree without any trouble in 1922 at the *Realgymnasium* in Würzburg, and then my medical degree at the University of Würzburg, the Julius Maximilians Universität, which is probably still its name today. There I already came into contact with anti-Semitic professors.

Your household must have been very religious, given your father's profession.
Of course. That was my first big problem. My father wanted his son Willy—
they called me Willy—to be a rabbi and I started to rebel against that idea. To
have to go to synagogue and say all those prayers every day wasn't for me.
Despite having become a Jewish man at age thirteen—Bar Mitzvah is like
confirmation. And despite his orthodoxy, my father was a liberal man, open to
all currents of thought, to philosophy, politics. One would call him progressive, though not left wing. He accepted that fact that his son Willy didn't want
to be a rabbi.

When I think of my mother, I see and hear her playing the piano—back
then. Do you know, the first melody I still remember, what still comes to
mind, is Lehar's *Merry Widow*. And she was already so progressive, the rabbi's
wife, that she played the waltz from *The Merry Widow* over and over on the
piano. And little Willy sat next to her—that was my first musical experience.
I never became a musician, but I'm a big fan of opera, of German opera. *Der
Freischütz*, of course, and many other operas, the Wagner operas too.

Your decision to be a doctor—was that a coincidence of your "background"?
Oh no! In Schippenbeil the only doctor was a Dr. Wolson, who was Jewish. He
made a big impression on me. And very early I began . . . I won't say
dreaming of medicine, but wanting to practice medicine. I didn't have much
idea what medicine was other than healing. But that's where I got my interest
in survivors. My later work here was with [Holocaust] survivors. I am on this
planet in order to help, to help sick people, people in distress, in emotional
distress—physical, psychophysical, and psychosomatic distress.

*[After completing his studies in Würzburg in 1929, William Niederland took a
position in a sanatorium in Beelitz near Berlin, but left Germany in 1933 for Italy
where he practiced medicine as a neurologist until 1939. In May 1939, with the help
of a refugee organization, he succeeded in emigrating to England, where he worked
for four months as a physician in a refugee camp, and then to the United States.]*

In August 1940 I arrived in San Francisco where I didn't know a soul, but in
New York I had my elder brother Paul, who now lives in Utica, the musician.
He had managed to get a visitor's visa to America as a musician and to live in
New York. So, because it was the cheapest way, I took a Greyhound bus right
across America, five days and six nights. And here things were simple. Here I
had to take the Medical Board Examination again, and I set up practice on
86th Street . . .

When the first inmates of the concentration camps were released and came
to New York, many of them came to Mt. Sinai Hospital where I work with

nightmares*, with—how do you say it?—*Alpträumen*, with stomach dis-
orders, tachycardia. And all of us made incorrect diagnoses, myself included.
These people are depressed, without roots, they suffer from severe depression.
We always prescribed antidepressants, tranquilizers, Elavil.

Until I realized—and that took me ten to twelve years—that these people
weren't just having anxiety dreams and nightmares. They see themselves
hunted and persecuted by people in uniforms and arrested at the last moment.
Or they see a pile of corpses, and hide themselves behind a mountain of
corpses. The depressed patient is melancholic. With these patients life itself is
sad. I call that here "wordless sadness."

So I realized that this was a new illness that wasn't in any of the medical
textbooks. The people suffer from guilt feelings. The majority of them come
to me and say:

I shouldn't be here.
Where would you like to be?
I should not be here in that office.
Where?
Where my parents are. Or where my brothers and sisters are. Where my wife is.

In saying this they deny that, even were they to return to Auschwitz, they
wouldn't find any graves, only bits of dust. But those are by far not the most
serious cases. I have a patient who says, "*I have been selected, selected to be the
King of England.*" He's referring to the selection in . . . Do you know what
selection was? Right side, left side . . . I call that "*Survivor Syndrome.*"

Today I still have patients who, if they see a policeman in a dark blue uniform, run into a side street or hide themselves in a lobby. They're reminded of
the SS. Although of course they know they're in New York. Or they start
trembling when the doorbell rings early in the morning. That doesn't happen
often here, but sometimes it does—and then it turns out to be the milkman
who wants to settle the bill.

I have a patient who is no longer young, but when he first came to me he
was a young man, a Hungarian Jew. He still trembles so much that he often
can't drink a cup of coffee or a beer. He was ashamed of going into a bar or a
coffee shop. Diagnosis: *hysterical tremor*. But I managed to pierce through
these symptoms—sometimes it takes a quarter of a year or six months before
the patient can talk about it—and he said to me: "I was with the death crew,
I had to bury people who were still living. With these hands. People who had
been shot dead, hundreds were dead, but ten or twenty were still alive, and
some were very much alive . . . With these hands!" This patient I wasn't
able to cure. Today he's fifty-eight years old. Then he was sixteen.

So, I realized that wasn't depression, but a new type of illness: *Survivor*

---

*In English in the original.

Syndrome. The sickness of those who survive, in a double sense. People suffer chronically from guilt feelings or unresolved persecution fear. Or the sickness is a consequence of unresolved concentration camp trauma. I should mention an important aspect: "hypermnesia," acute memory.

The images, the images of persecution, how dogs were running after you, or . . . That stays with them and is experienced as if it had happened last week and not years ago. One's memory becomes overly sharp. There's a good man in Munich, Paul Mattusek, who expresses it differently. He says that a part of the ego of these former concentration camp inmates has remained in the camp. And will stay there until they die.

Today I can help people in two ways. As individuals, so that they can have confidence in a person for the first time after having been persecuted.

At first they're suspicious, even of me. One patient once said to me: "*Who knows if you were not the commandant of Auschwitz.*" Now I can understand these people, and they feel they're understood and so they can *pull the heart out*, how do you say this in German? All experiences, even the little ones, such as how they managed to survive—and the others didn't: *the survivor guilt*. One of my patients is the only survivor in a family of eighteen people: that he or she [died], why didn't I . . . ? One was in Mauthausen, the other in Bergen-Belsen or Dachau.

I've never had a case of a complete cure. I have to admit it. A complete cure where the nightmares disappear completely, the depressive states disappear completely, where the hypermnesia completely disappears—I never managed to do it.

Very often the survivors, while still in the *displaced camps* or when they came to America, would only marry other persecution victims. In the beginning they tell each other their story, and then that's that. And then comes the *state of wordless sadness*. Speechless, wordless feelings of mourning. With anxiety dreams and with . . .

[This often comes] in connection with a recent death, although it doesn't have to be a death, it can also be the loss of a business. Let's take someone who has opened a little store, perhaps even with reparations money [from Germany]. Often a couple start a small stationery store somewhere in Brooklyn or the Bronx or New Jersey. If the store fails for financial reasons, these people fall back into their earlier "failures" [in Germany], when they were driven from their stores or their jobs, from their positions. That comes back with devastating power, all at once. Hypermnesia. That is the opposite of amnesia, which means forgetting. Hypermnesia is the overly acute capacity for memory. The loss of a business is associated with the previous loss of a business. With everything from back then, with the worries, the terrible fear they had when the SS came and they hid in the pantry or were thrown into the ghetto and had nothing to eat. All that comes rushing back. With sudden intensity and sharpness.

The nightmares are different. They see themselves being persecuted or in a ditch or behind piles of corpses. The image of piles of corpses is frequent. And when they wake up from these nightmares, in Brooklyn or Manhattan or the Bronx or Queens or wherever it is, these people are awake for a half hour or three quarters of an hour, or sometimes a whole hour and they run up and down in their bedrooms without stop because they're no longer sure they're not there where the nightmare [is] . . . Although rationally of course they know: I live in Queens.

Is there a case that particularly disturbed you?

All my cases! I was the official physician in charge of certifying such cases for the German Consulate General here in New York. And for this work I received every week three, four, sometimes more piles of such cases. There is a Dr. Frank, the head medical certifier in Frankfurt, who says, the certifier in New York, Niederland, he's blowing *Kristallnacht* all out of proportion.

How do you account for the obduracy of the certifiers, for the cynicism that, in part, is expressed in such reactions?

If a patient's case is approved, reparations must be paid from the deportation in Auschwitz or Dachau or Stutthof or Mauthausen or wherever, until now. Although the survivors only get small sums—sixty or a hundred-twenty dollars per month—that quickly adds up to ten thousand dollars. Some of them buy a small stationery store with the money or establish some sort of living. There are also people who say I don't want any money from them, from Germany.

Six months ago a man came to me who had been in a camp in Dachau and never applied for reparations money; who thought, "Here in America I'll free myself from all that." He built a *garment center* all on his own, built himself a life. A year ago he collapses, a nervous breakdown with total insomnia, nightmares where he sees hundreds of skulls grinning at him. His son brought him to me: a typical case of *survivor syndrome*. But it had remained latent for thirty years, and only now, in advanced age, did it come back. He won't get any reparations money. For they will object that there's no connection. I didn't even fill out a form. I'm simply treating him. The man can't manage his own living, he had to give up his *garment center*, and is now living in a small town, in New Brunswick. [. . .]

You also reported about a boy who always had to be moving . . .

Yes—as a child he wasn't in a camp but hidden in a cellar, in the house of Polish farmers. And he couldn't yell because the SS would pass by with their dogs. So his father would clamp his mouth shut and his mother would jump on top of him. For two and a half years. I couldn't cure him. He's still running from one neighborhood to the next. I treated him for about eight years, without success. Finally, with the help of a social worker, I got him a job as a messenger. But he still goes into some basement bar on Eighth or Tenth Avenue and makes noise. Those are incurable cases.

Another particularly tragic case. It was a man who had already been diagnosed with persecution depression. On a Jewish holiday, around Easter, he hanged himself from the fire escape of a synagogue in Brooklyn. His widow and children made a request to have his death recognized as the result of persecution [but it was] rejected by the State Court of Munich. And this is because the certifier from Munich, a Professor Frick at the Munich University Clinic for Psychiatry, said, "Well, if only one knew why he had chosen exactly that day and that place, then perhaps one could see a relationship with his persecution." In a synagogue in Brooklyn, on a Jewish holiday—that's no reason to see a relationship with persecution, that's unrelated to persecution. He hanged himself on April 4, 1970. And what day was that? Passover. To be precise, the last day of Passover, the day for remembering the dead. The day of remembering the dead is the memorial day for [Holocaust] victims. And he was the only survivor in a family of thirty people with cousins, aunts, brothers and sisters, thirty people . . .

There are also the children of survivors.
Yes, that's a new problem. They don't have these nightmares. They are disturbed in a different way. That isn't survivor syndrome but the result of their parents' survivor syndrome. It shows up in their restlessness and frightening fantasy life. Of course the children know their parents were in a concentration camp. Many of them still have these Auschwitz numbers tattooed into their arms. And then they get suspicious of their parents. I once had a patient, her four- or five-year-old daughter asked her: What's that mommy? *That's my telephone number*. Four years later the child learns that was a lie.

So this problem is expressed in a lack of trust, in suspicion, in a frightening fantasy life. In fact, they have the fantasy that their parents survived because they killed. That's why the Nazis let them go. The Nazis were murderers, and the parents were murderers too; otherwise they wouldn't have survived— that's what one of these children told me.

They suffer too, but there are no legal means of assisting them. Only psychiatric treatment. *It goes across the generations*, as a condition of mistrust or lack of trust—lack of trust of the children in the surviving parents . . .

What kind of relationship do these people have today with Germany?
When they get their monthly reparations check in the mail, it's not only the value of the money that is important. More important is that the Germans themselves recognize that they have done wrong, have committed a crime. That's in the check. And that is also a positive mental process, a curing. Do

you understand? For then, slowly but surely, comes the thought: they aren't all *murderers*, are not all criminals! So then many people can think back about Germany perhaps not with positive feelings but at least with neutral feelings. German punctuality plays a positive role here. The survivors know that the check will arrive exactly on the thirtieth, or whenever that is. Each check is so to speak the admission of wrongdoing that they suffered. And that lessens their feelings of rejection [for Germany], I would almost say it lessens the origin of their hatred.

Is there still hatred?
Yes. Some people, American Jews, can't accept it when my wife and I say: "*Oh, we had a very nice time in Freiburg, on Lake Constance.*" [. . .] My wife says that particularly well, and my wife loves Germany very much. We're at a party for twenty-five people, all sitting around a big table.
Where were you last summer?
Oh, we were in Germany.
How did you like it there?
Oh, we had a very good time, my wife says.
Then everyone is silent. So it's still there. Not with the new generation, but the older people. And not always.

I feel a certain nostalgia for Europe. Indeed, even nostalgia for Würzburg. When I think of the Main River and the Main bridges, the Steinburg, the old fortress, the cathedral and chapel of the Virgin Mary. Although I'm Jewish. The synagogue isn't there anymore, they tore the whole thing down. They didn't burn it down because it was in the middle of the old town, right between the old houses, but they tore it down completely. Now they've built a new synagogue outside the town, in a suburb of Würzburg. That interests me less. But I still like to go back there and especially, *believe it or not*, I always like visiting the spa in Kissingen. A health cure in Bad Kissingen. Why? Every year my parents visited the spa in Bad Kissingen. It's about one and a half hours away by train from Würzburg. That's the sentimental, emotional part of me. A certain nostalgia for Europe. My wife is especially quick to notice it: "You're speaking German again." I'm always slipping back into German. Here you have proof, you see, here are twelve volumes of Goethe. Here twelve volumes of Heinrich Heine. And upstairs, my real library is upstairs, everything is in German. I admit my sentimentality, you don't have to destroy it. As analysts we know that feelings are often stronger than thoughts.

My relation to Germany has gone through a change. When I first came back to Würzburg, it was in 1947 or 1948, you could already go by airplane to Frankfurt, though not nonstop; you had to land in Newfoundland, in Gander and in Shannon, Ireland, and then you arrived in Frankfurt. And then you took the train to Würzburg. Often I had the feeling, My God, maybe the hand that these people are holding out to me is stained with blood, with

Jewish blood. People shake hands more often over there than they do here. I'm sure you've noticed that. We once celebrated a high school reunion in Würzburg, in the restaurant called Black Whale at Askalon. Now it's called The Whale. There a man once drank for three days until he was lying on the marble table, stiff as a broomstick. People don't sing those songs anymore, do they? So often I had a feeling not of foreignness but of worry. The worry: so here is where the Holocaust took place. Here is where they murdered all those people. *Mercilessly*, completely *mercilessly*, no one stood up for them. Or only a few did. So sometimes I was relieved, I must tell you, when I crossed the border to Switzerland in Constance. In the first years—not anymore today. Today I accept Germany, although not with the feeling of love I once had.

FALSE YOUTH

Günther Anders (whose real name was Günther Stern) was a brilliant and precocious philosophy student who fled to Paris after the burning of the Reichstag and emigrated to the United States in 1936. First married to Hannah Arendt, he maintained close contact with the leading philosophers of emigration (Adorno, Horkheimer, Marcuse) and writers such as Brecht and Döblin, writing often for the Aufbau and other German-language journals.

New York, 1948

Yesterday I was invited to L.'s fiftieth birthday. Six couples. All pretty much the same age. The men about fifty, the women about forty. The celebration had begun, people were in the best of moods, when suddenly Mrs. D. stood at the door, blushing with embarrassment, excusing her tardiness with her four children, regaling us with silly jokes and nonsense.

A tomblike silence settled over the table.

For a while she continued in her bubbly, joyful manner. But after a while Mrs. D. began to sense the stillness. And after shifting into a hesitant, questioning register, she broke off in the middle of a sentence. "Is someone sick here or something?"

"Nothing of the kind," L. reassured her politely. "You've been very entertaining."

"*Honestly?*"*

"*Honestly.*"

Only with difficulty could we get the conversation started again. About a completely different subject. In English, for the sake of Mrs. D. But our friendly efforts were useless for *we* were controlling the English conversation. Half suspicious, half alarmed, she looked around at us in a circle, wondering whether we were hiding something from her or whether she had made a faux

---

* Italicized words indicate use of English in the original.

pas. And no doubt there arose in her, this friendly, helpful, unprejudiced woman, something like a feeling of resentment against *"those queer refugees."* Before she had even touched her piece of cake, she was out the door.

The ones left behind, who only slowly regained their composure, were . . . six childless couples.

Explanation: The six couples were educated, cultivated people, but cultivated only in a narrow sense, incapable of understanding their flight from Germany in 1933 as a (tiny) part of a global historical event. They interpreted it rather as a personal catastrophe forcing them to abandon their homeland. Their single attitude toward the state of world affairs was one of irritation, and in the intervening years nothing had fundamentally changed this outlook.

At least during the first years of emigration, before arriving in America, in various European countries, they had lived from hand to mouth. Or rather, from *her* hand to *his* mouth. They could no longer count on anything in their lives. How they would pay for their food fourteen days from the present had always been uncertain; equally uncertain whether they would still have legal permission to "reside" in a particular country; equally uncertain where they would be living a half year later; and finally equally uncertain whether one would be living at all in a year. The natural result? All of them had remained—and all unintentionally—*childless*. In the ten, fifteen years that followed, this state of affairs became the "normal state." No one mentioned it, just as no one in a school for the deaf and dumb needs to mention his deafness and dumbness. But once in a while it can happen that someone unwittingly exposes the latent spot. And that's what Mrs. D. had just done. The result of this unnatural state? Despite years of continual vexations day after day, the men as well as the women have remained "younger" than people of the same age in earlier generations. But "younger" in a deceptive sense, the sense of "less adult." For adulthood, first of all in a man, is neither a biological condition, nor that which in our university seminars on the novel (how many light years ago was that?) we used to call the "stage of intellectual and moral development." "Adulthood" is much more a social status. Part of which, for instance, is being a father. An adult individual is *the* one who can count on his precise role within a precisely defined social order, one who can take particular actions based on this role, and with whose precise function society itself must reckon. In short: *Adulthood is one's social identity.*

The six couples have therefore been robbed of this identity. Although chock full of experiences—things that not one of their fathers or grandfathers could have even imagined—they are not truly "men," but look rather like overextended youths, boys with faces of "character." The fact that many of them appear to be artists from the nineteenth century is not an accident. For the artists also, as outsiders, were robbed of their adulthood. Even the most boring of the lot had strong, interesting features . . . Which only goes to show with what randomness history drags its harrow through all our faces.

Three of the six couples are still (or rather, since until now nothing has come through, once again) working *for* a profession. *For*, not *in*, a profession. So they are still in the phase of *preparing* for life, a fact which is no less embarrassing than if they had just begun to show signs of puberty. Five decades for the overture, one decade for the opera. In an age in which our fathers and grandfathers enjoyed great security, stood at least at the height of their powers or already were approaching old age (whether willingly or not), these three couples were still looking "ahead." Here in America, where people repress the thought of death, and where, as the book titles testify, *"life begins at seventy,"* this manner of looking ahead may seem quite attractive. But for men who knew how to grow old, the sight of these emigrants would bring a lump to their throats.

January 25

If you can only break camp late in the afternoon, start climbing at sunset and meet hikers who, adorned with flowers from the mountain top, are already running down the mountain and who, in place of a greeting, only shout out the question how far it is to the hut below, not even waiting to hear your answer—no, if you have to climb under these conditions you won't be able to muster much enthusiasm. When you get to the top, the peak will be covered over, like the view into the valley below—assuming that you even get there. To be able to spend the night in the hut down below—no one can have that many illusions.

January 26

The expression "false youth" applies even more to women than to men. For the women, less resistant to change, the effect is even more embarrassing, like an artificial, cosmetically induced impression of youthfulness. They represent a peculiar intermediary type. They certainly have nothing in common with old maids (who, compared to these women, would be clear-cut types). But they also have nothing in common with mothers. They have been robbed not only of children, but of the natural manner of being maternal, robbed of the opportunity to experience that which every woman is entitled to experience. Thus they remain "young women" who grow older every day. We try to avoid imagining how they will look at sixty. That two of the six, although by character not inclined to do so, have slipped into an aggressive, blue-stocking manner, is not their fault—but it cannot be denied. One has a particularly strange appearance. According to her interests and character she is actually a "family person." But she has no family. Her parents were gassed to death, she didn't have children, and her husband is neither paternal nor childish enough to replace what is missing. And in this way her need to love is showered into empty space. Her gestures resemble the movements of those intolerable dancers who dance as if they were carrying something without actually having anything in their hands, or who try to make us believe they're dragging something heavy without an actual rope. It's a wonder that the terrible discrepancy between disposition and reality, between offer and demand, has made so few of these women sick in a psychiatric sense.

And yet in terms of the experience and worldliness of these women, they infinitely surpass the horizon of their mothers and grandmothers. They surpass them in such a way that the advantage of the men over their fathers and grandfathers becomes uninteresting. In a certain sense these women have gained more experience and more insight during their emigration than the men. How many of them were able to find illegal work in the various emigration countries (as secretaries, nannies, cleaning ladies) while their husbands desperately searched for working papers as if these papers signified a permanent job? And in this way they came to know the countries, the milieus, the way of doing things, the thousand nuances that come with being humiliated, while the men were ushered out the door with the noble-sounding words: "But my dear sir, one cannot possibly offer you such a lowly position"—and thus condemned as the legitimate gigolos of their wives to enjoy the luxury of a writer's misery or some other idle occupation. Between the paragraphs of their books, written for no one, they would listen at the door to see if the hotel clerk had gone out. And if so they quietly got out the gas burner hidden behind the wash-table so they could cook some spaghetti. Because the wives had to "go out" into the "cruel world," it became natural for the men to become, economically as well as morally, the housewives of their furnished attic hotel rooms. But it wasn't great for the relation between husband and wife.

So there they are, the six couples: young couples with gray hair. The unequal distribution of the financial burdens has evened out somewhat over the years. But their childlessness, which they never intended, has forced them into a loneliness à deux which at this age (in which normal couples have already sent their children out into the world) is completely abnormal. It's no wonder then that with some of them the relation between the sexes (that is, the love problem), still plays a role in their lives as a problem. Again, at an age in which that simply isn't natural and in which the problem for previous generations had long been resolved, for better or for worse. Even in cases where habit or a common job has long led to mutual dependency, the lack of a family—which previously had strengthened marriage after the initial passion—was keenly apparent.

For those emigrants with a delicate or an inventive streak, it may have been possible to forge relationships with greater solidarity between husband and wife than earlier couples had had or needed to have: taking on the role of a child for each other, or of several children, performing the three- or four-role play with only two actors and (as in Goethe's novel *Wilhelm Meister*) at least providing for each other the *appearance* of what they had missed out on together. But how many are there who were able to put on this play for moral reasons, who were able to mobilize their imaginations in order to comfort their partners, who knew how to disguise themselves out of love and thoughtfulness?

No, for most of the couples in this age group, the exclusively two-person family was simply too difficult. And they had no role models for overcoming it. Again and again they thought they had buried these difficulties once and for all. But in reality they were lying just below the surface, and the slightest wind would uncover them.

To expect that the bubbly Mrs. D. could see all this would have been ridiculous of course. But it strikes me as likely that she felt herself suddenly hemmed in, as if she were surrounded by ghosts. Does anyone wonder why she raced back so fast to her four kids?

CHAPTER SIX

Looking Homeward

Peter Gay }

ON BECOMING AN AMERICAN

The following piece is part of a larger essay written in 1976 as the author's tribute to the American Bicentennial.

In Denver, where my father and I settled to be near my mother, who was hospitalized there, I worked to help support my parents and, after two years, went to college. My mother's misfortune was, in a sense, my fortune. It propelled me to mid-America, far from the rest of my family, who had found a home in the South, and far from the massive colonies of German refugees huddled together in New York and San Francisco.

In Denver I lived and worked mainly among Americans, although there were hundreds of German refugees in that city too. They made something of an extended family, drawn together by the common experience of acculturation and by a shared and growing anxiety over those German Jews still in Nazi hands—unable, as we put it, "to get out." Then, after Pearl Harbor, we acquired a common stigma: we were all declared enemy aliens, a status leniently perceived by the authorities and more absurd than onerous. The German exiles in Denver formed, as refugees will, a kind of government in exile; they read the same refugee newspaper, the indispensable *Aufbau*; they discussed American politics and military events, and explored over and over again, helplessly, with almost total futility, strategies for rescuing relatives and friends left behind. For many, their little world within a world, natural and benign as it was, became an obstacle to assimilation. It was a community of rumors and nostalgia. Everyone spoke German. Everyone retained a certain distance from the golden land to which we had come and which, on inspection, proved to be a demanding and not altogether generous democracy. Educated and cultivated professional men—doctors, lawyers, professors—found that their credentials counted for little. They were compelled to take menial jobs and undergo humiliating retraining, while their once spoiled and idle wives, who in Germany had never cooked or swept floors, heroically acquired domestic skills, working as maids or in factories to keep their families afloat.

I too worked hard, at jobs I could not have imagined in my gloomiest dreams. With my mother in the sanatorium and my father painfully learning English and unable to provide for us, I had to drop out of high school half a year before graduation. For more than a year I was a shipping clerk in a cap factory at sixteen dollars a week, stupidly packing officers' caps and GIs' overseas caps, standing among wrapping materials in a dirty work shirt, and living a deeply private fantasy life. It was the year of Joe DiMaggio's unprecedented fifty-six-game hitting streak, and day after day I listened to the Yankee baseball broadcasts—rather vague about the game, nostalgic about the soccer games of my childhood, and hoping for a better life. I did not complain. I was protected from self-pity by the vigorous assaults my father liked to launch on the "Byunskis" among the refugees, for daring to find anything good about Germany or anything wrong with America. The epithet came from a cliché to which all too many refugees resorted: *"Bei uns in Deutschland war alles besser."* (With us in Germany everything was better.)

Besides, my belief in my own future never wavered. I do not think that I consciously told myself, as I packed shipment after shipment of caps, that I would not always be doing such menial work. I simply knew it. And this confidence was in itself a tribute to America. It represented a confluence of causes: from some unarticulated inner resources, from my parents' insistent high opinion of my talents, and, powerfully, from the American world in which I was so rapidly learning to find my way. [. . .] And everywhere— well, almost everywhere—there was American kindness. Not intrusive charity or offensive inquisitiveness, but a consistent decency, a receptivity to whatever gifts I might possess. Shabby in my appearance, awkward in my behavior, far from certain in my English, I could have been a figure of fun; and for the well-scrubbed high school girls I was trying to impress, perhaps I was. But both of the teachers in whose classes I sat during my fleeting attendance at East High School in the fall and winter of 1941 seemed to see some promise in me, and they exercised their power for my benefit. The first, George Cavender, a most unorthodox teacher of civics, introduced me to Thurman Arnold; I think the first book I ever bought in the United States—a solemn moment in view of my poverty—was a one-dollar edition of Arnold's *Folklore of Capitalism*. It became a treasure to me, a bracing foretaste of many books I would buy in later years, buy—and write. Arnold's irreverent, tough-minded analysis of the political process captivated me, and I promptly began to work on a book-length manuscript of my own, boldly entitled "New Measures, New Men." I have only the faintest recollection of what this ambitious essay was supposed to demonstrate, but it is a measure of my unquenchable self-confidence that I sent it off to a publisher, to Harper, I think. They did not publish it, of course, and the manuscript is, fortunately, lost. But the force that generated it—Mr. Cavender's interest in me and his trust in my capacities— was not lost; it formed the kernel, however small, of all I would later dare to do.

A second East High teacher, Helen Hunter, who was lame and known by heartless youth as "Step-and-a-half Hunter," redirected my life in even more drastic fashion. One day, some months after I had had to exchange school for a job, she suddenly appeared at my mother's bedside in the National Jewish Hospital. I still do not know how she found her, but there she was, exuding authority and telling my mother it was a shame that someone like me should go through life without a diploma. Surely one day I would go to a university, and then I would need proof that I had graduated from high school. And she volunteered to arrange for that diploma by giving me a private tutorial in English. Accordingly, we met several times; I read Shakespeare with her and wrote a paper proving that Hamlet's madness was real, not feigned.

In the summer of 1943 I could appreciate her genial intervention, for I was admitted to the University of Denver. There, as I made friends among the students and faculty, my Americanization continued. I kept on working, in the evenings, on weekends, during vacations, fantasizing my way through ill-paying and mindless jobs. I sold shirts in a men's store, manned the cash register in a shoe store, dished out ice cream in a creamery. I walked through these jobs—doing them, no doubt, badly at times—unviolated and invulnerable, cherishing my mother's expectation that, with my interest in writing, I should become someone like Walter Lippmann. In fact, after only a year or so at the University of Denver, I began to write a weekly column on national and international politics, filled with confident and often ill-informed commentary on everything from the future of American liberalism to the prospects of the United Nations. Sometime during these years I read a news story about the daughter of a Supreme Court justice—William O. Douglas, I think— who spent her summer vacations earning pocket money as a soda jerk. It put my own working life into perspective. And in 1945 I even ran for student president, losing to an immensely popular football player by only six votes: 261 to 255. When, in May 1946, at the earliest legal moment, I became a U.S. citizen, I had already been a citizen in my mind for some years. Where but in America was such rapid acceptance even thinkable?

[After the war Peter Gay studied history at Columbia University and began his academic career. But he often found himself at odds with the political extremism and "myopia" of his friends and colleagues, who oscillated between McCarthyism on the one hand and an intellectual anti-Americanism on the other.]

One fine summer day at Wellfleet [Massachusetts] I had my epiphany. I understood, I thought, the causes of this double myopia. I was visiting the Hofstadters, and we were all on the beach, clustered in a large informal group, close friends and recent acquaintances drifting together to chat, to sunbathe, even to go swimming. And in this idyllic setting, one such acquaintance, an American teaching sociology at Princeton, got up, surveyed the drowsy, cheerful scene, and intoned in his euphoria: "Goyim, go home!" It was a self-isolated word that made islands of Jews hostile to the surrounding world, a word my father had taught me to detest. I got up and walked away.

This became more than an insignificant, if unpleasant, incident—a marker, I now see, on the way to my own bicentennial—because at that moment I overcame my irritated and self-satisfied reflection that I was above such vulgarity, and recognized that this sociologist was expressing a profound uneasiness. I could never have made such a remark because, ironically enough, I was at home in America and he was not. In a decade I had learned to have confidence that other Americans would help me, would see me not as an interesting and alien curiosity but as myself—in short, would accept me. To see America not as a treasure house to be exploited, but as a home in which to find my place, was equivalent to seeing all gentiles not as potential participants in pogroms but as possible friends. Paradoxically I, the immigrant, could live in this country with less fear, with less suspicion than this American-born social scientist, driven, perhaps in joke but anxiously enough, to construct barriers where there should only be free traffic.

But these reflections did not resolve the paradox; they only pushed it one step further. Why should I feel at home in America and he, American-born, feel himself an alien? I found the solution hard to accept; in fact, it took me many years to glimpse it. I was at home in America because I had been at home in Germany; he was not at home in America because his forefathers had not been at home in Poland or in Galicia. He had absorbed, and unconsciously perpetuated, the wariness of his ancestors. He was successful, he was settled, he commanded a good salary and a wide public, but he was still living out of his suitcases. I had unpacked mine.

In many ways this insight was nothing more than a return of what had been repressed. My father, for the first forty years of his life, had been a German, unquestioning, comfortable, cheerful. I was nearly ten in 1933, and fully as German as he. He would remind me, during the war and just after, when I persisted in mouthing clichés about collective German guilt and incurable German viciousness, of those Germans who had remained our friends through it all, taking great risks for our sake. Only after my memories of having been at home in Germany—memories that I had repressed with single-minded ferocity—reemerged, could I interpret that scene on the Wellfleet beach in all its rich and puzzling significance.

Henry Pachter]

ON BEING AN EXILE

Henry Pachter (1907–80) fled Germany for France in 1933, was interned in a work camp there, and managed to emigrate to the United States where he had a long career as a political scientist at the New School for Social Research and the City University of New York. The following remarks are from "On Being an Exile: An Old-Timer's Personal and Political Memoir," written in the late 1960s.

Being an exile is not a matter of needing a passport; it is a state of mind. I discovered this but gradually. In the beginning I did not experience exile as a universal mode of existence. I still attributed my stance entirely to the specific and, so it seemed, transitory phenomenon of Hitler. We all felt that Hitler was something extraordinary, irregular, unforeseeable and, if rightly considered, impossible. According to the German philosophy which still was most commonly accepted and to which the Marxists also paid their tribute, this unthinkable phenomenon had no right to, and therefore did not, exist. Not really. Ernst Cassirer, the philosopher who was to be my neighbor in New York, once expressed it in a classical way which I repeat every year for my undergraduates' edification: "You know, Mr. Pachter, this Hitler is an error (*Irrtum*) of History; he does not belong in German history at all. And therefore he will perish." This is what all decent people felt at the time. But History cared not for human decency—or German philosophy for that matter.

While I still felt that History owed us a rectification of her mistakes—a faith on which hinged our confidence in the eventual triumph of anti-Fascism—yet I delivered my message that Hitler would last five years and that the condition of our rebirth was recognition of our defeat. They almost lynched me. Bertolt Brecht said: "How can you maintain that we suffered a defeat when we did not even fight?" He was capable of such sophistries on behalf of the Party, and I never found out whether he believed them or whether he really was an unpolitical person. But other comrades' answers were no better; all the has-beens expressed the fervent belief that nothing had happened to debunk their prophets. None of the political groups that met in somber backrooms of a brasserie or bistro to deliberate the fate of the world knew its own fate yet. Each was trying to prove to the others that its special brand of Marxism should have been followed and that others should not have betrayed the cause. There is nothing as inconsequential as émigré *querelles*, and in the midst of all that activity I soon felt more isolated than I had been in Nazi Berlin. I formed an alliance with Arkadj Gurland, who also had managed to be alienated from all groups and who was prepared to start thinking anew—that is if he was not reading whodunits, which he considered an appropriate occupation for us.

Many of us indeed fell silent. The myth that exile produces Dantes, Marxes, Bartóks, and Avicennas certainly is not justified in the mass. More often exile destroys talent, or it means the loss of the environment that nourished the talent morally, socially and physically. Even the musicians, whose idiom one might suppose is both personal and international, were surprised to find out how little their values were appreciated in a culture just next door. Only the few who already had world-famous names were able to carry on—living on reduced royalties, but not reduced to starting from scratch; yet, even in this category we have Thomas Mann's comically pathetic complaint that he had to live in a hotel room! Lucky also were those young enough to claim that their studies had been interrupted: benevolent committees provided the means for them to complete their education, and some endured hunger for the opportunity of a new start in intellectual life. But for most of us a new country meant more than a new language. Few found jobs in their field, and most not even jobs that might be termed tolerable. No one had a working permit, and the kind of work one could do illegally was poorly paid, never steady, and often demeaning. The more pleasant opportunities were "nègre" (ghosting), i.e., a dentist, lawyer, engineering consultant, research chemist, etc., did the job of a Frenchman who lent his name and took most of the pay. Many of the jobs I had were fraudulent, ridiculous, or repulsive. Having been taught by my puritanical father that work ennobles, I now learned that work can be more degrading than anything else. People who once had taken money for granted shared my feelings. One day Rudolf Hilferding, former finance minister and author of *Das Finanzkapital*, asked me with a sigh: "Did you ever have to work for a living?"

Each of us solved this problem in his own way, and not all did so honorably. Many had to rely on their wives, who could always find maids' jobs; but over this many marriages broke. Others made an art of persuading backers and committees that we had a claim on their respect and money: even those of us who had not produced a line yet represented that thin veneer of culture which stood between Western civilization and the new barbarians. Our physical and moral survival attitude we developed toward moneyed institutions prepared us for the games we later had to play with American foundations. We may even have helped to develop the art of thinking up research projects and writing outlines which has now become the mark of the academic operator in the

Western world. (I suspect this because the percentage of German problems in American research, notably in the 'forties and 'fifties, far exceeded our share in the academic population.) While one could not beat the Nazis one could still analyze them—hoping in one act to keep the question of the century before the public eye and to justify one's existence.

It is no exaggeration to say that at that time we needed the Nazis as our *raison d'être*. They had become our obsession. Their omnipotence could not be illustrated more poignantly than by the way Nazism or Fascism affected our professional careers. Erich Fromm, a psychologist, wrote *Escape from Freedom;* Theodor Adorno, who had sparked the modern interest in Kierkegaard and was interested in the sociology of music, instead studied *The Authoritarian Personality;* Hannah Arendt, a gifted philosopher with little talent for politics, gave us the book on the origins of totalitarianism; Ernst Kris, Freud's co-editor of *Imago,* studied Nazi propaganda; Ernst Cassirer, who detested the entire area of politics and statecraft, nevertheless had to write *The Myth of the State.* Remote fields like philology were raked over in efforts to discover strands of Nazi ideology in early German literature or in the structure of the German language. Having published an analysis of Nazi grammar, I was deeply touched when after the war I discovered that two scholars inside Germany had collected evidence of totalitarian corruption of the German language—a handsome example of parallel ideas among internal and external exiles.* (How even the purest of sciences had been affected became apparent only much later when it was revealed that Einstein, Meitner, Bohr, Bethe, and other pacifists had contributed to the development of the atomic bomb.)

[. . .] Going to America was in itself an admission of defeat; but we were fortunate in preserving our lives, and we were glad that so many of us were able to escape from the destruction of Europe. Many had preceded us to these shores and prepared the mold for a different kind of émigré existence: here one tried to find a place in a society that was prepared to accept the immigrant. One had the right to work and no need to feel excluded. Moreover, American society was engaged in a great revolution which seemed to continue where the Popular Front in France had failed, and that revolution offered the progressive intellectual a special opportunity to experiment with Utopias. An enlightened government was transforming the Republic into a social democracy whose ideology was at the opposite pole from Hitler's and Stalin's.

At the same time, America was on the verge of a great reorientation in her foreign policy. She had been isolationist and secure in her own strength between two oceans, but FDR's vision, combined with the shock of the fall of

---

* One was Victor Klemperer, the Romance philologist and author of *LTI* (The Language of the Third Reich) as well as of extensive diaries detailing daily life in Nazi Germany. Ed.

France, gradually produced the change which we refugees—perhaps erroneously—interpreted as a conversion of America to our political philosophy. We felt that anti-Fascism and international security were really two facets of one policy and that we were able to explain her mission to America while helping FDR to educate his country for this new responsibility.

But to do this we also had to learn and to unlearn a lot. Americans did not react to the same appeals that could move us. Americans do not easily respond to abstract ideas. They don't admire a man for what he proposes but for the way he carries it out. They are forever trying out something new but are careful to keep it in the framework of old institutions which, however, are capable of infinite reinterpretation. They think that the term "pragmatic" implies something honorable and laudable and they conceive of their laws as of mere guidelines that one circumvents, modifies, disregards, or adapts to. To a European mind all of this can be exasperating, most of all the ambiguity of that experimenting and temporizing: one never can tell whether "flexibility" will lead to utter corruption or to greater efficiency. Americans are gamblers, and to provide some European solidity for our program we had to gamble too.

The immigrants tried their best to understand this climate of general permissiveness and to blend into it, to prosper in it personally, and to gain profit from it for their special cause. To enlist our new country in the service of humanity (and its good war) we were able to appeal to its own ideals, which we embraced ardently; but we also had to overlook some of its glaring blemishes and crying injustices. (Few of us then were aware of the full depth of the Negro problem.) To exploit the political naiveté of America, we had to flatter its consciousness of history which we knew it did not have. But we loved America for its promise, its youthfulness, its strength, and also because it was different from Europe in one important respect: America allows the individual to retreat from society and to have ties to various associations and bodies in many different ways; Europe always assumes that one is part of a social group whose every attitude and opinion one shares. In America a religious crisis does not entail a political collapse; an economic depression may leave the social structure intact; a revolution at the universities need not involve other strata. A man may be a racist and yet support the welfare state, or he may be a civil rights fighter and yet hate labor unions. This was almost incomprehensible to me in the beginning. Later I found that herein lies the true secret of America's domestic security: each group is revolutionary in its own field at one time; no convergence toward a total revolution ever threatens the system as a whole. Because the refugees had no desire to be revolutionary in America, they thankfully embraced this system which permitted them to be dynamic reformers each in his own field. They accepted the so-called conformism which sits so lightly on most Americans' shoulders—precisely because it never seems to affect vital interests of the individual; politics does not involve

Americans with the totalitarian intensity of European party life. In the beginning of this century, European Socialism immigrated into New York's sweat shops with the immigrants. The refugees of the thirties and forties by contrast had no quarrel with the American government; it had saved them from destruction and, they hoped, would help to defeat their enemies—first Hitler, then Stalin. Eagerly they absorbed the gospel of opportunity. Many went into business or found positions that might not have been open to them in their old countries. In that respect they were no different from earlier waves of immigrants, except that their rise to prosperity was steeper and faster.*

Beyond these purely personal and mundane reasons, however, the American creed held the promise of another mission for us especially: we would return to postwar Europe as apostles of a global new deal. For once it was possible to identify with a living state, and we gladly exchanged European ideologies for the absorbing and fascinating adventure of American pragmatism. I don't know what would have happened if we had arrived here under Hoover. But FDR and after him Truman persuaded us that our fight and America's were one, not only against Hitler but against all forms of totalitarianism, against hunger and backwardness, against colonialism and power politics.

During the war I worked for intelligence—no cloak-and-dagger operations but desk work, which is ninety-five percent of the job—and later found employment in market research. In contrast to many intellectuals I know a little about American business, but though I was a pretty good economist I found economics less and less rewarding, the people I met positively boring, their manners appalling, and their outlook distressing. I had considerable difficulty in getting "adjusted"—an American word which had not been in my vocabulary before; but this hardly was America's fault. My upbringing and experience probably would have made it hard for me to adjust to any business community or to live by business-oriented values in any country. Yet America seems to have developed the purest strain of that culture, unadulterated by aristocratic or intellectual impurities. To make things worse, whiskey does

---

* Unlike the Irish and Puerto Ricans, we did not have to start from the bottom and work our way up. Thanks to benevolent committees, general prosperity, and the war, many of us were able to join the social class we had left in Europe. This was particularly true of intellectuals. In the beginning many of us had to take positions that might be described as "academic proletariat"; but eventually, many reached positions they might not have obtained in the old country. "Upward social mobility" is no myth, and despite a few cases of failure the percentage of successful careers is truly astounding. Even my friend W. J., whose charms are not of the kind that goes with efficiency and whose academic credentials are doubtful, achieved tenure. Observation: one could be very poor and yet be sure that upward mobility exists for us; one might also be quite sensitive to discrimination and yet not be aware of the absolute limits to the social mobility of Negroes.

not agree with me, I loathe loud noise, television and cocktail parties where one has to shout over the din of other people's chatter. I find baseball the most boring of sports to look at. I agree with Brecht and Sartre that the consumer culture of the American middle class represents a low point in taste and "engagement." Had my naturalization depended on my acceptance of the "American way," I would scarcely have passed. The same is true of some of my friends, though others have mastered the arts of socializing in this country.

When I turned to teaching, my worries were not over. American students were not used to the freedom that was the pride of European universities. They were poorly informed, provincial, grade-conscious, and difficult to interest in problems of universal significance. When our daughter went to school, however, I began to understand why American education fails to stimulate and to slake the thirst for knowledge. What is wrong with the college in the United States is the American high school and elementary school. My idea of education was based on the European model of élite culture to which, one hopes, the masses can be lifted up. American education seems to strive for an optimum which neither develops the highest cultural potential for the élite nor the maximum useful and relevant knowledge for the masses. The result is that the cultural avant-garde moves in a vacuum, unrelated to yesterday's cultures which may or may not be taught in the schools and colleges, unrelated also to itself. I did not find in the United States, as in other countries, a cultural capital where a constant circle of conversation is spinning a web of intellectual relations. There were no coffeehouses—and college cafeterias are notoriously unconducive to talk. Writers in this country don't seem to congregate; they emerge from their respective farms or college residences with a book every two or three years, and then disappear from public view, except on speaking tours for enormous fees. Academic departments, of course, congregate; but not with each other. They hardly mix for lunch.

I also found it difficult to land a desirable position because I do not fit into any of the approved slots; I have written on Fascism, on Renaissance medicine, on foreign policy, on propaganda—which makes people uneasy. I am no culture snob, but I find myself saying "we" when I am referring to Europeans of the period I happen to teach, and my students have learned to accept me as a witness or as an exhibit of what I am trying to demonstrate. Friends and other refugee scholars who have written memoirs report similar experiences, and unless those who are well adjusted are not talking, the Americanization of refugee intellectuals seems far less perfect than their outward success. Yet, this is not the whole story . . .

How much of an American one has become he notices only on his first return "home," where everything now appears so small, so petty, so mean, so oversophisticated, that one is prepared to praise everything American, even the shortcomings; I took offense at the servility, the class spirit, the maid's constant "Ja, Herr Doktor," the chauffeur's heel-clicking, the over-correctness of officials, and the air of importance in every business executive's anteroom. No matter how heavy the cultural heritage one carries on one's back, "you can't go home again." No matter how close the friends to whom you return, you come home as a stranger, or at least as a different person. Back in Europe I loved America's freedom.

As a result, I found myself constantly caught between two camps—explaining Europe to Americans and explaining America to Europeans. I am writing for European papers and I am teaching in America. Carl Friedrich and Hans Rothfels are in a similar position, holding chairs in this country and in Germany. Others who have permanent positions at American universities like to spend a summer semester or a year at some European academy. Still more make it a habit to go to Europe at least for their vacation, or even own a house in the Alps—not to speak of the conferences and congresses they have to attend in Europe. This jetting about seems to indicate, not that European scholars have caught the American virus of restlessness but that they still live in two worlds. Despite success and adjustment, they seem to need a yearly replenishment with their previous cultural resources even while they have elected to stay in this country.

In discussing this strange paradox of outstanding successes in American academic life despite a nostalgic attachment to European culture, one easily comes upon two interconnecting observations: perhaps we can be better Europeans in the United States than anywhere in Europe—unencumbered by special interests—and perhaps precisely this purity of our European idealism makes us marketable in the United States. Both sides of this equation are also related to my earlier remark on the permissiveness of American society and government: America does not either absorb or reject a person but allows many hundreds of flowers to bloom in its garden. Divergency, dissent, even strangeness can be allowed to produce the sweet poison from which this enormously resourceful society may yet distill some useful drug.

Bibliography

The following bibliography lists only works that were useful for the present volume or are of interest to the general reader. No attempt has been made to include the vast number of personal memoirs or specialized accounts.

PRIMARY SOURCES

CRAWFORD, REX, ed. *The Cultural Migration: The European Scholar in America*, Philadelphia: University of Pennsylvania Press, 1953.

GONG, ALFRED, ed. *Interview mit Amerika. 50 deutschsprachige Autoren in der neuen Welt*. Munich: Nymphenburger Verlangshandlung, 1962.

GREFFRATH, MATTHIAS, ed. *Die Zerstörung einer Zukunft. Gespräche mit emigrierten Sozial-wissenschaftlern*. Hamburg: Rowohlt, 1979.

HARTWIG, THOMAS, AND ROSCHER, ACHIM, eds. *Die verheissene Stadt: Deutsch-jüdische Emigranten in New York*. Berlin: Das Arsenal, 1986.

HEMPEL, HENRI J., ed. *Wenn ich schon ein Fremder sein muß: Deutsch-jüdische Emigranten in New York*. Frankfurt a.M.: Ullstein, 1984.

KESTEN, HERMANN, ed. *Deutsche Literatur im Exil. Briefe Europäischer Autoren, 1933–1949*. Vienna/Munich/Basel: Verlag Kurt Desch, 1964.

KORMAN, GERD, ed. *Hunter and Hunted: Human History of the Holocaust*. New York: Viking Press, 1973.

LIXL-PURCELL, ANDREAS, ed. *Women of Exile: German-Jewish Autobiographies since 1933*. NY/Westport, CT: Greenwood Press, 1988.

LOEWY, ERNST, ed. *Exil. Literarische und politische Texte aus dem deutschen Exil, 1933–1945*, 2 Vols. Stuttgart: J.B. Metzlersche Verlagsbuchhandlung, 1979.

NEILSON, WILLIAM ALLAN, ed. *We Escaped: Twelve Personal Narratives of the Flight to America*. New York: Macmillan, 1941.

RICHARZ, MONIKA, ed. *Jewish Life in Germany: Memoirs from Three Centuries*. Transl. Stella P. and Sidney Rosenfeld. Bloomington: Indiana University Press, 1991 (condensed and translated version of *Jüdisches Leben in Deutschland*.) 3 Vols. Stuttgart: Deutsche Verlags-Anstalt, 1982).

ROTHCHILD, SYLVIA. *Voices from the Holocaust*. New York: NAL Books, 1981.

SCHABER, WILL, ed. *Aufbau-Reconstruction. Dokumente einer Kultur im Exil*. New York: Overlook Press, 1972.

SCHÖFFLING, KLAUS, ed. *Dort wo man Bücher verbrennt. Stimmen der Betroffenen*. Frankfurt: Suhrkamp, 1983.

SCHOPPMANN, CLAUDIA, ed. *Im Fluchtgepäck die Sprache. Deutschsprachige Schriftstellerinnen im Exil*. Berlin: Orlanda Frauenverlag, 1991.

SCHWARZ, EGON AND WEGNER, MATTHIAS, eds. *Verbannung: Aufzeichnungen deutscher Schriftsteller im Exil*. Hamburg: Christian Wegner Verlag, 1964.

SPIERS, BENJAMIN, ed. *I am an American — By Famous Naturalized Americans*. Freeport, NY: Book for Libraries Press, 1941.

Um uns die Fremde: die Vertreibung des Geistes, 1933–45. Berlin: Sender Freies, Berlin, n.d.

WINKLER, MICHAEL, ed. *Deutsche Literatur im Exil 1933–1945*. Stuttgart: Reclam, 1977.

ZADEK, WALTER, ed. *Sie flohen vor dem Hakenkreuz. Selbstzeugnisse der Emigranten. Ein Lesebuch für Deutsche*. Hamburg: Rowohlt, 1981.

SECONDARY SOURCES

BARKAI, AVRAHAM, *From Boycott to Annihilation: The Economic Struggle of German Jews, 1933–1943*, tr. William Templer, Hanover and London: University Press of New England, 1989.

BARRON, STEPHANIE, ed. *Exiles and Emigrés: The Flight of European Artists from Hitler*. New York: Harry N. Abrams, Inc. and Los Angeles County Museum of Art, 1997.

BENTWICH, NORMAN. *The Rescue and Achievement of Refugee Scholars. The Story of Displaced Scholars and Scientists, 1933–1952*. The Hague: Martinus Nijhoff, 1953.

BENZ, WOLFGANG (ed), *Die Juden in Deutschland, 1933–1945*, Munich: C. H. Beck, 1989.

BOYERS, ROBERT, ed. *The Legacy of the German Refugee Intellectuals*. New York: Schocken Books, 1972.

COSER, LEWIS. *Refugee Scholars in America: Their Impact and Their Experiences*. New Haven, CT: Yale UP, 1984.

DAVIE, MAURICE R. *Refugees in America: Report of the Committee for the Study of Recent Immigration from Europe*. New York and London: Harper and Brothers, 1947.

DUGGAN, STEPHEN, AND DRURY, BETTY. *The Rescue of Science and Learning: The Story of the Emergency Committee in Aid of Displaced Foreign Scholars*. New York: Macmillan Company, 1948.

EDGCOMB, GABRIELLE SIMON. *From Swastika to Jim Crow: Refugee Scholars at Black Colleges*. Malabar, FL: Kireger, 1993.

FEINGOLD, HENRY L. *The Politics of Rescue: The Roosevelt Administration and the Holocaust, 1938-1945*. New Brunswick, N.J.: Rutgers UP, 1970.

FERMI, LAURA. *Illustrious Immigrants: The Intellectual Migration from Europe, 1930–41*. Chicago: U. of Chicago Press, 1968.

FRIEDMAN, SAUL S. *No Haven for the Oppressed: United States Policy toward Jewish Refugees, 1938–1945*. Detroit: Wayne State UP, 1973.

FRY, VARIAN. *Assignment: Rescue*. 1945 (reprinted by Scholastic; condensed version of *Surrender on Demand*).

———. *Surrender on Demand*. 1945 (reprinted, Boulder: Johnson Books, 1997).

GAY, RUTH. *The Jews of Germany: A Historical Portrait*. New Haven, CT: Yale UP, 1992.

GROSSMANN, KURT R. *Emigration: Geschichte der Hitler-Flüchtlinge, 1933-1939.* Frankfurt: Europäische Verlagsanstalt, 1969.

GROTH, MICHAEL. *The Road to New York: The Emigration of Berlin Journalists, 1933–1945.* Munich: Minerva, 1984.

HEILBUT, ANTHONY. *Exiled in Paradise: German Refugee Artists and Intellectuals in America.* New York: Viking Press, 1983.

JACKMAN, JARRELL C., AND BORDEN, CARLA M., eds. *The Muses Flee Hitler: Cultural Transfer and Adaptation, 1930–1945.* Washington, D.C.: Smithsonian Institution Press, 1983.

KALNAY, FRANCIS, ed. *The New American: A Handbook of Necessary Information for Aliens and New Citizens.* New York: Greenberg, 1941.

KAPLAN, MARION, *Between Dignity and Despair: Jewish Life in Nazi Germany*, New York and Oxford: Oxford University Press, 1998.

KROHN, CLAUS-DIETER. *Intellectuals in Exile: Refugee Scholars and the New School for Social Research.* Trans. Rita and Robert Kimber. Amherst: U. of Massachussetts Press, 1993.

MARRUS, MICHAEL R. *The Unwanted: European Refugees in the Twentieth Century.* New York: Oxford UP, 1985.

PALMIER, JEAN-MICHEL. *Weimar en exil: le destin de l'émigration intellectuelle allemande antinazie en Europe et aux Etats-Unis.* Paris: Editions Payot, 1988.

PFANNER, HELMUT. *Exile in New York: German and Austrian Writers after 1933.* Detroit: Wayne State UP, 1983.

QUACK, SIBYLLE. *Zuflucht Amerika. Zur Sozialgeschichte der Emigration Deutsch-jüdischer Frauen in die USA, 1933–1945.* Bonn: J.H.W. Dietz, 1995.

———, ed. *Between Sorrow and Strength: Women Refugees of the Nazi Period.* Cambridge and New York: Cambridge UP, 1995.

RADKAU, JOACHIM. *Die Deutsche Emigration in den U.S.A.: Ihr Einfluss auf die amerikanische Europapolitik, 1933-1945.* Düsseldorf: Bertelsmann Universitätsverlag, 1971.

ROBINSON, MARC, ed. *Altogether Elsewhere: Writers on Exile.* Boston and London: Faber and Faber, 1994.

SAENGER, GERHART. *Today's Refugees, Tomorrow's Citizens: A Story of Americanization.* New York: Harper and Brothers, 1941.

SIMPSON, SIR JOHN HOPE. *The Refugee Problem: Report of a Survey.* London and New York: Oxford UP, 1939.

SPALEK, JOHN M., AND HAWRYLCHAK, SANDRA H., eds. *Guide to the Archival Materials of the German-Speaking Emigration to the United States after 1933.* 3 Vols. Bern and Munich: Saur Verlag, 1997.

SPALEK, JOHN M., FEILCHENFELDT, KONRAD AND HAWRYLCHAK, SANDRA H., eds. *Deutschsprachige Exilliteratur seit 1933. Bibliographien.* 3 Vols. Bern and Munich: Saur Verlag, 1994

SPALEK, JOHN M. *Guide to the Archival Materials of the German-Speaking Emigration to the United States after 1933.* 2 Vols. Charlottesville: UP of Virginia, 1978–92.

SRUBAR, ILJA, ed. *Exil, Wissenschaft, Identität. Die Emigration deutscher Sozialwissenschaftler, 1933–1945.* Frankfurt: Suhrkamp, 1988.

STERN, ERICH. *Die Emigration als psychologisches Problem.* Boulogne-sur-Seine: Stern, 1937.

STRAUSS, HERBERT A., ed. *Jewish Immigrants of the Nazi Period in the USA.* 6 Vols. New York/Munich/London/Paris: K.G. Saur, 1978–92.

TARTAKOWER, ARIEH, AND GROSSMANN, KURT R. *The Jewish Refugee*. New York: Institute of Jewish Affairs of the American Jewish Congress and World Jewish Congress, 1944.

THOMPSON, DOROTHY. *Refugees: Anarchy or Organization*. New York: Random House, 1938.

TROMMLER, FRANK, AND MCVEIGH, JOSEPH, eds. *America and the Germans: An Assessment of a Three-Hundred-Year History*. Vol. 2, *The Relationship in the Twentieth Century*. Philadelphia: University of Pennsylvania Press, 1985.

WISE, STEPHEN S., ed. *Never Again! Ten Years of Hitler: A Symposium*. New York: Jewish Opinion Publishing Corp., 1943.

WYMAN, DAVID S. *The Abandonment of the Jews: America and the Holocaust, 1941–1945*. New York: Pantheon, 1984.

Permissions

Alfred Döblin, "The Reichstag is Burning" originally appeared in German in *Schriften zu Leben und Werk* (Freiburg-Olten: Walter-Verlag, 1986), p. 265–267. Reprinted by permission of Walter Verlag, Zurich; translation by Mark M. Anderson.

Käte Frankenthal, "Berlin, 1933" originally appeared in German in *Der dreifache Fluch: Jüdin, Intellektuelle, Sozialistin.* The manuscript is in the Houghton Library, Harvard University, shelf #bMS Ger. 91 (67). Reprinted by permission of Campus Verlag, Frankfurt; translation by Mark M. Anderson and Dorothea von Moltke.

Ernst Toller, "An Open Letter to Herr Goebbels" originally appeared in German in *Gesammelte Werke*, edited by John Spalek and Wolfgang Früwald (Munich: Carl Hanser Verlag, 1978), Volume 1; translation by Mark M. Anderson.

Anonymous, "A Farmer from South Germany" has appeared in *We Escaped: Twelve Personal Narratives of the Flight to America*, edited by William Allan Neilson, transcription and translation by Caroline Neilson (New York: Macmillan, 1941).

Marta Appel, "From the Eyes of a Mother" is from a previously unpublished manuscript in the Memoir Collection of the Leo Baeck Institute, New York. Reprinted by permission of the Leo Baeck Institute, New York.

Anonymous, "Underground" is from an unpublished manuscript in YIVO. Reprinted by permission of the YIVO Institute for Jewish Culture, New York.

Peter Gay, "The 1936 Berlin Olympics" is reprinted by permission of the author.

Hertha Nathorff, "A Doctor's View" originally appeared in German in *Das Tagebuch der Hertha Nathorff*, edited by Wolfgang Benz (Munich: Oldenbourg Verlag, 1987). The manuscript is in the Houghton Library at Harvard University, shelf #bMS Ger. 91 (162). Reprinted by permission of Oldenbourg Verlag, Munich; translation by Mark M. Anderson.

Annemarie Wolfram, "From the Eyes of a Child" has appeared in English in *Women of Exile: German-Jewish Autobiographies since 1933*, edited by Andreas Lixl-Purcell, translated by Gabriele Koch (Westport, CT: Greenwood Press, 1988). The manuscript is in the Houghton Library at Harvard University, shelf number bMS Ger 91 (247). Reprinted by permission of the Houghton Library, Harvard University.

Anonymous, "Vienna: To the West Station" has appeared in English in *We Escaped: Twelve Personal Narratives of the Flight to America*, edited by William Allan Neilson, transcription and translation by Caroline Neilson (New York: Macmillan, 1941).

Arnold Bernstein, "The Trial of a Shipping Magnate" is from a previously unpublished manuscript in the Memoir Collection of the Leo Baeck Institute, New York. Reprinted by permission of the Leo Baeck Institute, New York.

Alice Salomon, "An Invitation from the Gestapo" is from Chapter 24, "A New Lease on Life," of the unpublished manuscript *Character is Destiny*. A German translation has been published (Basel: Beltz Verlag, 1983).

Elisabeth Freund, "Waiting" is from the unpublished manuscript in the Memoir Collection of the Leo Baeck Institute, New York. It has appeared in English in *Jewish Life in Germany: Memoirs from Three Centuries*, edited by Monika Richarz, translated by Stella P. and Sidney Rosenfield (Bloomington, IN: Indiana University Press, 1991). Reprinted by permission of the Leo Baeck Institute, New York and Indiana University Press.

Lion Feuchtwanger, "The Grandeur and Misery of Exile" originally appeared in German in *Das Wort*, Volume 6 (Paris: 1938). © Aufbau-Verlag GmBH, Berlin, 1994; translation by Mark M. Anderson.

Ludwig Marcuse, "Resisting America" originally appeared in German in *Mein zwanzigstes Jahrhundert* (Munich: Paul List Verlag). Reprinted by permission of Diogenes Verlag AG, Switzerland; translation by Mark M. Anderson.

Alfred Kantarowicz, "An Ordinary Day" originally appeared in German in *In unserem Lager ist Deutschland. Reden und Aufsätze* (Paris: Edition du Phénix, 1936); translation by Mark M. Anderson.

Hermann Kesten, "Letter to Ernst Toller" originally appeared in German in *Deutsche Literatur im Exil. Briefe Europäischer Autoren, 1933–1949*, edited by Hermann Kesten (Vienna/Munich/Basel: Verlag Kurt Desch, 1964). Reprinted by permission of Steidl Verlag, Göttingen; translation by Mark M. Anderson.

Käte Frankenthal, "Paris-Switzerland-Prague" originally appeared in German in *Der dreifache Fluch: Jüdin, Intellektuelle, Sozialistin*, edited by Kathleen M. Pearle and Stephan Leibfried (Frankfurt/New York: Campus Verlag, 1981). Reprinted by permission of Campus Verlag, Frankfurt; translation by Mark M. Anderson and Dorothea von Moltke.

Marta Appel, "Amsterdam-Paris" is from a previously unpublished manuscript in the Memoir Collection of the Leo Baeck Institute, New York. Reprinted by permission of the Leo Baeck Institute, New York.

Hilda Branch, "Verona-Brussels" has appeared in English in *Voices of the Holocaust*, edited by Sylvia Rothschild.

Hans Sahl, "On Varian Fry" originally appeared in English in *The Few and the Many* (New York: Harcourt, Brace and World, 1962). Reprinted by permission of Harcourt Brace and Company.

Ellen Schoenheimer, "Refugee Life in France" has appeared in English in *Women of Exile: German-Jewish Autobiographies since 1933*, edited by Andreas Lixl-Purcell, translated by Lussia Neumann (Westport, CT: Greenwood Press, 1988). The manuscript, entitled "In Lieux [*sic*] of a Title," is in the Leo Baeck Institute, New York. Reprinted by permission of the Leo Baeck Institute.

Max O. Korman, "The Ill-fated Steamship St. Louis" has appeared in English in *Hunter and Hunted: A Human History of the Holocaust*, edited by Gerd Korman, translator unknown (New York: Viking Press, 1973).

Stefan Zweig, "Two Letters to Hermann Kesten" originally appeared in German in *Deutsche Literatur im Exil. Briefe Europäischer Autoren, 1933–1949*, edited by Hermann Kesten (Vienna/Munich/Basel: Verlag Kurt Desch, 1964). Reprinted by permission; translation by Mark M. Anderson.

Lessie Sachs, "Advice from the Midwest" originally appeared in German in *Aufbau*, March 1, 1938, and was published in German in *Central-Verein-Zeitung*, supplement "Das Blatt der jüdischen Frau," Berlin; translation by Mark M. Anderson.

Hilde Walter, "Everything is Always Different" originally appeared in *Verbannung: Aufzeichnungen deutscher Schriftsteller im Exil*, edited by Egon

Schwarz and Matthias Wegner (Hamburg: Christian Wegner Verlag, 1964); translation by Mark M. Anderson and Dorothea von Moltke.

Josef Thon, "Seder on a Refugee Ship" originally appeared in German in *Aufbau*, May 16, 1941; translation by Mark M. Anderson.

Heinz Natonek, "The Last Day in Europe" originally appeared in German in *Aufbau*, April 4, 1941. Courtesy of Paul Zsolnay Verlag, Vienna; translation by Mark M. Anderson.

Marta Appel, "The Sight of New York" is from a previously unpublished manuscript in the Memoir Collection of the Leo Baeck Institute, New York. Reprinted by permission of the Leo Baeck Institute, New York.

Arnold Bernstein, "Starting Over in New York" is from a previously unpublished manuscript in English in the Memoir Collection of the Leo Baeck Institute, New York. Reprinted by permission of the Leo Baeck Institute, New York.

Hertha Nathorff, "Arriving in New York" originally appeared in German in *Das Tagebuch der Hertha Nathorff*, edited by Wolfgang Benz (Munich: Oldenbourg Verlag, 1987). The manuscript is in the Houghton Library at Harvard University, shelf #bMS Ger. 91 (162). Reprinted by permission of Oldenbourg Verlag, Munich; translation by Mark M. Anderson.

Sibylle Ortmann, "'So Utterly Connected'" is from a previously unpublished manuscript in English, copyright Peter Crane. Reprinted by permission of Peter Crane.

Klaus Mann, "My Last Day with Ernst Toller" originally appeared in German in *Deutsche Literatur im Exil. Briefe Europäischer Autoren, 1933–1949*, edited by Hermann Kesten (Vienna/Munich/Basel: Verlag Kurt Desch, 1964). From Klaus Mann, *Zweimal Deutschland* © 1994 by Rowohlt Verlag. Reprinted by permission; translation by Mark M. Anderson.

Ludwig Marcuse, "Ernst Toller's Last Day" originally appeared in German in *Deutsche Literatur im Exil. Briefe Europäischer Autoren, 1933–1949*, edited by Hermann Kesten (Vienna/Munich/Basel: Verlag Kurt Desch, 1964). Reprinted by permission of Diogenes Verlag, Switzerland; translation by Mark M. Anderson.

Bermann-Fischer/Mann, "The 'Enemy Alien' Question" originally appeared in German in *Bedroht-Bewahrt. Weg eines Verlegers* (Frankfurt: Fischer Verlag, 1967). Reprinted by permission of S. Fischer Verlag, Frankfurt; translation by Mark M. Anderson.

Albert Einstein et al., "Open Letter to President Roosevelt" originally appeared in English in *Bedroht-Bewahrt. Weg eines Verlegers* (Frankfurt: Fischer Verlag, 1967).

Hannah Arendt, "We Refugees" originally appeared in English in *The Menorah Journal* (January 1943), copyright 1943 by the Menorah Association, Inc. Reprinted by permission of Harcourt Brace and Company.

Thomas Mann, "The Exiled Writer's Relation to His Homeland" has appeared in English in *Altogether Elsewhere: Writers on Exile*, edited by Marc Robinson, translator unknown. (Boston/London: Faber and Faber, 1994). Reprinted by permission.

Alfred Polgar, "Life on the Pacific" originally appeared in German in *Aufbau*, September 4, 1942. From Polgar, *Kleine Schriften* © 1982 by Rowohlt Verlag, Rheinbeck bei Hamburg. Reprinted by permission; translation by Mark M. Anderson.

Alfred Döblin, "Letter from the L.A. Public Library" originally appeared in German in *Deutsche Literatur im Exil. Briefe Europäischer Autoren, 1933–1949*, edited by Hermann Kesten (Vienna/Munich/Basel: Verlag Kurt Desch, 1964). Reprinted by permission of Walter Verlag, Zurich; translation by Mark M. Anderson.

Carl Zuckmayer, "A Part of Myself" has appeared in English in *A Part of Myself*, translated by Richard and Clara Winston (New York: Harcourt Brace Jovanovich, 1970). Reprinted by permission of Harcourt Brace and Company.

Bertolt Brecht, "Exiled from Our Era" has appeared in English in *Bertolt Brecht Journals*, edited by John Willett, translated by Hugh Rorrison (New York: Routledge, 1993). Copyright 1973 Stefan S. Brecht. Translation copyright 1993 Stefan S. Brecht. Reprinted by permission of Routledge, Inc.

Alice Herdan, "A Second Childhood" originally appeared in German in *Interview mit Amerika*, edited by Alfred Gong (Munich: Nymphenburger Verlagshandlung, 1962). Translated by Dorothea von Moltke and Mark M. Anderson.

Anonymous, "An Immigrant Family" is from an unpublished manuscript of an oral interview conducted February 14, 1945 in YIVO. Reprinted by permission of the YIVO Institute for Jewish Culture, New York.

Hertha Nathorff, "An American Life" originally appeared in German in *Das Tagebuch der Hertha Nathorff*, edited by Wolfgang Benz (Munich: Oldenbourg Verlag, 1987). The manuscript is in the Houghton Library at Harvard University, shelf #bMS Ger. 91 (162). Reprinted by permission of Oldenbourg Verlag, Munich; translation by Mark M. Anderson.

Richard Plant, "Becoming Jewish" is from an unpublished interview conducted by Dorothea von Moltke in 1996. Reprinted by permission of the author.

William Niederland, "Caring for the Survivors" originally appeared in German in *Die verheissene Stadt. Deutsch-jüdische Emigranten in New York*, edited by Thomas Hartwig, Achim Roscher, Das Arsenal, 1986. Reprinted by permission of Arsenal Verlag, Berlin; translation by Mark M. Anderson.

Günther Anders, "False Youth" originally appeared in *Lieben gestern. Notizen zur Geschichte des Fühlens* (Munich: C.H. Beck, 1989). Reprinted by permission of C.H. Beck Verlag, Munich; translation by Mark M. Anderson.

Peter Gay, "On Becoming an American" has appeared in English as "At Home in America," in *Salmagundi*, Winter 1976/77 copyright Peter Gay. Reprinted by permission of the author.

Henry Pachter, "On Being an Exile" has appeared in English in *The Legacy of the German Refugee Intellectuals*, edited by Robert Boyers (New York: Schocken Books, 1972), copyright Skidmore College. Reprinted by permission of *Salmagundi*.

Every attempt has been made to contact the original copyright holders of each piece. The editor welcomes any additional information; he may be contacted in care of the publisher.